WOMEN IN EARLY MODERN
1500–1700

◆

The Longman History of European Women is a pioneering new history in six volumes, ranging from the early medieval period to the present day.

European Women, 500–1200
Janet Nelson and Pauline Stafford

Women in Medieval Europe, 1200–1500
Jennifer Ward

Women in Early Modern Europe, 1500–1700
Cissie Fairchilds

European Women, 1700–1800
Margaret Hunt

The Making of Modern Woman: Europe 1789–1918
Lynn Abrams

European Women in the Twentieth Century
Jill Stephenson

WOMEN IN EARLY MODERN EUROPE, 1500–1700

CISSIE FAIRCHILDS

Harlow, England • London • New York • Boston • San Francisco • Toronto
Sydney • Tokyo • Singapore • Hong Kong • Seoul • Taipei • New Delhi
Cape Town • Madrid • Mexico City • Amsterdam • Munich • Paris • Milan

Edinburgh Gate
Harlow CM20 2JE
United Kingdom
Tel: +44 (0)1279 623623
Fax: +44 (0)1279 431059
Website: www.pearsoned.co.uk

———————————

First edition published in Great Britain in 2007

© Pearson Education 2007

The right of Cissie Fairchilds to be identified as author
of this work has been asserted by her in accordance
with the Copyright, Designs and Patents Act 1988.

ISBN: 978-0-582-35718-1

British Library Cataloguing in Publication Data
A CIP catalogue record for this book can be obtained from the British Library

Library of Congress Cataloging in Publication Data
A CIP catalog record for this book can be obtained from the Library of Congress

10   9   8   7   6   5   4   3   2   1
10   09   08   07

Set by 35 in 11.5/14pt Garamond
Printed and bound in Malaysia (CTP-VVP)

The Publishers' policy is to use paper manufactured from sustainable forests.

CONTENTS

———◆———

PUBLISHER'S ACKNOWLEDGEMENTS

We are grateful to the following for permission to reproduce copyright material:

Plate 1: Topfoto/The British Library/HIP; Plate 2A: Corbis/Summerfield Press; Plate 2B: The Detroit Institute of Arts, USA/Bridgeman Art Library; Plate 3a: AKG Images/Cameraphoto/Galleria dell' Accademia; Plate 3b: Corbis/Arte & Immagini sri; Plate 4: Fratelli Alinari; Plate 5: Topfoto/Topham Picture Point; Plate 6a: Mary Evans Picture Library; Plate 9: AKG Images/Rijksmuseum, Amsterdam; Plate 10: Szepmuvesz eti Museum, Budapest; Plate 11: Mary Evans Picture Library; Plate 12: Giraudon, Louvre, Paris, France/Bridgeman Art Library.

In some instances we have been unable to trace the owners of copyright material, and we would appreciate any information that would enable us to do so.

INTRODUCTION

———◆———

This book deals with the lives of European women from 1500 to 1700. Both the place and the period it covers need some explanation. The women whose lives I discuss did not think of themselves as Europeans; indeed, they rarely thought of Europe as a geographical entity. Instead, they thought of 'Christendom', by which they meant the largely Christian* areas of western and central Europe: England, Scotland, France, Spain and Portugal (and their overseas empires), the Dutch Republic, Switzerland, the various states of what are today Italy and Germany, the territories ruled by the Austrian Hapsburgs, Poland and the Christian parts of Hungary. These areas shared not only their Christian religion but also a common intellectual and artistic heritage rooted in the classical culture of ancient Greece and Rome, plus more or less common economic, social and political attitudes and institutions. Early modern Europeans did not usually include in Christendom the peripheral areas of Europe like Iceland, Ireland, Scandinavia, and Russia (then called Muscovy) because, while Christian, they had rather different economic, social and political institutions and were not fully integrated into the European state system.[†] Also not included in Christendom were Greece, the Balkans and the rest of eastern Europe because, while most of their inhabitants were Christians, these lands were ruled by the Islamic Ottoman Empire, Christendom's greatest foe. This book reflects these attitudes in that it concentrates on the women of Christendom. Historical authenticity is not the only reason for this; there are practical reasons as well. Most of the research in women's history has been done on that area and its essential similarity allows the results to be synthesized in a relatively clear and straightforward narrative. By contrast, much less is known about the lives of women in Scandinavia, Russia and the Ottoman Empire and what little is known often deviates from the general pattern.

---

* 'Christendom' included a few Jews, mostly in Spain, Portugal and Germany and a few Muslims, again in Spain. Although they lived within the borders of Christendom, they were definitely not part of it.

† This would change in the seventeenth century, with the English conquest of Ireland and the rise of first Sweden and then Russia as western-style absolutist states and great powers.

Therefore this book concentrates on the experiences of Christian women in western and central Europe. The others are discussed much less thoroughly, often only when their experiences diverge from the norm.

The period this book covers – from about 1500 to about 1700 – also deserves an explanation. In traditional European history, these years form a distinct and cohesive period, 'early modern Europe', characterized by the spread of Renaissance culture from Italy to the rest of Europe, the voyages of discovery and the beginnings of overseas empires, the religious conflicts of the Reformation and Counterreformation and the growth and modernization of armies and bureaucracies and the rise of absolutist states. But women's history has its own rhythms, which often differ from those of mainstream history. Do the years from 1500 to 1700 form a distinct and cohesive period in women's history as well?

The answer is yes. Even before there was a distinct field of women's history, one of the first historians to research women's lives, Alice Clark, concentrated on this period. Her *Working Life of Women in the Seventeenth Century*, first published in 1919,[1] established the early modern period as a distinct one and, in fact, a major turning point in women's history. It also provided what is still the most widely held interpretation of the changes in women's lives during the period: that the years from 1500 to 1700 saw an erosion of women's power and autonomy and of the respect accorded to them by society. As its title suggests, Clark's book dealt with the working lives of women in seventeenth-century England. She found that employment opportunities for women were shrinking, at least in comparison to those available in the Middle Ages. Women were increasingly forced out of the guilds which controlled the production and sale of many goods and men took over lucrative traditionally female occupations such as midwifery and brewing. Further, as production moved out of individual households into larger workshops, the economic role of the housewife changed from productive worker to consumer and lady of leisure. Clark suggested that when women contributed less to the family income, they lost power in society and received less respect. Thus Clark pictured the early modern period as one of decline for women, at least when compared to the Middle Ages.

Thirty years ago, when women's history was just starting to be considered a legitimate field of historical inquiry, another famous pioneer, Joan Kelly-Gadol, extended Clark's thesis of the early modern period as one of decline for women to areas beyond the economy. A specialist in the history of Renaissance Italy, Kelly-Gadol famously asked, did women have a Renaissance?[2] Her answer was no, at least not in the sense of enjoying a golden age of human civilization. Instead, Kelly-Gadol followed Clark in painting the Renaissance as a period of decline for women vis-à-vis the Middle Ages. Comparing the housewife of Renaissance treatises on women to the medieval lady of courtly love lyrics, Kelly-Gadol argued that during the Renaissance elite women lost the autonomy, power in the public sphere and the ability to choose their lovers they supposedly had enjoyed in the medieval period. They became mere housewives, secluded in their homes to protect their reputations for chastity, their sole useful function the production of heirs for their husbands' family lineages.

In the decades following Kelly-Gadol's work, the field of women's history grew tremendously and historians uncovered many other changes in women's lives during the early modern period. These included the redefinition of the married state which stressed the necessity of love and equality between husband and wife, a new emphasis on motherhood as woman's primary function, the spread of literacy and the growth of female self-expression in literature and the arts, changes in the legal status of women and new roles for women in the churches and the state, including a remarkable cluster of female rulers and the first demands by women for political rights equal to those of men. Despite the fact that most of these changes advanced the status of women, and despite mounting evidence that the Middle Ages were not a golden age for women, as the Clark and Kelly-Gadol interpretations suggest, such was the power of their work that today the early modern period is still usually depicted as one of setbacks for women.

I contend that is not true. In this book, I emphasize the positive changes in the lives of European women from 1500 to 1700, especially the ones that underlay and influenced all the others: the challenges to and eventual destruction of traditional misogynist notions that women were inferior to men, less intelligent, more wilful and inclined to sin and that therefore they had to live under the authority of male patriarchs (heads of families), whether their fathers or their husbands, confined to the household and the domestic roles of housewife and mother and barred from participation in the public spheres of government, religion, and intellectual life. Supported by the Church and deeply embedded in laws, institutions and social customs, these notions, which I call the *patriarchal paradigm*, undoubtedly restricted women and were responsible for many of the negative features of the early modern period usually emphasized by historians. Yet from 1500 to 1700 the patriarchal paradigm was not only increasingly challenged by intellectuals, both male and female, it was also routinely ignored or subverted by ordinary men and women going about their daily lives.

Thus the period from 1500 to 1700 saw constant tension between the principles of patriarchalism and the forces subverting it, with the latter finally winning out. This dialectical relationship between patriarchy and the factors subverting it was, I believe, the most important force shaping women's lives in early modern Europe. Therefore it provides the organizational scheme for my book, which is divided into five parts. In the first, I define the patriarchal paradigm, examine its origins and explore the intellectual challenges to it during the *querelle des femmes*, the great debate over the nature and roles of women that preoccupied intellectuals in the period.

In Part II, I turn from the realm of ideas to the realm of the realities of women's daily existence. These I explore in four chapters divided among the stages of women's lives as defined in the early modern period. Because women were viewed not as autonomous individuals but as subordinate members of patriarchal households, their lifecycles were not divided according to chronology (childhood, 'youth', etc.) or according to their work experiences and professional development (apprentice, journeyman, master craftsman), as men's were. Instead, they were defined by their changing relationships with male patriarchs. Therefore women were daughters, wives, mothers, and widows or elderly women and, in Part II, I devote a chapter to each of these female life stages.

In the final parts of the book, I explore different aspects of the public sphere, the world outside the female space of the household. In early modern Europe, the public sphere was defined as masculine and was therefore one in which women fit only uneasily.

Part III of the book is devoted to the world of work. In theory this was masculine; women's work was housework, performed in the feminine domestic space of the household. But since the household was the basic unit of production in most of Europe in this period, women's work went far beyond housework. Many women even had independent careers outside the home. In Part III, I devote a chapter to women's work in the countryside, where most of the population lived, and another to employment opportunities for women in cities and towns. A third chapter deals with the new careers for women that began in this period: as actresses, artists, musicians, writers, scientists and intellectuals of all sorts.

Part IV deals with religion, another supposedly 'masculine' realm in which women fit uneasily. All three great religions of the period, Christianity, Judaism and Islam, considered women the spiritual equals of men, yet all barred women from their priesthoods and all taught that they needed to be under male guidance and control to avoid sin. After briefly considering the position of women in Judaism and Islam, I devote the bulk of this part to their position in Christianity in this period when what had been a universal Christian Church was split into the two warring groups of Catholics and Protestants by the Reformation. One chapter is devoted to the Protestants. It examines Protestant teachings about women, the family and sexuality and explores the roles of women in spreading the Reformation and in the new Protestant churches. A second chapter is devoted to the Catholic response to Protestantism, detailing the Church's new teachings about women and the family, the new female religious orders that emerged during the Counterreformation, and how these orders combated the Protestant challenge. The last chapter in this section covers witchcraft and the prosecution of witches. The early modern period was the heyday of the witch trials; probably around 60,000 people, three-quarters of them women, lost their lives during the witchhunts. This topic falls under the rubric of religion because people thought about witchcraft in religious terms. Most witches were prosecuted not for the harm they supposedly inflicted but for religious heresy: they had chosen to worship the Devil over God.

The final part of the book deals with a final masculine realm in which women fit uneasily: the state. In the patriarchal political theory of the time, the state was the household writ large; the power of kings and other rulers over their subjects was like that of a patriarch over his household. Therefore political power was gendered masculine; it was against nature for women to rule over men. Yet early modern Europe had an enormous number of female rulers. The first chapter in this section is devoted to them. The second is devoted to their female subjects. Patriarchal households were not only the models for politics in this period; they were also its building blocks. Such households were considered the basic units of society and only their male heads were full citizens of the state, with full legal and political rights. Yet women were citizens too, although their political rights were limited, and they had to obey the law, although often the law did not recognize their existence. Chapter 13 explores these paradoxes of female citizenship. The final chapter in this section examines women's roles in two of the most important activities of states in this period, both strongly gendered masculine: war and overseas colonization.

A word about sources. This is a work of synthesis, not original research. It attempts to present the findings of an immense amount of research done on the women of early modern Europe since the emergence of women's history as a credible historical field 30 years ago. Therefore I have borrowed extensively from my fellow practitioners in women's history. Every sentence of this book should be adorned with long footnotes. But because this is a text-book, citations were kept to a minimum. To everyone from whom I borrowed, my apologies and my gratitude.

My gratitude also goes to those who made this book possible. They include the historians whose friendships sustained me over my 35 years in the field, especially Lenard Berlanstein, Linda Clark, Fred Marquardt and Carole Shammas, and the graduate students at Syracuse University whose interest in European women's history kept my own fresh: Eric Estes, Denny Frey, Megan Hickerson, Holly Hurlburt, Sherri Klassen, Johanna Moyer, Janaki Nair and Eric Reed. I also owe thanks to the Inter-Library Loan staff at Bird Library, Syracuse University, who found me hundreds of books and articles, and to the others who helped get me books: Linda Clark and Bill Weber, Bill and Mary Ann Meyer, Norman Kutcher, Fred Marquardt and Liz Conger. And I owe more than I can say to Fran Bockus, who typed the manuscript not only accurately but cheerfully, patiently putting up with my endless changes.

Finally, I owe the biggest debt to the person to whom this book is dedicated, my late mother, Eleanor D. Fairchilds. This is her book, not only because I wrote the proposal for it while sitting at her bedside during what turned out to be her last stay in the hospital and began the research for it in the after-math of her death. It is also her book because she was very like the women I write about. Like them, she lived in a time when society's expectations for women were very restrictive, yet like them she made for herself within those parameters a full and meaningful life. She grew up in America in the 1920s and when the Depression hit she had to leave college, although her family scraped together enough to keep her brother in school. Like most 'career girls' of the period, she worked as a secretary – a legal secretary, although she would have made a fine lawyer. And when she married she stopped working and became a typical suburban housewife of the 1950s. But she was never the pathetic creature depicted by Betty Friedan in *The Feminine Mystique*. She actually enjoyed housework and did it with great skill. She managed the family finances, revelled in a vast and supportive network of female friends and, even in her nineties, remained interested in and connected with the world through reading and travel. Above all, she raised and sustained a daughter whose life, thanks to the new opportunities for women that opened up in the 1960s, turned out to be very different from her own. So this book is dedicated with love to the late Eleanor D. Fairchilds, 1906–97.

Part I

◆

THE PATRIARCHAL PARADIGM

Every society has a set of beliefs, deep seated and often unarticulated, which people use to make sense of their lives. In early modern Europe, one of these sets of beliefs was what I call the *patriarchal paradigm*. Its basic tenet was that women were born inferior to men and therefore destined to live under male guidance and control. Women were assumed to be less intelligent than men and more wilful, with less self-control, a greater tendency to sin and a daunting array of negative personality traits. Historian Ruth Kelso lists them:

> [L]icentiousness, instability, disloyalty and gluttony, pride, vanity, avarice, greed, sedi-tiousness, quarrelsomeness, vindictiveness, and evidently the most irritating of all, talkativeness. To end with the favorite summary of weary cataloguers: if all the seas were ink, land and fields parchment, trees pens, and all who know how to write were to write without ceasing, all the evil in women could not be expressed.[1]

Because of their lack of intelligence and self-control and their greater tendency to sin, women had to live under the authority of men, specifically of the male patriarchs (the word means male head of a household or family) who ruled the households into which they were born and into which they were married. These households, in which patriarchs ruled and guided not only their womenfolk but also their sons and other male relatives and their employees and servants, were according to patriarchal theory the basic build-ing blocks of human society. A state was just a collection of households and a ruler's powers were those of a patriarch writ large.

These households, according to patriarchal theory, also formed the boundary of women's lives. In the patriarchal paradigm, the world was divided in two.

There was the public sphere, the world of work, politics, and learning, which was the domain of men, and there was the private sphere of household and family, which was the domain of women. A woman's duty was to run her household efficiently, care for her family and provide it with heirs. These, and these alone, were acceptable social roles for women.

In this part of the book, we will examine the sources for this cluster of beliefs about women and their social roles and we will see how these notions were challenged and eventually undermined in our period, thanks to an enormous intellectual debate over the nature of women called the *querelle des femmes*.

Chapter 1

◆

INFERIORS OR EQUALS? IDEAS ABOUT THE NATURE OF WOMEN

SOURCES OF THE PATRIARCHAL PARADIGM: CHRISTIAN TEACHINGS ABOUT WOMEN

The people of early modern Europe believed that women were inferior to men and that they had to live under the control of male patriarchs because they thought these doctrines were in the Bible. To a society which was, except for the Muslims in Spain and the Balkans and a scattering of Jews in the Iberian Peninsula, Italy, and Germany, uniformly and profoundly Christian, the Bible was the Word of God, revealing His plan for mankind. That the people of early modern Europe found the patriarchal paradigm in the Bible is at first puzzling, because the basic premise of Christianity was the spiritual equality of all human beings of all races, nationalities and genders – all were equal in the eyes of God and all had equal opportunity to gain salvation. Yet this part of the message of Christianity was in medieval and early modern Europe routinely ignored in favour of biblical texts that seemed to support the patriarchal paradigm.

The prime example of this involves the most important text dealing with gender and gender roles, the story of Adam and Eve in the Book of Genesis. Genesis contains an egalitarian version of the creation story (Genesis 1:27), which states that men and women were created equal:

So God created man in his own image, in the image of God created he him; male and female He created them.

This version of the creation story was, however, usually ignored in favour of the longer version found in Chapter 2 of Genesis. In this version, Adam, usually taken to represent the male sex, was created first, from the dust of the earth. Eve, representing women, was only an afterthought, created from Adam's rib when he asked for a companion. Adam was created in God's image; Eve in Adam's. Therefore she was further removed from God. And, of course, it was Eve who was tricked by the serpent and lured Adam into disobedience and sin, leading to the fall of mankind, the stain of Original Sin and the expulsion from Paradise. This version of the Creation story is replete with supposed evidence of women's inferiority. It was the weakness of the female intellect that allowed the serpent to beguile Eve and female wilfulness made her disobey God's command. And because Eve used her physical charms to entice Adam into sin, the story supposedly showed the wantonness of women and proved the common assumptions that women were the lustier sex with stronger sexual appetites than men's and that their outward beauty masked inward corruption and lured men into sin. Further, the punishments God allotted to Adam and Eve affirmed woman's inferiority and subordination to men in no uncertain terms. Adam's punishment, to work by the sweat of his brow, was interpreted as giving men dominance in the world of work and the public sphere, while Eve's punishment, to bring forth her children in sorrow, was thought to confine women to the domestic sphere of home and family. Finally, the Bible clearly stated that men were to rule women, for God told the erring Eve: 'Thy desire shall be to thy husband, and he shall rule over thee.'

The patriarchal lessons of this all-important Old Testament text were reinforced by well-known and often quoted passages from the New Testament. Again the choice was selective. The New Testament contained the classic statement of that bedrock doctrine of Christianity, the spiritual equality of all believers:

There is neither Jew nor Greek, there is neither bond nor free, there is neither male nor female, for ye are all one in Christ Jesus. (St Paul's Epistle to the Galatians 3:28)

It also contained much evidence that Jesus himself had treated women as equals, regarded them primarily as intellectual and spiritual beings, not housewives and mothers (the story of Mary and Martha) and gave them important roles in his ministry (he appeared after his resurrection first to Mary Magdelene, not to a male disciple). But again all this was ignored in favour of texts that seemed to sanction women's inferiority and subordination:*

> Wives, submit yourselves unto your own husbands, as unto the Lord. For the husband is the head of the wife. (Ephesians 5:22–3)

> Let your women keep silence in the churches: for it is not permitted unto them to speak; but they are commanded to be under obedience . . . And if they will learn anything, let them ask their husbands at home. (1 Corinthians 14:34–5)

> I suffer not a woman to teach, nor to usurp authority over the man, but to be in silence. For Adam was first formed, then Eve. And Adam was not deceived, but the woman being deceived was in transgression. (1 Timothy 2:12–14)

These misogynist texts emphasize that women must submit to male author- ity and that they should be excluded from the public sphere, especially the Church. This is not surprising, because these texts were probably products of the period when the Church was shedding its early, informal, egalitarian organization, in which women were allowed to preach, prophesy and baptize, in favour of an all-male bureaucracy organized on the models of the Roman Empire's bureaucracy and army. This change was probably necessary when the Church evolved from an illegal underground cult into the official religion of the late Roman Empire, but it nonetheless meant that the egalitarianism of the early Church was forgotten.[1]

Another trend in the early Church, the rise of celibacy (abstaining from sex), also had unfortunate consequences for women. Almost as revered as the Bible by later Christians were the writings of the Church Fathers, leading theologians of the early Church like St Augustine, St John Chrysostom and Clement of Alexandria. Most of them tried to remain celibate and most of them found that difficult. To them every woman was a sexual temptress, a lure to sin. Unfortunately, this is how they portrayed women in their writings. Tertullian asked them:

> And do you not know that you are Eve? God's sentence hangs still over all your sex and His punishment weighs down upon you. You are the devil's gateway.[2]

Although a few of the Church Fathers praised marriage and the virtue of faithful wives, most counselled women to remain virgins, for only by refrain- ing from sex could they avoid the curse of Eve and gain salvation. St John

---

* I say 'seemed to' because today biblical scholars interpret them differently. So did some of the defenders of women during the *querelle des femmes*, as we shall see.

Chrysostom explained that Adam and Eve's sexual act stripped them of their virginity and:

> made [them] subject to death and every other form of curse and imperfection . . . Do
> you see where marriage took its origin? How it had of necessity to be preceded by the
> breaking of the divine commandment, by malediction and death? For where there
> is death, there too is sexual coupling; and where there is no death, there is no sexual
> coupling either.[3]

Thus, by the Middle Ages, Christianity had changed from a religion stressing the spiritual equality of all human beings to one whose message to women was of their essential sinfulness and their God-ordained subordination to men. This evolution took place because texts emphasizing female inferiority were frequently cited while those emphasizing equality were ignored. This suggests that people found what they wanted to find in Christianity – that they found the patriarchal paradigm there because they already believed in it. And this is true. Both the intellectual and the social contexts from which Christianity arose were intensely patriarchal and they form the other sources for the patriarchal paradigm.

SOURCES OF THE PATRIARCHAL PARADIGM: ANCIENT MEDICAL AND SCIENTIFIC BELIEFS

Christianity arose in a world whose medical and scientific beliefs were derived from the writings of the ancient Greeks, especially Aristotle and Galen. Their teachings, which shaped the way people viewed themselves and the natural world until the scientific revolution of the late eighteenth century, were profoundly patriarchal and misogynistic. They were based on what historians have labelled the 'one-sex' model of human nature: there was only one standard human body and that was male.[4]

The ancient Greeks taught that the universe was formed of four basic elements: earth, air, fire and water. These were arranged in a hierarchy according to their qualities, with fire (hot and dry) and air (hot and moist) at the top, because heat was active, lively and necessary for life, and earth (cold and dry) and water (cold and moist) at the bottom. In human beings, these elements took the form of humours. Yellow bile was hot and dry, blood was hot and moist, black bile was cold and dry and phlegm was cold and moist. The proportion and balance of these humours determined a person's sex and personality. Men had a preponderance of the preferable warm and dry humours, which made them active and intelligent, while in women the less preferable melancholy and lethargic cold and moist humours prevailed (see Plate 1).

[Because women were cold and moist and lacked heat, their sexual organs, thought to be identical to men's, were not fully developed. Women were therefore, in effect, failed men, 'mutilated men', 'monstrosities of nature'.]As Galen, the leading medical writer of the ancient world, explained:

> Now just as mankind is the most perfect of all animals, so within mankind the man is more perfect than the woman, and the reason for his perfection is his excess of heat, for heat is Nature's primary instrument . . . the woman is less perfect than the man in respect to the generative parts [sexual organs]. For the parts were formed within her when she was still a fetus, but could not because of the defect in the heat emerge and project on the outside [as men's do].[5]

If Galen thought women's sexual organs were misplaced, he thought they were nonetheless equivalent to men's: the vagina was like the penis, the ovaries were equivalent to the testicles, etc. And he thought that women as well as men produced a seed and it was the mingling of the two seeds, male and female, that made a child.

Aristotle, the leading scientist of the ancient world, denied women even this tiny bit of equality in nature. Aristotle had a different explanation of human reproduction. He maintained that women did not produce a seed. Instead, the embryo was fully formed in the seed of the male. A woman's womb was only the 'fertile field' in which the seed was planted. A mother contributed only nourishment to the child to be, whose body, mind and personality were totally shaped by the father.[6]

Women's minor and inferior role in reproduction mirrored what Aristotle saw as their minor and inferior role throughout nature. [Aristotle's writings about animals, birds and insects, given a Christian framework by St Thomas Aquinas in the twelfth century, were the main source of people's beliefs about the natural world through the Middle Ages and deep into the early modern period.]Unfortunately, Aristotle showed that in every species of living thing, the male dominated the female. He was often larger and stronger and had more attractive plumage or markings; he was also more active and intelligent:

> [The male principle in nature is associated with active, formative and perfected characteristics, while the female is passive, material, and deprived, desiring the male in order to become complete.[7]]

Thus female inferiority and subordination were from the ancient world on considered laws of nature. No wonder Christians looked for texts which proved them laws of God as well.

SOURCES OF THE PATRIARCHAL PARADIGM: CONTEMPORARY SOCIAL INSTITUTIONS

⌐If they needed proof that female inferiority and patriarchal control were⌐ indeed laws of nature and of God, inevitable and right, the people of early modern Europe had only to look around them at their own society. For in that period the patriarchal paradigm functioned as a self-fulfilling prophecy. Its assumptions of women's sinfulness and lack of intelligence and self-control were used to restrict their opportunities for education, careers and power in the public sphere and then the consequences of these restrictions – that there were few female writers, that women did not hold public office, etc. – were cited as evidence of female inferiority.⌐

Women's education is an example. As we shall see in the next chapter, women were often denied educations on the grounds that they were less intelligent than men and that their roles in life – wife, mother, household drudge – did not require book learning. [Their lack of education meant that women could not be lawyers, officeholders or intellectuals. In turn, the fact that they *were not* lawyers or intellectuals was taken as evidence that they *could not* fill those roles because they lacked the intelligence to do so.]

The legal disabilities of women worked in a similar fashion. The laws under which the women of early modern Europe lived were a complex mixture of customary law, derived from the laws of the early Germanic tribes, which treated women as the property of men and denied them the right to inherit land or bring lawsuits in court, and Roman law, which recognized women as legal persons and allowed them to own property, make wills and bring lawsuits but denied them any power over others, meaning that they could not hold public office, act as legal guardians or as witnesses in court.[8] The result was an extraordinary hodgepodge of laws which varied not only from country to country but also from region to region and town to town. A woman's legal rights also varied over the course of her life; wives usually had fewer rights than spinsters or widows. But everywhere and at all times it was more difficult for women than men to own property and to defend it in court. This meant that it was difficult for women to compete with men in business, especially in large-scale enterprises which needed lots of capital, and for them to own land, the most prized sort of property in this period, which brought not only profits but also power and prestige. Therefore women in commerce were confined to the lowest paying and least profitable occupations and female landowners were denied power in the public sphere. And, of course, the fact that few women commanded great wealth and power was

[margin note:] TRG → why all the female characters or the social structures are prostitutes. TRG

used as evidence that women were incapable of running a profitable business or managing a great estate.

Even the unpleasant personality traits attributed to women had elements of the self-fulfilling prophecy. Women were often accused of deceitfulness and guile and of relying on their looks and sexual attractiveness to manipulate their menfolk. But what else could they do? Restricted in their ability to own property and earn enough to support themselves, most had to marry and, once married, they were under the control of their husbands, who had the right to punish them physically for disobedience. In this situation, they had to manipulate men to survive. Deceit and guile are weapons of the weak. Similarly, the talkativeness of women that so annoyed men grew out of the patriarchal paradigm. Too weak to defend themselves physically and often unable to defend their rights in court, what weapon did women have but their tongues?

Thus the people of early modern Europe found proof that the standard beliefs about women and gender roles were true all around them. Therefore it is not surprising that they accepted the assumptions of the patriarchal paradigm, which permeated every level of late medieval and early modern culture, from the learned treatises of churchmen and humanists through the courtly love romances of the poets to the folktales, fables and proverbs of the common folk. What *is* surprising is that so many people, men as well as women, began in the early modern period to question its assumptions and argue for equality of the sexes.

CHALLENGES TO THE PATRIARCHAL PARADIGM: CHRISTINE DE PISAN

The first person to challenge publicly traditional assumptions about women was, appropriately enough, a woman, Christine de Pisan (1365–1429). Her defence of women's nature, which earns her the title of the 'first feminist', was not the only 'first' she is credited with in women's history; she was also the first woman known to have earned her living as a professional author. As her name suggests, she was Italian, the daughter of a Renaissance humanist*

---

* Humanists were scholars who knew Latin and Greek and the works of ancient Greek and Roman authors, especially in the 'humanities' – history, poetry, rhetoric and other literary subjects that everyone in that period considered the height of mankind's intellectual achievements. Humanists enjoyed the same sort of prestige that scientists enjoy today.

who was appointed official astrologer to the French king. Educated (unusually for a woman) in Latin and the classics by her father, Pisan married a minor French noble. When he left her a young widow with three children, an aged mother and a niece to support, she put her unusual education to work by churning out poetry and historical works in praise of her royal patrons and hackwork like a military manual and a history of heraldry commissioned by wealthy clients.[†]

Pisan's challenge to the patriarchal paradigm might have begun as an attempt to gain publicity and thus more commissions.[9] At any rate, she attacked the author, Jean de Meung, of part of the most famous poem of her time, *The Romance of the Rose*. This was a courtly love poem in which, as in all such works, a young unmarried knight fell in love with an older, nobler, married woman, his desired lady. Pisan attacked de Meung for praising adulterous love and painting women as prey to their insatiable sexual desires. Pisan's attack was praised by the Archbishop of Paris and she became famous. Meanwhile de Meung's fellow poets defended him and an intellectual debate over the nature of women, the *querelle de femmes*, was born. It would last for almost 300 years and produce hundreds of works on women and their roles in society.

Pisan herself contributed the first major work in the debate – and the first major attack on the patriarchal paradigm – with her masterpiece *The Book of the City of Ladies*, probably written around 1404 or 1405. In its opening pages she explained how she came to write it. She was sitting in her study reading a treatise against marriage by one of de Meung's followers:

> [That] made me wonder how . . . so many different men – and learned men among them – have been and are so inclined to express . . . so many wicked insults about women and their behaviour.[10]

Although these descriptions didn't match the way Pisan and the women she knew behaved, they plunged her into such gloom that she wondered why God had bothered to make so worthless a thing as women. She was consoled in her despair by the appearance of three female allegorical figures representing Reason, Rectitude and Justice, who reassured her about women's nature and helped her to build an allegorical walled city, the City of Ladies, to house virtuous women.

[†] Pisan wrote before the invention of printing (c. 1453). In her time being commissioned to write a specific work by a royal or noble patron or receiving a pension from a king or noble to live at court and contribute to its intellectual life were the only ways lay writers and intellectuals could support themselves.

As a good medieval Christian, Pisan was most troubled by the widespread belief that women as a sex were so sinful that none could gain salvation. Therefore her first concern in *The City of Ladies* was to restore the spiritual equality of the two sexes inherent in Christianity. This meant that she had to reinterpret the story of Adam and Eve. According to Pisan, the fact that Eve was created from Adam's rib did not signify that she was an afterthought created in man's image, not God's. Instead it signified 'that she should stand at his side like a companion and never lie at his feet like a slave'.[11] Eve *was* created in the image of God:

> God created the soul and placed wholly similar souls, equally good and noble in the feminine and in the masculine bodies.[12]

Therefore it is not women as a sex who are sinful, but *individual* women – and also individual men. Both men and women might be sinful and therefore damned, but both could be virtuous and attain salvation:

> The man or the woman in whom resides greater virtue is the higher; neither the loftiness nor the lowliness of a person lies in the body according to the sex, but in the perfection of conduct and virtues.[13]

In fact, the City of Ladies was a metaphor for Heaven and Pisan peopled it with the Virgin Mary and female saints whose virtue and salvation could not be doubted.

But what of ordinary women and their earthly lives? Did the spiritual equality of women imply that they were men's equals in other ways as well? Did the fact that sinfulness was a trait of individuals, not a sex, hold true for other supposedly 'masculine' or 'feminine' qualities? And if men and women were equally likely to be virtuous, intelligent or whatever, did that mean that they were equally able to rule states and contribute to learning? Were gender roles not dictated by natural or divine law but simply the product of social custom?

Pisan clearly believed all this, but she dared not come right out and say it. Instead, she used various oblique devices to convince her readers of these truths. For instance, she cited examples, culled from her classical learning, of men who displayed 'feminine' traits (women are supposedly inconstant, but look at the Emperor Nero) and of women who successfully filled 'masculine' social roles (ruling a state was men's work, but the ancient queens Semiramis, Nicaula, Zenobia and Artemesia all did it very well).[14] Pisan also tried to discredit beliefs in inherent gender traits and the inevitability of gender roles by showing where they came from. Supposedly 'inherent' female traits were products of nurture, not nature. Women were not innately less intelligent than men. 'If it were customary to send daughters to school like sons . . . they would learn as thoroughly and understand the subtleties, of all the arts and sciences as well as sons.'[15] Many commonly held notions about women were simply totally false. Writing about women was done by men and they often ascribed negative qualities to women out of envy, hurt pride (when rejected by a woman) and even guilt (remorseful over their sexual sins, they blamed the women they found alluring).[16]

Thus Pisan tried to undermine the notions of innate gender traits and natural gender roles. But she never simply stated her basic argument that men and women were equal and that women should be allowed to do anything that men could do. Neither did she call for the social changes that these ideas seemed to demand. Ever tactful, as befitted someone dependent on court patronage, Pisan accepted the patriarchal conventions of her society and urged women to conform to them. In *The City of Ladies*, Pisan advised wives to obey their husbands and all women to guard their chastity. And she stated that although women were capable of filling any social role, society worked better when patriarchal gender norms were maintained: 'God has . . . ordained men and women to serve Him in different offices.' God gave men strong bodies and loud voices so that they could rule states, while women's gentle, loving dis-positions made them suited to motherhood.[17]

THE *QUERELLE DES FEMMES* IN THE FIFTEENTH CENTURY

Pisan's caution is understandable, given the early period in which she wrote. It would take a century of debate before her key premise that men and women were equal and that they should be judged as individuals, not as representatives of their gender, would be widely accepted and it would take another century for intellectuals to go beyond Pisan and call for changes in their own society. During the fifteenth century, the period in which Pisan wrote, hundreds of humanists contributed to the *querelle*, but most of them ignored Pisan's work and simply repeated the standard assertions of the patriarchal paradigm, using the standard sources – religious texts, Galen, Aristotle, examples from their own society – to support them. There were only two types of dissenting argument. One, propounded by the so-called 'civic humanists', accepted most of the premises of the patriarchal paradigm: women were inferior to men, for instance, and they had inborn qualities that barred them from the public sphere but made them suitable for the domes-tic roles of wife and mother. They simply argued that women were slightly less inferior and their domestic roles slightly more useful to society than was usually thought.[18]

As their name implies, the civic humanists were primarily interested in politics. Their vision of politics was patriarchal. Patriarchal households formed the basic units of society. A state was a collection of households and a well-run household mirrored a well-run state. This vision of politics inspired the civic humanists to write extensively about marriage, the family and household management – in short, about women. Their works, like Francesco Barbaro's *On Marriage* (1415) and Leon Battista Alberti's *On the Family* (1434–37), followed the patriarchal paradigm in defining separate spheres for the two sexes and confining women to the domestic sphere, where they were to be chaste, silent and obedient to the patriarchal household head.[19]

Yet the civic humanists departed from the patriarchal paradigm in some significant ways. Because the family was so central to their thinking, they acknowledged the importance of the domestic sphere and of women as wives, mothers and household managers to the proper functioning of society. They also acknowledged that playing these roles properly required that women be both virtuous and intelligent – qualities usually denied them. They thought that it required that they be educated, again something traditional patriarchy denied women. The civic humanists were great proponents of education. They thought it was their intellect that separated human beings from animals and that everyone should cultivate his or her intellect, even women, who needed education to strengthen their virtue so that they would be faithful wives and to teach their children properly. The civic humanists believed women did not need to know Latin or Greek, the marks of the truly educated in this period, or to read the classics to learn how to be a good citizen, because they had no role in the public sphere. But they did need to know how to read and write in their own language. Many humanists wrote treatises on women's education; Juan Luis Vives' *The Education of a Christian Woman* (1523) is the most famous.[20] Humanists thought that educated, intelligent and virtuous wives were fit companions for their husbands and should be treated respectfully.

The civic humanists advocated only modest – though significant – changes in the patriarchal paradigm. This was not true of the other group of dissenters in the fifteenth-century *querelle*. They stood traditional patriarchy on its head by arguing that women were superior, not inferior to men – more intelligent, more virtuous – and that they should rule the world. Not surprisingly, only a handful of treatises, beginning with Juan Rodriguez de la Camara's *The Triumph of Women* (1438), and including Bartholommeo Goggio's *In Praise of Women* (c. 1487) and Galeazzo Flavio Capra's *On the Excellence and Dignity of*

Women (1525) took this radical and controversial position. In fact, the notion that women might be superior to men was so radical that historians wonder if those who advocated it were completely sincere. They might have been writing tongue-in-cheek, or to please a female patron, or they might have been trying to make names for themselves by taking an unexpected stance in a familiar debate.[21]

AGRIPPA'S DECLAMATION ON *THE NOBILITY AND PRE-EMINENCE OF THE FEMALE SEX* (1529)

Nonetheless it was one of these suspect treatises that demolished the traditional arguments for the patriarchal paradigm and gave a new direction to the *querelle des femmes* in the sixteenth century. This was *A Declamation on the Nobility and Pre-eminence of the Female Sex* by the humanist Henricus Cornelius Agrippa, written in 1509 but not published until 1529. Historians have not decided whether Agrippa was sincere in advocating female superiority. Arguing against it is the fact that he wrote for a female patron. On the other hand, Agrippa was known for taking the unpopular, controversial sides of the intellectual debates of his day. He was Europe's leading propagandist for occultism, which rejected the observable 'truths' of nature in favour of its hidden connections and meanings, and he supported Protestantism, argued for the study of Hebrew despite Church opposition and defended accused witches. His feminism fits this pattern and may therefore have been sincere.[22]

At any rate, Agrippa's strategy in the *Declamation* was to take the traditional texts and beliefs of the patriarchal paradigm and show that they could be interpreted in an opposite way, to support female superiority, not inferiority. Take the Adam and Eve story. Agrippa not only cited the almost forgotten egalitarian version of Genesis, he also reinterpreted the standard version to favour Eve. She was created last not because she was an afterthought but because she was the ultimate end of Creation, its finest product. Her creation from Adam's rib did not signify that she was further removed from God; instead it showed that she was made from a finer material than man, human flesh, not mere dirt.[23]

Agrippa also overturned the traditional scientific arguments for female inferiority, that women were incomplete men with underdeveloped sex organs and only a minor role in reproduction. Agrippa argued that women's sexual organs were inside their bodies not because they were undeveloped or shameful but because women were more modest than men. This was also shown by the fact that their heads, the most noble part of the human body, were covered with hair, while many men were bald! As for women's role in reproduction, Agrippa not only supported Galen, rather than Aristotle, he also asserted that it was the female seed, not the male, which shaped the offspring. He even stated that some females could reproduce without male help – female vultures, for example.[24]

Agrippa also attacked all the clichés about woman's character. Men are more intelligent than women, who never contributed anything to civilization? Nonsense. Women are as smart as men and the classics yield many examples of female poets and philosophers. Women are the more sinful sex? Not true. The most perfect human being who ever lived was a woman (the Virgin Mary), while the most sinful (Judas Iscariot) was male, as were, the Bible tells us, the first murderer, the first drunkard, the first fornicator and the first person to commit incest. In Eden, only Adam was specifically forbidden by God to eat the forbidden fruit, so technically only he sinned. And because a man had sinned, Jesus came to redeem fallen mankind as a man, not a woman.[25]

Thus Agrippa undermined the patriarchal paradigm by showing that the texts on which it was based had 'various figures of speech and meanings' which allowed them to be interpreted in different, even opposite, ways.[26] He also exposed the 'self-fulfilling prophecy' elements of arguments based on the position of women in society. Yes, women do not rule states and they have contributed little to intellectual life, but that is not surprising:

[W]omen [are] in our day obstructed by unjust laws, suppressed by custom and usage, reduced to nothing by education. For as soon as she is born a woman is confined to idleness at home . . . and, as if incapable of functions more important, she has no other prospect than needle and thread. Further, when she has reached the age of puberty, she is delivered over to the jealous power of a husband, or she is enclosed forever in a [convent]. She is forbidden by law to hold public office; even the most shrewd among them are not permitted to bring a suit in court . . . They are excluded also from preaching the word of God, in contradiction to Scriptures where the Holy Spirit, by the mouth of Joel has promised them: 'Your daughters also will prophesy'.[27]

All this happened simply because men had the power in society and they used it to establish laws and social customs that kept women oppressed and inferior. In fact, they were *not* inferior. God had created men and women equal:

Women are not inferior to men either in the quality of their minds or in their phys-ical strength . . . they can do everything that men do.[28]

And, Agrippa strongly implied, they should be allowed to do so.

THE *QUERELLE DES FEMMES* IN THE SIXTEENTH AND EARLY SEVENTEENTH CENTURIES

Agrippa's widely read *Declamation* changed the course of the *querelle des femmes*. After his work, the type of treatise predominant earlier in the *querelle*, one that used the standard texts to argue that women were inferior to men, almost completely disappeared. The few such treatises published were promptly refuted with Agrippa's arguments and examples, often by female humanists defending their sex. That is what happened to Guiseppe Passi, for example. His *On the Defects of Women* appeared in 1599. The next year the female poet and biographer Lucrezia Marinella demolished his arguments in her Agrippa-like *The Nobility and Excellence of Women and the Defects and Vices of Men*.[29] Even arguing female inferiority with tongue-in-cheek invited instant refutation. In 1595 an anonymous pamphlet (actually written by the German humanist Valeus Acidalius) used the usual texts for 'proof' not just that women were inferior but that they were not even human. If women were different from and inferior to men and men were the standard for human beings, as they were in the one-sex model, then women were not human! But Acidalius' ingenious argument was not admired; instead, a Protestant minister accused him of blasphemy in denying the humanity of women.[30]

This attack provides a clue to one of the great mysteries of the *querelle des femmes*: why did Agrippa's attack on the notion of female inferiority succeed while Pisan's very similar arguments failed? The answer is simple: Agrippa wrote a century after Pisan and by then European society had changed. As we saw, social reality was often used as evidence to support the patriarchal paradigm, but there was much in European society that did not fit the patriarchal pattern and this became more true as time went by. For example, by the mid-sixteenth century, the Protestant Reformation was well under way and the Protestants, inspired by the Renaissance humanists to go back to the text, in their case the Bible, had rediscovered and proclaimed the basic spiritual equality of men and women inherent in Christianity. Protestants taught that men and women were equal in the eyes of God and that both were essential parts of the Creation. Both were equally liable to sin and equally able to attain salvation. (For more on Protestant teachings on women, see Chapter 9.) Thus the spread of Protestantism made ideas of female equality more acceptable.

So too did other social developments. By the sixteenth century courtly society was growing in importance as most of the self-governing city-states of Italy became princely domains and the new monarchs of western Europe used their ever larger and more lavish courts as instruments of power. In courtly society men and women were almost equal. Baldesar Castiglione's famous handbook on how to succeed in court, *The Courtier* (1528), noted that male and female court attendants needed essentially the same qualities. Both had to be physically attractive, fashionably dressed, witty, tactful and discreet, appreciative of the arts, skilled in drawing, singing, dancing and playing a musical instrument and well educated, with a thorough grounding in the Latin and Greek classics with their lessons in civic virtue, necessary in case they had to advise rulers. Only the requirements of chastity for women and good horsemanship and swordsmanship and courage in battle for men differentiated the male and female court attendant. Therefore it is not surprising that *The Courtier* eloquently defended the equality of men and women:

> For just as no stone can be more perfectly a stone as regards the essence stone, nor one piece of wood more perfectly wood than another piece ... so ... the male will not be more perfect than the female as regards their formal substance, because the one and the other are included under the species man, and that in which the one differs from the other is an accident and is not of the essence.[31]

Both Protestantism and the courtly ideal required that women be educated and rising rates of female literacy and the consequent growing numbers of women writers, scientists and intellectuals gave yet more evidence that men and women were equal, as did the surprisingly high numbers of female rulers in sixteenth-century Europe. Here were women playing men's roles and playing them well. In fact, it was these women in men's roles who became the focus of the *querelle* in the sixteenth and early seventeenth centuries. After Agrippa, no intellectual could seriously defend the notion that women were fundamentally inferior to men, although that notion lingered on in popular culture throughout the early modern period. But for those involved in the *querelle*, the end of the notion of female inferiority brought the rest of the patriarchal paradigm into question. If men and women were created equal, did they, as Pisan and Agrippa maintained, have essentially the same qualities and were they capable of filling the same social roles? Or were they spiritually equal but physically different, with inborn gender traits, and did those of women ban them from the public sphere and confine them to the domestic roles of wife and mother?

As we have seen, the latter is what the humanists had argued in the earlier *querelle* and, in the sixteenth century, the Protestants also supported this position. Although they emphasized the spiritual equality of all human beings, Protestants also drew a sharp distinction between the spiritual world and our temporal one. In the God-ordained spiritual world, men and women were equals, but in the temporal world, whose order was not dictated by God but shaped by nature and the needs of human society, men and women were physically different and destined for different social roles. As Protestantism's founder Martin Luther explained:

> Men have broad shoulders and narrow hips, and accordingly they possess intelligence ... Women ought to stay at home; the way they were created indicates this, for they have broad hips and a wide fundament to sit upon, keep house and bear and raise children.[32]

This humanist–Protestant position, which might be called the 'equal but different' argument, kept most of the patriarchal paradigm intact. Not surprisingly, it became the conservative majority position taken by most of the participants in the sixteenth-century *querelle*. But a minority of the debaters were convinced by Pisan's and Agrippa's questioning of innate gender traits and naturally dictated gender roles, especially since the number of women who seemed to have 'manly' qualities and play 'manly' roles was growing so dramatically. These exceptional women, known in the period as *femmes fortes*, women of strength and fortitude, became the new focus of the debate.

The *femme forte* had haunted the *querelle des femmes* from its beginning, when Christine de Pisan pillaged Giovanni Boccaccio's *Of Famous Women*, a compendium of notable women in ancient history and mythology, for examples of female writers, artists, rulers and other women playing men's roles. To her this proved that there were no inherent gender traits or naturally dictated gender roles. But most people did not agree. For according to the universally accepted one-sex model of human nature, there was a wide continuum of possible sexual identities. The right combination of humours produced a man and the opposite a woman, but other combinations might produce hermaphrodites (people with both male and female sexual characteristics), 'womanly' men with some female characteristics or 'manly' women with some male features. For most people, the last explained the *femmes fortes*, who showed 'male' traits and played 'male' social roles: they were women with more masculine humours than were found in the usual female.[33] In early modern Europe every woman of accomplishment was labelled 'manly', starting with Christine de Pisan herself, whom the Archbishop of Paris praised as 'distinguished woman, manly female'.[34] Thus the existence of *femmes fortes* did not necessarily undermine the belief that women and men had distinct personality traits and social roles; instead, it strengthened it.

So, too, did the way these 'manly' women were portrayed in art and literature. Throughout the sixteenth and well into the seventeenth century, the *femme forte* was a favourite subject for artists and writers. At first she was portrayed in ways that reaffirmed the existence of separate gender traits and roles. The *femmes fortes* portrayed were usually examples from the Bible or classical learning – Jael, Judith slaying Holofernes, the goddess Minerva, the Amazons and Lucretia were favourites – and they were usually depicted not in female dress but with helmets, swords and armour, which indicated to contemporary viewers that they were not claiming their heroic traits for *women* but instead were temporarily acting as *men*. Of these standard *femmes fortes*, the Amazons and Lucretia were especially reassuring to those worried about the gender order.[According to legend, the Amazons, female hunters and warriors, had renounced their womanhood. They lived chastely without men and amputated one breast (an obvious symbol of femininity) to make drawing a bow easier. And Lucretia, a Roman matron and rape victim who committed suicide rather than bring disgrace on her husband's family, had displayed her manly fortitude in defence of the female virtue most important to traditional patriarchy, wifely fidelity.[35]]

Yet the *femme forte* had potential to subvert the gender order. Unsurprisingly, her image was often employed by actual women who had to act as men – artists, writers, rulers. For example, Marie de Medici, who ruled France in the early seventeenth century as regent for her son Louis XIII, had herself portrayed, helmeted and with one breast bared, as Minerva. Marie's daughter-in-law, Anne of Austria, another regent, was also portrayed as Minerva, by a female artist, Artemisia Gentileschi. Gentileschi herself, also a woman playing a man's role, found the imagery of the *femme forte* useful. Not only did she often paint her, she also used her as a role model. Frequently in letters to potential clients and patrons she presented herself as a lone woman forced to play a man's role in the world.[36] Aristocratic court ladies in seventeenth-century France also modelled themselves on *femmes fortes*, posing for their portraits in bits of armour and even donning it when they invaded the masculine sphere of politics and became military leaders of various noble factions during the revolt of the Fronde.[37]

But this adoption of the image of the *femme forte* by living women was dangerous for the gender order. As more and more living women adopted the image of the *femme forte*, she was increasingly identified with *them* rather than Lucretia or the Amazons. In the *querelle*, authors increasingly cited living examples of *femmes fortes*. Anna Maria van Schurmann, a seventeenth-century Dutch woman who knew six languages and was deemed the greatest linguist of her time, not the mythical Carmentis, supposed inventor of the Roman alphabet, was cited to show women's facility with language, and Elizabeth I of England and Isabella of Castile, not Semiramis and Zenobia, were used as examples of successful female rulers. When the famous Spanish playwright Calderon created a strong-minded female ruler he named her Cristerna, after his contemporary, Queen Christina of Sweden.[38] These living, breathing women were *women*, far more obviously than their shadowy ancient counterparts, and the ways they used the imagery of the *femme forte* often emphasized their femininity. Marie de Medici had herself portrayed in the feminine guises of Ceres, goddess of the harvest and fecundity, and Juno, consort of Jupiter, as well as Minerva, and Artemisia Gentileschi presented herself as a highly skilled *female* painter as well as a *femme forte*. And the *femmes fortes* she painted were not the lifeless embodiments of manly virtues portrayed by male artists but instead real women with real emotions, as a comparison of her Judiths (Plate 2) with those of male artists (Plate 3) shows.

DEBATES ABOUT WOMEN'S SOCIAL ROLES

Thus the ubiquity of the *femme forte* and her symbolic use by women raised basic questions about the gender order. Was the *femme forte* indeed an exceptional woman or was she a normal female whose achievements were within reach of many of her sex? Were the qualities underlying her achievements 'manly' or simply human and likely to be found in people of either sex? The sixteenth- and early seventeenth-century *querelle* was full of debates over these questions, as numerous writers examined the various 'masculine' social roles and asked if women could possibly fill them.

The best known of these debates is that provoked by the numerous female rulers – Elizabeth I, Mary Tudor, Mary Queen of Scots, Catherine de Medici – of the period. (For more on them, see Chapter 12.) It began in 1558, when John Knox, a Protestant Scot who disliked having to obey his Catholic queens, Mary Queen of Scots and her mother Mary of Guise, published his *First Blast of the Trumpet Against the Monstrous Regiment of Women*. Knox argued that women should not be allowed to rule because having a woman command men went against the laws of God and of nature. Furthermore, women were inevitably bad rulers, because they lacked the masculine qualities, like reason, prudence and a willingness to listen to advice, necessary to govern effectively. Knox's diatribe was answered the next year by John Aylmer, an English Protestant anxious to justify the power of his Protestant queen, Elizabeth I. He too accepted that men and women had different innate qualities that made women unfit for rule, but drawing on the principles of patriarchy and patriliny, Aylmer argued that when there was no legitimate male heir, daughters should inherit the throne and that their female weaknesses of mind and body no more disqualified them for rule than physical infirmity or feeblemindedness disqualified a legitimate male heir. Thus for Aylmer one part of the patriarchal paradigm, the patrilineal descent of property, trumped another, women's inherent faults.

Other contributors to the debate, however, attacked the idea of inherent gender traits. Frenchman Nicolas de Cholières pointed out the illogic of his country's Salic law, which mandated the appointment of queen mothers as regents for their underage sons but did not allow king's daughters to inherit the throne. Surely if, despite their inherent female qualities, women were fit to rule France as regents, they should also be able to rule as queens in their own right. And Lord Ormond, a Scottish courtier of and apologist for Catherine de Medici, simply questioned the notion of inherent gender differences. Like Agrippa, he argued that men and women were created equal, with the same qualities, including the two necessary for governing well, reason and prudence. Because of this, Ormond suggested that women should not only be allowed to inherit thrones but also to hold elective public office.[39]

Whether women should hold public office was also widely debated in the *querelle*, for that was part of a broader aspect of the patriarchal paradigm widely questioned in the sixteenth and early seventeenth centuries: woman's place as citizen and her status at law. Many legal treatises explored the last and pointed out its inconsistencies. Women were required to obey the law as individual human beings and they were individually held responsible for their crimes, yet they often were denied legal rights – to make contracts, bring lawsuits, inherit property – that men as individuals possessed. Further, women's legal rights changed over the course of their lives as their relationships with male patriarchs changed; a widow had different rights than those of a wife. Women's citizenship also differed from men's. While women born of citizen parents in a city or country inherited citizenship as men did, female citizenship did not encompass, as male citizenship might, the right to vote or hold public office.

Many contributors to the *querelle* argued that all this was illogical. If, as everyone agreed, natural law preceded and formed the basis of man-made laws, and if in natural law every human being, man and woman alike, had what Nicolas Estienne in his *Misères de la femme mariée* (*Miseries of the Married Woman*, 1619) termed a 'God-given right to self-government' based on their existence as human beings, then man-made laws should reflect and protect this, not deny women legal rights.[40] And if women were citizens, 'free burgesses of the same citie whereof their husbands are free, and free denisons in the same land wherein their husbands are free', as William Heale put it in *An Apologie for Women* (1609), then they should enjoy all the rights and duties that come with citizenship.[41]

Why then were women denied these rights? Why were they excluded from the public sphere of politics and confined to the home? The Italian Domenico Bruni da Pistoia answered (in his *Defence of Women*, 1559) that it was not 'because of lack of judgement' on their part but simply for 'public decency' – i.e. to protect their chastity. Husbands did not want their wives going out in public and mingling with other men. Bruni argued that the division of the world into a masculine public sphere of business and politics and a feminine private sphere of the home was based not on biblical injunction or natural law but simply on 'ancient custom'. Proof that God did not ordain or nature dictate that division was that other societies allotted gender roles differently; in ancient Egypt, according to Herodotus, men stayed home and did house-work.[42] Bruni also pointed out that only elite women were really confined to the home; lower class women were necessarily active in the public sphere of work:

> Every woman [artisan] does as well as a man in looking after her [business] affairs and organizing her life . . . And if we wish to speak of country women, we will see that they are in no way inferior to their husbands. For they are intent on the same basic rural tasks.[43]

THE END OF THE QUERELLE

In the sixteenth and early seventeenth centuries, almost every social role was debated and found fit for women. Therefore it is not surprising that the *querelle des femmes* ended with short, all-encompassing and *uncontested* statements of women's equality with men and their ability to perform any and every social role. Of these works, two stand out. Both came from France, for the *querelle* ended where it began. They are *The Equality of Men and Women*, by Marie Jars de Gournay, written in 1622, and François Poullain de La Barre's *Of the Equality of the Two Sexes*, first published in 1673.

Marie de Gournay's work is second only to Pisan's as a contribution to the *querelle* by a woman writer. Gournay, in fact, resembled Pisan; she too was a minor French noblewoman who supported herself by her pen. But Gournay's career differed from Pisan's in ways which highlight women's gains over the 300 years separating them. Gournay did not have to rely on her father for an education in the classics; she educated herself. She was not forced into an arranged marriage or into a convent. She supported herself as a single woman all her life and she relied on publisher's fees for her work as an editor, translator, novelist and poet, not just royal patronage, to do it.[44]

But Gournay was like Pisan in one very important way: she was devout and her main concern in the *querelle* was the issue of female sinfulness and the spiritual equality of women. Religion is the theme that runs through her work. She bases her argument for the equality of the sexes not on reason (which could be disputed) or examples (which were 'too common'), but on 'the authority of God himself': 'Man was created male and female – so says scripture.'[45] And while she is careful to dispute the existence of inborn gender traits (for those who believe in such things, 'the supreme excellence women may achieve is to resemble ordinary men') and to argue that women can be learned and rule states and that they were prevented from doing these things by their poor educations and by men, who used their greater strength to keep women 'confined to the distaff alone' and preserve their own supremacy, Gournay's greatest concern was with the spiritual equality of women and their role in religion.[46] Here she went further than anyone else had dared, putting forth not only the common argument that women had preached in the early church but also the uncommon one that since they were allowed to administer the sacraments (or at least *a* sacrament; midwives could baptize newborns in danger of dying), they should be eligible for the priesthood. Gournay dismissed the usual argument against this, that Jesus' incarnation as a man, not a woman, showed that God intended only men to be priests. Gournay argued that Jesus' male incarnation was only a convenience:

> It had to be thus for necessary reasons of decency, since he would have been unable without scandal to mingle as a young person and at all hours of the day and night among the crowds in order to convert, succor, and save the human race, if he had been of the female sex.[47]

While Gournay's emphasis is overwhelmingly religious, her successor, the last important contributor to the *querelle*, Poullain de La Barre, repudiated religion altogether. De La Barre's work was not published until 1673 and by then the scientific revolution had cast doubt on the 'truths' of religion. Poullain was a follower of René Descartes, one of the founders of modern science and, like Descartes, he was sceptical of any 'truths' unproved by human reason. Reason was the key to Poullain's views, as religion had been for Gournay's. Nature, not God, had created men and women equal and it was their reason, not their souls, that made them so. Men and women were equal because they were equally intelligent. Their brains worked similarly, receiving and processing the sense impressions which, according to the new scientific ideas, were the only basis of true knowledge:

> [T]he most exact Anatomy remarks . . . no difference . . . between *Men* and *Women*, their brain is altogether like to ours: the impressions of sense are received, and muster themselves there in the same fashion.[48]

Because their minds were the same as men's, women, when properly educated, were capable of filling any social role demanding intelligence. This principle allowed de La Barre to claim the last remaining male outposts for women. Women could not only rule states and hold elective public office; they could fill the post of government bureaucracies as well, 'as Vice-Queens, Goverants, Secretaries, Counsellors of State, and Treasurers'. And they could 'teach with success' at universities.[49] And because de La Barre, in the standard Enlightenment fashion, rejected the spiritual side of religion as mere belief unfounded in fact and thought religion should simply provide a moral code of conduct, he saw no reason why women could not be pastors or priests.[50] De La Barre even envisaged a role for women in that last bastion of masculinity, warfare:

> For my part, I should be no more surprised to see a *Woman* with a helmet on her head, than to see her with a Crown; preside in a Council of war, as well as in a Council of State . . . The military Art hath nothing beyond others, whereof *Women* are not capable . . . The Eyes are sufficient to learn from a Mapp . . . all the High-ways of a country, . . . and the places most proper for surprises, and encampings . . . A *Woman* can do all this, and can invent Strategems to surprise the enemy . . . And *Women* testifie no less heart, and resolution when their honour is concerned, than is requisite to attack or defend a Place.[51]

As our own society shows, de La Barre's radical notions about women's roles in society were not widely accepted. Ironically, this was due to the same factor that gave rise to his ideas in the first place: the scientific revolution of the seventeenth century. If the rise of modern science helped women by throwing all traditional assumptions into question, it also hurt women by suggesting that they were biologically destined solely to be wives and mothers. The scientific revolution destroyed the old one-sex model of human nature, in which women were inferior men. Replacing this was a new two-sex model, which emphasized the physical differences between men and women and suggested that these differences meant that they were destined by nature for different social roles. Men, with their physical strength and competitiveness, were destined for the public spheres of work, government and war, while women were, of course, destined for motherhood. Thus the scientific revolution prolonged the notion that women should be confined to the domestic sphere and the social roles of wife and mother.[52]

Although it did not change women's social roles, the *querelle des femmes* nonetheless transformed accepted views of the nature of women. It challenged every aspect of the patriarchal paradigm. It destroyed the notion that women were inferior to men, lustier and more sinful and therefore incapable of gaining salvation. Instead, it gave women a new identity as rational human beings whose education was not just possible but desirable. It at least raised the possibilities that inborn gender traits did not exist, that women, like men, should be judged as individuals and that at least some women were capable of fulfilling 'masculine' social roles. And if most women continued to be destined for the domestic sphere and the roles of wife and mother, the *querelle* invested these with a new dignity and social importance. It is significant that most female contributors to the *querelle* did not argue that women should be rulers or army officers; instead, they argued for women's education, attacked arranged marriages and tried to find alternatives to marriage for respectable women. Their desire was to improve the domestic roles that, despite the *querelle*, most women still accepted as their proper ones. It is to these that we now turn.

Part II

◆

WOMEN AND THE FAMILY

In early modern Europe, her family was the centre of a woman's life. Society viewed her not as an autonomous individual but as a subordinate member of a patriarchal family and her major social roles were family centred: she was to perpetuate her family through the production of heirs and to love and care for its members. How she fulfilled these duties changed over the course of her life, but the very stages of her life were defined by her position in her family. Men's lives were divided chronologically (they were children, youths, mature men, elderly) or by the stages of their working lives (apprentices, journeymen, masters; students, professionals, retired), but women's lives were divided by their changing roles in the family and changing relationships with its male head; women were daughters, wives, mothers, widows. In this part of the book, we will examine women's roles in and relationships with their families, with a chapter devoted to each stage of their lives.

Chapter 2

◆

GIRLS AND MAIDENS

RAISING A DAUGHTER

In her pioneering feminist work *The Second Sex*, published in 1949, the French intellectual Simone de Beauvoir wrote that women are made, not born.[1] She meant that for women gender identity is not biologically determined but instead inculcated by society from a girl's earliest days. In the early modern period, as in ours, the making of a woman – and indeed a man – began at birth. From the moment she was born, a girl was treated differently from a boy. For one thing, her birth was often greeted with less rejoicing than those of her brothers. Early modern Europe was a patrilineal society; property generally descended through male heirs. Therefore, everyone from poor peasants to kings on their thrones wanted sons as heirs to the family fortune and bearers of the family name. Daughters were liabilities, draining away family resources because of the dowries necessary to marry them off. In seventeenth-century France, a noblewoman, the Comtesse de Grignan, apologized to her husband for giving birth to a daughter instead of the son and heir he desired: 'If my good health can console you for only having a daughter, I will not ask your forgiveness for not having given you a son.' Madame refused to care for the disappointing child, leaving her first to servants and then to her own mother, the famous writer Madame de Sévigné, and finally putting her into a convent at age five. When she was eight, the little girl announced that she wanted to become a nun, thus removing herself permanently from her mother's sight and life.[2]

Madame de Grignan was not the only mother to abandon a disappointing female baby. In early modern Europe, poor parents were often forced during hard times to abandon one or more of their children, either to an orphanage or foundling home, from which they might be retrieved in better times, or simply on the streets. There is much evidence that girls were more likely to be abandoned and less likely to be taken back by their families than boys. For example, in 1700 the Inclusa, a foundling home in Madrid, received more abandoned girls than boys (67.6 percent of the children entering were female) and while 53.2 percent of the boys were eventually reclaimed by their parents, only 46.4 percent of the girls were.[3]

If they kept their daughters, parents of all social classes faced a challenge, for girls were considered harder to raise than boys. This was due to two intertwined factors: their deficiencies of intellect and will and their destiny, which was to marry. Girls were thought to lack the sharp minds and strong willpower of boys, which made them harder to educate. Also, they were destined to marry and to do so they had to be virgins. The preservation of their daughter's chastity, a difficult task given girls' supposedly strong sex drive and weak moral sense, obsessed many parents, who were extremely watchful over their daughters and restricted their movement and contacts.

I say 'parents', but, in fact, it was mothers who were primarily responsible for childrearing, especially the raising of daughters. Fathers, as patriarchal heads of households, in theory bore the ultimate responsibility for the moral guidance of their children, as indeed they did for that of their wives, apprentices, servants and any other members of their households, but the daily, hands-on tasks of childrearing, especially caring for the child's physical needs, fell on the mother, because women were thought destined by nature for childcare. And despite their own lack of education and feeble feminine intellects and moral instincts, mothers were also responsible for the first steps in the education of their children. This was true because 'education' in our sense of the word, that is, booklearning acquired in school, the heart of our experience of childhood, formed only a minor part of that stage of life in the early modern period even for boys, and for the majority of women, who never went to school and could not read and write, 'education' in our sense of the word was nonexistent. In the sixteenth and seventeenth centuries, 'education' was defined as training for the child's future life. This included moral training so that the child would lead an upright life and practical training in the skills necessary for his or her future occupation.[4] A seventeenth-century English farmer's son explained that he had been educated 'sometimes at school, sometimes with herding, and tending of Sheep, or Cattel, sometime with the Plow, cart, or threshing Instrument or other lawfull labor'.[5] Those whose adult roles required literacy – future doctors, lawyers or bureaucrats, for example – were educated in our sense of the word, but many boys and most girls were not. In any case, mothers were considered capable of and responsible for laying the foundations of moral and vocational training in early childhood.

The vocational training of boys eventually took them 'out of the hands of women' and into the hands of male schoolmasters and role models. But this did not happen with daughters, whose adult vocations would be wifehood and motherhood. These entailed skills their mothers could teach them. Mothers therefore remained central throughout the 'education' of their daughters, and a virtuous daughter capable of running a household efficiently reflected well on her mother (see Plate 4). As François de Grenaille put it in his work on the education of girls, *L'Honneste fille*, published in 1639:

> [T]he virtuous daughter seeing her mother has a perfect description of what she must one day be . . . the virtuous daughter is the image and the masterwork of the virtuous woman . . . Women serve not only in forming them [daughters], but since they use themselves as models, and since in order to produce a daughter the mother makes her own image, one can further say that they have the same right over their work as a painter over his self-portrait.[6]

For both boys and girls, 'education' was accomplished in three stages, the stages into which childhood was routinely divided in early modern Europe. The first stage lasted from birth until age six or seven. In this stage children were considered animal-like and incapable of true intellectual thought, but appealing in their childishness and helplessness. This was true of both boys and girls. In fact, after the crucial first days of life, when frailer boy babies were more likely to die than girls (this is true in all human societies), there was little to differentiate a girl's life from a boy's. In western Europe, while they were toddlers, both sexes wore a unisex baby dress. Both boys and girls had to survive the perils of wet nursing, swaddling, learning to walk, toilet training and corporal punishment. (For more on these matters, see Chapter 4.) Only in their play was gendered treatment of boys and girls apparent. Then, as now, children were directed (often unconsciously) by adults to gender-specific play which would help prepare them for their adult roles. One seventeenth-century German writer noted:

> Little daughters do not know yet that they are girls, even less why they are such. Still they play with dolls made from rags. They cradle them, caress them, and care for them, while boys horse around, build houses, and even altars.[7]

Because girls' play was quieter and gentler than that of boys, and because girls were cuter, with more of the winsome childish graces adults found appealing in young children, at this stage of life the earlier gender imbalance was redressed and daughters often inspired deep love in the parents who had not especially welcomed their birth. An example is the disappointing daughter of the Comtesse de Grignan, who never succeeded in winning her mother's love but did gain the devotion of her grandmother, Madame de Sévigné, through her winning ways. De Sévigné wrote of her as a 2-year-old:

> She does a hundred little things, she speaks, she caresses, she hits, she makes the sign of the cross, she asks for forgiveness, she curtseys, she kisses the hand, she shrugs her shoulders, she dances, she flatters, she raises her chin; in a word, she is pretty in every way. I have fun with her for hours on end . . . I do not know how someone could manage not to love her daughter.[8]

Most of the surviving parental laments for children who died young concern daughters, not sons.

SCHOOLING AND LITERACY

Unfortunately, the advantage tipped again in favour of boys when children entered into the second stage of childhood at age six or seven. It was only then that children were thought capable of analytical reasoning and therefore it was only then that their education in our sense of the word – their school-ing – normally began. Both boys and girls were often taught the alphabet and their numbers and perhaps even basic reading skills at an earlier age, by their mothers if they themselves were literate or, in the case of royal and some aristocratic children, by hired tutors. For example, the educations of Queen Isabella of Castile and Princess Mary Tudor, sister of Henry VIII, both began when they were given tutors at age four. But this sort of learning was rote memorization accomplished by repetition and habituation, the methods used for training animals, which such young children were thought to resemble. Only at seven was it thought children could actually reason. Therefore that was the age at which most schools accepted pupils and most children's educa-tions began. This meant that when their offspring turned seven, parents were faced with important decisions: should the child be educated? Should he or she be sent to school?

If the child was a girl, the answers were usually no. Only among Muslims was there a strong motive for educating girls: the religious one that all believers should be able to read – or at least memorize – the Quran, the Muslim holy book. The major cities and towns of the Ottoman Empire had primary schools for girls, staffed by female teachers, and many girls were doubtless proud of having, like their brothers, earned the religious title *hafiz* by memorizing the Quran.[9]

Christian Europe, by contrast, until the Protestant Reformation at least, lacked a religious motive for educating girls and had inherited from the Middle Ages strong arguments against the practice. First, there was the supposed incapacity of the female brain for logical thought, a supposition which, as Christine de Pisan noted, was usually 'proved' by the fact that women had made few contributions to learning.[10] Pisan tartly pointed out that this was a circular argument and a self-fulfilling prophecy: women made few contributions to learning because they were not educated and they were not educated because they had made few contributions to learning. Another, more persuasive, argument was that most women had no need of reading and writing. If education were defined as preparing a child for adult life, why should girls be taught to read and write? Only a few adult female roles really required literacy. Nuns had to know how to read and so did queens and noblewomen, who might have to stand in for their male relatives as estate managers, judges in seigneurial courts and even rulers. Pisan thought all noblewomen should not only read and write but also have some legal training. But even she could see no point in teaching a future peasant's wife to read and write. A final argument against women's education was that it was not only unnecessary for most female roles but detrimental to the most important one: that of faithful wife. If women could read, they would have access to courtly love romances, with their glorification of adulterous passion. And given women's impressionable nature, strong sex drive and weak moral sense, wives would soon be imitating their favourite fictional heroines and cuckholding their husbands!

By 1600 these medieval arguments against teaching girls to read and write had lost much of their force, as new factors arose to promote the spread of literacy even among women. The first was the invention of printing, which greatly multiplied and cheapened books and made the world of learning accessible to many more people. Another factor was economic and social change. As the economy expanded in the sixteenth century, urban artisans, producing more goods for a geographically broader clientele, increasingly found it necessary to be able to read, write and keep accurate records. And because production took place in the household and involved the whole family, it was important that artisans' wives and daughters were literate as well.

A final factor promoting the spread of literacy was the new theories about the value of education propounded by the Renaissance humanists and, later, by the theologians of the Reformation and Counterreformation. The humanists were traditional in that they viewed education as a training for adult roles. This meant that women had no need of what the humanists considered the highest form of education, the study of the humanities, especially the Latin and Greek classics of the ancient world, because the classics prepared people to be good citizens – to understand public issues, to make moral choices in such matters, to communicate their ideas effectively to others. Most women had no need of these qualities, for they were not citizens in that sense (see Chapter 13). But the humanists thought all human beings, men and women alike, should be literate, because literacy promoted moral behaviour. To the humanists, the essence of human nature, the thing that set human beings apart from animals, was their capacity to tell good from evil and their desire to lead a moral life. They thought that every human being should be trained in morality so that he or she would behave well in this life and gain salvation in the next. The best way to learn moral behaviour was to read the Bible in the vernacular. As the most famous of the Renaissance humanists, Desiderius Erasmus, put it:

> I absolutely dissent from those people who don't want the holy scriptures to be read in translation by the unlearned – as if, forsooth, Christ taught such complex doctrine that hardly anyone outside a handful of theologians could understand it ... I should prefer that all women, even of the lowest rank, should read the evangelists and the epistles of Paul ... I would hope that the farmer might chant a holy text at his plow, the spinner sing it as she sits at her wheel ... It makes no sense when baptism ... along with the sacraments and the final reward of immortality are open equally to all, that doctrine should be confined to just a handful.[11]

The emphasis on women in this vision of universal Bible reading is significant: Erasmus and the other humanists were firm advocates of education for females. They turned the traditional arguments against educating women inside out. Finding examples of learned women, even poets and philosophers, in their beloved ancient Greece and Rome, they maintained that women were men's intellectual equals and fully capable of learning. They also argued that the ability to read was a vital part of women's major social role as wife and mother. A literate mother could teach her children and a literate wife would not only be a true intellectual companion to her husband but also a more faithful spouse, for if women could read they could read the Bible and other moral works which would inspire them to guard their chastity.

The educational theories of the humanists were important for two reasons. First, they inspired the foundation of schools, especially in Italy, the centre of humanist learning. For example, in sixteenth-century Venice, 26 percent of the city's boys between the ages of six and 13 attended schools.[12] The educational writings of the humanists were also important because they shaped the educational theories of the Protestant Reformation, the most important force for schooling and literacy in our period. (For more on this, see Chapter 9.) Protestants like Martin Luther thought that all Christians had to be literate so that they could read the scriptures. This would not only help them to act morally in this world but also bring them salvation in the next, because Protestants believed that salvation came not through performing good works or gaining the intercession of the Virgin Mary and the saints, but by faith alone. And the source of faith was the New Testament, the very words of Christ. Therefore every Christian should be able to read the New Testament and absorb its lessons. To facilitate this, Protestants urged their rulers, whether kings, princes or city magistrates, to build schools. And these schools were to teach girls as well as boys, for the Protestants regarded women as the spiritual equals of men and just as capable of gaining salvation. The English Protestant and advocate of female education, Thomas Becon, wrote:

> It is expedient that by public authority schools for women-children be erected and set up in every Christian commonweal . . . If it be thought convenient . . . that schools should be erected and set up for the right education and bringing up of the youth of the male kind, why should it not also be thought convenient that schools be built for the godly institution and virtuous bringing up of the youth of the female kind? Is not the woman a creature of God so well as the man? And as dear unto God as the man?[13]

Its advocacy of female literacy was one of the attractions of Protestantism for women. And because it was losing so many to the new faith, the Catholic Church revised its position on this issue. After the reforming Council of Trent (1540–1563), the Church began promoting at least basic literacy for all its flock, men and women alike. It was thought that if Catholics could read they could more easily learn their catechism and they could read devotional works which would strengthen their faith and inoculate them against Protestantism. So the Catholic Church too began to promote the spread of schooling, although, unlike the Protestants, it did not urge civil authorities to establish schools but instead founded its own, run by its own personnel. Parish priests ran catechism classes which taught basic reading skills, male orders like the Jesuits and the Christian Brothers founded schools for boys and the new orders of nuns of the Counterreformation like the Ursulines and the Daughters of Charity ran schools for girls (see Chapter 10).

Therefore the sixteenth and especially the seventeenth century, when the Catholic programme really got under way, saw an explosion of schools throughout Europe. In England, for example, at least 410 and maybe as many as 800 schools were founded between 1480 and 1660. The German state of Württemberg had only 50 schools in 1534 but 270 by 1581.[14] Naturally this wider availability of schools fuelled a dramatic rise in literacy. But even by 1700 literacy was still far from universal. Instead its incidence varied by geographic region, religion, social class and especially by gender. Because being able to read and interpret the Bible was more central to Protestantism than Catholicism, Protestants were more likely to be literate. In France in 1690, for example, in a Protestant village in the Dauphiné, 65 percent of the male artisans and 44 percent of the male peasants could sign their names, compared to 55 percent of the male artisans and only 10 percent of the male peasants in a nearby Catholic village.[15] This meant that predominantly Protestant countries like England and Holland had the highest literacy rates. England and Holland were also highly literate because they were highly urbanized. Towns and cities, with their concentration of schools and of magistrates, lawyers, merchants and artisans who needed to be able to read and write, always had higher literacy rates than the countryside. In Spain in 1635, about one-third of the male household heads in major cities were literate. In country towns, the figure was one-quarter, but in rural areas it was less than one-tenth. Social class was another major variable: the higher the class, the more literacy was likely. In Spain between 1580 and 1650, all churchmen and government bureaucrats were literate, as were the wealthiest nobles and merchants, but some poor nobles, the *hidalgos*, could not read and write. Between one-third and one-half of male artisans, shopkeepers and well-off peasants could sign their names, but almost all male day labourers could not. Similarly, in sixteenth-century Poland 91 percent of officials and middle-class townsmen were literate, but only 78 percent of the noblemen and 12 percent of the male peasants.[16]

Cutting across all these factors was the most important variable of all: gender. Whether Protestant or Catholic, town or country dweller, noble or peasant, a man was far more likely to be literate than a woman. In seventeenth-century Amsterdam one-third of the men but two-thirds of the women who married could not sign the parish register; in Madrid in the same period the figures are one-third and three-quarters. Three-quarters of the women in seventeenth-century Provence were also illiterate and in seventeenth-century Muscovy female illiteracy was almost total. Only a handful of nuns and noblewomen could read and write. The Princess Sophia, who ruled for a time as regent, apparently was literate, but it is not clear that her sisters were.[17]

TRAINING FOR LIFE

This suggests that despite the efforts of the humanists to redefine education as booklearning, most people still thought of it as acquiring the skills necessary for later life and that, despite all the efforts of the religious reformers, basic literacy was still not considered essential for the prime roles of women in later life: wife, mother and homemaker. Indeed, even the staunchest advocates of literacy for women acknowledged that little girls should learn other things as well – how to handle wool and flax, according to Vives; sewing and spinning, according to the German educational reformer Christoph Hager. Thus while books and schooling played a growing role in girls' education, they were still optional rather than central to the process.

Because the adult lives of women varied by social class, the patterns of their 'education' did too. As Richard Mulcaster, yet another famous educational reformer, explained:

> If a young maiden is to be brought up with a view to marriage, obedience to authority and similar qualities must form the best kind of training; if from necessity she has to learn how to earn her own living some technical training must prepare her for a definite calling; if she is to adorn some high position she must acquire suitable accomplishments; if she is destined for government . . . the greatness of the position calls for general excellence and a variety of gifts.[18]

As this suggests, for girls of the lower classes occupational training rather than book learning was the rule. This was especially true of peasant girls, who were of all people the least likely to have any formal schooling. Their destiny was to become good peasant wives and they learned the skills involved in this – hoeing, weeding, making butter and cheese, harvesting, preparing and spinning flax, sewing, cooking, laundering, raising livestock and children – simply by watching and helping their mothers (see Chapter 6).

The girlhood and 'education' of lower-class townswomen, the daughters of day labourers and artisans, was different. Because they lived in towns, they might have a chance to attend a free charity school, where children in Catholic countries were taught by monks and nuns and in Protestant countries by hired schoolmasters and mistresses. Or they might attend at least a catechism school taught by the local minister or parish priest. There, with 30 to 60 other pupils of all ages, they might be taught to memorize the alphabet and recognize its individual letters and then, if they were allowed to stay in school for a few months, to identify syllables, phrases and words, and eventually learn to read. In most such schools, books were few – usually only one ABC and one more advanced reader, filled with pious moralizing stories, to serve the whole class. Pupils, especially girls, were less likely to learn how to write than how to read, because writing was taught only in the third or fourth year of school, by which time many girls had left, and because learning it required expensive paper and quill pens poor parents could rarely supply. In Finland, children learned to form their letters by drawing them with a stick on sand in a sand-box and elsewhere they practised with chalk on a slate before they dared use the expensive pens and paper.[19] Because more people learned to read than to write, our literacy statistics, which are based on the percentages of people who could sign their names to legal documents, are probably underestimates.

For daughters of urban artisans and day labourers learning to read and write was less important than learning a trade. Artisans' daughters were often trained by their fathers in their crafts; sometimes they were even apprenticed by their father to a fellow master, as was Ana Grener of Barcelona in 1578. Her father, a *tapiner* (maker of cork soles for ladies' shoes), hired a fellow *tapiner* to teach her.[20] An artisan's workshop was a family enterprise. The craftsman, usually a master in his craft's guild, was assisted by his apprentices and journeymen and also by his wife (who often helped make the goods, supervise the apprentices, deal with customers and keep the books) and by his children. Training a daughter in your craft had two advantages: her work increased the family income in the short run and her skills made her an attractive marriage prospect in the long run. Artisans frequently married the daughters of fellow craftsmen because they knew such women had the skills necessary to help them make their family business a success.

Sometimes, however, artisans' daughters were taught a trade or craft different from their fathers', a 'women's' trade that would support them while single and that they could continue to practise when they married. (For more on this, see Chapter 7.) Many 'women's trades' – laundressing and petty commerce like street peddling and selling from market stalls – were low-pay and low-prestige occupations not organized into guilds. Therefore they had no apprenticeships. Girls learned to be laundresses simply by being hired to wash clothes. But the more prestigious and lucrative of the women's trades, like dressmaking and midwifery, might be organized in guilds and fathers paid for their daughters to be apprenticed to a guild mistress. The apprenticeship was often long; in sixteenth-century Bristol 12 to 15 years was the norm.[21] During this time the young girl lived in the mistress's house and learned the trade; the food, clothing and occasional sums of money she received were usually spelled out in the apprenticeship contract. Sometimes contracts also stipulated that apprentices not be beaten or otherwise abused or forced to do housework. Mistresses were sorely tempted to use their apprentices as domestic servants and to neglect teaching them their trade. Thus when Mary Tristam, a soap maker's daughter, was apprenticed to Mrs Susan Beeke to learn seamstressing in 1626, the contract specified that Mrs Beeke would always have a servant to do the household chores, so 'that the said Mary may better ply her needlework'.[22] In the seventeenth century, apprenticeship contracts for girls increasingly specified that they be taught to read and write. In 1632 Sara Gwin's mistress was required to give her 'time and libertie at sometimes in the weeke for her to learn to reade' and in 1658 Mary Bussell, apprenticed to a seamstress, was to be taught both sewing and writing.[23] This suggests that literacy was increasingly regarded as useful for artisans' daughters. But the heart of their education remained learning a trade, either a women's trade they could pursue independently or a man's trade they could help their husband practise in later life.

The education of middle- and upper-class girls was different because their destinies as adult women were different. Women of these classes were destined for marriages in which their role would be solely that of wife, mother and housewife, not, as with peasants' and artisans' wives, working partner in the family enterprise. Although a merchant's wife might help with her husband's business when he was alive, middle-class girls were usually given no special training for this. And wives of professionals – doctors, lawyers, clergymen, government bureaucrats – usually could not help with or inherit their husbands' careers; they were solely housewives. So the practical training of middle-class girls was confined to housewifely skills – cooking, cleaning, sewing, spinning and the like. These were, however, formidable skills in an era when at least some households aimed for self-sufficiency and housekeeping included making butter, cheese and candles and weaving and dying cloth (see Chapter 6). Occasionally girls received this training through apprenticeship; Anne Colston was apprenticed for five years to learn parchment working, lace making and fancy sewing.[24] And sometimes teachers were hired to come to their homes. But usually they were trained in housewifery by their mothers.

Mothers were also responsible for an even more important aspect of their education: moral training. Middle-class girls had to be socialized to be good Christian mothers and faithful, obedient wives. Thanks to the humanists and the religious reformers who emphasized the usefulness of devotional literature to women's moral training, the first step in this moral training was the acquisition of basic literacy. Middle-class girls usually learned basic reading, writing and counting skills between the ages of seven and 12, considered the prime learning period for children. They might be taught at home, often along with their brothers; the teacher might be their mother, their father or a hired tutor, usually male, in Protestant areas often a young clergyman. Or girls might attend school, in Catholic areas often a convent school. Sometimes girls even attended a local grammar school and learned the rudiments of Latin and Greek along with their brothers.[25]

MAIDENHOOD

Around age 12, however, the educations of elite boys and girls diverged. At 12, a child embarked on the final stage of childhood: adolescence (for girls called maidenhood), with its onset of sexual maturity. For young men, adolescence brought more rigorous educational training, often at boarding schools, in Latin, Greek and the classics, to prepare them for their future careers. But the onset of sexual maturity and sexual awareness was thought to dominate the lives of adolescent girls to the exclusion of all else and to make them uninterested in and almost incapable of further learning:

> Here mothers I should tell
> That you should teach your daughters well
> While they are still young in years
> Before the flame of love appears.[26]

So the onset of adolescence usually marked the end of a girl's formal schooling and a concentration on moral training. Moral training was considered vital at this stage of life because of women's supposed lustiness; if not well armed against sin, a sexually mature maiden might lose her virginity. Then not only her chances of marriage but also the honour of the family would be ruined, for a family's reputation depended on the ability of the men of the house to guard the sexual virtue of their womenfolk. This was done not only through moral training but often through literally confining them to the home. The degree to which maidens were secluded varied. In the Ottoman Empire and Muscovy, daughters of the middle and upper classes were confined to the women's quarters of their homes and were veiled on the rare occasions when they ventured forth in public. Respectable girls in Italy, Spain and Portugal were almost as secluded. Because wandering the streets would proclaim that they were unprotected and sexually available to all, and therefore ruin the family honour, they were rarely allowed out of the house and were always accompanied when they ventured forth. Testimony from the trial of the rapist of the great artist Artemisia Gentileschi (for her career, see Chapter 8) shows that she, as an unmarried girl of a respectable family, passed most of her time within her father's house. On her rare excursions out into the world, mostly walks to church, she always had a female chaperone. Her rapist was an artist her father hired to come to the house to give her painting lessons.[27] In northern Europe, where codes of honour were slightly less strict than in Mediterranean countries, respectable girls had slightly more freedom to leave home and wander the streets unescorted, but they were admonished not to do so too often. As the author of a German advice book for maidens explained, girls who showed themselves too often in public 'will look like an item for sale, whereas serious suitors will want merchandise that does not lie in the shop window but is carefully kept in the back of the store'.[28]

Remaining contentedly at home was only one aspect of the modest, decorous behaviour expected of a respectable maiden. She was also supposed to be silent, obedient, pious, industrious and self-effacing. The psychologist Carol Gilligan has argued that modern American girls undergo dramatic changes in personality and behaviour in their early teens, as they are socialized to abandon the tomboyish habits, the fierce competitiveness and the physical and intellectual adventurousness of their girlhood years and turn themselves into the quiet, unintellectual, uncompetitive, self-absorbed beauties they think society expects women to be.[29] Probably similar personality changes occurred as maidens of the early modern period were constantly admonished to be chaste, silent and obedient. As a girl, the sixteenth-century Spanish saint Theresa of Avila dreamed of running away from home with her brothers and going off to fight the Moors in the Holy Land, but she spent her adult life as a cloistered nun.[30] The seventeenth-century Englishwoman Lucy Hutchinson as a girl was so eager to learn that she preferred lessons to games and so competitive that she outdid her brothers in Latin. Loud and bossy, she lorded it over her siblings and the children of the neighbourhood. But when grown, she painted this word portrait of her younger self not in a boastful autobiography but as a modest aside in a flattering biography of her husband, Colonel Hutchinson.[31] These women, and most of their early modern sisters, seem to have internalized the constant admonitions about maidenly behaviour:

> Nobody wants an ill-behaved daughter, a wild thing, a mad Ursula, a tomboy, a rude creature, an uneducated child, a cheeky animal, a nosy thing, a big mouth who avoids home like it was on fire, who runs in all directions, goes to fairs and markets, who stuffs herself in secret, borrows eggs and butter, hits the bottle, drinks with bad companions, does nothing all day, and when she is sent on an errand takes her sweet time in coming home, who snaps at everyone, is a foul mouth at home, and does not listen to her mother. Such a girl, such a maiden, will be passed by come marriage time.[32]

LEARNED LADIES

That passage is from one of the many advice books written for middle- and upper-class girls in early modern Europe. Adolescent girls were encouraged to read such books, along with the Bible and other religious works which would teach moral lessons, between bouts of sewing as they meekly sat at home and learned how to behave. But they were not usually encouraged to do other reading, to follow their intellectual interests and pursue knowledge for its own sake. Further education in our sense of the word was likely to occur only under certain conditions: in families of the intellectual bourgeoisie – clergymen, lawyers and bureaucrats, scholars and humanists – in which the father either taught his children or supervised their education and was willing that his daughters learn along with their brothers. This pattern occurs again and again in the biographies of 'learned ladies', the middle- and upper-class women who dazzled their contemporaries with their 'masculine' learning (see Chapter 8). It was even found in the Ottoman Empire, where Arabic and Persian, not Latin and Greek, were the learned languages. The handful of women writers in those languages shared the experience of the poet Zeinab, who was educated by her father, an intellectual, after he noticed 'the rare jewels of her talent'.[33] Similarly, in Germany the humanist Ulrich Ellenbog personally taught his five sons and four daughters Latin, Greek and the sciences and Juliana Schultt was taught Greek, Hebrew, Latin, French, arithmetic, geography and German poetry by her father, a member of the Privy Council of Darmstadt.[34] In England the humanist Sir Thomas More was very interested in education but had only daughters to practise on, so he turned them into intellectual prodigies. His daughter Margaret especially became famous throughout Europe for the precision and stylistic elegance of her Latin and Greek.

Learned ladies like Margaret More Roper were objects of curiosity but not always of admiration. It was generally felt that their learning was unsuitable for women in general and middle-class women in particular:

> For the nobility, learned women might be a good thing. A knowledge of history and political science will help them in carrying out their representational duties. But for the burger daughter, it will cost a great deal and the girl will never be able to use her newly acquired knowledge in a profession. Furthermore, it will hurt a girl's chances at marriage. It will be hard to find a decent and wealthy husband for someone like that, especially if she is not beautiful, because men want a wealthy wife who is also good at housekeeping, not one who sits over her books all day.[35]

As this passage from yet another German educational theorist suggests, advanced learning was considered useful – and even necessary – for noblewomen. The daughters of kings and princes might have to substitute for their husbands, sons and brothers as rulers or even have to rule themselves (see Chapter 12), so obviously they needed a good grounding in politics and the lessons of political morality which people thought only the Latin and Greek writers of the classical period could teach. And noblewomen might become attendants at a royal or princely court or in a great noble household and there they would need a formidable array of skills (see Chapter 12 again) to hold their own, advance the interests of their families, make a worthy marriage and perhaps tactfully nudge their royal or noble master or mistress to embrace the sensible policies and virtuous conduct of a worthy ruler. Again a thorough knowledge of the classics was necessary, as was a mastery of modern languages and an ability to appreciate the works of the poets and playwrights at court. Noblewomen also had to have good taste in art (many were important patronesses of artists) and to draw and sketch themselves. They had to appreciate music and to sing, play a musical instrument and dance with grace.

As we saw in Chapter 1, these were the same skills necessary for male courtiers, and indeed the sons and daughters of princely and noble families were often taught together, with only the training in fancy sewing for girls and horsemanship and swordsmanship for boys differentiating the sexes. As in families of the intellectual bourgeoisie, this teaching was likely to take place within the home, although it was often someone else's. In the Middle Ages, young nobles, both men and women, had been sent to great noble households to be trained in their future roles and in the sixteenth and seventeenth centuries this old custom was often still followed, especially in England. Anne Boleyn, for example, was sent to the French court at age seven and, lower down on the social scale, young Margaret Dakins, daughter of a country squire, was educated in the household of the Countess of Huntington.

Whether in their own home or someone else's, the teaching of academic subjects was usually done by male tutors, who were often distinguished intellectuals, especially if the pupils were of princely rank. Juan Luis Vives himself tutored the Princess Mary, eldest daughter of England's Henry VIII, writing a basic Latin grammar book for his royal pupil. Anne, the daughter of the Earl of Somerset, the Lord Protector of England during the brief reign of Henry's son Edward VI, was tutored by the great Protestant cleric Archbishop Cranmer and John Foxe, the famous author of the *Book of Martyrs*, taught Lady Jane Howard, so effectively that 'greke and lattyne was vulgar unto her, her composycon in verse notable'.[36] In Italy, Cecilia Gonzaga, daughter of the Duke of Mantua, was schooled by the great educational theorist Vittorio da Feltre.

The result was a series of famously learned royal and noble ladies: in England Queen Mary, Queen Elizabeth and the tragic Lady Jane Grey, who knew Latin, Greek, French, Italian and smatterings of Hebrew, Arabic and Chaldean. Even Mary Queen of Scots, known more for her beauty and her love life than her learning, could write poetry in French and gave a speech in Latin on women's capacity for knowledge. In France, Marguerite de Navarre, sister of Francis I, wrote the *Heptaméron*, one of the first French novels. Her daughter Jeanne d'Albret and granddaughter Catherine de Bourbon were also well educated in humanism, which led them to favour the Protestants in France's religious wars (see Chapter 9). Humanistically educated royal women were often drawn to Protestantism. In fact, the religion spread in central Europe largely because of their protection. For example, Mary of Austria and Isabella Jagellion, successive queens of Hungary in the sixteenth century, protected Calvinists there.[37] In the German states, royal women were less likely to be taught the Latin and Greek of the humanists; one of the many things Henry VIII disliked about Anne of Cleves, the German princess he married sight unseen and quickly divorced, was her ignorance. But even there royal women were educated along with their brothers in religion, modern languages and statecraft. The princesses Maria and Maximiliana Wittelsbach were taught 'German and Latin, writing and rhetoric' by their brother Ernst's tutor and Elizabeth Charlotte of the Palatinate was carefully instructed in religion, German and French.[38]

CHANGES IN GIRLS' EDUCATION AROUND 1700

Such royal 'learned ladies' were more likely to be found at the beginning of the sixteenth century than at the end of the seventeenth. The period from 1500 to 1700 was one of change in women's education, with two distinct trends, one positive and one negative. On the plus side, more and more lower-class women acquired basic literacy, especially in cities. But this was balanced by a deterioration in the quality and rigour of the intellectual training given to women of the elite.

Many factors lay behind this decline. One was the spread of the absolutist state on the French model, with its vast, all-male bureaucracy. As absolutism spread, the political power of the nobility declined – or at least it ceased to be exercised independently and was instead wielded in concert with and often within the royal bureaucracy. Therefore noblewomen were less likely to exercise political power and they were thought to have less need of rigorous humanist educations. The absolutist states also brought expanded royal courts on the model of Louis XIV's Versailles, which set fashions in art, music, literature, dance and dress throughout Europe. Therefore a knowledge of modern languages, especially French, of fashion and the courtly graces became more important than a knowledge of the classics and such matters increasingly dominated the education of great noblewomen.

There were also changes in the educations of girls of the lesser nobility and the middle class. The settlement in the mid-seventeenth century of the religious struggles of the Reformation made giving women a proper grounding in morals and religion less urgent; therefore girls' education became increasingly secular. This trend was furthered by two other factors: the growth of secular reading material – newspapers, novels, advice books on manners, cookery and childrearing – available to women and the spread of what historians call 'companionate marriage' – the notion that people should marry for love or at least grow to love their spouses after they are wed. This was thought more likely to happen if a woman was physically attractive and also witty, amusing and well informed on the fashionable topics of the day – qualities furthered by the new secular reading matter. To elite men of the late seventeenth, eighteenth and nineteenth centuries, the ideal wife was an attractive and amusing companion rather than the chaste, silent and obedient spouse, the thrifty and efficient household manager and the pious childrearer of an earlier era. This brought yet another change to the education of elite girls: the teaching of serious housewifely skills gave way to the acquisition of showy but useless feminine 'accomplishments'. In the sixteenth century elite girls were taught to sew, spin, oversee the preparation of flax, preserve food and cure the basic illnesses of their household members, but from 1650 on they were increasingly taught just fancy craft work (see Chapter 6). The late seventeenth-century governess Hannah Woolley listed in her newspaper advertisement a long list of such crafts she could teach:

> All works wrought with a Nedle, all Transparent works, Shell-work, Moss-work, also cutting of Prints and adorning Room or Cabinets or Stands with them. All kinds of Beugle [bead]-Works upon Wyers or otherwise. All manner of pretty toyes for Closets. Rocks made with Shells or in Sweets. Frames for Looking-glasses, Pictures or the like. Feather of Crewel for the Corner of Beds.[39]

Mrs Woolley is indicative of yet another trend in the education of elite girls: its feminization. Among the Muslims of the Ottoman Empire, with their strict segregation of the sexes, girls had always had women teachers. Now this became true in western Europe as well. If girls were taught at home, the male tutor increasingly gave way to the female governess. Male music and especially dancing masters might still be employed, but the other subjects taught to girls were well within the capacity of a female governess, both because these subjects were now less academically rigorous and because the governesses, often drawn from the professional bourgeoisie, were themselves increasingly well educated. By the seventeenth century even princesses might have female teachers; in England Bathsua Makin, sister of a famous mathematician and linguist, was governess to Charles I's daughter Princess Elizabeth and to many aristocratic girls. She could teach her pupils French, Italian, Latin, Greek, Hebrew, mathematics, science, music, cooking and needlework.[40]

Mrs Makin eventually opened a girls' boarding school. This reflects the final change in the education of elite girls: by 1700 it often included a year or two at school, not as a child to learn to read but as a teenager at a boarding school (a convent school in Catholic countries or a secular boarding school in Protestant areas) to acquire ladylike accomplishments. This too was a feminized education. Convent schools were staffed by nuns and secular girls' boarding schools were usually founded and run by ex-governesses like Mrs Makin; their staffs were largely female.

The archetype of the new girls' boarding school was the famous St Cyr, founded in 1684 to provide free education to the daughters of poor French nobles by Mme de Maintenon, mistress and secret wife of King Louis XIV. Unusually for a royal mistress, Mme de Maintenon was a born teacher; she won the king's heart while governess to his bastard children by an earlier mistress, Mme de Montespan. Most royal mistresses demanded clothes and jewels from their lovers; La Maintenon asked for a school for 250 girls, to be taught religion, French and foreign languages and courtly accomplishments. In the 1690s, Mme de Maintenon came under the influence of the pious Archbishop Fénélon, author of a treatise on girls' education, who advocated an old-fashioned training in religion and housewifery. Mme de Maintenon then turned St Cyr into a convent school and adopted Fénélon's curriculum. But the earlier, more worldly St Cyr was the model for girls' boarding schools throughout Europe.[41]

There is much to deplore in these changes in the education of elite girls. In the 1790s the feminist Mary Wollstonecraft railed against the girls' education of her day, which taught nothing of substance and created empty-headed women who cared for nothing but looking pretty and trapping a man. But while the educations of elite girls in the eighteenth century was less intellectually serious and rigorous than that of the sixteenth century, it nonetheless had some positive aspects. The rise of the governess and the girls' boarding school opened new careers for middle-class women as teachers, giving them a way to support themselves without being forced into marriage (see Chapter 8). And the fact that many genuinely learned women like Bathsua Makin filled these posts indicates that at least some women, especially daughters of the intellectual bourgeoisie, continued to receive educations with some intellectual content. Indeed, the blossoming of women diarists, novelists, poets, play-wrights and journalists, and the growing number of women who contributed to the religious and political debates of the day, suggests that most middle- and upper-class women, despite the deficiencies in their education, were increasingly comfortable with literacy, accustomed to express themselves in writing, interested in the events of the world around them, even those in the 'masculine' public sphere, and self-confident enough to venture into the 'masculine' and 'public' realm of print to express their opinions about them. This intellectual curiosity and self-confidence resulted from the new trends in elite women's education, especially the rise of the boarding school. Their few years at school got girls out of the house and out from under the control of their families and often at school they formed friendships with other girls that would sustain them throughout their lives. The eighteenth century is the first period in history when we find widespread evidence of such sustaining female friendships. When Mme Roland, an important political leader, was executed during the French Revolution, one of the last people she saw on her way to the guillotine was her friend Sophie Grandchamps, who risked the dangers and disorders of the bloodthirsty crowd and the emotional trauma of watching her friend die so that Mme Roland would see a friendly face dur-ing her last moments on earth. The two women had been best friends since the day they met as teenagers in a convent boarding school.[42]

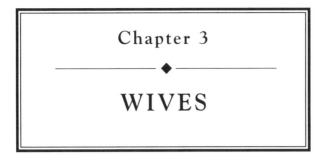

WIVES

THE 'EUROPEAN' MARRIAGE PATTERN

A girl's childhood ended when she became engaged to be married. The age at which this happened varied according to where she lived. In 1965 the demographer J. Hajnal discovered what he called a uniquely European marriage pattern: in Europe from at least the sixteenth through the early twentieth centuries, men and women were most likely to marry relatively late in life, in their mid- to late twenties on average, and around 20 percent of the adult population did not marry at all. This differed from all other human societies, where early and nearly universal marriage was the norm. The 'European' marriage pattern did not, however, prevail throughout Europe. As Hajnal specified, it was predominant only west of a line running from St Petersburg to Trieste. East and south of that line, in Russia, the Balkans, and areas of southern Italy and Spain, the 'non-European' pattern of early marriage prevailed.[1]

Why this difference? Two factors seem to have been at work. 'Non-European' areas had religious traditions that accepted as valid the marriages of very young people (at puberty or even earlier) arranged by their parents and social traditions that provided shelter and support for the new young household until it could stand on its own feet economically. The 'European' areas, by contrast, had a religious tradition that insisted that the unforced consent of the couple was necessary to make a valid marriage and a social tradition that newlyweds form their own separate economically viable household. Both these factors, especially the latter, delayed marriage until well into adulthood and forced some to stay single.

YOUTHFUL MARRIAGES IN 'NON-EUROPEAN' AREAS

Youthful marriage was most deeply embedded in social customs in the Ottoman Empire, where Islam prevailed. Islam had a long tradition of child marriage, dating back to the prophet Mohammed himself, who took as his fourth and last wife Aisha, the daughter of one of his earliest followers. The marriage was consummated when she was only nine. According to Islamic law, the marriages of people who were legally of age (that is, had reached puberty) required their consent to be valid, but matches could be arranged for minors by their parents and guardians without their consent. If a woman objected to her marriage when she came of age, she could get a divorce if it had been arranged by her guardian, but if her father or grandfather had made the match, there was no escape. Islamic law forbade the consummation of child marriages before the spouses were physically mature, but a girl's physical maturity was measured not by puberty but by her attractiveness to men. Even if she was not yet menstruating, a girl who was 'an object of desire', 'fleshy' or 'buxom', was deemed capable of 'enduring intercourse'. By the seventeenth century, actual child marriages were rare, but the tradition of youthful unions guaranteed that most girls were married at or shortly after puberty. So did the financial arrangements for marriages. While the wife's family provided her with a dowry of clothes and household goods, the major financial provision for the new couple was the groom's contribution, the dower or *mahr*. Consisting of household goods, cash and/or real estate, it belonged to the bride after the wedding and had to be large enough to support her if she was divorced or widowed. While she was married, the husband could use it to pay her living expenses. That, plus his obligation at law to support his wife (she could divorce him if he didn't), usually guaranteed that a couple married only if the groom's parents provided adequate resources for the young couple or housed them themselves.[2]

Jewish laws and customs also promoted youthful marriages. Parents were free to arrange matches for their offspring and the *kest*, the custom that the groom's parents house the newlyweds for the first year of marriage and the bride's parents the second, allowed couples to marry when too young to support themselves. Jews usually married at or shortly after puberty.[3] Glikl Leib, a female Jewish merchant of seventeenth-century Hamburg who wrote a famous autobiography, was betrothed at 12 and married at 14; her husband was only a few years older.[4]

Early marriage was also customary in areas where Orthodox Christianity prevailed. In the Balkans, most of the population was Greek Orthodox with a minority of Muslims; in Muscovy, the religion was Russian Orthodox. In both, the Church controlled marriage and a church ceremony made a marriage valid. For a valid marriage, church law (canon law) required the permission of the parents but not the consent of the couple, so it is not surprising that parents arranged marriages for their offspring, often when they were very young. Canon law prohibited marriage before the age of 12 for girls and 15 for boys, but children could be betrothed while younger and marriages usually took place as soon as the couple reached the legal ages.[5]

These youthful marriages were possible because the newlyweds could move into existing households. Eastern Europe was the homeland of the *zadruga*, found in its purest form in Serbia and Bulgaria. A *zadruga* was a multigenerational household consisting of an elderly patriarch and his wife, plus his grown sons and their wives and often their grown children. They lived in a large house with two rooms, one where food was prepared and eaten and one where everybody slept together for warmth, although wealthy *zadrugas* might also have small rooms or even separate cottages where the couples might live privately in the spring and summer. Land was owned in common and work was divided by gender, the men working together under the direction of the *zadruga*'s head and the women together directed by his wife. Usually it was only when the *zadruga* needed more female labour that a young man was allowed to take a wife, picked for him by the *zadruga*'s patriarch. The new daughter-in-law became the drudge of the household, rising first, going to bed last and assigned all the most unpleasant tasks, until the birth of a son to her or the arrival of another daughter-in-law moved her up in the *zadruga*'s hierarchy.[6]

Classic *zadrugas* prevailed only in Serbia, Bulgaria and Albania. In Romania, sons had separate houses near their father's and Moscovy had a mixture of *zadrugas* and small, nuclear family households. But everywhere in eastern Europe the marriage pattern was the same: early matches arranged by the parents for family advantage. The young people had little say in the matter. They were legally forbidden to arrange their own marriages or marry without their parents' permission; if they did so in Russia, they could lose their property and face a large fine. In theory, they had to consent to the proposed match, but consent was defined as not objecting when the marriage was first proposed and there was much pressure on a young person, especially a daughter, to obey. A Serbian law stated: 'If a maiden refuses to marry the young man to whom her parents promised her, she shall be considered shameless and dishonorable among her friends and before the people.'[7]

The only way a daughter could escape marriage was to remain celibate and become a nun. As we shall see, this could be an attractive option in western

Europe, but it was less so in Orthodox Christianity, where marriage was more prized than virginity for women. (Unlike western Christianity, in which most female saints were virgins, Orthodox Christianity abounded in saintly wives and mothers.) Only upper-class girls could become nuns. And nuns were not guaranteed an education in Orthodoxy, as they were in the west; neither did they live in an autonomous, female-run world. Orthodox convents were not cloistered and therefore men managed their finances.[8]

An Albanian girl had another option if she disliked the groom her father chose for her: to become an 'honourary man'. She could vow publicly to remain a virgin and stay in her paternal *zadruga*, dressing, working and fighting like a man, eating at the male table and attending the male assemblies, although she could not vote.[9] But this alternative existed only in remote Albania. Elsewhere in the Orthodox world girls married early and as their parents wished.

MARRIAGE IN 'EUROPEAN' AREAS: CHURCH DOCTRINE

In western Europe, women married later and had more input in their choice of spouse. This was because in Catholic Christianity the consent of the couple – and that alone – made a marriage valid. [According to the medieval Catholic Church, marriage was a sacrament, the only sacrament that did not require a priest. Although a public ceremony with witnesses, performed usually in front of rather than inside a church, was preferable, a couple could marry themselves simply by expressing their consent to be wed. This was done either by exchanging vows in the present tense ('I marry you'), or by vows in the future tense ('I will marry you') followed by the sexual consummation of the match. If it met the Church's other criteria (if the couple were of age, that is, 12 for girls and 14 for boys, were not related in the prohibited degrees of kinship and had not taken monastic vows or been married to a spouse still living), it was a valid marriage.]

 ⌐ This doctrine that consent made a marriage had an immense effect on marriage practices in western Europe. Not only did it provide, in the 'clandestine' or private marriage performed by the spouses themselves, a way for young people to escape arranged matches they disliked, it also laid the foundation for the gradual growth of the notion that love, both romantic and sexual, was necessary for marriage and that therefore people should be allowed to pick their own mates. This notion conflicted with the widespread conviction that marriage, as the occasion for the transfer of property and the formation of a new patriarchal household, the basic unit of society, was too important a

business to be left to young people in the throes of romantic passion. Therefore marriage in western Europe became a matter of negotiation between parents and children, family interest and personal inclination. Marriages in western
Europe ran the gamut from those arranged by parents with no input from
their offspring to those where the couple was left free to choose. Where an individual marriage fell on this gamut depended on the geographical location and
the religion, wealth and social status of the people involved. Generally marriages in southern Europe and among Catholics were more likely to be arranged
than those among Protestants in northern Europe. And the greater the wealth
and prestige of the families involved, the less likely they were to leave the
choice of their spouses to their children. Some specific examples will illustrate
the variety and complexity of western European marriage arrangements.

MARRIAGE AMONG NOBLES IN ITALY

Marriages were most likely to be arranged among the nobility of Italy. There
a girl not only could not choose her husband, she also could not choose
whether to marry at all or to join a convent. In the early modern period Italian
nobles fought economic hard times by using the *fede commissa*, a legal arrangement that let them bypass inheritance laws which dictated that all children,
male and female, were entitled to share their father's estate and instead pass
it all to the eldest son. Only he was allowed to marry and he often waited
until he was quite old to do so. By 1700 in Florence the average age of marriage of male nobles was 36. Younger sons were forced into the Church, the
army or the law or simply given yearly pensions and sent to live in the country. Their sexual needs were met by mistresses and maidservants.[10]

This policy of marrying only one son very late created a shortage of noble
grooms, which in turn created dowry inflation, as noble families competed
to marry off their daughters by giving them ever-larger dowries, so large that
families often had to mortgage their estates and borrow heavily to raise
them. In Florence there was a public dowry fund to help fathers meet their
obligations. In such circumstances noble families could afford to marry
off only one or two daughters. Because it took time to accumulate a dowry
and because the elderly bridegrooms preferred young brides (noble girls in
Florence in 1700 married at 18 or 19), usually the youngest, not the oldest,
daughter was allowed to marry. The others were placed in convents.[11] It is
estimated that in 1581 three-fifths of the patrician women in Venice were
in convents, which had become, as the archbishop complained, 'public ware-
houses' for upper-class daughters.[12]

Actually life as a nun was not a bad alternative to an arranged marriage. At least nuns avoided sex with someone they might dislike and the perils of childbearing. Because they did not face the risks of giving birth, nuns on average lived longer than lay women. Further, a convent was familiar territory to a noble Italian girl. She had probably been schooled in one and she would have often visited female relatives – aunts, cousins, older sisters – who preceded her in taking the veil. Convents could be very comfortable. Even after the Council of Trent (1540–1563) insisted that nuns be strictly cloistered and actually keep their vows of poverty, chastity and obedience (see Chapter 10), convent life was far from austere. As Plate 5 shows, the South American nun, poet and feminist Sor Juana de la Cruz had a large, comfortable cell with a kitchen and a sitting room filled with books, musical and scientific instruments and her collection of folk art. Sor Juana's example also shows that in the Catholic Church, unlike the Orthodox, nuns had to be taught to read and write and were often encouraged in intellectual and artistic endeavours. As we will see in Chapter 8, nuns were often singers, musicians, composers, writers and poets, even scientists. An ambitious woman could also make a career out of simply being a nun and eventually rise to the status of mistress of novices or even abbess of her convent.

If she was chosen to marry, a noble Italian girl did not get to choose her husband. She might not even get to meet him until the betrothal, when the marriage contract was signed. Often, however, she knew him, because cousins married cousins, back and forth over generations, to keep the enormous dowries in the family. Another common pattern was for a brother and sister of one family to marry a sister and brother from another, again to conserve dowries.[13]

The dowry's size and, even more importantly for the bride's father, how it would be paid (in a lump sum or instalments spread over the course of the marriage) were worked out in negotiations between the fathers or guardians of the couple. So too was the groom's contribution to the match, which everywhere but Florence took the form of a provision for the bride if her husband died. In Naples, for example, where Spanish law prevailed, a widow was entitled to two-thirds of her husband's estate. (For more on provisions for widows, see Chapter 5.) When all the financial details were ironed out, the parties shook hands or kissed to seal the bargain.

The next step in the marriage was a visit by the groom to the bride in her home.[14] Sometimes this was their first meeting. The groom usually brought her gifts, often of jewellery; as we shall see, these gifts, survivals of pagan bride purchase, were important in lower-class as well as noble marriages.

For the upper classes, the next step in marriage, the formal signing of the marriage contract spelling out all the financial details of the match, was the vital one. In this, the *sponsalia* or betrothal, the groom and the male members of the bride's family met, usually in a church, and signed the contract drawn up by a notary, who presided over the proceedings. The two families also exchanged public, witnessed promises that the marriage would take place. Breaking these was a serious offence leading to feuds and vendettas.

The next step in the process included the bride: this was the marriage itself, when the couple exchanged their vows 'in the present tense'. Before the Counterreformation this took place in the bride's home and was presided over by the notary. After the Council of Trent tightened Catholic marriage law, the ceremony had to take place in a church and a priest had to officiate.

Although the exchange of vows made the marriage valid, it wasn't the end of the process. The formation of a new household had to be proclaimed publicly and accepted by the community. This was done by a procession in which the bride, dressed in her wedding finery and accompanied by her trousseau and an escort of her husband's friends, went from her father's house to her husband's. There she was led to the nuptial bed and, amid much lewd joking, the marriage was consummated.

If the bride did not object to the groom at the very beginning of this process, the only way she could stop it was to run away from her father's house and marry someone else clandestinely, à la Romeo and Juliet. This occasionally happened. In seventeenth-century Faenza, the 16-year-old son of noble Paolo Spada fell in love with an older woman (of 21!) whom his parents deemed unsuitable. Determined to marry her, he ran away from home, negotiated the financial terms of the marriage with the bride's family himself and married her in church with a compliant priest and notary presiding. His parents had the notary arrested, but the Church refused to annul the marriage and the couple lived happily ever after.[15] Most matches, however, proceeded inexorably and the most a bride could hope for was that her parents had chosen wisely.

MARRIAGE AMONG THE ENGLISH
PEERS AND GENTRY

Although the steps on their road to the altar were similar, an English gentlewoman had much more input into her marriage than her Italian counterpart. For one thing, she was more likely to be older and therefore better able to stand up to her parents. From the sixteenth through the eighteenth centuries, the average age of wealthy brides in England was 19 to 23; for their grooms it was 24 to 29.[16] For another, she lived in a Protestant country, where the Church emphasized that love was the basis of marriage and criticized parents who forced their children to marry against their will (see Chapter 9). Therefore the marriage strategies of the English upper-class parents had more complicated goals than those of Italian nobles: while they wanted to enhance the resources and influence of their family, as Italian nobles did, the English also wanted to provide for the future happiness of *all* their children.

Like the Italians, the English hoped to pass their estates down intact to the eldest son generation after generation. To guarantee this, increasing use was made of the entail, the English equivalent of the *fede commissa*, which kept the estate in the male line. But this did not necessarily cut daughters out of their fathers' estates, as was done in Italy. English patriarchs customarily made generous provisions for all their children, either in their wills or through marriage settlements and deeds of gift during their lifetimes. Younger sons were trained for the socially acceptable professions (the law, the Church and the army) and/or given annuities to live on, while daughters received their 'portions' of their father's estate in cash or goods, sometimes even in land. For example, seventeenth-century gentleman Sir Edmund Verney's lands and title went to his eldest son Ralph, but his three younger sons received annuities and his four daughters were supposed to get marriage portions of £1000 each.[17] As this suggests, most English patriarchs treated their children, except for the eldest son, even-handedly. Daughters got as much or more than younger sons and they were treated equally. The English did not follow the Italian custom of giving one daughter a huge dowry and denying marriage to the rest.

In England a daughter's portion often became her dowry, but it might also be used to support her as a single woman. Earlier generations of historians of women assumed that when the Reformation closed convents in Protestant countries, women no longer had the option to remain single. Today we know otherwise. About 20 percent of early modern Englishwomen never married and among the gentry generous portions from their fathers allowed them to live independently and well.[18] Admittedly single women lacked the protection of a husband and the social status conveyed by the married state. Yet spinsterhood had its advantages: single women avoided the perils of childbirth, retained control of their property and did not have to obey a husband. Little wonder that the single life was celebrated in ballads and poems:

Whilst you are single, there's none to curb you.
Go to bed quietly and take your ease.
Early or late there's none to disturb you,
Walk abroad where you will and when you please.
(A Fairing for Maids, 1639)

I live well contented as any Maid can.
What need I entangle my self with a Man?
I need not say 'Shall I, pray shall I husband?'
Now I have my self to guide and to rule.
(Tobias' Observation, 1687)[19]

These sentiments were echoed by actual single spinsters. Twenty-three-year-old Alice Wandesford replied when people suggested she marry: 'I was exceedingly sattisfied in that happie and free condittion, wherein I enjoyed my time with delight.'[20]

Pressured by her family, Wandesford did eventually marry. Her match typified marriages among the English gentry. Because her father was dead, Alice's widowed mother arranged the match, after asking Alice if she was willing to wed. Mrs Wandesford investigated various potential grooms of appropriate social and financial status and William Thornton emerged as her choice. The couple was introduced and a period of getting acquainted and 'courtship' – the exchange of visits and gifts such as gloves, stockings, jewellery and books – ensued. Finally Thornton proposed to Alice and she, convinced that he 'seemed to be a very godly, sober and discreet person, free from all manner of vice, and of a good conversation', with 'a handsome competency' of an estate, accepted him. If this suggests she was not in love with him, it also shows that she freely chose him because he had the traits she wanted in a husband.[21]

This mixture of family connivance and free choice by the couple was probably typical of upper-class English matches. In some, the woman had no choice. The 13-year-old heiress Mary Blacknall was married to Sir Edmund Verney's young heir Ralph without having met him.[22] In others, the couple fell in love and married in defiance of their families. Thomas Thynne and Maria Marvin, both 16, were the offspring of feuding families in Wiltshire who fell in love and, defying their families, ran away to marry; their story apparently inspired Shakespeare to write *Romeo and Juliet*.[23] Thus England had a variety of marriage patterns, but in most the bride seems to have had at least a veto power over a potential groom, if not the right to choose him herself. A study of 21 well-documented gentry marriages shows only four arranged or forced matches; in all 17 of the others, the bride at least had veto power and, in six, the match was initiated by the couple themselves.[24]

Once the match was arranged, the next step was negotiating its financial details: the nature and amount of the bride's portion and, on the groom's side, provision for the bride during widowhood. Most common was the join-ture, in which the groom's family gave a piece of property or a cash sum valu-able enough to generate an income to the couple jointly (hence the name). The husband had use of it while he lived; after his death it supported his widow and when she died it passed to their children. The bride also received 'pin money', a specified sum for her own expenses, especially clothes and jewellery. Jointures were usually substantially smaller than dowries and the trend in our period was for further shrinkage, but if a widow survived her husband for a number of years, she in effect got back her dowry and more. Among the gentry the average widow got back her dowry if she lived from five to seven-and-a-half years after her husband's death; among the peerage the figure was 10 years. But since most widows outlived their husbands by 12 to 16 years, their join-tures were in reality generous.[25]

Before the Reformation, the next step in the marriage process was a public betrothal ceremony, the spousal or trothplight, similar to the Italian *sponsalia*. But after England became Protestant, this was gradually abandoned by the upper classes, because the Protestant churches dismissed spousals and emphas-ized the actual marriage ceremony. So instead the couple experienced a few months of 'engagement', when their banns (plans to wed) were called in church and they received the congratulations of family and friends. The bride-to-be was queen in this period, showered with gifts and attention from relatives and her intended. Then came the wedding ceremony, celebrated in church and very similar to Protestant weddings today. After that, the company sat down to a lavish feast that might last for days. Finally the couple was led to a flower-strewn bed, undressed, given a strengthening drink and left alone to consummate the match.[26]

COURTSHIP AND MARRIAGE AMONG THE LOWER CLASSES

Elsewhere in Europe, aristocratic courtship and marriage fell between the Italian and the English models, the general rule being that freedom of choice was more likely in Protestant areas. It was also more likely lower down on the social scale. Among peasants and artisans, marriage was an economic necessity, as we shall see in Chapters 6 and 7; usually peasants, artisans and day labourers, men as well as women, were more prosperous as part of a 'family economy' than as single workers. Marriage was also a mark of maturity. A man came into true manhood and independence only when he married and a woman became a woman and took her rightful place among her female neighbours only as a wife. In the eyes of their married neighbours, those who remained single were perpetual adolescents. Given its importance, marriage was not undertaken lightly. Peasants waited until they inherited land or could rent a plot before marrying and artisans waited until they had a mastership and shop. Postponing marriage until they could afford it was deeply engrained in the lower classes. When Joan Wigg's fiancé pressed her to marry, she said, 'Shall we marry so soon? It were better for us to forebear and [have] some house-hold stuff to begin withal.'[27] Because they married late (men in their mid- to late twenties, women in their mid-twenties), the lower classes often did not have parents alive to guide or object to their choice of a mate. This reinforced the freedom of choice traditional at this level of society.

But this freedom of choice was always hedged with prudence. Even if they were legally above the age when they needed their parents' consent to the match (in France, for example, according to a law of 1556 men over 30 and women over 25 could marry without their parents' consent), potential spouses often sought the advice of family and friends and used them as intermediaries in courtship. Seventeenth-century Englishman Roger Lowe, a mercer's apprentice whose parents were dead, could have done his own courting. Instead he relied on male and female friends to suggest potential mates and approach them for him. Lowe's choices always had financial as well as personal attractions. Ellen Marsh 'had a house and a liveinge'; another young woman was 'worth 11 li [pounds] per Annum in house and ground'.[28] Lowe's hardheaded approach to marriage conformed to folk wisdom. Throughout Europe folk sayings emphasized prudence in choosing a mate. Physical beauty and charm were less important than character and the ability to work hard:

Catalonia: Pretty girl, stupid and vain.
England: Marry for love and work for silver.[29]

Young people met eligible mates at *veillées* and *Spinstuben*, the winter evening gatherings where the whole village came together to spin, carve and tell stories, at markets and fairs and at dances and festivals like May Day, when the young people of the village stayed up all night to gather flowers and branches to place at the doorways of marriageable girls. These were group activities, characteristic of youthful socializing in early modern Europe. When a couple paired off, the pattern changed to long walks alone and the exchange of visits (sometimes overnight) and love tokens. Rings and gloves were favourites, although one Englishman bestowed garters, cloth, furniture and Puritan religious tracts on his beloved. Eventually there was a proposal and a public betrothal, often at a tavern, where, in the presence of friends and family, the couple vowed to marry, exchanged gifts (again rings and gloves were favourites) and drank a toast, often from the same cup, to the future union.[30] The gift exchange and the toast were what anthropologists called 'rituals of union', powerful public symbols that the couple seriously intended to wed. They were accepted as such by the courts. In 1580 in Neuchâtel a church court upheld the breach of promise suit of Claude Borrel against Elise Simonin. Borrel conceded that Simonin had never verbally agreed to marry him, but he maintained that she had publicly accepted a belt from him and drunk a toast to the match.[31] Thus lower-class betrothals did not highlight the property arrangements of the marriage, as upper-class ones did; instead they sent signals to the community that the couple seriously intended to wed and that it would have to make room for a new household.

The months between the betrothal and the marriage were a time when the community could object to the match. They were also a time when the couple could get to know each other better. Often this meant having sex, because people had long accepted the Church's teaching that public vows to wed, even if in the future tense, made a marriage if the match was consummated and they therefore viewed engaged couples as virtually married. This accounts for the high percentage of pregnant brides characteristic of early modern Europe. In England in 1550 the figure was around 30 percent, and while Protestantism emphasized the importance of the wedding over the betrothal and tried to eliminate pre-marital sex, in the seventeenth century the figure was still 15 percent. In some places in Scotland, a wedding took place only *if* the bride was pregnant, for that gave proof of her fertility.[32]

At the wedding, as at the betrothal, there were folk rituals to incorporate the new household into the community. Both the Reformation and the Counterreformation tried to suppress these 'superstitions' but failed, because they served an important purpose: they signalled that the community would accept the new household and that it would function according to community norms.

Marriages usually began with separation rituals, symbolic leave takings by the bride and groom of the still-single friends of their youth.[33] In some places, these friends were given gifts. In others, it was the friends who escorted the couple to church, the noise they made on the way a symbolic protest against their loss. In still others – Russia and Wales, for example – the bride hid and the young men of the village hunted for her and escorted her to her husband, signalling their acceptance of her loss as a potential mate.

Once the couple arrived at the church, the rituals changed to symbolize the formation of a new household that would function according to community norms. In many places the bride spread her apron as she knelt at the altar and the groom knelt on it. This symbolized the sexual union to come and also that the husband would rule the household, with his wife's consent (she had voluntarily spread her apron). It further signified that she would be a good housewife (the apron again). Multilayered symbolism also surrounded the wedding ring. In many areas, the husband tried a number of times to push the ring over the bride's knuckle but failed, although he finally succeeded. This symbolized the husband's dominance as well as the bride's sexual deflowering. Because of the latter, the bestowing of the ring was the point in the marriage ceremony when someone ill-disposed toward the couple performed a counter-ritual, the 'tying of the knot'. Knotting a thread or cord as the ring was given supposedly rendered the groom impotent, preventing the consummation of the marriage.

After the ceremony, the bride and groom were escorted by friends and relatives to their new home, where again rituals symbolizing both their sexual union and the ordering of the new household occurred. In some places a broom was placed on the front step. If the bride stepped over it, she would rule the roost and neglect her housewifely duties, but if she picked it up and started sweeping, she would be a good housekeeper. In other areas, she was handed a spindle, again symbolizing her new status, and, in still others, she was given a tour of her new house by the groom's family. Then, after a wedding feast, the couple was ceremoniously put to bed with much lewd joking. Finally, the guests departed, only to continue laughing and joking until the couple threw out coins, a symbol of fruitfulness, to make them go away. This serenading of the bridal couple was called rough music in England and *charivari* in France.

GENDER ROLES AND BEHAVIOUR IN MARRIAGE: IDEALS

As marriage rituals suggest, people had firm opinions about the proper roles and behaviour of husband and wife. These corresponded surprisingly well to what learned humanists and clergymen wrote in treatises about marriage. [They were promulgated at the village level by rituals and proverbs, and enforced by *charivaris* and by gossip against those who did not conform.] Village gossip, spread primarily by women, determined one's reputation, and that in turn determined one's economic well-being; few would employ a man who could

TRG

not keep his household in order or a woman who was a slovenly house-keeper. Because gossip was so important, its victims often filed slander suits to protect their reputations and, from these, as well as from proverbs and learned treatises, we can deduce popular expectations about the proper behaviour of husband and wife.[34]

What were these expectations? First and foremost, the husband should rule the household and guide and correct his wife. Learned commentators traced this to God's punishment of Eve: 'Thy desires shall be subject to thy husband, and he shall rule over thee.' That God ordained that husbands rule wives was reinforced by other biblical texts, like St Peter's *Ye wives, be ye in subjection to obey your own husband* (1 Peter 3:1) and St Paul's *Let women be subject to their husbands, as to the Lord; for the husband is the head of the woman, as Christ is the head of the Church* (Ephesians 5:22–23). Popular proverbs repeated and enlarged this. Their use of natural metaphors implied that female subjection was ordained by nature as well as God:

> When the cock has crowed, the hen should be silent. (Picardy)
> The household is going very badly when the hen plays the cock. (Provence)[35]

[These proverbs suggested that if wives ruled husbands, the natural order was subverted and the world turned upside down. It would be as if a fish caught a fisherman or a rabbit shot a hunter. In fact, there was a genre of cheap engravings, widely popular, called 'the world turned upside down', depicting such reversals (see Plate 6). In those showing unnatural marriages, the wife is dressed in symbols of masculine authority like trousers, hat, and gun and performs manly tasks, while the husband wears feminine dress and spins and tends the baby.]Popular proverbs echoed these themes:

> Neither trousers for the woman nor skirts for a man. (Catalonia)
> The hat must master the bonnet. (Brittany)
> A man spinning and a woman leading the horses make an absurd household. (Picardy)[36]

So absurd was it that households ruled by wives were subject to *charivaris* and rough music by which communities expressed their disapproval.

Both learned commentators and popular proverbs agreed that a husband should rule his household with moderation and phrase his corrections in loving and tactful language, mindful not only that he was correcting a lover and helpmeet who deserved tenderness but also a 'weaker vessel' whose limited intelligence and stubborn will necessitated careful handling. As the Anglican Church's homily on marriage explained:

For the woman is a weak creature, not endued [endowed] with like strength and constancy of mind [to men's] . . . These things must be considered of [by] the man . . . so that he ought to wink at some things and must gently expound all things and to forebear . . . reasoning should be used and not fighting . . . she is the weaker vessel, of a frail heart, inconstant, and in a word soon stirred to wrath.[37]

[If gentle admonitions failed, both learned and popular opinion agreed that a husband had the right, indeed the duty, to use force against his wife, so long as he did it in moderation and did not endanger her life.] At Russian weddings, the groom was often given a whip to symbolize his right of correction.[38] In the beginning of our period, all European law codes allowed wifebeating. In English common law, it was acceptable so long as the husband did not use a stick thicker than his thumb; hence, our expression 'rule of thumb'. Popular proverbs said women were better for a little beating:

[Women are like chops, the more you beat them the tenderer they are. (Languedoc)
A spaniel, a woman, and a walnut tree, the more they're beaten, the better they be. (England)[39]]

Church courts granted separations to abused wives only if their lives were in danger and sometimes not even then. In July 1603 the episcopal court of Constance heard the case of Appolonia Meckhen, a noblewoman, and her husband Hans Caspar Ingolstetter, the *Bürgermeister* of Freiburg. Appolonia claimed that Hans beat her severely and would soon kill her. The judges refused to break up the marriage and told the couple to live together peaceably. Hans agreed but Appolonia did not. Telling the judges they had condemned her to death, she went to jail rather than return to her husband.[40]

Luckily for women, attitudes to spousal abuse changed over the course of our period, thanks largely to the Protestant Reformation. As we shall see in Chapter 9, Protestants redefined marriage as a loving union between spiritual equals. Although husbands were still supposed to correct their wives, Protestants thought violence had no place in marriage; Puritan William Becon wrote that beating your wife was like beating yourself. In Calvinist Geneva wifebeaters were punished and, elsewhere, Protestants made extreme physical abuse grounds for divorce. The challenge of Protestantism prompted the Catholic Church to change its attitude as well; during the Counterreformation the Church promoted Saint Rita as patroness of abused wives. Eventually popular opinion followed suit. By the seventeenth century French peasant proverbs suggested that only bad wives needed beatings ('The bad horse needs the spur, the bad wife needs the stick') and that beatings did no good ('Beating your wife is like beating a sack of flour, the good flies out, the bad remains').[41] And by 1800

English rural communities aimed their rough music at wifebeaters, not at men who failed to control their wives.[42]

In addition to his duty of moral correction, a husband was expected to provide for his wife's physical needs – food, clothing and shelter – in a style suitable to their social status. This duty stemmed from God's curse that Adam work by the sweat of his brow. Failure of a husband to perform this manly duty was thought to justify feminine misbehaviour. A sixteenth-century German world turned upside down woodcut has the dominant wife explaining her refusal to obey her husband:

> How can one expect beautiful young women
> To maintain their wifely dignity
> When they are forced to go about naked,
> Begging from door to door, hungry,
> Subsisting on water?
> If you will not work to support me,
> Then you must wash, spin, and draw the cart
> And be beaten upon your back.[43]

Church and local courts punished husbands who failed to provide adequately for their wives, as did public opinion. In Neuchâtel, in 1604, David Tissot Robert was imprisoned for three days because he spent his money on drink while his wife and children starved.[44]

The husband's responsibility to support his wife was taken so seriously because in most areas of Europe, on marriage, he got control not only of his wife's dowry but also of her property and of anything she earned or inherited while they were wed. Only under Islamic law did a wife's property remain separate from her husband's.[45] In most of Christian Europe marriage made man and wife not only one flesh but also one legal entity, whose sole recognized representative at law was the husband. A seventeenth-century English legal commentator likened a married woman to a stream which joins a mighty river and loses its identity in the greater flow. So too did a wife lose her identity at law when she was joined to a husband. In English common law, husbands got complete control over any property a wife brought into a marriage plus anything she inherited or earned during it. And anything they acquired jointly while wed was his to administer and dispose of as well.[46] Similarly, the customary law of Douai made all property acquired by either party during marriage part of a community or common fund. While he lived, the husband administered it; when he died it went to his widow.[47] In some customary law areas, at least some of a wife's property could be protected from her husband by having it declared lineage property of her family in her marriage contract; it would then be kept intact and passed on to her heirs. In Roman law areas, too, a wife's property might be kept separate from her husband's by provisions in the marriage contract.[48] But in general, marriage meant a pooling of financial resources under the control of the husband, and this gave him the duty to support his wife properly.

In return for his guidance and financial support, what did a wife owe her husband? Wifely duties are easily summed up in three words: a good wife was 'chaste, silent and obedient'. Let us begin with chastity, which meant not abstinence from sex but sexual fidelity. Because the Church traditionally defined the purpose of marriage as reproduction, husband and wife owed each other sexual services; inability or refusal to perform such services could get a marriage annulled. Similarly, spouses owed each other sexual fidelity. Adultery by either party fractured beyond repair the loving union that supposedly made a marriage. Innocent spouses in adulterous Catholic or Orthodox marriages could demand legal separations although they could not remarry and for Protestants adultery was grounds for divorce. The law codes of most cities and states made it a crime as well.

Yet in practice adultery by husbands usually went unpunished; indeed, a husband's routine infidelities – visits to prostitutes, seduction of the family maidservant – were not legally defined as adultery. Only husbands who seduced other men's wives or humiliated their own by publicly parading a mistress were likely to be tried for adultery, and their punishment usually was light – often just a small fine.[49]

Wives, contrariwise, were expected to be totally faithful to their husbands and failing in this was severely punished. Many law codes – Spain's, for example – allowed husbands to kill adulterous wives if they caught them in the act.[50] This differential treatment of husbands and wives arose from the different consequences for the family of their infidelities. A husband's adultery did not destroy his family, but a wife's might, because all the children she bore while married were at law considered her husband's and were legally his heirs. If they were sired by someone else, the patriliny had no true heirs and its patrimony would be illegally hijacked.

Thus a wife's sexual fidelity was vital to her new family; it was, as the Germans put it, the 'honour of the house'.[51] As this suggests, it had a public face: to have honour, a wife not only had to be faithful to her husband, she had to be seen to be faithful. For this she had to project a public image of wifely fidelity, leaving the house only when necessary, avoiding immodest apparel and behaving with extreme decorum in public. Peasant proverbs explicitly associated a wife's sexual fidelity with her confinement in the house:

> Whoever lets his horse drink at every ford, and takes his wife to every festival, makes his horse into a nag, and his wife into a whore. (Languedoc)[52]

Because it was manifested in public behaviour, chastity merged with the other characteristics of a good wife, silence and obedience. The need for obedience was obvious; it was enjoined on women as part of God's punishment of Eve. Women's silence was also grounded in the scriptures, specifically in the passage from St Paul's letter to the Corinthians where he says that women must be silent in churches and that if they have any questions about religion, they should ask their husbands at home. This passage was interpreted in a number of ways, none of which would probably have pleased St Paul. One was that women should remain silent at all times. In early modern Europe, speech was considered woman's weapon, the counterpart of male physical strength; it was powerful and widely feared. Eve had seduced Adam into sin through honeyed words as well as her physical charms, and so too could ordinary women use what the English called the 'bolster lecture' – sweet words in bed – to make men act against their better judgement. And women's words had public as well as private power. In the form of neighbourhood gossip, they determined the reputations of men and women alike and having a bad reputation could have disastrous social and even economic consequences. Therefore women's speech had to be regulated. In England 'scolds' – people who publicly harassed and insulted others – could be punished with exposure in the pillory, a ducking in the ducking or cucking stool, or by the 'scold's bridle', a muzzle like those of vicious dogs. Although few people were actually punished this way – and some of them were men – this nonetheless reveals society's deep-seated fears of women's speech.[53]

Unfortunately for women, 'speech' in this period included all forms of self-expression. Women were therefore discouraged from writing, as well as speaking, especially about their own experiences (see Chapter 8). And they were even more firmly discouraged from publishing their work, because that was a form of public speech. Self-expression through art or music was also considered public speech, so women were discouraged from becoming artists or musicians. When they did, they, like female authors, put their sexual reputations at risk, for in speaking in public a woman exposed herself to strangers and drew their attention just as she would if she dressed and behaved wantonly. Chastity and silence were coupled in people's minds; both demanded that women stay out of the public gaze. A woman who expressed herself in public opened herself to attacks on her sexual reputation, as many female writers and artists discovered.

[This was especially likely to happen if a woman expressed opinions about matters deemed masculine: religion, politics, philosophy and the higher reaches of thought in general.] For a final layer of meaning distilled from St Paul's admonition was that religion and other such things were men's business. [His words could have been interpreted as suggesting that women should be interested in such things and ask questions about them, but they were not. Instead they were taken to signify that women should not be curious about masculine matters but instead should confine themselves to female concerns, specifically the household and its functioning.] For good wives had one further duty, not included in the formula 'chaste, silent and obedient': they were to be efficient and thrifty housewives, managing the household so that it functioned smoothly on the least possible expense.]

As we shall see in Chapters 6 and 7, this was no easy task. In rural areas, where at least 80 percent of the population lived, the responsibilities of the housewife were not just confined to the house itself and the cooking and cleaning that define housework today. Instead the housewife was responsible for all work on the farm except plowing and harvesting grain and raising livestock and driving them to market. Housewives milked cows, made butter and cheese and ale, raised bees and made candles, grew flax or hemp and spun and wove them and wool into cloth and made clothes, grew, processed and stored fruits and vegetables, made medicines and tonics and cared for their health needs and/or trained servants to do all these tasks and supervised them as they did them.

Urban housewives also had a wide range of responsibilities. Although their households were not as self-sufficient as rural ones, many still made their own cloth and candles. Artisan households included craft workshops and artisan wives were expected to supervise apprentices, help produce goods, man the shop counter, guard the till and peddle unsold goods on the street corner or in the market. Merchants' wives were often partners in their husband's enterprises, handling clients when their husbands were away. They might also have their own career, as surgeon or midwife. Wives of professionals – doctors, lawyers, government officeholders – could not share their husbands' duties, but they often handled the family finances and investments. As this suggests, housewives were expected to be able to manage money and, like the other qualities expected of a good wife, this was manifested in a way which shaped a wife's public reputation. A wife's management skills were shown not just by her well-run household but also by her dress, which, while it could be of costly material and fashionable cut if she were of high rank, had nonetheless to be dignified, modest and sombre. Colourful, expensive dress on the cutting edge of fashion marked a wasteful, extravagant and selfish wife. So strict were these expectations that even queens could not flaunt them. Isabella of Spain loved colourful clothes and jewels but wore them mostly in private; in her portraits she is dressed soberly, as befits a proper wife.[54]

GENDER ROLES AND BEHAVIOUR IN MARRIAGE: REALITY

Obviously, to fulfil her housewifely duties properly a woman had to be energetic, knowledgeable, decisive and active in the public sphere – qualities opposite to those of the chaste, silent and obedient 'good wife'. This suggests that gender role ideals often bore little resemblance to reality. This is true. Roles and relationships within marriage, like patterns of courtship, ran a gamut, from those that rigidly conformed to societal expectations to those that totally reversed them.

At one end of the scale were those relationships in which the husband took his duty to correct his wife too seriously and abused her. Clearly many wives were abused and neglected. The seventeenth-century French mystic Madame de Guyon, forced into an arranged marriage at 15, almost never saw her husband; denied any authority in her mother-in-law's household, she was frequently beaten and abused even by the servants.[55] Englishwoman Elizabeth Freke had to spend most of her marriage in bored isolation on her husband's estate in Ireland while he enjoyed the pleasures of London society. He visited her only to tap her large fortune; in 1702 she wrote, 'My dear husband borrowed of me not without force or cruelty £1560.' Her story is all the sadder in that she had married for love, against her father's wishes.[56]

More frequent than neglect and abuse was a simple adherence to the expected roles of husband and wife. This seems to have been the reason for the success of the 50-year-long marriage of Sir Anthony and Lady Grace Mildmay. A 14-year-old bride in an arranged marriage, Lady Grace never complained about her husband's bad temper or his frequent absences at court. Instead she busied herself learning to be an expert housewife; she was especially good at brewing and administering remedies for illnesses (see Chapter 6). Sir Anthony, in turn, valued his wife's hard work and made lavish provisions for her widowhood. Lady Grace summed up her formula for a successful marriage thus:

> I carried always that reverend respect toward him . . . I could not find in my heart to challenge him for the worst word or deed which ever he offered me in all his life, as to say why spoke you thus? or why did you that? but in silence passed over all such matters betwixt us.[57]

Probably most common of all were those marriages in which wives consciously or unconsciously used the standard expectations of proper wifely behaviour to get their own way. Typical of these marriages was that of Sir Ralph and Lady Mary Verney. A 13-year-old heiress, Mary Blacknall was married to Sir Ralph, aged 26, in an arranged match in 1629. Throughout their marriage, Sir Ralph, who seems to have been what we would today call a control freak, wrote fussy letters of instruction to his young wife, who accepted them with outward meekness. When he complained that she failed to respond to his every suggestion, she wrote:

> My dear . . . truly I am confident tis by chance if I miss answering of every particular, for I always lay thy letters before me when I write.

When she herself offered him suggestions, again it was done with a proper wifely diffidence: 'Tis only because you bid me do it that I trouble you with my silly advice, for I am sure thy own judgement is much better.' This deferential stance allowed her to insist on having her own way in things that really mattered to her, like the naming of her children, and it eventually earned her the devotion of her husband, who remained inconsolable for 40 years after she died:

> [S]uch was her goodness that when I was most peevish she would be most patient and, as if she meant to air my forwardness and frequent follies by the constancy of her forbearance, studied nothing more than a sweet compliance.[58]

Another wife who manipulated stereotypes of wifely deference to get her own way was Magdalena Paumgartner, whose husband Balthasar was a widely travelled and successful merchant in Nuremberg. While Balthasar was away on business trips, Magdalena stayed home and dutifully ran the house and the company, but she longed to be invited to accompany her husband on his travels. She wrote of this desire in a letter that reminded her husband of her devotion, obedience, and good housekeeping and thus artfully suggested how closely she conformed to the ideal of the 'good wife':

> I know nothing else to say to you, dear Paumgartner, except to ask that you take care of yourself. I do not know how you will be provided for in the kitchen. May it always be well with you! I have long wanted to hitch the three horses and . . . come to you. But then I have thought better of it, [remembering that] you have not given me

permission to do so, and it would also be expensive . . . so I have restrained myself. Otherwise, I have devoted my week to cleaning and scrubbing.

Take my greetings into your heart of hearts, you chosen treasure, until God helps us come together in joy.[59]

So usual was it for wives to play on the stereotypes of the 'good wife' to get their own way that marriage manuals even gave advice on how to do it. A German advice book of 1702 described how a wife could effectively oppose one of her husband's decisions; she should speak to him:

in a modest tone, choosing a pleasant time and occasion so that all is said in strictest privacy, and let her words be chosen with such care that he will recognize that her action is no impertinent attempt to control him or any presumption to power over him, but rather an expression of her love and concern for his own best interest. For this reason, it is better that such a conversation proceed with demonstrative entreaty and pleading on the part of the wife – if the circumstances require, even with tears – than that a wife give the impression of asserting authority or severity against her husband.[60]

If most wives either accepted their deferential roles or used them as strategies to get their own way, there were a few marriages in which husband and wife regarded each other as equals and spoke their minds without reservation, as couples do today. An example of a marriage with such egalitarian give-and-take is that of Maria Marvin and Thomas Thynne, the couple whose elopement inspired *Romeo and Juliet*. Both husband and wife wrote frankly of their sexual pleasure in each other and Maria Thynne rarely displayed proper wifely submissiveness. When her husband tried to tell her how to run her household, she complained that that showed 'a contempt of my poor wits' and she even made fun of the deferential posture expected of wives:

Mine own sweet Thomken, I have . . . last night written such a large volume in praise of thy kindness to me, thy dogs, thy hawks, the horse and the foxes and also in commendation of thy great care of thy businesses in the country that I think I need not amplify any more on that text.[61]

Finally, at the other end of the spectrum from those matches in which wives were routinely neglected or abused, were the marriages in which the world was turned upside down and the wife, not the husband, ruled the roost. As popular proverbs recognized, these tended to be of two types: marriages of an older husband, often a widower, to a young bride, and matches between an older woman, often a wealthy widow, and a younger man. In the latter, the woman's age, wealth and sexual experience were thought to give her the self-confidence to assert herself and rule her husband; in the former, elderly husbands were thought to be sexually in thrall to their pretty young wives, who could twist them around their little fingers. A sixteenth-century German print entitled *The Old Man and the Young Girl* says of the young girl:

> She gave the old man a friendly stare
> And promised what he desired:
> She would hold him in love and honor.
> She thought, however, only of cold cash.
> Stroking him with sweet words,
> She draped a fool's cape
> About the old dandy's neck,
> And taking him in tow,
> She led him away on a fool's rope,
> As happens still to many an old man.[62]

A real-life example of an indulgent older husband was 52-year-old William Cavendish, Duke of Newcastle, who married the 18-year-old Margaret Lucas when both were in exile with the Royalists in Antwerp during the English Civil War. Unlike the young girl in the poem, Margaret Cavendish apparently genuinely loved her elderly husband and well she might, for he indulged her every whim. Not only did he shower her with clothes and jewels, he also indulged her intellectual pretensions. Although poorly educated and, like many women, an atrocious speller,* Margaret dreamed of being both a writer and a scientist. She wrote poetry, over 21 plays and a utopian novel in which the heroine becomes the empress Margaret I of an imaginary island, learns all about science and founds schools and scientific academies. As this suggests, her real interest was science, not writing. Without either reading the works of others (she boasted, 'I have never any Guide to Direct me, nor Intelligence from any Authors . . .'; and when she had herself painted at work in her library, its bookshelves were conspicuously empty) or performing experiments in the spirit of the seventeenth-century scientific revolution (she believed knowledge gained through experiment and observation was both fallacious and useless: 'The inspection of a Bee, through a Microscope, will bring him no more Honey'), she came up with an atomic theory of the universe which she promulgated in over 20 published works. Her egotism, her eccentricities, her flouting of convention and her bizarre theories made her the object of public ridicule. She was nicknamed 'Mad Madge' and the diarist Samuel Pepys called her a 'mad, conceited, ridiculous woman'. But her indulgent husband not only

---

* In this period the French had a phrase, 'women's spelling', meaning spelling out words as they sounded rather than using their proper form.

encouraged her to risk the family honour by publishing her theories, he risked his own honour by publicly defending her in print, praising her, as one author put it, as 'cleverer than Homer, beyond Aristotle, more modern than Hippocrates and more eloquent than Cicero; her writing, he said, put Virgil and Horace to shame'.[63]

The example of the Cavendishes suggests, with the ridicule Margaret garnered, the strength of the conventions of the 'good wife', but also, with her husband's encouragement to break her silence, the fact that these conventions were often ignored. In early modern marriages, husbands clearly had a dominant position, yet this does not mean that all husbands were tyrants and all wives helpless victims. Wives could play on or subvert the 'good wife' stereotype and carve out for themselves happy and satisfying relationships. Historian Sara Mendelson has read the diaries of seventeenth-century Englishwomen to see if their marriages were happy. Of the 21 with enough information for analysis, she judged 15 to be happy. They included two love matches, three marriages where the bride had the power to choose, two arranged marriages in which the bride had veto power and one arranged marriage in which the bride was only 13. The six unhappy marriages included two forced marriages, one arranged match, one in which the bride had free choice and one elopement. While this suggests that the more choice the bride had, the more likely it was that she would be happy, it also shows that arranged matches could be satisfying.[64] In early modern Europe, her marriage was what a woman made of it.

Chapter 4

◆

MOTHERS

Today, with their small families and high life expectancy, European women spend only a small portion of their lives as active mothers, bearing children and caring for infants and toddlers. But in early modern Europe, when many women died in their forties or fifties instead of in their eighties, motherhood took up a larger portion of their lives. Indeed, a woman who married at 25 and died at 40 might well spend *all* of her married life either pregnant or nursing an infant. To the people of the sixteenth and seventeenth centuries, this was as it should be. The purpose of marriage was procreation, and the purpose of woman was motherhood. As a Russian proverb put it: 'A wife is given to a man for a single purpose, to bear children.' A childless woman was thought to be not yet truly a woman; another Russian proverb said: 'Just as a field withers without rain, so does a childless woman wither.'[1]

Little wonder then that marriage rites included thinly disguised fertility rituals and newly wedded brides were vigilantly watched for signs of pregnancy. Today married couples often worry about having too many children, concerned that they do not have enough time or money to raise them properly. But in the early modern period, with its high levels of childhood deaths, parents usually worried about having too few offspring. Children were desired for economic reasons, as potential contributors to the family economy and as caregivers for their parents in old age. They were also desired for emotional reasons, as objects and bestowers of love and affection. But above all, they were desired for reasons of family pride, as heirs to the family property and perpetuators of the family name. This was as true for peasants as it was for kings and nobles. Therefore it is not surprising that, as the seventeenth-century English midwife Jane Sharp wrote: 'To conceive with child is the earnest desire if not of all, of most women.'[2]

Because children were so desired, the focus of reproductive medicine was not, as it is today, on birth control, but instead on infertility. This was usually blamed on the woman, despite the fact that both the Aristotelian and the Galenic versions of reproduction gave the husband the more active and important role. Male impotence was known and acknowledged; a man's inability to consummate his marriage was grounds for its annulment in the western, Greek, and Russian Orthodox Christian churches and, if it lasted for more than a year, under Islamic marriage law. In France cases of suspected male impotence were judged by 'trial by congress': the suspected husband had to demonstrate publicly in front of a court or its appointed experts that he was not impotent.[3] But impotence was considered not necessarily the man's fault: he might well have been bewitched by a magic spell ('tying the knot') cast by an ill wisher at his marriage. That happened to the unhappy sixteenth-century French peasant Martin Guerre, who was so ashamed that he eventually ran away from his wife and neighbours and joined the army.*

A wife's barrenness was, however, her own fault (probably a punishment from God for her sins) and it was up to her to do something about it. Infertile wives spent much time and effort trying to conceive, eating foods such as eggs, beans, and peas thought to promote conception; using magical remedies like drinking mule's urine or swallowing the ground-up umbilical cord of a first-born son; praying and making pilgrimages to shrines like France's Notre Dame du Puy, whose wonder-working Black Madonna was thought to make her petitioners fertile. Such shrines often pre-dated Christianity and contained obvious fertility symbols like phallically shaped rocks and bubbling springs.[4]

PREGNANCY

It might be hard to know at first if these efforts to conceive were successful. The medical profession had no sure test for pregnancy until the nineteenth century. Before that, doctors and midwives went by the same signs that women passed down from generation to generation: cessation of periods, morning sickness, weight gain. Most women were not really sure they were pregnant until the baby moved in the womb and even that might be misinterpreted.

---

* His eventual reappearance set off the most famous case of identity theft in early modern Europe, a story marvellously recounted by Natalie Davis in *The Return of Martin Guerre* (Cambridge, MA, 1983).

Unwed mothers, who often found it hard to face up to the fact that they might be pregnant, sometimes ignored that warning sign; they often stated that they had been surprised to find themselves giving birth. Male doctors, who in our period had only recently begun to treat women, knew so little about pregnancy that until the eighteenth century most thought it had no fixed term but could instead last anywhere from seven to 10 months.[5]

Once her pregnancy was recognized, a woman was perceived as entering into a special and unique state of life. Pregnancy sanctified women, cancelling out their sins and in a sense restoring their lost virginity. It also put them in danger of death. The writer of one medical text described pregnancy as 'a rough sea on which a big-belly'd woman and her infant floats the space of nine months and labour, which is the only port, is full of dangerous rocks'. Many expectant mothers, conscious of the threat of death, made their wills; Elizabeth Joceline bought a new winding sheet, just in case. Jane Josselin, wife of the seventeenth-century English clergyman Ralph Josselin, spent most of her many pregnancies telling him 'thou and I must part' [soon, through her death], and another seventeenth-century Englishwoman, Alice Thornton, recorded during her pregnancy her fears about 'the sad estate I was to pass and dangerous perils my soul was to find, even by the gates of death'.[6]

How dangerous were these perils? Accurate statistics are difficult to find, but in the sixteenth and seventeenth centuries probably about 15 of every 1000 pregnant women died in childbirth. In England the rate was 15.7 per 1000; in Geneva 15–19 per 1000; in Rouen 12 per 1000. This is, of course, far more than today, when the rate for European women is only 0.1 per 1000 and more than the nineteenth-century rate of 4.6 per 1000.[7] But it is not especially high. In fact, in early modern Europe women stood as great a chance of dying from disease as they did of dying from childbirth. Why then the fears associated with it? They probably arose because death from childbirth was so obvious and conspicuous. The diseases which killed women were many, varied and often mysterious in their operation, but when a woman died in childbirth the cause of death was obvious. Perhaps too death in childbirth was thought more unfair, for the mother had voluntarily put herself at risk. At any rate, women were very conscious of the dangers of pregnancy and childbirth.

Luckily, apart from recommending frequent bleeding (pregnancy was thought to thicken the blood and therefore impede its circulation), medical advice to pregnant women was quite sensible. Again it chimed in with traditional female folk wisdom. Pregnant women were advised to eat and drink in moderation, get plenty of exercise in sensible, low-heeled shoes and avoid tight corsets, sexual intercourse, hot baths (thought to open the womb) and overexertion.[8] The Russian Orthodox Church forbade priests from demanding that pregnant women make the usual deep genuflections before the altar.[9] Above all, pregnant women were told to avoid anything that might induce a miscarriage or cause birth defects in the foetus. In both the humoral and the Paracelsian theories of the body prevalent in the early modern period, the body was thought to be easily affected by spiritual forces and psychological states. Spontaneous miscarriages were quite common because of the poor diet and health and overwork of many expectant mothers, but they were usually attributed to psychological factors: loud noises, bad smells, unpleasant sights. These were also thought to cause birth defects. In Stuttgart in 1659 a coppersmith's wife who gave birth to a boy with only one foot attributed that to having seen a lame beggar on her way to market and in 1677 another German traced the deformed hands and feet of her child to the shock she received when a dog and her puppies jumped up on her unexpectedly while she was doing the laundry.[10]

Pregnant women were advised to avoid such shocks if possible and protection from them was deemed their right. A Nuremberg city ordinance of 1478 required beggars to hide their deformed limbs so they would not frighten expectant mothers and in 1630 the district court of Wildberg forbade Claus Saalen's daughter from leaving her house because her appearance 'was so disgusting that pregnant women might be shocked'. Scenes of violence and death were especially harmful; many German towns therefore placed their gallows in inconspicuous places. The fact that hangings were harmful to pregnant women led, in German cities at least, to the custom of allowing them to plead for the lives of condemned felons. In 1620 in Constance, no fewer than 52 pregnant women begged the judge to spare one offender's life.[11] Pregnancy thus gave women special rights and privileges. Peasant villages often demanded the right to fish in their lord's stream or gather acorns in his woods because pregnant women needed nourishment and abused wives often falsely claimed to be pregnant to stop the beatings. Russian law explicitly forbade husbands to strike pregnant wives and such abuse was frowned on elsewhere.[12]

CHILDBIRTH

Communal concern for pregnant women increased as the birth drew near. Whether or not a medical professional would be called in and whether this would be a male physician or surgeon or a female midwife depended on the period, location and social class of the expectant mother. By the late seventeenth century it was fashionable among the nobility and wealthiest of the urban bourgeoisie in England and France to have a so-called 'male midwife' – a male physician or surgeon who specialized in treating women – in attendance. In France, for example, in 1663 King Louis XIV employed a physician to attend the confinement of his mistress Mlle de La Vallière, starting a fashion of using male midwives among the court nobility.[13] But most of the provincial nobility and gentry, plus all but the richest and most fashionable of townswomen in western Europe, employed female midwives, who were the standard providers of health care for women in the urban areas of western Europe in the early modern period. The Prussian court employed female midwives throughout the eighteenth century.[14] Usually trained by apprenticeship, midwives were some-times organized into guilds, but more often they were tested for competence, licensed and supervised by town governments, as in Paris, Nuremberg, Frankfurt and Stuttgart. German cities often paid midwives to provide free care for poor women in labour; such women might also receive from town governments free food and bedding and a small cash grant, the 'lying-in florin'.[15] Poor women in rural areas were not so lucky. In the countryside, properly trained midwives were few and far between and most expectant mothers had to make do with the help of the local lady of the manor (who, as we shall see in Chapter 6, was the usual healthcare provider in rural areas) or the local wise woman with her herbs and spells, plus the assistance of female friends and neighbours.

There has been much debate among historians of women over which type of help – male medical 'knowledge' or the female folk wisdom of midwives, wise women, and friends and neighbours – was better for the mother and child. In the 1970s and 1980s, when women's history was largely written by committed feminists struggling to give the women of their own time an alterna-tive to sterile, impersonal, uncaring hospital births by supporting midwives and home births, the entrance in the seventeenth century of male doctors and surgeons into the hitherto all-female world of birth was depicted as a disaster. Male doctors, desiring to rid themselves of female competition and monopolize the world of medicine for men, were said to have wrongly ridiculed the usually highly trained, experienced and professional midwives as drunken incompetents relying on outmoded superstitious and magical practices. Further, their own vaunted modern medical 'knowledge' was said to be actually more harmful for women than traditional folk practices. For example, male doctors demanded that women give birth prone in bed, instead of kneeling or sitting upright on the traditional birthing stool (see Plate 7), where the force of gravity helped the delivery, and they were said to show off their new instruments like the forceps by surgically intervening in normal births, with disastrous effects.

Today, with the contemporary battle for alternative birthing safely won, historians are more nuanced in their interpretations. Most acknowledge that birthing stools were giving way to births in bed even before male midwives appeared on the scene and that some of the midwives' traditional practices, like reaching into the birth canal and forcing an infant's arm or leg back into the womb if it appeared before the head, endangered mother and child. Today the consensus seems to be that midwives and female folk wisdom were preferable for normal births, but that male doctors, with their new instruments and superior strength, could probably intervene more effectively when there were complications.[16]

There has been a similar reinterpretation of the rituals surrounding births. When they were first studied, historians thought they were not only exclusively female but also, in a sense, directed against men, for birth was seen as a privileged time when women could get together and through their 'gossip', a word derived from birth rituals,* enunciate and enforce standards of female behaviour separate from and often in opposition to those of the male patriarchy. Not to be invited to attend a neighbour's giving birth was an insult and often the basis of hard feelings and even witchcraft accusations. Today, however, historians take a more cautious view, pointing out that the standards of womanly behaviour shaped by these female gatherings differed little from those in the patriarchal society at large and that while husbands and their male friends were excluded from watching and helping with the actual birth, they nonetheless had an important place in its rituals. When his wife's time grew near, a husband was expected to rearrange the family's work schedules to spare his wife heavy labour, to provide meat, wine, a bed and decent linens for the birth and, if possible, to hire an assistant, either a physician or a midwife, for the birth itself, and a nurse or lying-in maid for the period after.[17] Above all, husbands were expected to remain nearby and display love and concern when the labour started. When Margaret Hobart's husband refused to prepare for her lying-in, concerned friends wrote to her father and one German town government arrested a man for leaving on a business trip when his wife was about to go into labour. Most husbands did not need to be goaded by the community into displaying concern. In 1630 Englishman Edward Dering spoke for many husbands when he wrote to his wife in labour: 'God in heaven blesse thee, and oure hopefull burthen, for I carry in my heart ye paynes thou

---

* Gossip originally meant 'god-sib' or 'god-sibling', that is, someone suited to be a godparent – i.e. a guest at a birth ritual. Later it evolved through 'female friend' to 'the talk of female friends' to its present meaning.

sufferest for me.'[18] Some felt their wives' pain elsewhere than in their hearts: in southwestern France, in the folk ritual of the *couvade*, an expectant father, supported by his male friends, was expected to simulate the labour pangs of his wife.

Most of the rituals surrounding births were all female, however. Like most rites of passage, births took place in a special space set aside for that purpose: in Russia, in bathhouses; elsewhere, in the largest and warmest first-floor room in the house, closed off from its everyday use and the outside world by drawn curtains. Fires were lit and the lying-in bed, sometimes rented for the occasion, prepared. Women might give birth lying in bed (that was the norm by 1700), but they might also take advantage of the force of gravity by using the midwife's birthing stool, kneeling down or sitting on another woman's lap. Medicinal remedies like senna bark, orange peel, white wine, rue and sabine were administered to hurry the birth and magical objects said to ease labour (a snake skin tied around the belly, the father's hat placed on top of it, an 'eagle's' stone worn on the arm) applied. In Catholic countries, women prayed to the saints traditionally associated with childbirth: the Virgin's mother, Saint Anne; Saint Margaret, who survived being swallowed by a dragon; St Leonard, patron of prisoners wishing deliverance; Saint Honorine; Saint Hyacinth; and, above all, the Virgin Mary herself. Protestants could not invoke these traditional protectors (see Chapter 9) and had simply to pray to God for a safe delivery. Women in labour were encouraged to yell and scream, for this was thought to help labour along. Those who didn't were considered unnatural. In 1597 in the German town of Sulz, Catharina Springer was denounced to the authorities for 'not having acted during her labour as she should'.[19]

Once the baby was born, the midwife cut and tied the umbilical cord and washed and swaddled the child. She also removed the placenta (it was often preserved to be used in magical rituals), washed the mother and fed her a special celebratory food prepared by the women in attendance. The food varied from country to country (in England it was often oatmeal, in Italy a nourishing soup) but the custom was universal.

So too was the lying-in period, lasting a month or even 40 days, if the mother could be spared from her housework and other chores for that long. These were performed by the lying-in nurse, usually a poor elderly woman hired not to care for the mother but to do her work. For the first three days after the birth – sometimes longer – the new mother remained in bed, in the still darkened and secluded birth chamber. Then came what the English called her 'upsitting', when she got out of bed and its bloody linen was changed for the first time since the birth. This was a time of celebration, when the women who had attended the birth were invited back for food and drink. After this the mother was allowed to sit up, but she stayed in her room for another week or 10 days. Then she was allowed to leave her room and do light household tasks, but she was confined to the house for the whole month.[20]

The new mother ended her lying-in and re-entered local society by leaving her house to go to church. In Russia, this was to undergo a ceremonial purification after the pollution of childbirth. According to the Russian Orthodox Church, during her 40-day lying-in period a new mother was impure. She was forbidden to attend church or receive communion. Her husband could not have sex with her and no Christian was supposed to eat in her presence, not even her infant, which in theory made it impossible for a mother to nurse her child. In practice, this was circumvented by delaying the newborn's baptism until after the purification ceremony. While unbaptized, the infant was technically not yet a Christian and therefore could eat in its mother's presence.[21]

Western Christendom too had required purification after birth in the Middle Ages, but by 1600 the Catholic Church found the notion that childbirth defiled a woman insulting to the female sex and substituted for the purification ceremony a service of thanksgiving for having survived the perils of labour. The more radical Protestant denominations banned even these services but were often forced to reinstate them under pressure from the women of their congregations.[22] This suggests that women found the 'churching', as it was called in England, and indeed all the rituals surrounding childbirth, meaningful. Having friends around and using the traditional prayers and rituals alleviated the horrors of labour. The long lying-in period, while not what doctors would advise for today's healthier mothers, gave the often undernourished and overworked women of early modern Europe a respite from their gruelling daily chores and a chance to recover from difficult deliveries and bond with their new babies. And the churching was a chance to celebrate all this with female friends – one of the few public rituals that celebrated a uniquely *female* accomplishment with women at centre stage. No wonder women were the main force behind its continuation.

The final ritual surrounding childbirth was the new baby's baptism. When this took place varied widely. In Russian Orthodox Christianity, as we have seen, it did not occur until after the 40-day lying-in. Protestants too delayed baptism, usually until two weeks or a month after birth. The delay was possible because while Protestants thought baptism a sacrament by which God's grace was transmitted to mankind, they did not believe it necessary for salvation. The almighty Protestant God could save whomever He pleased, including unbaptized babies. The central meaning of baptism for Protestants was the acceptance of Christian doctrines by the baptized and his or her entrance into the community of Christians. That was why some of the more radical Protestant sects practised adult baptism; only an adult could truly understand what he was accepting. But for mainstream Protestants, the acceptance was done by godparents on the child's behalf.

Catholic beliefs about baptism differed. To Catholics baptism was absolutely essential for salvation; the unbaptized, even innocent babies, would spend eternity in limbo. Given the frail health of many newborns, this meant that baptism had to take place quickly. The Council of Trent, which laid out Church doctrine during the Counterreformation, mandated three days after birth. Newborns in danger of dying might be given emergency baptisms right after birth or even in the womb. The Church reluctantly allowed midwives to perform this ceremony – reluctantly because women should not take on priestly roles and administer the sacraments. If a man – a male doctor, the baby's father – were present, he was supposed to do it. But usually there were no men at births, so the Church bowed to necessity, requiring that bishops supervise the midwives of their dioceses to make sure they baptized properly. Sometimes even emergency baptisms came too late. Catholic Europe was scattered with shrines where mothers of dead infants prayed to the Virgin Mary to revive them just long enough to be baptized.[23]

Despite these variations in timing, baptisms in Christian Europe had two constants: godparents and gifts. The relationship of godparent to godchild was much closer in early modern Europe than it is today. In fact, it was so close that marriage between them, or between the godparents of one individual, was forbidden; such matches were considered incestuous. Godparents were expected to provide material as well as spiritual gifts and guidance to their godchildren: a gift at the baptism, a financial contribution to the apprenticeship of a young man or the dowry of a girl, a legacy in a will. The fairy godmother of folktales thus had a basis in fact. Because the protection and favours granted to the child were extended to its family as well, people often sought for their children godparents of a higher social class. Nobles were godparents of numerous offspring of their peasants; an urban artisan might ask a town councillor to sponsor his child. Godparenting was considered an equivalent to actual parenting and therefore the childless, especially childless women, were often asked. Childless Anna Bauer was godmother to 57 children between 1535 and 1555.[24]

The other constant in baptisms was gift giving. Godparents provided a tip to the midwife and a gift for the child, even if, among the very poor, it was only a prayer. The infant's parents provided gifts – usually food, ranging from sweets and sweetmeats to a full-blown banquet – for the guests. Anthropologists would say that this was to propitiate the community, so that it would welcome yet another member competing for its scarce resources. Baptism signified and celebrated the entrance of a new member into the family (at the baptisms of children of the Polish nobility hired poets recited verses recounting the glorious lineage and history of the families the babies were joining)[25] and into the local community.

UNWANTED PREGNANCIES AND CHILDREN

Not all children were welcome, however, and pregnancies did not always produce a proud mother to be churched and a healthy baby to be baptized. Probably around 3 to 5 percent of the babies born in this period were illegitimate.[26] Unwed mothers – rape victims, maidservants sexually abused by their masters, courting girls whose lovers refused to marry them – were usually appalled when they found themselves pregnant. They hid their condition as long as possible. One English servant told her friends she was just 'pot-bellied', a trait that ran in her family. Unwed mothers often refused to face up to their condition even when they were about to give birth. Another English servant persistently denied she was pregnant, gave birth in her bed in silence and then killed the baby and hid its body.[27] She behaved this way because the consequences of an illegitimate pregnancy were severe: loss of honour and reputation; public disgrace and shaming (bastard bearers were publicly beaten in England and had to perform public penance in German towns); immediate job loss (female maidservants and the like discovered to be pregnant were almost inevitably fired); long-term unemployment (it was difficult to combine the sorts of employment available to dishonoured women – mostly casual heavy labour – with infant and childcare); and therefore lifelong poverty. One unwed mother summed it up: her pregnancy spelled 'certain ruin to her for life'.[28]

It had not always been so. In the Middle Ages illegitimacy and unwed motherhood were regarded leniently. Kings, nobles and rich merchants often acknowledged their bastards and took them into their households and communities tolerated courting couples who had sex before marriage. In fact, because verbally expressed consent made a marriage, especially if followed by sexual intercourse, communities considered such couples as good as married. In some places marriage took place only when the woman had proved her fertility by becoming pregnant. In medieval Scotland unmarried girls were actually encouraged by their families to have sex and bear bastards, for that not only proved their fertility and therefore enhanced their chances of marriage but also added members to their clans.[29] But after the Reformation and Counterreformation, with their disapproval of all sex outside marriage (see Chapters 9 and 10), popular attitudes changed and unwed motherhood everywhere became a disgrace.

In many places – German cities, for example – bearing an illegitimate child was a crime, leaving the mother subject to public shaming and banishment. In some areas of Germany in the sixteenth century the punishment for bearing a bastard was death by drowning.[30] Everywhere but Scotland and the Basque country, with their clan-like households that could absorb new members, it brought dishonour on the mother and her family. Therefore many pregnant women ran away from their native villages to give birth in the anonymity of a town or city. Consequently, they spent much of their pregnancies on the road. This was especially true in England, where they would be chased out of village after village. The English poor laws entitled those born in a village to public assistance from the village funds; therefore pregnant women were run out of town before they gave birth so their infants would not be entitled to relief. The records of English poor relief abound in stories of pregnant women stoned from village to village and giving birth in roadside ditches.

If they finally found a place that would accept them, unwed mothers might face official interrogation about the circumstances of their pregnancies. In France, for example, they were required to make a *déclaration de grossesse* – a declaration of pregnancy. Its purpose was threefold: to shame the woman; to identify the father so that he could be made to support the baby; and, above all, to prevent infanticide. It was feared that women who tried to conceal their pregnancies might kill their babies. Actually infanticide was not very common. Brittany had only one or two cases per year; in Nuremberg there were only 42 cases in the two centuries from 1500 to 1700.[31] But infanticide was a high-profile crime, for it was considered especially unnatural and heinous and, while relatively infrequent, it nevertheless formed a large portion (usually around 20 percent) of all the murder cases in early modern Europe. Because people were so concerned about it, most countries had very strict laws about infanticide, which instructed judges to find unwed mothers who had not made a declaration and could not produce a live baby guilty of infanticide, even though the child might have been stillborn or died shortly after birth of natural causes. Occasionally, if there were evidence (like the purchase of baby linen) that the mother was planning on caring for a live baby, death by natural causes was assumed and the woman acquitted; more usually, however, she was convicted.[32]

Unwed mothers did not usually kill their babies outright, but they often abandoned them. If they left them in places where they were unlikely to be noticed, this was tantamount to infanticide. This happened fairly frequently. When a drain was opened in Rennes, France, in 1721, the skeletons of over 80 abandoned babies were found.[33] But usually mothers left their babies in conspicuous places – church steps, market squares – hoping that they would be found and taken to the special institutions like the Hôpital des Enfants-Trouvés in Paris or the Inclusa in Madrid which cared for orphaned and abandoned children. In 1700 the Inclusa took in 443 abandoned babies.[34]

Not all the children killed or abandoned by their parents were bastards. Thirteen percent of the infants admitted to the Inclusa were probably legitimate and historians estimate that throughout Europe about 20 to 30 percent of abandoned children were legitimate also.[35] This suggests that, despite society's celebration of fertility in marriage, not all children were wanted. Like unwed mothers, married women sometimes endured their pregnancies in a state of denial and refused to care for their infants. In German towns, they could be imprisoned and fined for this dereliction of maternal duties, as Anna Maria Krauth was in 1657. Krauth was unhappily married; her husband was disabled and ugly, 'with thighs big as tree trunks'. Despite beatings by her husband and admonishments by her mother, her priest and her female neighbours (who even showed her a dead baby to try to arouse her maternal feelings), Krauth refused to care for herself properly during pregnancy and to prepare for giving birth. When labour began, she would not go to bed or use a birthing stool and throughout it she swore incessantly and said she wanted to die.[36]

Even women more happily married than Krauth might be dismayed to find themselves pregnant, either because of fears for their health and safety during pregnancy and childbirth or because of the financial burden of caring for an additional child. Obviously that consideration weighed most heavily on the poor, who might be forced to abandon the newborn so that there would be enough money to feet the rest of the family. Abandonment of legitimate children often rose when food prices did. Unlike abandoned bastards, who were almost always newborns, legitimate children were usually several months old when they were left at an institution – old enough to have bonded with their mothers, who had tried to keep them. And again unlike bastards, legitimate babies were usually left with identifying objects like ribbons and notes proclaiming their parents' intention to reclaim them when they could:

> This child was borne the 11 of June 1708 of unhappy parents wich is not abell to pro-
> vide for it: therefore I humbelly beg of you Gentell man hoever hands this unfourtunat
> child shall fall into that you will take that care that will become a feallow crattear and

if God makes me abell I will repaye the charge and reclame the child . . . her name is Jahn Bennett: shee is baptisead.[37]

Even well-to-do parents might worry about the financial burden of a large family. Mary Rich, wife of the younger son of an English earl, had two children early in her marriage and recorded in her memoirs her husband's dismay when she told him she might be pregnant again:

> [T]hough he was at as great a rate fond of his children he had, as any father would be, yet when he had had two he would often say he feared he would have so many as would undo a younger brother.[38]

Did such feelings prompt people to attempt family planning – to use contraception and abortion to limit the size of their families? Historians debate about this. Some say no, arguing that such measures were not only considered sinful by the Catholic Church (Protestants took a more lenient view) but were also unnecessary in most families, at least those in northwestern Europe. The late age of marriage (mid-twenties), the early onset of menopause (at about 40), the contraceptive effects of breastfeeding and, above all, the high rates of infant and child mortality (only about half the children born in this period grew to adulthood) kept the size of most families small without resort to abortion or contraception. The average woman in northwest Europe, married around 25 and, breastfeeding her children, would have been pregnant every two to three years until her late thirties and therefore would have borne four to five children, of whom only two or three would reach adulthood.[39]

On the other hand, there is much evidence from diaries and statements in court cases that women – and men too – tried to prevent or terminate pregnancies in both illicit relationships and marriage. Contraception was probably often attempted but usually ineffective. Two effective methods in use today, the sponge inserted into the cervix and the condom, were used then, but only in illicit sex. Only prostitutes used cervical sponges to prevent conception and their clients were the main users of condoms (made out of sheep's guts). In early modern Europe, condoms were used not as a contraceptive but to guard against sexually transmitted diseases. For contraception respectable women relied on amulets and charms begged or bought from wise women; their efficacy is doubtful. The only really reliable methods were intercourse in positions that did not result in conception and *coitus interruptus*, male withdrawal before ejaculation – the famous sin of Onan mentioned in the Bible. Demographers think that in the few instances they have found where contraception seems to have been practised – during periods of especially severe economic crisis, for example – the latter was the method used. There is much evidence that contemporaries thought so too. One English writer of a gynaecological manual noted, 'for this God slew him [Onan]: I believe God hath been more merciful to many in *England* in the same case'.[40]

Abortion was probably more widely practised, both because there were more reliable methods available and because they did not, unlike *coitus interruptus*, require the cooperation of men. Herbs that induced abortion like rue and savin were widely grown, and it was common knowledge that tightly laced corsets, horseback riding, strenuous physical exertion, plus the almost universal practice of bleeding, might bring on miscarriages. Indeed, some historians think that the long lists in medical books of precautions against miscarriages were really coded hints on how to induce abortions or at least were read as such by women.[41] The Jeringham family in England had a recipe of a herbal brew 'to cause miscarriage' that was handed down from generation to generation.[42] Apart from these do-it-yourself efforts, abortions were also performed by medical personnel. Midwives could lose their licences for performing abortions, yet many did; a male midwife complained that he was tricked into aborting a client who told him she had a false pregnancy. Finally, a few illegal back-alley abortionists existed, especially toward the end of our period. An example is Eleanor Merriman, tried in London in 1732 for performing abortions with 'iron instruments'.[43]

INFANT CARE

Wanted or not, once born, infants had to be cared for. In the sixteenth and seventeenth centuries this was a real challenge. Around one-quarter of all children born died before their first birthdays and many died only days – or even hours – after birth. Ten percent of the babies born in seventeenth-century French villages lived for less than a day.[44] They died because, born of undernourished and overworked mothers, they were weak to begin with. They died because of the traumas of birth, strangled by their umbilical cords or suffocated as their lungs filled with liquid when they lingered too long in the birth canal. They died from the germs in their unsanitary surroundings. And above all, they died from lack of nourishment. Their vital first feeding was often delayed for hours or even days, either because of religious scruples about feeding an infant before baptism or because male doctors thought the colostrum (the mother's first milk) bad for newborns. Mother's milk was, nonetheless, the only possible food for them. They could not digest the animal milk or the various oatmeals given in the absence of mother's milk and the harsh laxatives administered to help the digestive process only worsened their condition. In eighteenth-century Finland, the village of Koivulathi had an infant mortality rate of 548 per 1000, much higher than the 173 per 1000 recorded in the villages of the province of Karelia. This was because Koivulathi was a fishing village where, in the absence of their fisherman husbands, women were responsible for planting and harvesting the crops. Unable to fit breastfeeding into their busy schedules, mothers weaned their infants at the beginning of summer, feeding them cow's milk instead.[45]

If a mother could or would not feed her infant, a slightly better alternative than animal milk was hiring a wet nurse, a woman who had recently given birth herself. Wet nurses were often hired by mothers of all classes whose milk failed. They were also usually hired by noblewomen and by the wives of officeholders and professionals who emulated the nobility, even if they were capable of nursing their own infants. Wives of urban merchants and artisans also often hired wet nurses. Medical opinion deplored the practice, blaming female vanity for its persistence. Doctors suggested that women, especially women of fashion, did not want the sagging breasts that came with nursing. In fact, however, the decision to hire a wet nurse was often made by the husband, who faced the loss of his wife's sexual services for a year if she nursed. (There were taboos against having sexual intercourse while lactating; it was thought to ruin the milk.) Nursing also took up a great deal of time and many women who hired nurses did not have that to spare. Both the noblewomen who managed their husbands' large households and estates and the artisans' wives who supervised apprentices, kept the accounts and served behind the counter of their husbands' shops were extremely busy. They thought they contributed more usefully to their family's welfare by continuing to do these jobs, which no one else could do, than by nursing, for which someone could be hired.

Yet consigning a baby to a wet nurse could be tantamount to condemning it to death. Only in the largest noble households did nurses live in. All other babies had to go to the nurse, who was usually a peasant woman in the countryside. This often meant a long journey in inclement weather, with the infant unfed while en route. At the nurse's there were other hazards. One was malnutrition, if the nurse's milk failed, if she took in too many babies (in eighteenth-century France one wet nurse had 17 infants at one time)[46] or if, as was only natural, she favoured her own baby over that of a stranger. Others grew from the nurse's carelessness; peasant women were busy too. Unwatched infants often died of dog bites or falls into the fire. Another hazard was 'overlaying': taken into the marital bed to keep them warm, babies were often killed when the adults rolled over on them. 'Overlaying' also killed babies in their own homes, even well-to-do ones.

The high death tolls from early weaning, wet nursing and overlaying made early historians of the family question parents' devotion to newborns and postulate that they were afraid to invest too much love in those frail creatures so likely to die. Some even suggested that these practices were unconscious, disguised forms of infanticide perpetrated by parents who wanted to limit the size of their families. Later research has cast doubt on this. Diaries and letters provide overwhelming evidence that parents loved even frail newborn infants and grieved when they died. When his second son died four days after birth, the sixteenth-century German lawyer Christoph Scheurl wrote:

> [He] lived exactly four days, and never was I richer than when I was with these two sons of mine. I have thus had a grievous rejoicing, as my happiness was turned so quickly to sadness. This happened, however, by the will of my Lord God, whom it has pleased to do this . . . He gave the son, and He has taken him back.[47]

Sending a baby to a wet nurse was a sign of parental care, not indifference. Most parents chose nurses very carefully, in part because their milk was thought to pass personality traits on to the infants they nursed. Medical manuals were full of advice on picking the right nurse: she should be healthy, with a ruddy complexion, a sweet breath, etc. Once the nurse was selected, most parents carefully monitored their baby's progress, demanding reports and paying visits or asking relatives, friends or the local clergyman to do so.

If they survived, children usually returned home from the nurse at around age one. From ages one to seven, their childhoods resembled those of today's youngsters. So far as we can tell, they passed through the same developmental stages at approximately the same time: weaning at about one year; walking at about 13 months; teething at about 18 months; producing their first words at around age two.[48] These developments were anxiously and proudly recorded in the diaries and letters of their parents. Christoph Scheurl worried that at age three his son Georg could say only five words, a 'very remarkable' lack of progress, while Nicolas Blundell proudly noted that his 31-month-old daughter could not just walk but run.[49]

Childhood in the early modern period did, however, differ from today's in a number of ways. All infants were routinely swaddled – that is, wound with strips of clean cloth, arms straight at their sides and legs straight out, forming a papoose-like bundle. Swaddling was thought to be good for babies: it kept them warm, protected them from dog bites and made their limbs grow straight, an important consideration when infants were thought animal like and the main goal of childrearing was to make them 'human' as soon as possible. Above all, swaddling allowed a mother to go about her work. She could put a swaddled baby down, do her chores and return, confident that the baby would be where she had left it. Swaddling was the early modern equivalent of daycare.

Early modern infant care differed from today's in other ways as well. In the sixteenth and seventeenth centuries, unlike today, great efforts were made to discourage toddlers from crawling and to teach them, with leading strings attached to the shoulders of their dress and wooden walkers to walk upright as soon as possible, because this too encouraged the child to be 'human'. By contrast, toilet training, an important and often traumatic aspect of modern childrearing, seems to have received little attention, as was natural in a society where adults of all social classes relieved themselves casually, in public, whenever necessary.

A final – and controversial – way in which early modern childhoods differed from those of today was in the use of corporal punishment. Many childrearing manuals advised that children be beaten early and often, especially during the period modern parents call 'the terrible twos', when children begin to assert their own wills and must be taught that they cannot always have their own way. In early modern Europe, this wilfulness was considered a sign of original sin and children were beaten not only to make them obedient (a necessity, after all, in a hierarchical society in which almost every adult had to obey a social superior) but also to give them a sense of their own sinfulness, make them repent and thus start them on the road to salvation.

Corporal punishment is controversial because historians do not know how widespread it was. Childrearing manuals insisted it was necessary, but often in tones that suggested that their authors doubted that parents would follow their advice. Undoubtedly, many children were beaten. A seventeenth-century Englishman, Richard Norwood, wrote that as a child, 'often on a Lord's day at night or Monday morning I prayed to escape beating that week' and Grace Mildmay noted that she was beaten to 'inculcate virtuous principles'.[50] Dutchwoman Isabella Hoogentoren, after being spoiled as a baby, was beaten by her mother when she entered 'the terrible twos'. Her mother believed the girl, born with a caul (a piece of the birth sac, thought to be a sign of supernatural gifts and witchcraft), was possessed by an evil spirit. The experience so traumatized Isabella that she not only remained frightened of her mother for the rest of her life but also wrote a 699-page autobiography 'to show the evil beating causes'. In it she argued that beating makes children worse, not better. A beaten child feels 'likened to the animals'; it is 'affronted and it is taught by nature not to suffer affronts but to avenge them', so it continues to behave badly and eventually strikes out at its parents.[51] Most parents agreed and used other forms of punishment: scoldings, fines, isolation, with corporal punishment employed only as a last resort. Some children, Nehemiah Wallington for example, were never beaten; he described his mother as 'very tender-hearted to her children'.[52]

Note that, in these examples, it was the mother rather than the father who decided on and administered the punishment, if any. This highlights the centrality of the mother in the care of young children. Mothers bore almost total responsibility for the care of children under six; they were not only expected to care for their physical needs but also to begin their education and their moral training. Fathers were supposed to love their young children, but at a distance: their prime tasks were to work to provide for their family's material needs and to see that their wives did their childrearing duty. Men were considered incapable of caring for infants and the smelly tasks involved were thought beneath male dignity. This was why widowers with small children were expected to remarry almost immediately and usually did. (For more on this, see the next chapter.) In 'the world turned upside down' engravings like Plate 6, men were portrayed with swaddled babies as well as spindles while women were given trousers, pipe and musket to symbolize the reversal of gender roles. As so often happened, these theoretical expectations about gender roles did not necessarily match reality. In fact, many loving fathers shared the daily chores of babycare. Even so dignified a patriarch as Martin Luther occasionally changed a diaper, although he noted that: 'When a man washes the swaddling clothes or does some other menial task for the benefit of a baby, someone will undoubtedly make fun of him and take him for a fool or at least henpecked.'[53]

MATERNAL INSTINCT AND MOTHER LOVE

Mothers were assigned prime responsibility for the care of young children because they were thought to be endowed by nature with maternal instincts that prompted them to do what was necessary to care for their child. In the early modern period motherhood was not as central to female identity as it would become in the nineteenth century, but it was nonetheless a vital role for which women were thought uniquely endowed by nature, with not only the physical equipment necessary for childbearing but also with maternal instinct and unlimited patience and love. It was thought that mothers would never knowingly harm their children and would always do what was best for them.

These beliefs could harm women, by limiting their options and by exposing those who did not live up to these high standards to prosecution as bad mothers. But they could also empower women. Belief in mother love might get a mother custody of her children, something that went against two of the most basic principles of early modern law: that women should not be allowed to exercise legal authority over anyone and indeed often needed legal guardians themselves (see Chapter 13) and that children belonged to the patriliny and should remain there, under the guardianship of their father or, if he were dead, of their uncles or other male kin. Most law codes followed these rules, but there were exceptions. In Muscovy, widowed mothers automatically became guardians of their minor children.[54] In the customary law of the area around Nantes, France, when a father died the paternal and maternal kin of the children met to appoint a guardian. A mother was to be chosen 'if she is adequate and wants to take charge'. In 90 percent of the cases, she was selected.[55] Even in Florence, where women needed male guardians to act at law and children remained with the patriliny, mothers were sometimes appointed guardians in preference to male kin. The rationale was mother love: in choosing a guardian, the Florentine courts looked for someone who would not harm the child to gain some advantage – kill the child to inherit its property, for example.[56] Mothers seemed the least likely to do that. Mother love even gained women the right to rule states. Ordinarily women could not be rulers (see Chapter 12). A woman ruling over men went against the will of God and the laws of nature, both of which dictated that males dominate females. It also went against public order, for women were considered incapable of grasping the complexities of public affairs. Yet an exception was made for queen mothers. When their sons were underage, they were allowed to rule in their place. It was thought their mother love would prompt them instinctively to choose the policies best for the interests of their sons and therefore best for the kingdom.

MOTHERS AND OLDER CHILDREN

Did the fierce protective instincts of mother love remain as children grew into adults? It is hard to say. Much less has been written about the relationships between mothers and older and adult children than about the relationships between mothers and their infants. In part this is because historians are less interested in mature mother–child relationships than in infant care. But lack of sources also play a role. These relationships are less frequently recorded in letters and diaries and depicted in advice books, perhaps because there simply weren't very many of them. The relatively high age of marriage and therefore of motherhood combined with high levels of mortality meant that relatively few mothers lived to see their children grow into adults. By the time they married, half the people in early modern western Europe had lost at least one parent; many had lost both.[57] Most widowers remarried, especially if they had children to care for, so children were almost as likely to be guided through adolescence by a stepmother as by their own mothers. Stepmothers were not expected to love their stepchildren; quite the contrary. While they were supposed to see to the basic necessities, food, clothing, cleanliness and discipline, it was thought only natural that they would lavish their love on their own children and that there would be conflicts between the children of the first wife and those of the second over who would inherit the father's estate. Thus the wicked stepmother in folktales such as Cinderella, first collected and printed for a learned audience by Charles Perrault in 1697, had many counterparts in real life.

What if a mother survived to see her children become adults? How would she feel? Because the childhoods of boys and girls diverged at age seven, with girls remaining with their mothers while boys were given 'into the hands of men', to answer these questions we must distinguish the relationships of mothers and daughters from those of mothers and sons.

Since mothers remained responsible for the education and guidance of daughters until they married, it was expected that their relationships would be warm and close; a daughter was, as we saw, a mother's 'mirror image', her 'masterpiece'. And in fact there are many examples of mothers of all social classes who remained close to their daughters even after they had married and moved away, writing and visiting them often, helping them through childbirth, and even protecting them from abusive husbands. Wife-abuser Anthony Pitts told his wife: 'If ye Bitch your mother come I will kick her downe stairs.' The mother heard him and said: 'The Bitch mother is come, kick her.'[58] The most famous example of mother love from our period concerns a mother's devotion to her grown daughter: Mme de Sévigné's love for the Comtesse de Grignan. Mme de Sévigné's daughter was the centre of her existence; her love for her was the emotional centre of her life. Mme de Sévigné wrote to her daughter almost daily, sometimes twice a day. Hundreds of her long, warm, loving letters survive and while they chronicle her own doings, they centre on her worries about her daughter: her health, her welfare, her pregnancies, how she was treated by her husband.

Far fewer of the Comtesse's letters survived and they are more measured in tone: many are aloof, impersonal, even off-hand. The Comtesse never displayed her mother's all-engulfing love; indeed, she often seemed embarrassed by it.[59] In this, she may have been typical of daughters, who seem to have been ambivalent about their devoted mothers. Few loving letters from daughters to mothers survive, although this may be due to low levels of female literacy and society's tendency to toss away papers concerning only women. There are also few examples of devoted daughters in diaries and autobiographies; Lady Anne Clifford, who grieved that she could not go to the bedside of her dying mother, is one.[60] Perhaps the most intriguing suggestion of tension between mothers and daughters comes from witchcraft accusations. Often such accusations were levelled by young women who had recently given birth against the older women who helped them through their ordeal: the midwife, the lying-in maid, the friends and neighbours who came to visit. While there were many possible reasons for this (see Chapter 11), one is that the young women identified the older ones with their mothers, whom they subconsciously resented. Historian Lyndal Roper has suggested that, immobilized in bed during their lyings-in, the new mothers regressed to their own infancy, when the mother figure, giving and withholding comfort and nourishment, was all powerful and much resented.[61] I would offer a simpler psychological explanation. As we have seen, mothers had the prime responsibility for educating their daughters, for turning them into the chaste, silent and obedient wives, loving mothers and efficient housewives their patriarchal society expected them to be. If they found these roles constricting, isn't it possible that young women might have subconsciously blamed their mothers and relieved their resulting resentment by making dangerous and harmful accusations against the surrogate-mother figures of the midwife and lying-in maid?

Relationships between mothers and grown sons were also fraught with psychological pitfalls, although they seem to have worked in the opposite way. With daughters, we expected closeness and found estrangement; with sons, we would expect estrangement but we often find warm and loving ties.

Our expectations of estrangement arise, first, from the fact that around age seven, sons of all social classes were deliberately detached from their mothers and put 'into the hands of men' for their education – an education that was, in effect, a training in manhood. Psychologists from Sigmund Freud on have pointed out how difficult it is for boys to achieve detachment from the maternal figure and a new sense of identity and identification with a masculine role model, the father. The estrangement between mother and son often increased as both grew older, especially if the mother were widowed and became the de facto head of the family. Sons often found it psychologically difficult to accept this; the biblical injunction to obey one's parents fought with their sense of manhood, which in that patriarchal society meant that men should guide women and not the other way around. Accepting his mother as head of the family was especially difficult for an elder son, who might well think he had inherited that position. These tensions intensified when there was money at stake. As we shall see in the next chapter, widows often inherited substantial portions of their husband's property outright or at least received the usufruct (use) of it during their lifetimes, after which it reverted to their children. The potential for discord here is obvious. There are numerous examples of mothers and sons quarrelling over property. In Nantes, for example, a very long and bitter battle between Jeanne Duchesne, widow of Jean Charier, and her eldest son, Pierre, was eventually settled out of court. They squabbled over the division of Jean Charier's property, even disputing who was liable for his funeral expenses.[62] Another example is the prolonged battle between the prominent Roman widow Olimpia Giustiniani Barberini and her eldest son Urbano, as she desperately tried to prevent him from squandering all the assets of the immensely wealthy Casa Barberini. She eventually wrote an account of this battle in a manuscript entitled, 'Papers in which Signora Donna Olimpia describes in her own hand the good for nothing conduct of Signore Principe Urbano her son in the governing of the Casa, and demonstrates the incivilities she receives from him'. The 'incivilities' included being denied the use of the family carriage and having her country house invaded and wrecked by Urbano's servants.[63]

Thus there was much potential for conflict between mothers and grown sons and often this potential was realized. Yet most mothers and sons seem to have maintained close and loving ties, despite societal conventions separating them. Many loving letters exist from mothers to sons away at school and vice versa. That of Dutch noblewoman Elisabeth Van den Boetzelaer tot Toutenburg to her son and his roommate at boarding school might (except for a Latin quote) have been written – or emailed – by a mother today. It began, 'I hope you both are studying hard' and ended, 'I am sending each of you your own packet of six Utrecht cakes, wrapped in paper . . . Take this as a token of love, and I'll try to do better next time.'[64] A mother's love and care did not lessen as her sons grew to maturity. Both Mary Rich and Jane Fretwell abandoned their other responsibilities to nurse their sons through serious illnesses; the boys were aged 19 and 18 respectively. Katherine, Duchess of Suffolk, moved her household to Cambridge while her sons attended the university there. Mothers continued to guide and advise their sons and work to promote their interests even when they reached adulthood. The best known of these powerful mothers was Lady Margaret Beaufort, mother of Henry VII, first Tudor king of England. Lady Margaret constantly plotted and manoeuvred to advance her son's claims to the throne; she even married a man, Thomas Lord Stanley, whom she did not love or indeed like very much, to gain his support for her son. In her letters she addressed her son as 'my dearest and only desired joy in this world' and 'my dear heart'. Henry for his part called his mother 'my most entirely well beloved lady and mother', lavished estates on her, appointed her to high public office (see Chapter 13) and named his first daughter after her.[65]

Henry Tudor was not unusual in his devotion to his mother. Indeed, sons seem to have been closer to their mothers than daughters were; perhaps the traumatic separation at age seven left them longing to restore their original closeness with their mothers. At any rate, the two most famous public protests against maternal indifference in this period were staged by sons, not daughters. When the widowed French noblewoman Jeanne de Chantal left for Annency to found an order of nuns (see Chapter 10) in 1610, she took her daughter with her but left her 14-year-old son in the care of her father. The young man begged her not to go and lay down on the doorsill so that she had to step over him to leave. Similarly, 11-year-old Claude Martin ran away from home for three days when his widowed mother told him she planned to leave him and enter a convent. She eventually became Sister Marie de l'Incarnation, missionary to the Iroquois, and Claude followed her into the religious life, becoming a monk.[66] For early modern women, motherhood was just one stage in their lives, but to her children, especially her sons, a mother remained a mother until she died.

Chapter 5

◆

WIDOWS AND ELDERLY WOMEN

When they were no longer able to become mothers – that is, at the onset of menopause – the women of early modern Europe entered into the last stage of their lives. They had become old. Because of poor nutrition, this happened earlier than it does for women today. Historians estimate that the average age for menopause was 40.[1]

The men of early modern Europe did not grow old so quickly. Sixty was generally regarded as the threshold of old age for men. This difference grew from the different ways the stages of life were calculated for men and women. Men's lives had chronological turning points, often calculated by multiples of seven: at seven they left the hands of women, at 21 they gained their majority, etc. But the stages of life for women were based on their familial and reproductive roles: they were maidens, wives and mothers, and widows. Because women's life stages were tied to their reproductive capacities, women who could no longer bear children were viewed as no longer women, no longer sexual beings with sexual needs and a sexually defined identity.[2] When they grew old, women were seen as androgynous, sexless beings or even, like celibate nuns, as 'honourary men'. This had its advantages. Elderly women were given power in their families, their communities and the state denied to younger women because it was thought that their sexual needs would no longer cloud their judgements and disrupt public order. But it also had its disadvantages. If an older woman wanted to continue her sexual life, she was considered pathetic and ridiculous, or worse, an evil witch. Thus for the relatively few women who attained it, the final stage of their life could be either the best or worst period, the time when they exercised the most power and received the most respect or the time when they were treated with contempt and even tried and executed as witches.

WIDOWHOOD AND REMARRIAGE

This paradoxical nature of female old age was heightened by the fact that it often coincided with widowhood. In most legal systems, widows gained the ability to act for themselves at law; as we have seen, they were frequently named guardians of their children. They also regained control of their property and often inherited substantial holdings from their husbands. Thus widows were often the wealthiest women in their communities. And they now had control of their lives and made their own decisions. Yet, as with old age, there was another side to widowhood. With autonomy came loneliness and lack of sexual satisfaction and with property came responsibilities. And, of course, not all widows had property; those of the lower classes often inherited nothing but debts. Whether young and burdened with children or aged, infirm and unable to work, widows were often the poorest as well as the wealthiest women in their communities and the major recipients of poor relief and charity.

Although widowhood added to the problems of old age, not all old women were widows and not all widows were elderly. Because some women married very young, and because husbands were often much older than wives, there were very young widows. Marie Guyart, a seventeenth-century French baker's daughter who would eventually become Sister Marie de l'Incarnation, missionary to the Iroquois in French Canada, was married at 16 and widowed at 19.[3] The fate of young widows differed from that of 'old' (40+) widows in that the younger ones often remarried while the older seldom did.

Both Islam and Judaism, with their acceptance of human sexuality and belief that all adults should be married, encouraged the remarriage of a surviving spouse when a match was broken by death. The ancient Hebrews had even practised the levirate, where a widow was automatically married to her deceased husband's brother, although the custom seems to have died out among the Jews of early modern Europe.[4] In contrast, Christianity, more distrustful of marriage and sexuality, was less enthusiastic about remarriage. This was especially true of the Orthodox churches. The Russian Orthodox Church, for example, permitted second marriages for both men and women, but frowned on third and absolutely prohibited anyone from marrying a fourth time.[5] This was one reason why remarriages were relatively rare in eastern Europe.

Western Christianity had no such prohibitions, although in Catholic France priests refused to give second marriages of widows the nuptial blessing.

Remarriage was quite common in the west, especially for widowers. In the French village of Crulai between 1674 and 1742, 45 percent of the widowers remarried within a year of their wives' death; some remarried within months and even weeks. In another French village, 14 of 17 widowers married again within four months of their wives' death.[6] This is testimony to the rigidity of gender roles in early modern society and the important contributions of peasant wives to the family economy (see Chapter 6). In peasant families tasks were rigidly divided between the sexes and men were reluctant to undertake the housework, childcare, spinning, dairying and other tasks of 'women's work' and they had little time to do so while keeping up with the 'men's work' of the farm. The large complex households of eastern Europe contained other women who could do the work of the dead wife; this is another major reason why remarriage was relatively rare in eastern Europe. But in the small nuclear households of western Europe a dead wife had to be replaced. The grieving husband could hire a female servant, but it was often easier and cheaper to remarry.

Lower and middle-class townsmen in western Europe were even more likely to remarry than peasants. They too needed a woman to do the 'women's work' of the household and raise their children and in towns they had a wider choice of potential mates. In eighteenth-century Tuscany almost twice as many urban widowers remarried than did rural ones.[7]

Widowers from the upper classes, however, felt less need to remarry. Among the gentry of seventeenth-century Holland, for example, only 18 percent did so.[8] Such men could hire servants to do the 'women's work' and raise their motherless children. Therefore elite widowers contemplated remarriage only if they were childless or needed more heirs or if a socially or economically profitable match appeared on the horizon. The companionship and sexual satisfaction provided by a wife usually did not enter into their decision, for these could be had by taking a lower-class woman, often a servant, as mistress. The servant–mistress who ran a widower's household was a standard feature of aristocratic life. A Dutch noble, Adriaen de Wael, lost his wife in 1560 and employed a servant who became his mistress, ran his household, kept his accounts, doled out money to his children and bore him a bastard child. De Wael acknowledged the relationship and provided for mother and child in his will.[9]

Whatever their geographical location or class, widows were less likely to remarry than widowers. Apart from Jews and Muslims, this was a universal pattern, found in both eastern and western Europe. In an eighteenth-century French town, for example, about half the widowers but only one-fifth of the widows remarried.[10]

Why were widows less likely to remarry than widowers? Part of the explanation lies in gender-differentiated social attitudes toward grief and mourning. Husbands were expected to have loved their wives and to mourn their passing. Despite the universally acknowledged need of widowers to find a new wife to do the 'women's work' of the household, rapid remarriage was frowned on. Some cities and states even passed laws setting a minimum period of mourning; in Sweden, for example, a law of 1686 forbade widowers from remarrying for six months after their wives died.[11] But eventually widowers were expected to put their grief behind them and marry again.

Widows, by way of contrast, were expected to stay single and mourn their husbands for the rest of their lives. This attitude had a long history, dating back to the Roman idealization of the *univera* (the woman who had known only one man sexually) and to the important role allotted to chaste widows in early Christianity. In our period staying single was presented to widows as a duty they owed to their husbands in recompense for all they received from them, especially the moral guidance that helped them avoid sin. This role of moral guide to the 'weaker vessel' was one for which a husband deserved life-long love and gratitude from his widow – and it was one he could continue to play from beyond the grave. As the humanist Juan Luis Vives explained:

> [A] good widow ought to suppose that her husband is not utterly dead, but liveth both with life of his soul . . . and beside her with remembrance . . . [therefore] let her live and do so, as she shall think to please her husband . . . let her take him for her keeper and spy, not only of her deeds but also of her conscience.[12]

In practice, this meant that women should continue to be as chaste, silent and obedient as they had been as wives, attitudes starkly depicted in Plate 8, an engraving of the Protestant reformer Martin Luther's widow, Katherine von Bora. We do not know whether she and other widows literally bandaged their mouth as the portrait shows, but the image suggests the power of these ideals. Because chastity, silence and obedience were even harder to achieve for widows, lacking male moral guidance, than for other women, widows were advised to lead quiet lives, withdrawn from the world and its temptations, and to devote themselves to prayer. 'Chastity requireth solitariness', as Vives wrote, and therefore:

> [I]n courts and in resort of men . . . a widow should not meddle . . . [because] abroad and afore many mens eyes and handlings . . . honesty and chastity commeth in jeopardy.[13]

Ideally, this withdrawal from the world would take place in a convent and indeed, in Catholic and Orthodox countries, many widows, especially those who had been drawn toward a religious vocation in their youth, spent their last years in convents, as nuns or paying boarders. Even a widow as illustrious as Empress Maria, daughter of one Holy Roman Emperor, Charles V, and wife of another, Maximilian of Austria, passed her years of widowhood in a Spanish convent. Although she never formally took vows, she wore a nun's habit, customary garb for elite Catholic widows.[14] Poorer Catholic widows who could not afford convents might enter either *beguinages*, communities of women who lived together and devoted themselves to charity and prayer without formal vows, or one of the many religious institutions designed to shelter poor widows like the Orbatello in Florence.[15] Protestant widows could not, of course, become nuns, but they too often led quiet lives devoted to charity and prayer, following the model of the widow in the early Church, celibate and responsible for visiting the poor and sick and preparing women for catechism. For example, Dame Joan Bradshawe spent almost 70 years as a widow; a memorial in her church says that she 'all her life was very charitable to the poore . . . and at her charges [expense] newlye builte this chappell'.[16]

Thus traditional expectations about pious widowhood discouraged widows from remarrying. But these social norms had the power to shape behaviour because they served practical purposes. There were practical reasons why remarriage was more difficult and complicated for widows than widowers and why society therefore discouraged it. These stemmed from the way the family was conceived in the early modern period: as a patriliny, with generations of fathers producing generations of male heirs to the family's name and property, who would marry and produce heirs in their turn. The remarriage of a widower did not disrupt this pattern. The new wife moved into an existing household and became part of her husband's patriliny and, if she bore him children, they shared his estate with the children of the first marriage.

The remarriage of a widow, however, did disrupt the pattern, for she in effect left the patriliny of her late husband and joined a new one. This created innumerable problems. What if she were pregnant when her first husband died and remarried soon after? How could anyone be sure to which patriliny the new baby belonged? Because of this, legislated periods of mourning before remarriage were invariably longer for widows than widowers – at least nine months, typically a year. The Swedish law of 1686, for example, made widowers wait six months before marrying again but mandated a year's wait for widows.[17]

Another problem with the remarrying widow was that she might take some or all of her husband's property into her new marriage, thus violating the basic principle of inheritance in the early modern period: that a patriarch's property stay within the patriliny. This principle was recognized even by those indulgent husbands who made wills leaving most of their estate to their wives and appointing them executor, which in effect allowed them to do as they pleased with the estate's assets. The provisions were usually that a wife was left use of the estate for her lifetime only; at her death it reverted to the children of the marriage.

Most husbands, however, did not leave wills, either because they died before making them or because they preferred the laws governing the distribution of intestate property to portion out their estates. These laws embodied two contradictory principles: that a widow should be supported by her husband's estate and that the natural heirs of a patriarch were the next generation of the patriliny, his children. How these contradictory principles were reconciled varied from place to place. In Florence, all the father's property went directly to the children; the widow only got her dowry back.[18] In northern Europe, where customary law prevailed, lineage property went to the children, but property acquired by the couple during their marriage (often the bulk of the husband's estate) was considered communal property and the surviving spouse was entitled to half or sometimes, as in the city of Douai, all of it.[19] Finally, sometimes widows even got a portion of the lineage property; in Spain, for example, their *arras* gave them one-tenth of what their husbands brought into the marriage.[20] English common law gave them one-third.[21] All these provisions – plus of course wills – put much of a husband's estate into the hands of a widow – and into the hands of a second husband and new patriliny if she remarried. Even if the second husband only got to manage her property during her lifetime, he could mismanage it so that nothing was left for the children of the first marriage. Not even the Florentine system kept all property safe within the patriliny. It was thought that a mother ought to leave her dowry to her children and a 'bad mother' in Florence was one who left it all to the children of her second marriage, ignoring those of her first.[22]

These problems provoked many ingenious solutions. The most common was a marriage contract providing the widow with a larger income than she would have from customary or common law – if she would renounce all other claims to her husband's property and/or not marry again. Another solution was laws protecting the rights of the children of a first marriage in the face of a second. In 1659 the Dutch Republic required widows and widowers to leave something to the children of their first match when they remarried; in 1560, France forbade widows from giving their second husbands any lineage property they received from their first and provided that any gifts of their own property to a new husband be no larger than the smallest legacy to their children by a first marriage.[23] But the easiest solution was to get widows to stay single. Hence all the emphasis on pious widowhood. Many a widow accepted and internalized these values, finding solace for her loss in continued devotion to her late husband and the interests of his patriliny. One was Katherine Austen, who wrote to a friend explaining why she would not consider remarrying: 'I doe no Injury to none by not Loveing. But if I doe I may doe real Injuries where I am already engadged: To my Deceased friends posterity' (by which she meant her late husband's children).[24]

Apart from these social pressures against remarrying, widows might have their own personal – and often unacknowledged – reasons to remain single. Many enjoyed the new-found independence and autonomy of their situation. Often they controlled enough wealth to live well and, for the first time in their lives, they could make their own decisions and run their households and their lives as they pleased. They were also free from the sexual demands of a perhaps unloved husband and from the perilous prospects of pregnancy and childbirth. Little wonder then that the French noblewoman Charlotte Arbaleste, married at 17 and widowed at 19, held out against a determined suitor for five years. As she explained in her autobiography, 'having lived alone', she '[wished] to continue this way of life'.[25] She expressed in a decorous way what the fictional widow Lady Haughty said more forthrightly in the play *The Triumphant Widow* (1677):

> I ne're will wear a matrimonial chain
> But safe and quiet in this Throne remain
> And absolute Monarch o're my self will raign.[26]

Charlotte Arbaleste eventually did remarry, as did many other widows, especially if, like Arbaleste, they were still young enough to bear children. If society frowned on remarriage, it also pushed young widows toward the altar. In early modern Europe, society was uncomfortable with women who were not under control of a patriarchal husband or father but lived independently, especially if they were wealthy and powerful, as many widows were. Therefore, they were encouraged to remarry, for then they would be again safely enclosed in a patriarchal household under masculine control.

Widows were also pushed into remarriage by their natal families, for the same sorts of family advantage which had inspired their first matches. This was especially true of well-to-do Florentine widows, who not only got their dowries back but also enjoyed the right of *tornata* – that is, returning to their natal home and being supported by their fathers or brothers. Rather than supporting her for the rest of her life while her dowry lay idle until her children could inherit it, the menfolk of a young widow's family usually decided to put the dowry to work by arranging another socially and financially advantageous match.[27] Although the *tornata* made them especially vulnerable to it,

Florentine widows were not the only ones under family pressure to remarry. And why not? The remarriage of a widow allowed the family to gain an important alliance at little cost, much of the money which made the widow financially attractive having come from her first husband.

A widow might also be pressured to remarry by her first husband's family, which often tried to arrange a match with male relatives of her late spouse to keep the woman and her dowry and inheritance within the lineage. This practice dated back to the levirate of the ancient Hebrews. In early modern Europe, Jews no longer practised the levirate but the idea remained. In early modern Albania widows were not allowed to leave the *zadruga*; instead they were married off to one of their husband's relatives.[28]

The levirate and its variants were justified on the grounds that they helped the widow as well as her husband's family: with a new husband a widow's financial future was secure. And this was yet another factor pushing widows toward remarriage: society's – and their own – belief that a new marriage would provide financial support for them. Not all widows were wealthy or even comfortably off. The vast majority, wives of peasants in the countryside or day labourers in towns, were left destitute when they lost the main pillar of their family economy. Many were not only deprived of a male wage earner but also burdened with debts. A study of inheritance in early modern England shows that one-quarter of all husbands left their wives in debt.[29] Such widows and their fatherless children had since the ancient world been considered part of the *personae miserabilis* who had a special call on charity from Christians and poor relief from the state. But cheaper than charity was urging them to find a new husband.

The problem of caring for poor widows was especially acute in the countryside, where poverty was abundant and organized charities were few. The majority of peasant families lived right on the poverty line and a disaster like the loss of the husband and father, who did the crucial 'man's work' in the household, could push the family over the brink into utter destitution. Most widows had to hire a man to do the 'man's work', not because their neighbours would disapprove of their crossing gender boundaries to do it (there was sympathy for women forced to do 'men's work' to survive), but simply because it was beyond their physical capacities. But hiring a man strained already meager family resources and the available 'women's work' like spinning, sewing, taking in laundry, nursing the sick and selling bits of food and firewood door to door brought in little money. And paid employment for children was scarce in the rural areas. The result was that widows, especially those with small children, usually headed the poorest households in most peasant villages. In the Castilian village of La Nava de Arevalo in the sixteenth century, for example, 79 percent of the widows heading households were classified as 'poor' or 'very poor', while only 36 percent of male-headed households fell into those categories.[30]

Poor widows and their children often stayed alive through charity, but unfortunately organized poor relief was scarce in the countryside everywhere but in England. There the poor laws required each parish to care for its own poor. Not surprisingly, widows were major recipients of such relief. In four eighteenth-century English towns, widow-headed households accounted for one-third of those receiving aid, although they formed only 15 percent of all households in the villages.[31] Elsewhere in Europe there was little organized charity in rural areas, although it was accepted that the community had obligations to poor widows. In many places they were the first allowed to gather the remaining grain in the common fields after the gleaners were done, and often they were paid slightly more for their work than married women.[32] Otherwise they depended on the casual charity of their neighbours – gifts of food, being hired to watch over a sick baby.

Little wonder then that society encouraged them to remarry. Unfortunately, this was difficult to do. Potential grooms were scarce in the countryside, land of the married, and those available were reluctant to take on a houseful of dependent children despite the attractions of the widow's land. So most rural widows remained unmarried and abjectly poor.

Life was easier for lower-class widows in urban areas, for there employment opportunities, organized poor relief and potential bridegrooms all were more abundant. In towns, a poor widow could patch together a living from street peddling, taking in laundry, baby watching and casual day labour on building sites, and children too could find casual labouring jobs and contribute to the family income. If that wasn't sufficient, the family could apply for poor relief. In Catholic countries, there were even special houses of refuge for poor widows. An example is the Orbatello in Florence. Founded in 1370, in 1552 it housed 154 people like Donna Antonia, a poor widow who entered in 1513 with her three children, one an eight-month-old baby. They shared a room with Donna Antonia's mother-in-law and sister-in-law, also poor widows.[33] But to many widows remarriage was preferable to that sort of existence and because single men were abundant in towns, it was more likely to happen. In eighteenth-century Sweden, 24 percent of the widows in one city remarried, while only 15 percent of widows in a rural parish did so.[34]

Working-class widows were not the only ones pushed to remarry. Many middle- and upper-class widows were left 'poor' by the standards of their social group and remarriage was thought an appropriate solution to their financial problems. In fact, for some social groups, institutional arrangements to care for widows pushed them toward second matches. Guild artisans are an example. Guildsmen clearly viewed their shops as their widows' major source of support and therefore allowed them to carry on their businesses and assume their masterships. But by, on the one hand, limiting the number of journeymen they could employ and apprentices they could train and forcing them to sell the business after a year, while, on the other hand, providing that a second husband could take over the mastership, they seem to have been pushing their widows toward remarriage with an ambitious young journeyman desiring to become a master. If so, this didn't work. A study of widows in the English town of Abingdon in the sixteenth and seventeenth centuries shows that guilds-women were not more likely to remarry than other urban widows. Only those in the catering or transport trades, which needed large numbers of male workers who might resent being bossed around by a woman, show high remarriage rates. Other guild widows either kept their businesses going despite the restrictions or sold them and invested the proceeds in loans, annuities, or real estate to provide themselves with an income (see Chapter 7).[35]

The widows of professionals – lawyers, doctors, clergymen, government bureaucrats, officeholders – were also sometimes institutionally pushed toward remarriage. Here we must distinguish between the poor widows of very lowly government employees – jailers, toll collectors and the like – and those of middle-class professionals. Minor government offices were, like a craftsman's shop, family enterprises in which the wife shared her husband's duties (see Chapter 13). Therefore both the widow and her employers thought it only natural that she continue in the office after her husband's death, although this was not, as in the guilds, a right. A widow had to petition for the job:

> The Humble Petition of Elizabeth Prince, Widow of John Prince late keeper of The House of Correction at Abingdon.
>
> That your Petitioner is left in very distressful circumstances with family of eight children, the eldest of which being a daughter of only 14 years old and 3 of them with natural infirmities which will probably render them ever incapable of gaining their livelihood.
>
> That your Petitioner's Husband and his Father and Grandfather have been keepers of The House of Correction at Abingdon for a great number of years and your Petitioner has a brother and a Brother-in-law very well qualified and willing to assist her in the future management of that prison [. . .]
>
> Your Petitioner therefore, humbly prays to be continued in the office . . . that she may be thereby able to provide bread for her Family which must otherwise be unavoidably thrown on the parish for maintenance.[36]

Note the threat that the family might have to go on public assistance if the widow were not employed. This petition and others like it were granted because continuing the widow in her husband's job was a relatively cheap and easy way to support the family. In England between 1688 and 1775 more than one-quarter of the jails had or had had female keepers.[37] Yet, like guildsmen, government officials were uncomfortable with women doing men's work; note Prince's assurances that her brother and brother-in-law would guide her. Many German towns allowed women to continue in minor government offices only for a year, during which they hoped the widows might find second husbands to support them, although they did not make this easier by automatically granting the new husband the office.[38]

Widows of upper level officeholders and professionals like lawyers, doctors and clergymen posed a different problem. They had not shared their husbands' jobs and could not take over when they died. Yet so widespread was the notion that a husband's business was part of his provisions for his family that widows had rights to their husbands' offices. In France, for example, where the purchase of government offices was very common and very popular, especially among ambitious men of the middle class seeking social status (offices usually brought their buyers nobility plus the tax exemptions nobles enjoyed), widows could retain these advantages. They also were guaranteed half the value of the office when it was sold.[39] When this was added to the rest of her husband's property, there was usually enough to maintain a widow with her accustomed dignity.

There were, however, poor widows of the professional classes whose husbands had no property, only the salary from their positions – Protestant clergymen, for example. Their widows could not take over their duties, yet their salaries were the sole family asset. Scandinavian churches solved this problem by a variant on the levirate called 'the conservation of pastors' wives', in which a new pastor was required to marry either his predecessor's widow or daughter. This practice lasted until the eighteenth century, when the ideal of marriage for love plus worries about the sincerity of pastors' callings put an end to it. German Protestants never adopted this practice. Instead, they invented in the sixteenth century what would eventually become society's major means of providing financially for the elderly, men and women alike: the pension fund. By 1800 governments had picked up the idea and most countries paid pensions to the widows of their army and navy officers and government bureaucrats.[40]

There were, of course, factors other than institutional provisions pushing widows toward remarriage. Hard as it may be for modern women to believe, some widows found their new independence and financial responsibilities frightening, not liberating, especially if they were unused to managing money or if their husbands' estates were especially complex or debt ridden. In such cases, widows often welcomed the guidance of the male guardians appointed in some areas to handle their financial and legal affairs. Some widows even willingly surrendered their position as executor of their husband's estate, rightly thinking that if court battles loomed on the horizon, a male litigant might be taken more seriously. Some looked for a second husband to assume these burdens.

More personal reasons also might push widows toward remarriage. Some wanted a father for their children. Others, especially the childless, were simply lonely. People did not often enjoy solitude or live alone by preference in early modern Europe. Those whose marriages had been happy missed the love and companionship of their husbands. English widow Thomasin Head lamented: 'I have lost that precious friend, who was the companion of my life, the joy of my heart, and the cause of my earthly contentment.'[41] And many missed having sex, although they rarely confessed this in writing.

This was, however, widely believed of widows. Women were, after all, the lustier sex, and widows were sexually experienced and used to having their sexual needs satisfied. Little wonder then that the lusty widow was the stuff of proverbs:

Spain: The widow's motto: to weep a little and look for another.
England: He that woos a maid must fain lie and flatter. But he that woos a widow, must down with his breeches and at her.[42]

In popular perceptions, the stereotype of the pious widow was accompanied by her mirror image, the merry widow, not chaste and withdrawn from the world but instead busily pursuing handsome young men with both sex and remarriage in mind. Advice books warned young men against succumbing to the merry widow despite her financial attractions. A widow would use her money as leverage to keep control in the marriage, denying her young husband his rights as patriarchal household head and, because she was sexually experienced, she could constantly make invidious comparisons between her second husband's sexual performance and that of her first.

This stereotype actually had some basis in fact. Widows did often choose younger husbands; a study of remarrying widows in sixteenth-century London found that on average they were four and a half years older than their new spouses.[43] And when they remarried, they often did deny their new husbands control of their property. Another study of English widows found that they were twice as likely as spinsters to make marriage contracts that kept their property separate from their husbands' and under their own control.[44] This often led to conflicts, many of which ended up in court. Stephen Bolton brought a suit against his wife Hester, alleging that she had promised him two houses she inherited from her first husband. Hester denied the promise and said that had she made it she would not have kept it, because Bolton was totally incapable of handling money.[45] And widows *did* taunt their new husbands sexually. Ellen Charnock complained to her neighbours that her new husband John was 'too young', too inexperienced and too effeminate to satisfy her: 'If she had not married him . . . he must have worn a Frock.' According to Ellen, poor John 'was no man, notwithstanding she was assured to the Contrary by having her hand in his Codpiece before the Marriage'. Ellen stated that, 'had she not had two husbands before she should not have known what belonged to a man'.[46]

Thus the stereotype of the merry widow had roots in reality. But the viciousness with which she was portrayed in popular culture suggests that she embodied something for which the people of early modern Europe had a deep-seated fear and revulsion. Certainly she represented the inversion of the proper gender order of society, 'the world turned upside down' in which wife ruled husband. But a comparison of the rather cheerful and accepting popular prints on that theme (see Plate 6) with the truly vicious portrayals of the experienced widow with the inexperienced husband suggest that something more was at work. That something was probably society's general revulsion toward the elderly, especially those still sexually active.

ATTITUDES TOWARDS THE ELDERLY

Probably less than 20 percent of the people born in early modern Europe lived to be 60, yet their achievement was not viewed favourably. This was because despite its relatively few elderly people, early modern Europe was a gerontocracy, in which the old, especially old men, held the reins of power. Elderly peasant patriarchs kept control of their lands, the guilds were run by elderly masters who denied ambitious young journeymen masterships and the marriage and manhood that went with them, and political power was in the hands of the elderly. In the sixteenth century, no fewer than 14 heads of state, including Suleiman the Magnificent and Elizabeth I, held office when they were 65 or older. And the two most important elective offices, the pope and the *doge* of Venice, were usually filled by men who were over 60 when elected and who held office for life.[47] A society teeming with young people – half the population was under 25 – expressed its frustrations in negative portrayals of the elderly.

Old age was pictured as a time of physical infirmities and illnesses so severe that one longed for death. At age 60 the French poet Ronsard wrote:

All that's left of me is bones. I resemble a skeleton
Unfleshed, unstrung, unmuscled and unpadded,
Unmercifully struck down by the delineaments of death . . .[48]

An elderly female compatriot also complained:

In pain I've lived so long
That I no longer wish to live[49]

Old age was thought to weaken the mind as well as the body, bringing life full circle by returning the elderly to the state of babyhood. The humanist Erasmus compared the old to infants:

There is really no difference between them except the old man's wrinkles and the number of birthdays he has. Otherwise they are exactly alike: white hair, toothless mouth, short stature, liking for milk, babbling, chattering, absurdity, forgetfulness, thoughtlessness, everything in fact. The nearer people approach old age, the closer they return to a semblance of childhood.[50]

Both the physical and mental infirmities of old age made sex among the elderly unseemly and ludicrous. It was thought that sexual feelings decreased with age and eventually disappeared. The Orthodox churches forbade the marriage of men over 70 and women over 60 because the essence of marriage was sexual union and the elderly were considered incapable of it.[51] When old people did indulge in sex they were the butt of popular jokes. Everywhere in Europe, elderly husbands with pretty young wives and elderly wives with strapping young mates were made fun of in satirical songs, poems and prints.

But an old man's lust for young girls merely rendered him ridiculous to his neighbours and this did not deter elderly widowers from remarrying, often to women 20 or even 30 years younger. The household in sixteenth-century Norwich of 70-year-old Valentine Leke was typical of the remarrying widower: his wife Curstance was 26 and his child 'vere yonge'.[52] The sexually active elderly woman, by way of contrast, was considered dangerous as well as foolish. Sexual appetite in elderly women was thought unnatural, akin to incest, as the eighteenth-century novelist Samuel Richardson explained: the idea of 'a Woman all hoary and grey – goored over by time' in 'the Embrace of a young Fellow' was 'next to a Degree of incest'.[53] It was also dangerous, for it led elderly women into that most fearsome of crimes, witchcraft. The Devil was thought to use sexual lures to gain followers and to seal his pact with them by sexual intercourse (see Chapter 11). Witches were usually portrayed as both elderly and sexually active. Given these negative images, it is not surprising that elderly widows were much more hesitant than elderly widowers to remarry. Age was the single most important determinant of whether a widow would remarry, far outweighing location and class. In London from 1540 to 1599, over 70 percent of young widows (that is, those whose marriages had lasted less than 10 years) remarried, but only 27 percent of old widows (those whose marriages lasted over 20 years) did so. By 1660–1720, the figure for young widows remained at 70 percent, but that for older widows had dropped to zero.[54]

GETTING CARE IN OLD AGE

Thus most women faced the difficulties of old age alone. In sixteenth-century Norwich there were only 12 single or widowed men over 20, but there were 127 widows over 50 and a further 58 elderly spinsters and deserted wives.[55] Therefore care of the elderly as they grew too old and infirm to feed and care for themselves was, then as today, primarily a problem of caring for old women. If they were wealthy widows, the problems of increasing infirmity were easily solved by hiring servants. In towns, households consisting of an elderly spinster or widow and her equally elderly maidservant were quite common. Often the women had lived together for much of their lives with great affection. In eighteenth-century Bordeaux, Marguerite Chauvel, widow of a judge, left a legacy to her chambermaid, Marie Philip, who, she wrote, 'has been near me for more than twenty-five years and who has always served me with the rarest of fidelity and affection'.[56]

Of course, most elderly women were not wealthy enough to have servants and this made the problem of their care acute. Relatively few elderly women lived alone, not only because if they did so they would have no one to care for them if they suddenly fell ill but also because it was difficult for them to support themselves if they had to depend on their own wages. The idea of retirement, a dignified retreat from a life of work, was spreading in this period, but not to the poor, who had few resources other than current earnings. 'Women's work' often did not yield enough to support a woman alone (see Chapters 6 and 7) and this was even more likely to be true if the woman worker were old and feeble. A 1579 census of the poor of Norwich shows both the expectation that the elderly would continue to work until they died and how difficult it often was to do so. A lame widow of 60 who 'worketh not' was disapprovingly termed 'unruly', while three other widows, aged 74, 79 and 82, were labelled 'almost past work'. Almost – but not quite; all three spun wool to earn their living.[57] Spinning, taking in laundry, doing housework and caring for the sick:

these poorest paid types of women's work occupied the poor elderly women who lived alone and supported themselves.

Obviously an elderly woman's financial prospects improved if she were a member of a household and a family economy, and if she lived with someone she would have a caregiver. Therefore it is not surprising that the majority of elderly women did not live alone. Most commonly they moved in with one of their grown children. Often the conditions of cohabitation were regulated by a formal written contract, especially if a transfer of property were involved. When a child married, the marriage contract might stipulate that he or she received the family property in return for caring for an ageing parent or parents. Or a father might leave his property to a child on the condition that the child care for his or her elderly widowed mother. Thus in 1610 an Englishman explained that by the terms of his father's will: 'I am charged to keepe Anne Barne my mother with meate drinke and lodgings.'[58] Or the woman might sign over her property by deed of gift in return for care; in 1650 old and blind Margaret Cully of Norfolk signed away her estate worth £40 in return for care for the rest of her life.[59] When little or no property was involved, such formal arrangements were unnecessary and the woman simply moved in with one of her children.

Sometimes the duty of caring for an elderly woman skipped a generation and fell on a grandchild. In sixteenth-century Norwich, for example, Alice Cotes, a 92-year-old widow who could no longer work, lived with a 'childes daughter' aged 18, who knitted stockings to support them.[60] If no family members were available, the elderly poor might create artificial households, taking in younger people who could provide care. Two examples, again from sixteenth-century Norwich: Elizabeth Tidemunde, aged 80 and widowed, took in a 14-year-old girl; both spun to earn money. And Elizabeth Petis, only 68 but 'very syk and feble', lived with a deserted wife who supported them both by spinning, sewing and helping women in childbirth.[61]

If they did not provide themselves with a caregiver, elderly women often had to enter charitable institutions. They were considered doubly entitled to charity, as widows and as part of the 'good poor', those unable to work (as contrasted to the 'bad poor', those who were physically able to work but refused to do so). In England, this meant receiving help at home; because what the elderly needed was care, the poor law authorities often housed an orphan child with them to provide it. Elsewhere in Europe, recipients of charity had to enter institutions like the hospitals-general of France, which cared for the voluntarily admitted 'good poor' like orphans, the infirm and the elderly as well as involuntarily confined able-bodied beggars. Life in such institutions was barely tolerable for those who entered on a private pension, a favourite way for employers to provide for faithful maidservants in their old age. Private pensioners usually had a bed to themselves and received more and better food than the average inmate. They were also exempt from the daily round of work – usually textile manufacturing – that lasted from dawn to dusk. Elderly inmates who entered without a pension shared a bed and worked until they no longer could. Then they were transferred to a hospital, where usually they promptly caught a contagious disease and died.[62]

The only institution in which life was tolerable for elderly women was the convent. In fact, a convent was the ideal place to spend one's twilight years. Nuns were not thought to age in the same way that ordinary women did, because their lives did not follow the typical female life course of maiden, wife, and mother. This, along with the rest of their former identity, was eradicated by the spiritual death nuns underwent when they took their vows and were reborn with a new timeless spiritual identity that persisted unchanged until their actual death. And this occurred later than it would have had they remained in the outside world. Because they avoided the perils of childbirth and were isolated against many contagious diseases, nuns often lived longer than other women. For example, in eighteenth-century Toulouse a lay woman who lived past 20 died on average at age 56.4, but for a nun who lived past age 20 the average age of death was 63.3.[63] Thus convents tended to be old people's homes; the elderly formed a fairly large portion of their population. Convents were also gerontocracies. Nuns were rarely elected to convent offices before age 50 and they retained these offices well into their seventies and eighties. Their obituaries show that these elderly leaders were respected for the skills and experience they had acquired with age. Like their leaders, ordinary nuns were expected to continue their normal routines into old age if their health permitted. If not, they were lovingly cared for. And unlike laypeople, nuns were, in theory at least, always spiritually prepared for death. Indeed, many welcomed it as the consummation of their marriage with Christ, their spiritual bridegroom so much more attractive than any earthly one. Their obituaries written by fellow nuns use sexual metaphors for death and mention their eagerness to join their divine bridegroom; one nun in Toulouse, for example, is said to have expressed in her last days an 'ardent desire to meet her divine spouse'.[64]

PREPARING FOR DEATH

Unlike nuns, lay women needed time to prepare for death and the elderly and sick were expected to spend their last days in doing so. In fact, that was how they were usually portrayed by artists. Because old age was considered ugly and demeaning, artists rarely painted the elderly and, when they did, they usually made solemn portraits of old but powerful men. There are only a few portraits of old women and even fewer that convey a sense of a lively individual personality. In most portrayals, elderly females are reduced to stereotypes, which, as always with women, divide into two: good and evil. The evil stereotype was the witch, already discussed. The good stereotype was the pious widow preparing for death. So strong was the association of old women and preparations for death that elderly women were often used as symbolic representations of the vanity of worldly concerns. This was the case in seventeenth-century Dutch Republic, whose prosperous burgers had a voracious appetite for portraits, still lifes and genre scenes to decorate their walls. Paintings of old women like that by Nicolaes Maes in Plate 9 reminded them that prosperity fades in the face of death. This is not an individual but instead a generic old woman, pictured in the proper female setting: the home. She is surrounded by objects suggesting two intertwined themes: the shortness of human life and the necessity of pious preparations for death. The hourglass suggests the former, as do the evanescent sheen on the metal funnel and the fact that the cat is about to bring the meal to an abrupt halt by pulling down the tablecloth. Religion is represented by the woman's prayer and her Lenten meal: fish, bread and no wine. Thus this painting was less a study of an individual old woman than a warning about the nearness of death and the necessity of preparations for it.[65]

To make a 'good death' one had both to straighten out one's worldly affairs and to settle one's account with God. The first step in the former was making a will. The wills of women tended to follow a pattern that made them different from men's wills. Men usually made their wills when they were fairly young: when they first married and wanted to provide for their wives and children in case they died suddenly or when the first of their children married and they had to decide how to divide their estates among their offspring. In either case, their legatees were usually immediate family members and their legacies were usually of real property: the family land or business. Women, by contrast, usually made their wills when they were elderly. The distribution of the family property had already been settled, usually by their late husbands' wills, and their children were often grown, occasionally even dead. Like men, women thought their children had first claim on their estate, but unlike men, they did not try to pass patrimonial property more or less intact to one son. Instead, they usually refused to play favourites among their children and either divided their goods equally among their offspring or else left them to any children disadvantaged in earlier divisions of the family property.

Once their children were taken care of, women, unlike men, were likely to leave further legacies to people outside their immediate nuclear families: grandchildren, brothers and sisters, nieces and nephews, cousins and other distant kin, godchildren, friends and neighbours.[66] Women's wills usually have long lists of bequests allotting their personal goods – their clothing, jewellery and the household items they so carefully tended during their lives – to people they thought would appreciate them or find them useful. Thus Mary Widd, a single woman and maltster, left two brothers £2 plus malt and made a third her executor. But her principal heir was her niece, who got 'a great spence [cupboard], a bedstead, a chest, a kettle, a buffet [low] stoole, two pewter doublers, a brasse box, and 4s. to change the kettle and buy a pan and a gimmer hog [yearling ewe]': enough to set up her own household.[67] Margaret Bankes gave her daughter Petronella a red rug and her daughter Margaret 'the bedstead in the parlor of the house wherin I now dwell and the curtain rodds' – but not the mattress, beddings, or curtains, which were given to Petronella; the mother had clearly thought about what each daughter needed.[68] Unlike men, women used their goods to thank those who helped them in their last illness or to perpetuate friendships beyond the grave. Widow Elizabeth Skaine had only £3 worth of goods when she died in a rented room, but she left them to her landlord rather than her brother because the landlord fed and cared for her during her last illness.[69]

Not only did women spread their wealth more widely among family and friends than men did, they were also more likely to leave something to charity. Perhaps this was due to the fact that, unlike men, they often made their wills when actually facing death and worrying about the fate of their soul or, maybe, with their families provided for from their husbands' estates, they could more easily afford to be generous. Or perhaps this reflected the assumption that charity was a female virtue. At any rate, women were generous to the poor and the church, sometimes spectacularly so. Catholic widows with religious aspirations and ample means often endowed or even founded convents. Mme de Bresets, widow of the seventeenth-century councillor in the Parlement of Bordeaux, left 60,000 écus to found a hospital for the poor.[70] On a more modest scale, English widow Anne Toynby, whose entire estate was only £35, nonetheless left 4d to every other widow in her village.[71] As this suggests, women and the institutions caring for them were often the objects of female charity. This may reflect a sense of sisterhood, a solidarity with the other members of the female community in which they spent their lives, but it also may simply reflect the fact that most of the poor were women.

Donating to charity and the church was part of the religious side of making a 'good death'. For Catholics this also included receiving the last rites and leaving a bequest for masses and prayers to be said for one's soul in perpetuity. Protestants were simply expected to see a clergyman, think about their sins, pray for forgiveness and express their faith in God's mercy and everlasting life. Both the last rites and the Protestant clergyman's visit were part of the rituals of the deathbed, the setting of the last act of both the religious and secular aspects of the 'good death'. After the visit of the priest or clergyman, family, friends and neighbours were summoned to say a solemn goodbye to the dying. Deathbed words and instructions, especially those from a dying mother to her children, were to be cherished and faithfully followed.

After death, the corpse was 'watched', usually for a night, by family members and friends; this was both a sign of respect and a precaution against premature burial. Then the corpse was undressed, washed and wound in a shroud. This was done by poor women hired for the task. Assisting at death was, like assisting at birth, women's work; in fact, lying-in maids were often also hired to prepare the dead for burial. Then came the funeral, in which the size and composition of the cortege of mourners, and the sumptuousness of the mourning garments and gifts (it was customary for the family to give gifts to the guests at funerals as at weddings, so they would have something by which to remember the deceased; black gloves were a favourite) and of the feast afterwards were significant markers of social status and prestige, so much so that many areas had sumptuary laws curbing excesses.[72]

Also a sign of prestige was the location of the burial plot, either in the churchyard or within the church itself. This was often specified in wills. In fact, choosing where she would be buried was the last chance a woman had to express her sense of self. She might express her religious aspirations by asking for burial apart from her family in a favourite church or convent. But families tended to be buried together. Most people in early modern Europe spent eternity as they had spent their lives on earth: as members of households and patrilinies. If she did not choose to be buried separately in a church or convent, a woman had to choose whether to be interred with her natal family or with her husband – and if she had been married more than once, with *which* husband. While some chose to return to their own kin, most opted for burial with their husbands – faithful and dutiful wives in death as they had been in life.[73]

Part III

◆

WOMEN AND WORK

The world of work is the first of the supposedly male spheres in which women fit uneasily. In early modern Europe, most women, even noblewomen, worked throughout their lives; the popular notion that women, especially married women, moved into the workforce in large numbers only in the twentieth century is simply mistaken. Yet the facts that women worked and in doing so often made possible the survival and prosperity of their families were not usually acknowledged. This is because in early modern Europe the world of work was viewed through two widely held and contradictory assumptions: that work was something that men, *and men alone*, did, and that the basic unit of production was the patriarchal household in which everyone, including women, worked together to support it.

That the world of work was a world of men was a conviction that had permeated western civilization since the dawn of time. In the Bible, work was the punishment God gave Adam for his sin ('In the sweat of your face you shall eat bread'). Eve's punishments of painful childbirth and subordination to her husband, by contrast, emphasized her familial roles. Thus the dichotomy, men: the outside world of work; women: the domestic sphere of the family, was created. Not just God but nature also seemingly allotted the world of work to men. Men's supposedly superior strength made physical labour a male task and their supposedly superior minds gave them dominance over intellectual work: religion, government, the professions and the production and dissemination of knowledge. Skilled labour was also thought to be a male task. Since ancient Athens, physical work that produced something, be it an agricultural crop or a hand-crafted item like a shoe, was considered a 'mystery', defined as something involving the application of esoteric, some-times secret knowledge and knowledge-derived skills to nature's raw materials to make a finished product. Because this seemed similar to the way the brain processed sense impressions to produce knowledge, and because knowledge was gendered masculine, skilled labour was too. Thus all occupations apart from housework and childcare were, in theory, 'men's work'.

This definition of work as something men, and men alone, did, was rein-forced by many aspects of early modern European culture. For example, the work he did gave a man his identity, while her roles in the family gave a woman's life its meaning. Surnames, relatively new in 1500 (they were not commonly used in Holland until the seventeenth century), were often derived from masculine crafts, like Smith or Miller. Thus men bore the name of a family trade, but women had the names of their fathers or their hus-bands. In official documents men's occupations were often given after their names, while women were listed as wives or widows. Skill at his trade and honesty in business dealings were important elements of a man's honour, while chastity defined the honour of a woman.

This identification of work with men and masculinity had one major prob-lem, however: it did not fit the realities of the early modern economy. In the pre-industrial era, most production took place in households, be they peasant smallholdings, artisans' workshops or noblemen's great estates. And within these households, everyone – men, women, children, servants – usually worked. In fact, most families survived only if all their members worked and con-tributed to what historians call 'the family economy'. The people of early modern Europe acknowledged this by embracing a second assumption about the world of work that contradicted the first: that patriarchal households were the basic units of economic production and that all their members worked to keep them afloat.

This assumption recognized the fact that women worked and indeed led to a second layer of gendering in the workplace, as tasks were considered 'men's work' or 'women's work' according to how they were parcelled out among the households' various members. But this second, more realistic vision of the workplace never displaced the assumption that the world of work was an essentially masculine sphere. This had a number of dire consequences for women.

First of all, the work that they did was often not recognized as work and they were not defined as individual workers, by their society. What men did was labelled work; what women did was not. As historian Mary Prior put it: 'Whatever a man did was work and what a woman did was her duty.'[1]

This failure to define women as workers and recognize what they did as work led to a second dire consequence for women: they were confined to the margins of the workforce and allotted the least prestigious, lowest paying jobs. In agriculture few women were landowners; most were casual day labourers. In manufacturing, few women were members of the prestigious craft guilds; most were hired workers making non-guild, low-prestige goods. And in retailing, few women were large-scale wholesale merchants or substantial shopkeepers; most sold cheap goods from market stalls or peddled them door to door. This confining of women to low-paying marginal jobs had especially dire consequences for single women trying to support themselves and widows trying to support their children. But it also disadvantaged the vast majority of adult women who were wives and mothers because it limited their earning power and therefore lessened their family income. This had wide-scale economic effects: society's refusal to use the full productive potential of its women limited its productivity and prosperity and held back its economic development.

Occasionally women could come in from the margins of the economy and take up 'male' occupations. But when they did they were almost always paid less than men. This too flowed from the gendering of the world of work as male. The association of work with manhood made the adult male the standard 'worker' and what he could do in a day determined the standard daily wage. All other workers – adolescent boys, elderly and disabled men, and women – were paid only a portion of the standard wage because it was assumed, rightly or wrongly, that they could not do as much as an adult man. This was true throughout Europe. Everywhere women were usually paid between two-thirds and three-quarters of an adult male's wages for doing the same work. This was true before our period (in Yorkshire in 1363 male reapers received 4d a day, women reapers $3\frac{1}{2}$d) and it is still true today.[2] The fact that women earned less than men for doing the same work is one of the great constants of women's history.

Apart from wage discrimination, the tendency to identify the worker as an adult male had other bad effects on women. For example, it justified excluding women from making decisions regarding work. In most peasant villages, female landowners could attend but not vote in the communal meetings that decided crop rotations, harvest dates and the like. Craft guilds also usually denied their female members the right to vote on new applicants and hold guild offices.

The definition of the world of work as male also justified something very common in our period: the invasion of the more lucrative types of traditional 'women's work' by men. In the second layer of the gendering of work, the boundaries between 'men's work' and 'women's work' were constantly shifting, but in general the area of 'men's work' expanded while that of 'women's work' shrank. In early modern Europe, it was difficult for women to do 'men's work', and even when they did it, and did it well, it remained men's work and the women who did it were simply labelled exceptional, 'manly' women. This is what happened to female writers, artists and scientists, for example. But because the whole world of work was male, men could invade and colonize jobs traditionally done by women, like ale brewing and midwifery, and eventually turn them into male occupations.

This invasion of traditionally female occupations by men, along with a decline in wages and working conditions in 'women's work' like textiles, growing restrictions on women in the guilds and an erosion of the productive functions of the housewife, prompted Alice Clark to label the early modern period as a time of setbacks for women in work, an interpretation which, as we have seen, later historians enlarged to cover most aspects of women's lives. We have argued that the extension of the Clark thesis does not fit the facts. Was Clark wrong about the decline in women's work as well? That is the question we will explore in the next three chapters.

Chapter 6

◆

HOUSEWIVES, SPINSTERS, HARVEST HANDS: WOMEN'S WORK IN THE COUNTRYSIDE

Despite their society's widespread conviction that work was something men, and men alone, did, most of the women in early modern Europe worked hard all their lives. This was especially true in the countryside, where most of the people – at least 80 percent of the population – lived. Agricultural labour was the largest single employer of women, as it was of men in that pre-industrial, agrarian economy.

What this work consisted of was remarkably uniform throughout Europe, because the basic crops and cultivation methods differed little from place to place. Only on the fringes of the continent were there deviations from the basic pattern. On the seacoasts peasants fished as well as farmed and along the temperate Mediterranean they raised a variety of crops, including grapes, olives, fruit and even silkworms. Mountainous areas like the Balkans were devoted to cattle and sheep raising. But in most of Europe the major crops were grains – barley, oats, rye and especially wheat – used for the bread that was the major food for most people, day in and day out. A typical peasant would eat bread plus a watery soup with a few vegetables floating in it for breakfast, have more bread washed down with ale, cider or watered wine for lunch and more bread and soup for supper. Fresh fruits and vegetables, fish, eggs and poultry and indeed any meat except bits of the family pig, slaughtered in the autumn and preserved over winter, were rare luxuries.

The grains that fed most of the population were cultivated on land held and worked in remarkably similar ways throughout Europe. Again variations from the standard pattern occurred on the fringes of the continent. In the Balkans, lands were owned and cultivated by the large, multigeneration *zadruga* households, which owed yearly tribute to their Muslim overlords. At the other end of Europe, the Dutch Republic and England boasted Europe's largest farms and most efficient agriculture. The substantial landowners in these areas, who worked their large farms with hired, often landless, wage labourers, could afford to experiment with advanced crop rotations combining arable and pasture that kept the land continually productive. But that was not true in most of Europe. The typical pattern was a wasteful one: the soil was replenished by leaving it lie fallow – that is, unplanted. In southern Europe, a simple two-field rotation was the norm: land would be planted one year, fallow the next. The heavier soils of northern Europe could support a three-field rotation: winter wheat, spring wheat and fallow.

In most of Europe, these fields were divided into estates, or manors, of a few hundred acres, usually but not inevitably owned by noblemen. The actual farming was done by the dozens of peasant families living on the manor. Each had its own plot of land. The peasants 'owned' their lands in the sense that they could sell them or pass them on to their heirs. But because their lands were part of manors, their freedom to do what they liked with them was restricted. First, a peasant's land was usually not a separate farm he could cultivate as he pleased. Instead, it was a claim to a part of the large common fields of the manor. What and when to plant there was decided by a meeting of the manor's landowners. Second, because the land was part of a manor, a peasant owed the manor's owner what were called manorial or seigneurial dues: usually a rent in money or kind, a fee when the land changed hands and special rights and monopolies (e.g. only the lord could fish or hunt game on the manor). East of the River Elbe, peasants might have other obligations to their lords, for there they were frequently unfree serfs, bound to the manor. This meant that they could not leave it without the lord's permission. Also, in addition to manorial dues, serfs owed their lord labour service – work without pay. This might be light – a few days a year – but it could be as heavy as two or three days each week. And in areas of serfdom the peasants' 'ownership' of their land was more precarious than in the west. A manorial court run by the lord dictated crop rotations and could oust tenants.

THE IDEAL OF THE RURAL HOUSEWIFE

Whether serf or free, the peasant household living on its land was the basic unit of agricultural production in early modern Europe. This shaped society's conception of 'men's work' and 'women's work'. A rural household was thought to contain two chief characters who divided its work between them, its patriarchal head, the 'husbandman', and his wife, the 'housewife'. Each worked in his or her separate sphere, the dividing line of which ran around the outside of the house. The 'husbandman', whose title implied both his married state and his agricultural labours, was responsible for the fieldwork away from the home, while the 'housewife', whose title also implied both her marital state and her tasks, was responsible for the house and its immediate vicinity. As Olivier de Serres, French author of an early seventeenth-century agricultural manual, explained: 'The affairs of the fields belong to the husband, those of the house to the wife.'[1] His English contemporary Thomas Tusser concurred poetically:

> The woman the name of a housewife doth win
> By keeping her house and of doings therein.[2]

Anthropologists have found similar divisions between male and female spheres of work in many human societies, especially those with sedentary crop raising. They speculate that men were allotted the fieldwork because of their greater upper arm strength and also because, unburdened by childcare, they were free to roam. Women, by contrast, were tied to their homes by their childcare responsibilities. Anthropologists also speculate that men could do their work in groups and that their co-operation might be the ultimate source of their dominance in government, religion and the creation of culture. Women, tied to their homes, tended to work alone.

What did the 'housework' consigned to women consist of? Much more than the cooking and cleaning that the word brings to mind today. Rural households in early modern Europe strove for self-sufficiency, that is, they tried to produce all they would consume. A sixteenth-century Russian household manual, the *Domostroi*, stated:

> A house run by a sensible, God-fearing master and mistress should contain everything the household will use during the year. This includes lumber, drink, food, grain, fat, meat (aged half-carcasses of red meat, ham, corned beef, dry-cured meat), winnowed grain, fresh and salt fish, biscuits, flour, oat flour, poppy seeds, wheat, peas, butter, hempseed, salt, malt, hops, soap and ashes – anything that can be stored in advance without perishing.[3]

The housewife was responsible for the raising, harvesting and processing, storing and doling out as needed of all this except the grains, which were the husbandman's responsibility. The housewife's sphere of activity included not just the house but also those areas adjacent to it. These included the garden, which meant that she raised vegetables and herbs and fruit to be made into jams. She was also responsible for the farmyard, where she raised pigs, chickens and ducks and geese and plucked the feathers and down of the last two for pillows. And she was responsible for the dairy, where she raised and milked cows and sometimes sheep and goats and made butter and cheese. She also raised bees, collected their honey and wax and made candles and she brewed ale. Finally, she was responsible for clothing as well as feeding her family and raised flax and hemp to be spun and woven into rough cloth for towels and shirts and spun and sometimes wove wool for clothing as well.

We can see the full range of these tasks in the diary of a sixteenth-century rural English housewife:

14 January, 1599. [. . .] after I had breakfast, I wrought [spun thread] til dinner time . . . til supper time I was busy in the grainary. [. . .]

15 January, 1599. In the morning at 6 o'clock I prayed privately: that done, I went to a wife in travail of child, about whom I was busy til one o'clock. [. . .]

28 Aug. 1599. [. . .] about one o'clock I gathered my Apples til 4, then I came home, and wrought til almost 6. [. . .]

1 Sept. 1599. [. . .] I walked about the house, barn, and fields and . . . then I went to take my bees. [. . .]

5 Oct. 1599. [. . .] after dinner I was busy about preserving quinces. [. . .]

9 Oct. 1599. [. . .] I went about and delivered Corn [wheat] and after received Rents. [. . .]

30 Oct. 1599. [. . .] After private prayer I did eat my breakfast, then I was busy to dye wool til almost dinner time. [. . .]

26 Nov. 1599. [. . .] I did see Lights [rush or wax candles] made almost all the afternoon. [. . .]

24 Sept. 1601. [. . .] I sealed a lease of the intake [the mill] to Stephen Tubley. [. . .]

26 Sept. 1601. [. . .] This day I . . . had sown of rye 5 pecks.[4]

THE RURAL NOBLEWOMAN

This hardworking woman was no downtrodden peasant. She was Lady Margaret Hoby, wife of Sir Thomas Hoby and mistress of Hackness Hall in Yorkshire. A wealthy heiress, Lady Margaret moved in the highest circles of Elizabethan society; her husband was a nephew of Lord Burghley, Queen Elizabeth's great councillor. Yet Lady Margaret's daily routine was ceaseless toil. This highlights an important fact about housewifery: the larger the landholding, the more work there was for the housewife to do. Noblewomen, mistresses of the largest estates, were not ladies of leisure in the sixteenth and early seventeenth centuries. They had to perform the full range of a housewife's duties or at least supervise the servants who did so. And noble housewives were responsible for the hiring of these servants and for their moral well-being. Lady Margaret, a pious Protestant, took these duties seriously and read the Bible to her assembled household, led them in prayer and admonished a man who had got one of her servants pregnant. Noblewomen were also responsible for the physical well-being of their families, servants and the people on their estates. This meant that they had to act as doctors and diagnose, dose and care for the sick. This could be very time-consuming, as the example of Lady Margaret's contemporary, Lady Grace Mildmay, suggests. Lady Grace took a scientific approach to her medical duties. She bought and read medical treatises and consulted male physicians on difficult cases. She made her own remedies, mostly herbal brews, in large quantities in a still room as well equipped as any apothecary's shop. (One recipe required 24 types of root, 68 different herbs, 10 spices, six gallons of wine and six pounds of sugar.) Lady Grace kept careful notes of her patients' progress so that she could adjust her dosage to their age, gender and physical condition. Over 2000 pages of these notes were found at her death.[5]

The duties of a housewife were difficult and time-consuming and the larger the estate the more onerous they were. In addition to their own work, many noblewomen performed tasks in theory relegated to their husbands, overseeing the planting and harvesting of field crops and hiring field workers, renting out land and collecting seigneurial rents and dues. Lady Margaret is an example, as her diary shows. Noblemen like Sir Thomas Hoby who had to be away from their land for long periods, whether for war or politics, often left the complete running of their estates to their wives, as did nobles who were incompetent or simply lazy.

By 1700, however, busy noble housewives like Lady Margaret were largely a thing of the past, especially in western Europe. Professionalized armies and government bureaucracies replaced noble amateurs and therefore many more noblemen stayed home and took pride in managing their estates themselves. The noble housewife also saw her duties shrink in other ways. Supervising servants became less time-consuming as new concepts of distance between master and servant gave servants more autonomy. Male physicians increasingly took over the noblewomen's healthcare responsibilities. And, above all, nobles no longer tried to make their estates self-sufficient. Growing numbers of fairs, markets and peddlers on the roads, plus the spread of shops in the countryside, allowed nobles to purchase items which formerly had to be made on the estate. Inventories of eighteenth-century country estates show far smaller stocks of food and household linens than those of earlier periods. Cheeses, candles, cloth, furniture and sometimes even clothing could now be purchased ready-made, as could the new colonial 'luxuries' which had rapidly become necessities: coffee, tea, sugar and tobacco.

All this dramatically changed the lives of rural noblewomen. In August 1783 the German novelist Sophie von La Roche described her life on her country estate in a letter to a friend:

> I rise at six o'clock and get dressed, write or read by myself until seven-thirty, when La Roche and Baron von Hohenfeld come to breakfast . . . Then I go into my kitchen and give instructions, since I myself am versed in the art of cooking. I check up on all work in the house, write my house accounts, and then work on *Pomona* [her novel] and write letters until noon. At half past twelve we go to table . . . From two o'clock, when we have coffee, to three o'clock, when the letters arrive, we stay together for all manner of conversation, and then everybody retires to his or her room. If there are visitors, or for as long as the men talk and read learned journals in my room, I diligently do needlework. At five o'clock I go back into my kitchen and arrange supper. My sons, who study French, geography, and history with me, arrive at seven. These are sweet hours, as we converse amiably and moral principles flow into their souls.[6]

Notice how different Sophie La Roche's daily routine was from Lady Margaret Hoby's two centuries earlier. Lady Margaret's days were filled with her housewifely duties, but for Sophie La Roche these had shrunk to planning menus, keeping household accounts and doing ornamental needlework while conversing with her husband and guests. Unlike Lady Margaret, Sophie La Roche had abundant leisure time, which she spent raising her sons and writing her novels. Alice Clark characterized these changes as the loss of the productive functions of the lady of the manor and as a setback for women, because when women contributed less to the economic functioning of the estate they supposedly were accorded less respect by their families and society at large.[7] But was this true? Lady Margaret, walking the fields and leasing them to tenants, may seem more powerful than Sophie La Roche, but was she really? Sir Thomas was the ultimate power at Hackness Hall and there is little indication that Lady Margaret had much influence over him. Theirs was an arranged marriage and they spent most of it apart. Sophie La Roche, however, married for love and had a profound influence on her doting husband. She also had power in the public realm through her novel writing, a career she could pursue because she did not have to spend all her time in housewifely duties. This suggests that while Clark was correct in characterizing the changes in the role of noble housewife in this period, her interpretation of the effects of these changes on the status of women is less sound. The loss of their productive functions did not necessarily mean that elite women lost status and power. If given a choice, most probably would have preferred ornamental needlework and conversation to plucking geese and making candles.

PEASANT HOUSEWIVES

Of course, most housewives in the countryside were not noblewomen. Instead, they were wives of poor peasant smallholders. This meant that their working lives often differed from that of the stereotype rural housewife. The women of the *zadrugas* of eastern Europe fit the stereotype best. There the men of the household worked away from home under the direction of the male patriarch, while the women stayed home and did housewifely tasks, directed by his wife.[8] The women of coastal fishing villages and some highland areas were least like the stereotype. There the men left the villages in the spring, to fish or to drive the cattle to high pastures, and did not return until late autumn. Hence *all* the agricultural labour, men's fieldwork as well as female housewifery, fell to the women. We saw that in the Finnish fishing village of Koivulathi, most babies died within a few months after they were born because their mothers weaned them early so they could work in the fields.

The typical peasant housewife fell between these two extremes. She rarely spent much of her time on traditional housewifery, for usually only a few households on each manor were prosperous enough to afford the dairy cows, ducks, geese, chickens, beehives and fruit trees that entailed. And her home, a one-room hovel with a dirt floor and no furniture except for straw-filled mattresses and a rough wooden table and bench, needed little cleaning. The only cooking she did was to keep a pot of soup bubbling on the open hearth; bread, mainstay of the family diet, needed a hot oven, lacking in most peasant cottages. Bread was therefore baked at the village baker's. And with swaddling, childcare too was minimal.

How then did the typical peasant housewife spend her time? She contributed to her family's income and well-being in two important ways that did not fit the housewife stereotype. One was by working in the fields. Fieldwork was in theory gendered masculine and, in fact, one aspect of it, ploughing, which required physical strength and costly equipment and had to be done continuously away from the home, was usually reserved for men. Indeed, ploughing was so firmly gendered masculine that it acquired sexual connotations; 'ploughing the field' was in most European languages a euphemism for sexual intercourse. But the rest of the fieldwork was shared between the sexes, with 'men's work' and 'women's work' allotted pragmatically according to local custom. Typically, hoeing weeds was masculine, pulling them up by hand, feminine. Collecting manure and spreading it on the fields was women's work. At harvest time, the whole village worked together to bring in the crop. If a heavy, long-handled scythe were used, the men did the reaping, with the women following to bind the grain and load it onto carts. But if the light, short-handled sickle were used, women might reap as well.[9]

FEMALE BY-EMPLOYMENTS

In addition to her work in the fields, a peasant's wife contributed to the economic well-being of her family in another way not recognized by the housewife stereotype: by taking on what economists call by-employments, extra work to supplement her income. Actually male peasants took on by-employments too, especially in the winter months when little could be done in the fields. They might work as carpenters or wheelwrights or, if they lived in highland areas and raised livestock, they might even leave their families for a few months and go to the lowlands to peddle cloth and trinkets along the roads. But because women's regular working patterns were more discontinuous than men's, it was easier for them to fit by-employments into their workdays and therefore such tasks formed a bigger portion of their contribution to the family income. Often it was absolutely crucial. Most peasants had so little land that they grew only enough to feed their families. A peasant's crops, especially grains, were usually consumed, not sold. Therefore a wife's by-employments usually brought in the only cash the family had to pay its dues to the lord and taxes to the state.

Although by-employments were not part of the housewifely stereotype, many of them grew out of it. A peasant wife too poor to keep bees or dairy cows herself was often hired to help with candle making and cheese making by wealthier neighbours. Peasant wives earned money by tending geese, nursing the sick and helping neighbours with their spinning, sewing or laundry. They might also be hired as lying-in nurses or, if they had recently given birth, as wet nurses to babies from nearby towns.

A farmer's wife might also sell her own produce or that of others. The vegetables she grew, the eggs and chickens she raised, the ale she brewed were often not consumed by her family. Instead they were destined for sale, either at the local market or, again, to more prosperous neighbours. And if she herself did not have anything to sell, she might buy her neighbour's surplus and then try to resell it for slightly more than she paid. This small-scale buying and reselling, called regrating, was a characteristically female type of commerce. It was probably the source of most of what was consumed in the countryside, where there were few shops or stores. Wealthy country families ordered luxury items – fine textiles, silver plate – from city merchants and they purchased cheaper goods from the male peddlers who travelled the country roads. (Most peddlers were men; women could not leave their families for long periods and it was dangerous for them to travel alone and sleep in the open.) But wealthy families bought their daily necessities from local female regraters. The account books of Margaret Fell Fox, mistress of a seventeenth-century gentry household in the north of England, show this pattern. The Foxes bought fine cloth and other luxury goods from shops in towns. Men bought and sold their livestock. But local women bought their excess eggs, butter, bread and cheese and sold them these items when needed.[10]

Yet another way for peasants' wives to earn money was to hire themselves out as farm labourers. As we have seen, fieldwork was in theory gendered male, and the amount of work an adult male could do was taken as a standard day's labour. He was paid the highest wage and all other labourers, including women, were assumed to be able to do less and were therefore paid less. But, of course, many peasant wives worked in the fields and because peasant husbands valued physical strength in their mates – a lustful neighbour said of a shepherd's wife, 'he would like to sleep with her, she was so pretty and strong'[11] – they were often able to do as much as men. This plus their lower wages made them bargains in the labour market. Therefore peasants' wives could easily find work as hired labourers, like the German wife who missed her day in court 'on account of the hay harvest'.[12]

The by-employments of peasants' wives both challenged and reinforced the stereotypes of the good wife and the good housewife. They reinforced the stereotypes because in order to be accepted into the networks of female buyers and sellers which honeycombed the countryside or to be hired as a lying-in nurse or even to help with the second haying a woman had to have a good reputation with her neighbours and that meant that she had to be known as a chaste and obedient wife and a hard-working and thrifty housewife. Little wonder then that women conformed to society's stereotypes and carefully guarded their reputations.

Yet in another way women's by-employments undermined the stereotype of the good wife and housewife, because in order to pursue them – to work for and sell things to her neighbours – a housewife had to leave her house and her children. In fact, much of a peasant housewife's working life was, despite the stereotype, spent away from home. Sheilagh Ogilvie has analysed the location of women's – and men's – work as revealed in seventeenth- and eighteenth-century court cases from two districts in Germany. Only about half of the married women in her sample were working in or near their homes; half were not.[13]

THE TEXTILE TRADE AND THE PUTTING-OUT SYSTEM

One final by-employment was so important for women's work that it deserves separate treatment. This was work in the textile industry. The making of cloth and clothing had been 'women's work' since the dawn of time; women probably invented weaving around 7000 BCE. Textiles were the major way women expressed themselves both figuratively, through the colour and design of the cloth they wove and, literally, through the quotes and proverbs they embroidered on their tapestries and samplers. Even princesses were taught how to spin and sew. In the early modern period, housewives were expected to produce most of the cloth used in their households: rough hemp cloth for towels, finer linen for sheets and shirts and wool for clothes and blankets. Making cloth was a long process: preparing the fibres, spinning them into thread or yarn, weaving that into cloth, fulling and dyeing it and cutting and sewing it into sheets or garments. Parts of this process were often done by men. In western Europe few women wove cloth, especially woollens, from 1500 to 1700. Looms were too large and expensive for most peasant homes, so after the yarn was spun, itinerant male weavers were usually hired to do the weaving. Similarly, male tailors were often hired to make the cloth into clothing. But the other steps in textile production were women's work. This was especially true of spinning, which was in many ways the ideal woman's task. Not only could it be started in an idle moment and stopped when the baby cried or some other urgent need appeared, it also could be done in the dark, by feel alone, so that it could fill the long dark winter evenings when other work was impossible. And if a spindle instead of a spinning wheel were used, it was portable as well. Women took their spindles everywhere, spinning as they walked to the fields or the market. Spinning was so identified with women that in early modern England, the word 'spinster', meaning one who spun, was applied indiscriminately to all women; only later did it take on its modern meaning of an unmarried woman.[14]

Most textiles produced by a peasant wife were for her own household, but if she made extras she would sell them to her neighbours or in the local market and if she had extra time, she might buy some raw flax or wool, spin it into yarn and sell that at the local market too. Or she might agree to spin for an urban textile merchant who supplied her with the raw wool and paid her for the yarn she spun. This arrangement, called the 'putting-out' system, was spreading rapidly in our period. Used since the Middle Ages in flax and linen manufacturing, because the thread had to be processed in water and this could be more easily done near the waterlogged fields where the flax was grown than in urban workshops, by the seventeenth century the putting-out system was coming to dominate woollen manufacturing as well. In the Middle Ages fine woollens had been manufactured in towns by mostly male artisans organized into craft guilds, one for each step in the process: carding, spinning, weaving, dyeing, etc. Their work was coordinated and the final product sold by wool merchants, who were among the wealthiest and most respectable of the town's businessmen. But the high cost of male guild labour spurred merchants to seek cheaper alternatives, so by the seventeenth century spinning, which mattered less to the final appearance of the cloth than weaving or dyeing, was frequently contracted out to the peasant women in the countryside, who could be paid less than guildsmen. This system of 'putting-out' parts of the manufacturing process was also used for stocking knitting and making lace.

In the putting-out system workers were paid piecework rates, that is, so much for every stocking knitted or length of yarn spun. These rates varied widely. Some sorts of lace making were highly skilled and paid well, but spinning was something most women could do and therefore paid very poorly. The spread of the putting-out system and the consequent loss of female autonomy and decline of wages in the textile industry was another of Alice Clark's major pieces of evidence for the decline in women's work in the early modern period.[15]

As with the elite housewife, Clark rightly identified an economic trend but misinterpreted its effects on women. It is undeniable that the putting-out system was spreading rapidly in early modern Europe and, although there were immense regional variations, generally wages tended to fall as more and more women in an area joined putting-out networks. But it is not clear that peasant wives saw this as an adverse development. It is especially unlikely that they grieved over their lost 'autonomy'; that is an attitude of a nineteenth-century male 'wage slave' that Clark projected back onto seventeenth-century housewives, who had little 'autonomy' to begin with and did not necessarily lose it when they worked for a woollen merchant. Joining a putting-out network did not necessarily mean that you stopped producing your own cloth. And even when it did, peasant wives may well have preferred working for a wool merchant at steady, if low, wages to the uncertainties of hawking their own work at the local market, where buyers might be numerous one day but non-existent the next. Indeed, so attractive was the prospect of steady work for cash wages to many peasants that in the late seventeenth and eighteenth centuries whole districts that were formerly agricultural became what economists call proto-industrial centres of putting-out industries, with men as well as women working at weaving, spinning and stock knitting. These proto-industries might allow peasants to marry, and therefore attain adulthood, earlier (they did not have to wait to inherit land, as true peasants did) and to have the cash to buy the new cheap but fashionable clothes and other consumer goods that replaced the land as marks of their identity.[16]

PEASANT WIDOWS

If the lives of peasant wives often departed from the housewife stereotype, there were other women in the countryside whom the stereotype fitted even less. Among these were widows, who combined the feminine role of house-wife with the masculine role of household head. As we have seen, widows were often richer or poorer than other women and in rural areas they tended to be very poor – often the poorest landowners in any village. This was because they had to somehow find the money to hire men to do the 'men's work' formerly done by their late husbands. Therefore they took on even more by-employments than peasant wives and were almost as likely to work away from home than wives were, even at the cost of neglecting their children.[17] In a German village in 1724 a widow who supported herself and her children by weaving was cited by the community for the 'tumult' in her house when she had to leave in the middle of the night to deliver the cloth she had finished.[18]

In theory, villages understood the plight of poor widows and granted them tax relief, rights to the common lands and special harvesting privileges. But not everyone sympathized. In 1787 a young male German peasant complained about poor widows who enjoyed these rights: 'He believes that the younger [male] citizens, who have all the burdens of citizens upon them and do not yet enjoy any common lands, would have a better right to the common lands than these persons.'[19] Sometimes German village councils deprived widows of their special privileges and they sometimes forced them into marriage or took away their land, handing it over to younger males. In 1592 Georg Lodholz's widow lost a field to her son and in 1624 Jan Roller's widow complained that her offspring had sold her meadow to the village bailiff without her permission. The bailiff admitted that he had bought it without her knowledge, asking 'what harm would it do if such an old animal [as the woman] should die of hunger?'[20]

Rural widows were even more likely to lose their land and rights in central and eastern Europe, where serfdom prevailed and the lords' manorial courts controlled the distribution of land. Landlords shared their society's convictions that a woman's place was in the household and work was something men did. Therefore they thought women were incapable of properly cultivating a holding, and they tried to get rid of female tenants. A study of serfdom in areas of Bohemia has shown that manorial courts were far more likely to evict female tenants than male. Although only about 4 percent of the tenants were female, they were the subject of 15 percent of the recorded eviction cases. And while male tenants were usually evicted for serious offences like failing to perform labour services or disobeying their lords, most female tenants were evicted for debt – or, in one-quarter of the cases, for no reason at all.[21] If they were not evicted, widows were often forced to remarry or give up their holdings. In 1604 a widow was ordered to 'provide the farm with a capable holder, sell it, or marry off the daughter, within a year and a day'.[22] Manorial courts even abrogated retirement contracts to get rid of female tenants. In 1650 a widow was allowed to use only one field, while 'the remainder of the retirement contract shall be altogether abolished . . . the sooner to secure a [male] purchaser for the farm'.[23]

TRUE SPINSTERS

In eastern Europe, housewives and widows were about the only sorts of women living in the countryside, but western Europe, with its late marriage and high rates of celibacy, had large numbers of unmarried 'maidens' in their teens and early twenties and also a substantial number of true spinsters – women over 25 who never married. The latter posed even more of a challenge to gender stereotypes than widows did, for, like men, they headed their own households and worked to support themselves. How did these women, whom the Germans called *Eigenbrötlerinnen* (literally, own breaders – women who earned their own bread) fare economically?

They fared best, of course, if they inherited land, money or at least some clothes and a few household goods, like English spinster Eleanor Cumpayne, who had been left an acre of land, a garden, a room in the family house, bedding, pots and pans, a cow, a mare, six sheep and a small cash allowance by her father.[24] Such a woman could easily piece together a living from the various female by-employments available in the countryside, as an English ballad from 1687 suggests:

I work for my living abroad and at home.
Sometimes I'me at home, to spinning of Yarn,
And sometimes abroad to reaping of Corn,
Sometimes in the Field to milk the Cow:
I get what I have by the sweat of my brow.[25]

As the ballad suggests, single women could do agricultural work, but employers were reluctant to hire them as they aged and lost their physical strength (and docility). Therefore older single women crowded into the other female by-employments, especially spinning. As we saw, the prominence of unmarried women in that branch of the textile trade gave 'spinster' its modern meaning. Spinning was in many ways ideal work for the spinster and vice versa: it could be done anywhere, even in the tiny rented rooms in someone else's house where many unmarried women ended up living, and, unlike wives and mothers, spinsters could come and go to pick up and deliver yarn as they pleased and devote their full time to the craft. Thus the spread of proto-industry in the seventeenth and eighteenth centuries, far from hurting women economically as Alice Clark suggested, allowed more and more single women to support themselves decently, especially if they moved in together to form an artificial family economy.[26]

While spinning was the most noticeable by-employment for single women, it was not the only one. Unmarried women were also prominent in buying, selling and regrating various goods and, because of their freedom of movement, they were frequently hired to run errands and tend the sick. In Germany in 1605 Judita Müller was employed by a weaver and his wife to take their yarn and cloth to a nearby town to be dyed and in 1652 Catharina Walz was paid a weekly wage by her community for 'tending Michel Zeller, who has been taken into the hospital-poorhouse'.[27]

Unfortunately, the very qualities – their ability to control their time and move around at will – that allowed single women to piece together a living aroused the distrust of their communities. *Eigenbrötlerinnen* defied both the patriarchal paradigm in which every woman lived in a patriarchal household under male control and the stereotype of the world of work as masculine, with women confined to the household and the tasks of housewifery. Communities expressed their disapproval by trying to force single women back into those stereotypes. This did not matter much in England, the Netherlands and France, where village councils had little power over individuals, but it did affect women in the German states. There village councils often denied single female landowners the right to use the village common lands, expelled single women as threats to communal morals and urged them to either enter service or marry to put them under proper male control. Thus in 1687 her village ordered 'Barbara Waltz as an *Eigenbrötlerin* . . . either to enter into service or, if she has an honourable offer, get married'.[28]

FARM SERVANTS

The service into which her village ordered Barbara Waltz was the employment of choice for the final group of women in the countryside: the young single 'maidens' who hoped to marry eventually. As we have seen, maidens were supposed to live modestly at home, helping their mothers with housewifely tasks. But this was impossible for most peasant girls, whose homes did not provide enough housewifely work for their mothers, let alone for them. So daughters usually left home in their mid-teens to find work elsewhere. This relieved their families of the burden of feeding them while they worked to save for the dowries that would allow them to marry. Peasant daughters were far more likely to leave home than peasant sons and they were the most likely of all the types of women in the countryside to work away from their homes and families.[29]

The fact that they no longer had a home shaped the sort of work they chose. Most female by-employments paid so little that they were viable options only if the worker already had a home and other sources of income, as widows and many spinsters did. But maidens did not and, of course, wandering the countryside, sleeping in ditches, while looking for work was dangerous. So most maidens chose to hire themselves out as servants on larger farms that needed extra labour, either helping with the dairying and other 'women's work' or, more usually, simply working in the fields. The great advantage of farm service was that it provided food and a place to sleep, if only in a shed or barn.

Unfortunately, farm service had many disadvantages as well. First, the room and board that attracted them to service might be all they got for their hard work; farm servants often received no wages. If they were paid, the wages were usually quite low (inevitably lower than those of male servants doing the same work) and they were frequently paid in kind, in the form of cast-off clothes, or in a lump sum when the servant left. This led to another disadvantage of service: employers controlled their servants' lives to an extent we would find intolerable today. They dictated what they ate, what they wore, where they slept and they controlled their leisure time, granting or withholding chances to visit the all-important fairs and markets where a servant might have a chance to meet and court a potential mate. Employers also interfered with their employees' private lives, for it was the duty of a patriarchal household head to oversee the morals of the members of his household, including the servants.

Live-in service had one other disadvantage: it exposed a servant to the sexual advances of her employer. Of course, any female worker, even a casual day labourer, might experience sexual harassment. In 1662 a German farmer hired a blacksmith's wife for the harvest and 'he gave her a half-Batzen and offered her another 3 Kreuzer, making it up to half the day-wage, if only she would let him reach under her skirt'.[30] But a live-in servant was especially vulnerable to sexual advances, not only because of proximity. Since ancient times servants had been regarded in law and fact as the sexual property of their masters. When a master set out to seduce a servant there was little she could do about it: she would be fired if she refused his advances. As one seduced and pregnant French farm servant explained, 'because he was my master I was obliged to consent' to his sexual advances.[31] In seventeenth-century Essex, 61 percent of the women who bore illegitimate children were farm servants and of these half had been seduced by their masters.[32]

Most of the rest were pregnant by young men their own age – often their fellow servants – who had promised to marry them. It is easy to see why this would be attractive. Marriage gave a woman status and the respect of her neighbours, the physical protection of a husband and the economic security of a family economy. A life of toil as housewife in your own household was preferable to that of toil as a servant in someone else's.

But for peasant girls in western Europe, marriage might be hard to achieve. The low wages of female farm servants made accumulating a dowry difficult and swains were scarce in the countryside and often had to wait to marry until their parents died and they inherited some land. Therefore it is not surprising that many of the most ambitious peasant girls left the country-side and moved to the nearest town or city, where both employment opportunities and potential husbands were more abundant. It is to women's work in cities and towns that we now turn.

Chapter 7

◆

CRAFTSWOMEN, MIDWIVES, SERVANTS: WOMEN'S WORK IN CITIES AND TOWNS

Early modern cities were deadly places. Although urban women often had higher fertility rates than their rural counterparts because they did not nurse their children (see Chapter 4), the filth and overcrowding in cities meant that deaths usually outnumbered births. Therefore towns grew only through a steady stream of migrants from the surrounding countryside. Although travelling was more dangerous for a woman than a man, the majority of migrants were young single women in their teens and early twenties. Most came from nearby, but great capital cities like London, Paris and Madrid, the fastest growing type of urban area in this period, drew ambitious migrants from all over their respective countries.

These young female migrants did more for their new homes than increase the population. Because they came to town to find a job that would allow them to save for a dowry, so they could return home and marry or acquire an urban husband, they contributed to the economy as well. But their economic contributions were limited by two factors. First, the best paying and most prestigious urban employments for women were usually restricted to native-born citizens of the town. Second, as in rural areas, female employments were restricted by society's vision of women as 'housewives' doing their duty to their families rather than as independent individuals who had to work to support themselves.

URBAN HOUSEWIVES

While equally restrictive, the ideal of the urban housewife differed from that of her rural counterpart. Although most towns still had vacant fields and many urban properties included gardens and even orchards, urban households did not strive for self-sufficiency. Instead of raising what they consumed, they bought what they needed at the numerous urban shops, markets and fairs or from the many peddlers who roamed the city streets. Therefore the main duty of an urban housewife was not production but consumption. Apart from her housewifery, an urban housewife was also, like her rural counterpart, expected to work to contribute to the family economy – as a Spanish humanist put it, to do 'anything necessary' to help her family live 'in prosperity'.[1]

As in the countryside, the duties of the housewife were most complex in the largest households – those of the upper layers of urban society – some nobles,* but mostly non-noble government officials, professionals like doctors, lawyers, intellectuals and, in Protestant countries, clergymen, and the richest of the town's merchants, usually those engaged in large-scale, long-distance overseas commerce. Their wives were literally 'housewives', wed to their homes, for, as we have seen, the ideal wife was expected to remain within the feminine space of the home and not wander the dirty and dangerous streets of the town; to do so would imperil the family's honour.

The family's honour was also at risk if the household did not function efficiently. The housewife was responsible for the hiring and training of the household servants. She was also responsible for their moral and physical well-being, although, unlike the rural noblewoman, she usually did not care for them herself when they were sick; as we shall see, cities and towns had a wide range of professional healthcare providers who could be called in when a servant fell ill. But housewives were expected to provide their servants with religious instruction, supervise their morals, contribute to the dowries or apprenticeships to set them up in life and see that they were cared for in old age. This was true not just for current servants but also former ones and for casual employees like wet nurses, washerwomen and seamstresses. Indeed, the responsibility of an elite woman for the well-being of her dependants extended to the poor women and children of the surrounding neighbourhood, which was viewed as an extension of the female space of the household. Most elite housewives took such responsibilities seriously. For example,

---

* In northern Europe, nobles rarely lived in towns, but southern European cities had substantial noble populations.

Anzola Rizzo, the wife of the wealthy son of a Venetian lawyer, in 1576 left legacies in her will not only to her husband, children and current and former servants; she also left the daughter of a poor neighbour 100 ducats for her dowry.[2] For many elite housewives their responsibility for their dependants extended over the city as a whole. Such women often founded and administered charitable institutions, especially ones caring for poor widows and orphans. Again a Venetian example: the Zitelle, a shelter for young girls in danger of falling into an immoral life, was founded by elite women and administered by an all-female board of governors, which selected and supervised the all-female staff.[3]

The most important responsibility of the urban housewife, however, was consumption. It was her duty to buy – and store – the vast quantities of food, clothing, linen (prosperous households had literally hundreds of sheets and towels), furniture and decorative accessories her household needed. And for each item she was expected to get the finest quality commensurate with her social status at the cheapest possible price. This was no small matter. In early modern cities and towns the social hierarchy was always on display. Most towns had yearly processions in which representatives of every social group marched, displaying symbols of their occupations and placed in line according to their social rank. One's house and possessions were expected to reflect one's social rank and everyone was expected to dress so that their social status was instantly obvious to all passers-by. So important was this that most cities and towns regulated consumption through sumptuary laws which forbade certain classes of people from buying certain types of goods. Sumptuary laws had many purposes, including strengthening the national economy by preventing people from buying expensive imported luxuries, but two of the main ones were preserving the social hierarchy by forbidding the lower classes to purchase high status goods and preventing the main consumers – women – from wasting the family patrimony through spending on expensive clothes and jewels to feed their feminine vanity and lust. Although the question needs much more research, many historians think that most sumptuary legislation was directed and enforced against women.[4] In early eighteenth-century Wildberg, Germany, for example, over 90 percent of those fined for sumptuary law violations were women and three-quarters of these were married housewives.[5]

Most elite housewives, however, did not need the threat of arrest to make them careful shoppers. An example is Magdalena, the wife of Balthasar Paumgartner, a wealthy, socially prominent long-distance merchant in sixteenth-century Nuremberg. While Balthasar was away buying textiles and other goods in Italy and selling them at the great fairs in Frankfurt, husband and wife corresponded constantly and the most common topic in their numerous letters was Magdalena's purchases. Salmon and melons, books and flax, silk vests and linen collars, gold thread and red satin, a silver toothpick on a chain she saw in the local market and bought for a relative and a fashionable fur coat 'like the one Wilhelm Imhoff brought his wife from Venice' she asks her husband to order for her: the list is endless and each item's quality, price and circumstances of purchase are carefully described.[6] The men of her family respected Magdalena's skills as a shopper. Her husband consulted her on his own purchases, even of so masculine an item as a new team of horses, and when her father-in-law wanted to give one of his other sons a fashionable suit, he asked Magdalena to buy the cloth and hire the tailor.[7]

Apart from her shrewd purchases, Magdalena also contributed to her family's prosperity by helping her husband with his business. Indeed, Steven Ozment, the historian who discovered and analysed their letters, described Magdalena as Balthasar's 'partner' in the family firm:

> When Balthasar was on the road, Magdalena became his Nuremberg distributor, book-keeper, and collection agency ... Over the years such responsibilities grew into a virtual partnership. In addition to regular shipments of Miltenberg wine, she received and disbursed to their Nuremberg clients and relatives a great variety of merchandise. The standard cloth items from Italy were linen and damask, but expensive velvet often arrived ... When regular shipments of flax arrived, she carefully inspected them for signs of damage, as flax did not travel very well. Then there were Milanese Parmesan and Dutch cheeses; ... a large whole salmon ... In one shipment he sends ... forty-nine pounds of Dutch cheeses ... seven pairs of shoes and two pairs of slippers; a German Bible ... newspapers ... and Cambrai flax. All such goods normally arrived in numbered crates, Balthasar sending crate numbers and brief descriptions of the merchandise ahead to Magdalena so that, knowing well in advance what to expect, she might prepare for storage and distribution.[8]

Magdalena also sold cheap goods to petty customers and collected rents from properties the family owned.

While merchants' wives like Magdalena could help their husbands with their work, wives of lawyers, government officials and intellectuals could not. But they too contributed to the prosperity of their families. Often their husbands were impressed enough with their skill at managing their households to turn over all the family's financial affairs to their wives and devote their minds totally to higher things. Thus in Martin Luther's household his wife had charge of the finances; she made ends meet by running a farm, breeding pigs, brewing beer and taking in lodgers.[9] And Florence Estienne, wife of the French humanist Isaac Casaubon, was such a good money manager that despite her husband's meagre income (mostly from not always promptly paid pensions from royal and noble patrons) and their 18 children, she managed to save 100 gold coins which she proudly presented to her husband as a birthday present. Therefore it is not surprising that when Casaubon, in religious exile in England, had debts to collect in France, he sent his wife to handle the negotiations and that he appointed her executor of his will.[10] Casaubon's reliance on his wife to handle all the family's finances was not unusual. Court records show that even in places where according to the law husbands controlled their wives' property and women needed male guardians for legal transactions, elite wives often appeared alone in court, administering not only their own property, but also their husbands'.[11]

Although they filled a role that society deemed masculine – that of money manager – elite women did it in a way that was distinctly feminine. Unlike men, they rarely ran their own business or invested in those of others. Instead they tended to invest in urban real estate or in loans and annuities, often arranged by notaries who specialized in bringing borrower and lender together.[12] Economic historians have seen these typically feminine investments, which brought small but safe returns, as timid and suggest that women's failure to command the heights of the early modern economy was due less to society's prejudices than to their own aversion to taking risks. But this is not true. In fact, given how difficult it was for women to travel, to defend their property in courts and to penetrate the social networks of male merchants that controlled long-distance commerce – plus the fact that elite housewives had other calls on their time – their tendency to invest in things that yielded a steady, safe return with little effort makes good economic sense.

Unfortunately, however, their investment patterns decreased the visibility of women in the financial world and therefore reinforced society's image of them as simply housewives. And by 1700 this was increasingly true. At the upper levels of urban society, the merchant's wife who helped her husband with his business and the professional's wife who handled the family finances were rapidly disappearing, replaced by a new model of the urban housewife derived from the aristocracy: the cultivated lady of leisure, devoted solely to her husband and children, for whom shopping in the newly attractively decorated stores was an amusing pastime, not a serious responsibility crucial to the family's prosperity and honour. Here Clark was probably right: the growth of capitalism was the major factor behind the change. On the one hand, it created new financial institutions like chartered companies that were totally masculine. On the other, the prosperity it brought to many merchant families allowed them the luxury of an economically idle wife and it created the new products and stores to fill her leisure time; the modern fashion industry was born in the eighteenth century. As with the similar change among elite rural housewives, most women probably preferred the new model. But it certainly reinforced the widespread notion that women had no place in the world of work.

THE GUILDSMAN'S WIFE

Right below the elite in the social hierarchy of cities and towns were the craftsmen organized into guilds. Urban areas were of course centres of commerce and of manufacturing in the literal sense of the word – the making of goods by hand. And the most lucrative types of commerce and manufacturing were regulated by the local governments through the guilds.

Guilds were important urban institutions in early modern Europe. Prevalent in western European towns since the late Middle Ages, from 1500 to 1700 they were dying out in England and the Dutch Republic, as proto-industry and free trade ideas spread, but they were still very strong in the German states and they were expanding into central and eastern Europe as well. Even the Ottoman Empire had guilds.

Guilds served many purposes: religious (guildsmen maintained altars to their craft's patron saint); social (guilds held dinners for their members and accompanied them to their graves); political (in most towns guildsmen were eligible to vote in municipal elections and hold public office and they, along with elite lawyers and merchants, dominated local governments), but, above all, economic. Guilds guaranteed that consumers received high-quality goods by supervising the training of apprentices and admitting as masters only those who had proved their skill by producing a 'masterpiece'. And they guaranteed the prosperity of their members by monopolizing the production of their goods, limiting the number of masters they admitted and limiting the number of apprentices and journeymen a master could employ and the number of shops he could open so that a few ambitious masters could not dominate the market. The guild ideal was that every master would earn enough to support his family comfortably. Like everyone else, guildsmen envisioned their society as a series of patriarchal households headed by men who were masters in both senses of the word, guild masters and household heads. They worked at their crafts, aided by their wives, children, apprentices, journeymen and servants, all of whom owed them obedience in return for the training, both practical and moral, they gave them.

Thus in the guild vision of a properly ordered world, a man's work was his craft. As for his wife – a person so important in urban life that she had her own title, *die Meisterin* (the female master) in German – she was, like all women, a housewife rather than a worker, but she was also expected to do 'whatever was necessary' to contribute to the prosperity of her family. For the guild-master's wife, as for her social superiors, housewifery was primarily organizing the household's consumption to maximize its income and social status, although the relative poverty of artisan households made this both less time-consuming and more important for the prosperity of their families than the consumption of elite housewives. But the most important duty of *die Meisterin* was to work along with her husband to contribute to the family income. A guildsman's wife was supposed to learn her husband's craft so that she could help him produce goods and supervise the apprentices and journeymen when he was out of the shop. She was also supposed to serve customers behind the counter and keep the shop's accounts. And while she, like all respectable urban housewives, was expected to stay within the domestic sphere of the home, she was also expected to venture out into the dangerous world of the urban streets to help the family economy. When business was slow, a guildsman's wife might sell her husband's goods from a market stall or even peddle them door to door. And craftsmen often sent their wives to buy supplies or collect debts from customers.

Many artisan households followed this stereotype. Sheilagh Ogilvie found that the majority of artisan households in her German samples did not include apprentices or journeymen and that many lacked working-age children as well.[13] Therefore the craftsman and his wife provided the only productive labour. Ogilvie also found numerous examples of wives performing the tasks assigned to them by the stereotype: a barrel maker's wife helping her husband collect wood to make barrel staves; a fountain maker's wife hired by the town to repair a public fountain; a weaver's wife fined for weaving on the Sabbath; a tailor and his wife arguing 'over the making of a bodice' (an argument which ended in his beating her 'because she always wants to have the last word'); a baker's wife peddling bread over hilly, icy roads when eight months pregnant; a weaver's wife cheating the buyers at her market stall; another weaver's wife pestering a customer for an unpaid debt four times in one day; a shoemaker's wife threatening to report a debtor to the district governor.[14]

But not all artisan households fitted the stereotype. The most prosperous could afford to hire apprentices, journeymen, and illegal workers and did not need the wife's labour, so she could devote herself to housewifery. Also, there were businesses – baking, beer brewing, running a stable – where heavy labour was required and hiring male workers rather than relying on the unpaid labour of a wife made economic sense. Finally, there were many businesses where the volume was so low that there was rarely enough to occupy one adult worker, let alone two. Shoemakers, for example, were the most numerous artisans in many towns and because there were so many of them, most made only a meagre living repairing their neighbours' footwear. Their businesses were too small to employ a wife. This meant that many artisans' wives had to 'do what was necessary' to help their families by pursuing independent careers. In a sample from sixteenth-century Paris, 23 wives of artisans shared their husbands' occupations, but 85 had their own trades, like Antoinette Pelourde, a carpenter's wife who was a linenmaker.[15] In a sample from seventeenth-century London, only 26 of the 256 employed wives worked with their husbands.[16]

If a guildsman's wife worked independently, her society's conviction that only men were truly workers severely limited her choice of occupation. Guildsmen's wives only rarely had their own careers as guild artisans, for example, because the guilds were largely closed to women. This had not been true when they were first founded in the Middle Ages. In thirteenth-century Paris 86 of the city's 100 guilds had female members; of these six were guilds of women only.[17] But even in the Middle Ages guilds discriminated against women. Most of their female members were daughters or widows who had inherited their masterships from a male master, not women who earned them through their own skills. The few women who followed the standard guild pattern of apprenticeship, journeymanship and mastership were usually concentrated in acceptably 'female' trades, especially textiles and food. And all guildswomen faced special restrictions: unless their guild was all female, they usually could not be elected to guild office, attend guild dinners or march with their guild in public processions.

By the early modern period guild discrimination against women had deepened. Very few places had guilds with female mistresses who had earned their masterships through their own skill; one was Paris, where a mixed-sex guild of vegetable, seed and grain sellers dating from 1595 actually specified that two of its four elected leaders had to be women, and a large and powerful all-female guild of seamstresses was founded in 1675.[18] More often, women were absolutely forbidden to join guilds; this was true in Barcelona, for example, and in most German towns.[19] Most typically, the only women allowed in guilds were daughters or widows who had inherited their masterships, and they were increasingly restricted in how – and how long – they could run their business. Usually they were not allowed to train apprentices and they were either forbidden to employ journeymen or required to employ them, so that a competent male craftsman produced their goods. This requirement could spell financial ruin for a small business because a journeyman's labour was expensive. Female masters also might be restricted in the types of goods they could produce – often tailors' daughters were only allowed to make children's clothes or to work with cheap fabrics – and in the prices they could charge. And, above all, they might be restricted in the time they could run their business; a year was the usual limit. As we have seen, this was to encourage them to marry, preferably a journeyman who would through his marriage acquire the mastership and take over the shop. If the widow married an outsider to the trade, she would usually be required to sell shop and mastership. Thus a mastership would open up for a journeyman who would buy and run the business. Either way, the proper gender order of society would be restored. The widow would again be a wife under control of a husband and the shop and mastership would be safely in the hands of a competent male artisan.

For Alice Clark, this proliferation of restrictions on guildswomen was yet more evidence that the economic position of women was declining in the early modern period, thanks to capitalism. According to Clark, the growth of capitalism moved production from the household to the factory, threatening the guilds, and guildsmen responded by closing their ranks to women. As usual, Clark was correct in discovering a trend but wrong in her explanation of it. Guilds had discriminated against women even in Clark's 'pre-capitalist' Middle Ages, and historians' local studies have failed to tie the new restrictions of the early modern period to the spread of specific capitalistically organized industries in various areas.[20]

A better explanation lies in the guildsmen's basic belief that, as one German master put it:

> Masculine sex is one of the indispensable basic preconditions for admission to a guild. The entire social order . . . is based upon each sex taking on those tasks which are most fitting to its nature.[21]

To guildsmen, their crafts were mysteries requiring esoteric knowledge only the masculine intellect could grasp. Of course, their daily experiences contradicted this. Their wives were usually untrained in their crafts until they married, but they quickly learned what was necessary to produce goods. So did daughters; guildsmen did not complain that they were harder to train than sons. And when they wished to flout guild regulations and expand their production, guildsmen usually did not hire expensive male journeymen but instead cheaper women workers. Yet nothing could shake their belief that only men could do their work. The denial of reality inherent in this belief became obvious when guildsmen tried to justify it:

Anyone who wants to learn a craft has to possess particular qualities, which are necessary because without them no one can be accepted as an apprentice and registered with a guild. Among these qualities is . . . masculine sex, since no female may properly practise a craft, even if she understands it just as well as a male person. [!][22]

MALE INVASION OF 'WOMEN'S WORK': BREWING AND TAVERN KEEPING

Guilded crafts were not the only respectable, well-paying employment option women lost during the early modern period. They also lost a number of other employment opportunities when jobs which had been 'women's work' in the Middle Ages were taken over by men.

One of these was brewing.[23] As we saw in the last chapter, many peasant wives brewed their own ale and had done so since the Middle Ages. In medieval Europe water was often dangerously polluted, so people in northern Europe, where wine was not widely produced, generally drank ale as their daily beverage. It was relatively easy to brew from readily available ingredients. Grain (oats or barley) was soaked to produce malt, which was then mixed with water to make ale. If a woman made more than her family needed, she did not store it because it spoiled quickly. Instead she sold it. In the English village of Alrewas in the fourteenth century, over half the women sold ale.[24] Thus brewing was yet another by-employment through which peasant wives contributed to the family economy.

Townswomen also brewed and sold ale, often branching out into tavern and inn keeping by providing their clients with a place to sit and drink their purchases. Brewing and selling ale were so much 'women's work' in the Middle Ages that when towns tried to police the trade, they appointed an alewife – as the name suggests, a woman, a female brewer – to do so.

But by the early modern period men had taken over brewing and tavern keeping. Part of the reason was that beer drinking grew in popularity. Unlike ale, beer needed expensive equipment to brew and an expensive imported ingredient – hops. Also unlike ale, beer could be stored over long periods and therefore made in large quantities and shipped over long distances. This meant that beer was most economically manufactured in large workshops and sold wholesale in large markets. Unfortunately, women usually lacked the capital, business experience and long-distance commercial contacts necessary for large-scale enterprises like beer brewing. Therefore it tended to be a masculine occupation and as beer grew more popular than ale, brewing stopped being women's work. In England, by the early modern period, brewing was often a regulated occupation, controlled either by an all-male guild or a licence from a town government and most towns, governed solely by men, granted licences only to male brewers.[25]

Men also took over brewing's lucrative sidelines: tavern and inn keeping. Playing on the stereotype of women as disorderly and lascivious, male tavern keepers persuaded urban officials that their female competitors ran disorderly houses given over to drunkenness and prostitution. Therefore many English towns – Chester is an example – banned women from running inns and taverns.[26] Others granted licences to do so only to men. The same thing happened in German towns and, indeed, throughout northern Europe. In the early modern period, rural women continued to brew and sell ale, but in towns, changes within the brewing industry plus male attacks on the character and competence of women changed brewing and its lucrative sidelines from women's work to men's work.

MALE INVASION OF 'WOMEN'S WORK': THE MEDICAL PROFESSION

Something similar happened in medicine. As we have seen, wives and mothers were traditionally responsible for the health of their families, and in the countryside during the early modern period medical care was mostly 'women's work'. Female neighbours helped each other through childbirth and 'wise women' sold herbs and spells to guard against and cure illnesses. The best medical care in rural areas was probably provided free of charge by the lady of the manor, who often made her own medicines and took careful notes of their effects.

In cities and towns, where the concentration of population made practising medicine more profitable, the situation was different. There people could choose from a wide variety of medical practitioners, many of them men. The most expensive and prestigious were licensed by either the local or the national government. At the pinnacle of the medical profession were the physicians, trained in universities by reading the classical medical texts of the ancient world. They specialized in what today would be called internal medicine. Next in the hierarchy were the surgeons, usually trained through apprenticeship and organized into guilds. They treated wounds, fractures and other external ill-nesses. Approximately equal to surgeons in pay and prestige were midwives, who, of course, attended women in childbirth. Trained by apprenticeship and sometimes organized into guilds, midwives were usually licensed by municipal governments. In some parts of Germany, a midwife who was paid by the town government to supervise the others and care for the poor women in child-birth was elected by the town's female citizens – the only elections in early modern Europe where women regularly voted.[27] Below surgeons and mid-wives in pay and prestige were the apothecaries, who dispensed medicine and advice, and the barbers, who pulled teeth and bled patients. They too were usually trained by apprenticeship and organized into guilds or licensed by town governments.

In theory, only these licensed personnel could practise medicine, but, in fact, towns and cities had many unlicensed practitioners, usually much cheaper than their licensed counterparts, who treated the bulk of the population. These ranged from itinerant tooth pullers to peddlers touting their medicines and ointments at fairs and markets to neighbourhood 'wise women' who, like their counterparts in rural areas, were known for mixing healing herbs, casting magic spells, and curing love sickness as well as stomach aches.*

As for gender, the rule was: the higher in the medical hierarchy, the less likely the practitioner was a woman. Women were scarcest among the physi-cians, largely because the universities which trained them were in theory closed to women. Nonetheless a few did manage to attend and other female doctors were trained by their physician fathers. In Florence between 1345 and 1444, of 350 licensed doctors, five were women. Two of these were physicians' daughters.[28] But male physicians, like male guildsmen, were never very welcom-ing to women, even in the Middle Ages, that supposed golden age of women's work. In the medieval kingdom of Naples, only 1 percent of medical licences were issued to women and most of these restricted them to treating only a few diseases or only female patients. No woman received the unrestricted licence usually given to male physicians.[29]

Women were more numerous and more respected at the next lower level of medical practitioners, those trained by apprenticeship and organized into guilds. Until the seventeenth century, they, and they alone, were midwives. There were also numerous female surgeons, apothecaries, and barber–surgeons. Of 1000 medical licences, mostly for surgery, granted in England in the Tudor–Stuart period, 66 went to women.[30] Many female surgeons were well-respected professionals with prominent clients. Sir Isaac Newton employed a female surgeon as his personal physician and the female surgeon Mrs Holder, sister of Sir Christopher Wren, was called in to treat a wound on

---

* An ill person in early modern Europe had one other option: he or she could turn to religion rather than medicine for a cure and invest in prayers to a healing saint or a pilgrimage to a healing shrine.

King Charles II's hand which his male physicians had failed to cure.[31] The testimony of midwives was accepted as expert in court cases involving pregnancy and rape and the competence of female surgeons and apothecaries was so widely accepted that they were often appointed to official posts in hospitals, orphanages and the like. For example, a Mrs Cook was the resident surgeon–apothecary in Christ's Hospital in London in 1576.[32]

Women were even more likely to be found among the unlicensed and poorly paid medical practitioners, as they were among the unregulated and poorly paid of every occupation. While the itinerant healers of fairs and markets were usually men, the neighbourhood healer with a local reputation for the efficacy of her herbs and spells was usually female. In the Italian town of Guagnano in 1565 there were eight unlicensed healers; five were men and three were women.[33] And, of course, it was women who filled the very lowest ranks of medical practitioners, as lying-in maids, nurses for the sick and caregivers for the elderly and infirm.

The attack on women in the medical profession began with attempts by licensed practitioners to ban unlicensed healers (usually called empirics). Beginning in the Middle Ages, licensed physicians and surgeons constantly attacked those whom the physicians of Salerno described in 1250 as 'the illiterate, the empiric, the Jew, the monk, the actor, the barber, the old woman – each pretends to be a doctor'.[34] As this suggests, women were not necessarily singled out in these attacks. But because so many empirics were 'wise women' who used magic spells as part of their cures, they were the easiest targets. They could be accused of witchcraft, as in an English law of 1511 banning unlicensed practitioners:

> Women, boldly and accustomably take upon them great Cures, and things of great difficulty, in which they partly use sorcery and witchcraft.[35]

This put individual female healers in jeopardy. Marietta Greca, for example, was tried for witchcraft by the Venetian Inquisition in 1620. She was a well-known healer, hired in the case which brought her to trial when the father of a teenaged girl suffering from severe stomach and chest pains asked the women of his neighbourhood who the best healer was. Greca cured the girl using both medicines and magic spells, but insisted to the Inquisition that she was a healer, not a witch.[36]

The association of female healers with witchcraft did more than put individual women in jeopardy. It also created an image of the female healer as an aged, disreputable crone who knew nothing of medicine and relied on spells and Satan for her 'cures' – in contrast, of course, to the respectable, rational, scientific male doctor. This image spread through the seventeenth century as more and more physicians and surgeons adopted the new ideas of Paracelsus about the human body and its diseases. As we saw in Chapter 1, traditional Galenic medicine traced illnesses to an imbalance of humours in the body. In contrast, Paracelsus believed that people fell sick when they were struck by a specific disease with its own unique cause and cure. While the gender lines were not rigid (some male doctors were staunch Galenians), in general, female practitioners tended to cling to Galenism and its traditional healing potions, while male doctors, who more easily than women achieved the extensive study Paracelsism required, converted to the new ideas. Thus the spread of Paracelsism deepened the image of the female healer as ignorant crone wedded to outdated, superstitious practices. This image provided both a means and a motive for male physicians and surgeons to attack not only unlicensed female empirics but also the women physicians, surgeons and midwives in their own ranks, whom they also pictured as ignorant crones.[37]

This attack was only partially successful. Midwives survived it best. As we saw in Chapter 4, in the sixteenth century male surgeons began to practise midwifery and by 1700 male midwives were often employed by the nobility and the most fashionable of the urban bourgeoisie. Nonetheless, most women still relied on the traditional female midwife. Considerations of cost and decorum kept midwifery a relatively well-paying and well-respected female employment through the eighteenth century.

The attack on female physicians, surgeons and apothecaries was more successful. When they were organized in guilds, surgeons and apothecaries followed standard guild procedure for getting rid of women, first allowing only the widows of male masters to practise and later barring even them. The Paris surgeons' guild, for example, as early as 1484 accepted only the widows of master surgeons as female guild members; in 1694 even they were banned.[38] In Württemberg from 1663 on, only widows of male masters could be female barber–surgeons and only if they employed assistants trained by men. Even then, they were forbidden from treating 'dangerous injuries'.[39]

Female surgeons and apothecaries had a better chance of surviving where practice was licensed rather than organized in guilds. In England women continued to be licensed as surgeons throughout the seventeenth century. Their male colleagues vouched for their skills. In 1687, for example, Elizabeth Wheatland was licensed as a surgeon after a male surgeon testified that she was 'a person sufficiently and fully qualified to be a Chirurgeon, we having by due examination found her able and expert in the art of physick and Chirurgery, And also that she is expert in boansetting.'[40] But while public authorities continued to grant licences to women, they stopped appointing them to lucrative posts in hospitals, orphanages and other public institutions. As we saw, such appointments were common earlier, but by 1700 local governments hired female healers only to care for the minor illnesses of the poor, especially ringworm, which for some reason was considered a female speciality.

This elimination of female medical practitioners from prestigious public posts not only reduced the income of individual women; it also deepened the image of the female healer as an ignorant, superstitious crone. By the end of the eighteenth century this was how the public viewed all women healers. The urban elites would no longer employ them. The final blows to women healers came around 1800, when a new type of medical education appeared: university training followed by an internship in a teaching hospital. Hospital staffs were, of course, all male, and when such hospitals opened dispensaries to treat walk-ins free of charge, female healers lost their last clients, for now even the poor had access to modern scientific male medicine.

URBAN TEXTILE WORKSHOPS AND
THE CLOTHING INDUSTRY

With brewing, medicine and the guilded crafts increasingly closed to them, where could guildsmen's wives find employment? As the examples of the seventeenth-century London tailors' wives who were seamstresses, washer-women and nurses suggest, only in the largely unregulated, marginal, low-pay, low-prestige jobs of traditional 'women's work'.[41] And for these they had to compete with the other female workers in the cities: the wives of casual day labourers, the unmarried women who had to work to support themselves and the numerous migrant maidens from the countryside.

Many guildsmen's wives worked in the textile and clothing industries. This is understandable, for these jobs were acceptable 'women's work' yet part of the guild world they knew. The few all-female guilds to survive from the Middle Ages were usually in the textile industry and the male guilds that controlled the manufacture of cloth and clothing often reserved parts of the process for their wives and daughters. In many towns only members of the all-male tailors' guild could make clothing for adults, but their wives and daughters had the exclusive right to sew children's clothes and sometimes adult clothing made from very cheap cloth. Guilds were so much a part of the textile industry that even non-guilded workers adopted their ways. In most towns seamstresses were not organized into an officially recognized guild, yet they often took on apprentices and registered the apprenticeship contracts with notaries just as guild masters did.[42]

As this suggests, employment opportunities for women in the textile and clothing industries went far beyond their guilded segments. There was, for example, piecework in putting-out systems. As we saw in the last chapter, the male urban guilds controlling textile and clothing manufacturing often farmed out parts of the processes to cheap female workers in the countryside. Townswomen also might be hired to spin thread or sew for male guild members. In Barcelona in 1628 female spinners rioted to stop the master woollen drapers from switching to women in the countryside.[43] Often the urban pieceworkers worked in their homes, as rural ones did; sometimes migrant women moved in together to work as a household and share expenses. But urban textile workers, unlike rural ones, might also be employed in large workshops, the ancestors of modern factories. In seventeenth-century Paris, for example, bonnet and stocking making was an unregulated trade dominated by 50 female entrepreneurs, who each ran workshops employing 40 to 50 women.[44]

Apart from legal piecework, women were also deeply involved in illegal manufacturing, sometimes at the behest of guildsmen and sometimes on their own. For example, in Barcelona the making of silk had once been women's work, but by the seventeenth century male guildsmen had taken it over and female silk weavers were allowed to make and sell only very small silk cloths. But the male guildsmen, restricted in the number of journeymen they could employ, often illegally hired these women to increase their production. And the women often illegally wove large pieces of silk on their own and illegally sold them at prices that undercut the legal, guild-produced merchandise.[45]

Seamstresses too often worked illegally. As we saw, the sewing of clothing was usually restricted to guilded tailors and their female relatives. But because most women knew how to sew, there was much illegal manufacturing of clothing. Male tailors illegally farmed out work to women and female seamstresses often ran their own illegal businesses, making and altering clothing for their neighbours. This was so common in seventeenth-century Paris that it was one of the arguments (the other was that it was indecent for male tailors to fit clothes on women) which Parisian seamstresses used to persuade the royal government, which licensed guilds in France, to allow them to legalize their work by forming their own all-female guild with a monopoly on the making of women's clothes. This guild soon became one of the city's largest and most successful. In the eighteenth century the hundreds of guild mistresses were prosperous enough either to marry well or to forgo marriage and head their own households of apprentices and servants.[46] But their prosperity was unusual. Because most textile and clothing industry jobs were unregulated and often illegal work for which all types of women competed, wages were generally very low.

PETTY RETAILING AND CASUAL DAY LABOUR

Another possibility for a guildsman's wife looking for an occupation was petty retailing – selling goods from a stall in a public market or peddling them from door to door. Like textile work, this had elements of the familiar world of the guilds. One of the duties of a master's wife was to sell the goods her husband produced behind the counter, in a market or door to door. It was a simple step to go from selling her husband's goods to selling those made by others. And this was a good choice because in most towns and cities at least selling at an established market was usually regulated by the local government, which restricted the right to do so to native-born citizens. Thus guildsmen's wives did not face competition from young migrant women. Neither did they usually have to compete with men. Petty retailing was recognized as 'women's work' and most towns usually granted market stall licences primarily to women. In a market in sixteenth-century Munich, for example, there were six male stallholders but 47 female ones (see Plate 10).[47]

Door-to-door peddling, however, was often unregulated and there guild wives faced competition from migrant maidens and from men. Anyone could buy a few cheap goods at a market and then try to sell them door to door at a small profit. This, plus the low earnings and erratic nature of the work, made it a bad occupational choice.

Casual day labour had the same disadvantages. Women did all sorts of casual day labour in early modern Europe. Not only did they hire themselves out as cleaning women, laundresses and nurses – acceptable female occupations – they also worked on construction sites and as stevedores and teamsters. In such jobs, they faced competition from adolescent boys and adult men, who inevitably got higher pay for the same work.

DOMESTIC SERVICE

The final legal job choice for women was domestic service. Actually this was not a choice open to guildsmen's wives, because most employers would not hire married servants. Service was also usually shunned by native-born single women; only in Rotterdam did they become servants in large numbers.[48]

Toulouse was more typical. There only 5 percent of the female servants were born in the city.[49] As this suggests, most women servants were young migrants. For them, domestic service was an obvious choice. Sometimes towns tried to make it their *only* employment option. In 1492 the city of Coventry legislated that all unmarried women take jobs as servants.[50] Many German cities had similar laws. The avowed reason for such legislation was the possibility that migrants would fall into prostitution and disrupt public order; in line with that, many towns forbade lodging-house keepers from renting rooms to single women. But behind these laws lay a fear of the independence of the 'self-breading' woman and a vision of society in which women were not workers but housewives confined to their households and guided by their husbands.

Actually domestic service had many advantages as a job for newcomers, most of which could be summed up in one word: security. First, domestic service provided a safe, easy way into the city. Female servants often avoided the difficulties of finding a job and an affordable place to live in a new and frightening environment because their employment had been arranged before they left home, by their parents, through a sister or cousin who had preceded them into town or through their lord, priest or pastor.

A second advantage of domestic service was that room and board was provided, so servants were immune from the usual lower-class hardships of seasonal unemployment and rises in the price of bread. And this led to a third advantage: because they, unlike most lower-class workers, did not have to spend most of their income on food and rent, they could actually put the bulk of their wages for their dowries.*

A final advantage of domestic service was that it might provide security in old age. Unlike rural domestics, urban servants often continued to work when they were elderly. Although their tasks varied (guildsmen's servants often helped produce goods, like the other women of the household), urban servants generally did housework, which was less physically demanding than farm labour. Therefore urban employers, unlike rural ones, did not automatically fire middle-aged or elderly domestics; their knowledge of the special ways of the household compensated for their declining strength. Indeed, urban

---

* Around 1500 there were still some urban servants in Europe who were unpaid slaves, Muslims in Venice and Christians in the Ottoman Empire. But these were fast disappearing and most servants were free wage earners. Some worked only for room and board, but most worked for cash wages and they were more likely to be paid these regularly than farm servants were.

employers often regarded servants as part of their families* and felt obliged to care for them in old age, leaving them legacies or buying places for them in charitable institutions.

But this security came at a price. Urban service had the same disadvantages – lack of independence, physical and sexual abuse – as farm service. These were heightened by the greater intimacy of master and servant in urban households. In towns servants did not sleep in barns or sheds; instead, they slept on cots or mattresses placed in odd corners or they shared a room and perhaps even a bed with their masters. This proximity, plus the intimate nature of the tasks they performed, made them very vulnerable. Samuel Pepys had a habit of propositioning his servants while they were delousing him.[51] When her pregnancy was discovered, a maid was not only almost inevitably fired; she also often faced arrest and punishment. In German cities pregnant servants were publicly shamed or beaten and then banished.[52]

The greater intimacy of urban households let masters exercise more control over their servants' lives and this often provoked resentment and misbehaviour. Masters probably subconsciously feared their servants, who after all cooked their food, raised their children and knew their most intimate secrets. This may have prompted them to pressure their town governments to bolster their authority over their servants. At any rate, theft and violence by servants were punished more severely than these crimes ordinarily were (see Chapter 13) and town governments passed numerous ordinances regulating servant behaviour. Domestics were forbidden to dress like their employers (a problem because many were given their masters' cast-off clothing as part of their wages); to leave their jobs even if offered higher wages and 'more freedom' by another employer; to drink in taverns; to pretend illness to avoid work, etc. This suggests that masters valued docility above all in a servant. So servants usually tried to keep their tempers while enduring insults and blows. They lived for their free time, when they could dress in the fine clothes they liked to buy (a signal of their earning power to a potential husband) and drink, dance and court. That, after all, was why they had come to the city in the first place.

CRIME AND PROSTITUTION

If none of their legal employment options appealed to women, or if, as often happened, they had tried legal work but failed to earn enough to support

---

* Sometimes they actually *were* family members. The English diarist Samuel Pepys employed his unmarried sister Poll as a chambermaid and ladies' maid to his wife.

themselves, they might step outside the law and take up crime or prostitution. As we shall see in Chapter 13, petty theft of clothing and household goods was one of the crimes most frequently committed by women in early modern Europe. Such thievery was the obvious expedient of the unemployed textile worker, the peddler who had not made a sale in days, the servant who had been fired for being saucy or pregnant. It was very easy for a servant to add some of her employers' clothing to her own when she left, since their employers' cast-offs often were part of her wages, and it was easy for a peddler to snatch a sheet or other bits of laundry left out to dry. These goods were taken to old-clothes dealers. They were central figures in the female networks of towns because they not only furnished clothing to the lower classes, who usually could not afford to buy cloth and hire a tailor to make something new, but also because they accepted it as collateral for short-term loans when hard times hit. This often made them fences for stolen goods.

Most urban theft fits this pattern. It was 'amateur' crime, done by women who were not habitual criminals but instead had been driven to crime by the simple need to survive. But there were also a few 'professional' female criminals in early modern towns who lived on the takings from their criminal activities. Examples are Margaretha Riechler of Memmingen, a thief who broke into homes and shops while their owners were out, and Barbara Meyer of Esslingen, a shoplifter who sewed a 'thief's bag' under her apron to conceal the goods she stole from market stalls.[53] Sometimes women were members of the criminal gangs that infested early modern cities. Although a few of these had female leaders, most of them had a strict sexual division of labour, with the men providing leadership and doing the actual robbing or killing, while the women scouted possible victims, disposed of stolen goods and provided sex for the male gangsters.[54]

Most of these female gang members were or had been prostitutes. Prostitution was the final employment option for young female migrants to cities. In the Middle Ages it had been a fairly attractive one. The Church regarded prostitution as a necessary evil, like sewers, as St Augustine famously said. Selling sexual services was sinful, but it was better that the young unmarried men in cities and towns patronize prostitutes than rape respectable girls and ruin their marriage prospects or seduce married women and imperil the lawful descent of property. Therefore municipal governments not only tolerated brothels (houses of prostitution) within their boundaries but often actually ran them themselves, paying the madam and her staff with municipal funds. Prostitutes were set apart from respectable women by laws making them

wear distinctive clothing and keep to certain areas of the city, but otherwise
they were an accepted part of urban society.[55]

[All this changed, however, with the Protestant Reformation, as we shall
see in Chapter 9. Protestants regarded all sex outside marriage as sinful and
thought prostitutes and their clients were equally guilty. To Protestants brothels
were not necessary evils but instead 'schools for sin' and they thought it
outrageous that town governments supported them.]Therefore, when Protestants gained control of a town, they usually closed down the brothels and
made both prostitution and the patronizing of prostitutes crimes. As we shall
see in Chapter 10, the Catholic Church of the Counterreformation soon
followed suit and brothels were shut down and prostitution criminalized in
most Catholic towns and cities as well. These measures did not of course end
prostitution, but they did end its role as a viable employment option for
women.[After the Reformation and Counterreformation, the 'professional'
prostitute – the woman who made her living primarily from prostitution
– more or less disappeared from early modern Europe.]She was replaced
by the 'amateur' – the unemployed servant or starving day labourer who,
when desperate, prostituted herself but when times were better resumed her
normal occupation.

Only in a few, mostly Italian, cities did prostitution remain 'professional' –
i.e. open and legal. The most important of these was Venice. Economically
declining in the early modern period, Venice increasingly lived off its reputation
as a tourist centre. Its greatest attraction was its prostitutes, said to number
20,000 (of a population of 150,000).[56] Most Venetian prostitutes were poor
migrants who could not make a more respectable living, but Venice also had
prostitutes at the high end of the sex trade, its famous courtesans. Often of
respectable, sometimes even noble, birth, these women modelled themselves
on the *hetairai* of ancient Greece, pleasing hired companions to rich and
cultivated men. They were not only beautiful, well dressed, tactful and witty;
they were also well educated in accomplishments traditional to the court lady.
Venetian courtesans could sing, play musical instruments, recite and write
poetry and even quote the classics. The nobly born Elisabetta Condulmer,
driven to prostitution because her family was too poor to dower her even
for a convent, let alone marriage, entertained her clients by playing the lute;
the patrician Veronica Franco was an excellent poet. So famous were these
Venetian courtesans that their homes, their accomplishments and even their
physical charms and their prices were listed in guidebooks to the city.[57]

Yet even for Venetian courtesans selling their sexual services was an
expedient of desperation rather than a viable employment option. Veronica

Franco gained international fame from her activities (the King of France asked to meet her when he visited Venice) and earned enough to support herself, her mother and her three illegitimate children in style. But the major theme of her writings was an attempt to create an alternate female honour to the lost sexual honour that isolated her from respectable society and left her vulnerable to charges of witchcraft and trial by the Inquisition. In her most famous writing she advised a friend to do anything to avoid making her daughter a prostitute.[58] In early modern Europe, prostitution not only was no longer an attractive employment for women, it also endangered some of their other occupational choices. As we shall see in the next chapter, one of the few bright spots for women's work in the period was the emergence of new jobs for women as singers, musicians, artists, writers and the like. But because these matched the accomplishments of courtesans, the women who practised them were open to charges of prostitution.

Apart from crime and prostitution, there was one other illegal expedient open to women trying to support themselves, that taken in seventeenth-century Holland by 15-year-old Maritgen Jens when she left her home in rural Zeeland to look for work in Amsterdam. She found a job in a silk-throwing workshop, but earned so little that she could barely stay alive. So she sold her women's clothes and began to dress as a man, although transvestism was illegal. Calling herself David Jens, she got a job in another silk workshop at much higher pay and was soon promoted to foreman.[59]

[Maritgen Jens' story is not unusual; researchers have found 119 documented cases of female transvestism in the early modern Netherlands alone.[60] (For more on this, see Chapter 14.) Most of these women were like Maritgen: they cross-dressed not because of their sexual orientation but because they could earn more as men. This points up the dismal employment opportunities available to women in early modern Europe.] Alice Clark was right to paint them as declining in this period as women were squeezed out of the guilds and men invaded lucrative fields of 'women's work' like brewing and medicine. But Clark was wrong in thinking that they had ever been good and in blaming 'capitalism' for their deterioration. A better explanation is the persistence of the patriarchal paradigm with its depiction of the world of work as a world of men and its confining of women to the home and the roles of wife and mother. Society's refusal to recognize women as independent and capable workers bore hardest on poor, young, single women like Maritgen Jens, who had to work to support themselves and save for their dowries. Their employment choices were limited to low-paying, low-prestige work at the margins of the economy. The refusal of society to recognize women as independent workers also hurt other women: artisans' wives and daughters barred from the guilds, female surgeons. But their situation was less dire and not simply because their families were better off. If middle- or upper-class women needed to work to support themselves or contribute to the family income, they could choose one of the new employment opportunities for women as artisans, musicians, actresses, writers or intellectuals. For the story of women's work in early modern Europe is not simply one of loss. It is rather one of a shift of boundaries between men's and women's work, with gains and losses on both sides. It is to the new jobs for women which opened in this period that we now turn.

Chapter 8

◆

ARTISTS, MUSICIANS, ACTRESSES, WRITERS, SCHOLARS, SCIENTISTS: NEW EMPLOYMENT OPPORTUNITIES FOR WOMEN

In 1516 the Italian poet Ariosto wrote:

> Women have arrived at excellence
> In every art in which they have striven;
> In their chosen fields their renown is apparent
> To anyone who studies the history books.
> If the world has long remained unaware of their achievements
> This sad state of affairs is only transitory;
> Perhaps envy concealed the honors due them
> Or perhaps the ignorance of historians.[1]

Ignorant no longer, today historians – and art historians, musicologists and literary critics – are busy recovering from centuries of neglect of the works of hundreds of hitherto unknown or forgotten women artists, musicians, writers, scholars and scientists. If many traditional lucrative employment opportunities for women were shrinking in the early modern period, new careers were opening up in the fields of art, literature and intellectual endeavours. Because they needed both education and talent, only a few women could take advantage of the new opportunities and they never fully replaced the jobs lost. But these new careers were better paying and more socially respectable than traditional women's work and therefore they allowed middle-class and elite spinsters to support themselves without help from their families. These careers also brought fame and prestige not only to the women artists and writers themselves but to the female sex as a whole. That women could paint, play music or write as well as men was one more very persuasive proof that men and women were equal and one more very effective argument against traditional misogyny.

WOMEN ARTISTS

Caterina van Hemessen is generally regarded as the first professional woman artist whose works survive today. She made her living as court artist to Mary of Austria, regent of the Netherlands in the middle of the sixteenth century.

There had, of course, been many women artists long before 1500. Since prehistoric times women had expressed themselves artistically through weaving and embroidering textiles and they continued to do so in our period. Even princesses were taught to embroider. Women were also active in the artistic crafts of the Middle Ages; we know of female stonemasons, goldsmiths and jewellers. As for painting, from the tenth century on nuns in their convents illuminated as well as copied manuscripts and they were the real ancestresses of the women artists of the Renaissance. When in the late Middle Ages manuscript copying and illumination moved out of the convent to become a secular industry, women practised it.[2]

And when manuscript illumination evolved first into the painting of miniatures and then into the larger easel paintings of the Renaissance, nuns pursued these new types of art. Throughout the Renaissance nuns like Andriola de Baracchis, Barbara Ragnoni and Plautilla Nelli produced religious paintings. But the Counterreformation and its rules of strict enclosure, which prevented nuns from having contact with the outside world (see Chapter 10), gradually destroyed art in the convents. Unable to get training (most artistic nuns were daughters of artists taught by their fathers before they took their vows) or to leave the cloister to undertake commissions or even to view the works of other artists, nuns had little knowledge of advances in style and technique and gradually dwindled into self-taught primitives producing works of much religious feeling but little artistic merit.[3]

The future of women artists lay in the court, not the cloister. A court's prestige depended on the skill of its artists in projecting a favourable image of its rulers and therefore during the Renaissance the artist was transformed from the humble, anonymous craftsman he had been in the Middle Ages to a creative genius sought after by kings and popes. Oddly, this elevation of the artist made it easier for women to become painters. While the new artistic genius was endowed with qualities defined as masculine – creativity, intellect, ambition, insight – it was also thought of as a sort of disembodied spirit that might appear in all sorts of unlikely people, even women. The talents of individuals were not taken as a reflection of the capabilities of their sex. Renaissance humanists also helped the emergence of the woman artist by unearthing examples – Thamyris, Irene and Marcia – of women artists from ancient Greece and Rome, a convincing argument that women could be artists to a culture that worshipped classical antiquity.[4]

But other aspects of the Renaissance made it difficult for women to have careers in art. The newly elevated artist had to fit in at court, which meant that he needed the qualities of a courtier: gentlemanly manners, tact, wit, a handsome appearance and some ability in and appreciation of music and poetry as well as art. Female courtiers – and therefore female artists – needed all of this plus an unblemished sexual reputation. But these qualities were hard to reconcile with the practical training necessary to produce a great artist, which during the Renaissance centred on life studies of nude male models, thought necessary for the large-scale historical and religious scenes that were considered the height of artistic achievement. How could a respectable young unmarried woman learn to draw nudes? How could she even leave her house unaccompanied for lessons or commissions?

Thus it is not surprising that the first generation of women artists whose works are known – Caterina van Hemessen (1528–1587), Sofonisba Anguissola (1532/5–1623) and Arcangela Paladini – emerged only at the very end of the Renaissance, around 1550. Neither is it surprising that most of them were the daughters of painters; training at home was the only kind that did not violate decorum. This generation of women artists did not compete with male artists for the lucrative and prestigious history paintings; instead it carved out its own little niche in the art market by doing portraits of or selling self-portraits to people intrigued by the novelty of a woman artist. Their self-portraits always project images of the ideal female courtier: absolute decorum plus an interest in all the arts. Anguissola depicted herself playing musical instruments and Paladini was as well known for her music and embroidery as for her painting.[5]

The first woman artist to break free of this court lady syndrome and compete directly with male artists for commissions of historical and religious paintings was Lavinia Fontana (1552–1614) of Bologna. The daughter of a painter who trained her, she preserved her sexual reputation by marrying a painter who became her assistant and bearing him 11 children. Fontana was unlucky to work in Bologna right before it changed from an artistic backwater to the centre of Italian art and to be trained in mannerism right before it was outmoded by the innovations of Caravaggio. For these reasons, art historians have never viewed Fontana as more than 'competent but unoriginal'. Yet her delicate, subtle palette and simple, unpretentious realism allow her best pictures to speak to the emotions without lapsing into sentimentality. While Anguissola, young, pretty, noble and no threat to male artists, was extravagantly praised during her lifetime, Fontana, a middle-aged mother of 11 directly competing with men, was fiercely attacked by art critics. Yet she garnered enough fame to be summoned by the pope to Rome (a noble family had its retainers fire salutes to her as she passed on her journey) and to make Bologna proud.[6] As the city, thanks to the Caracchis and Guido Reni, became the artistic centre of Italy in the seventeenth century, it remained hospitable to women artists. Prosperzia de'Rossi, the first woman sculptor, modelled statues for its cathedral and dozens of female easel painters, including the first-rate Elizabeth Sirani (1638–1665), followed in Fontana's footsteps. Sirani founded a school to train female artists, as did another female Bolognese artist, Chiara Varotari, who also wrote an 'Apology for the Female Sex'.[7]

The greatest of Fontana's successors – in fact, the greatest woman artist of the period – was not from Bologna, however, but from Rome. She was Artemisia Gentileschi (1593–1652/3).[8] Gentileschi is the only one of these early female artists to have rated a mention in art history texts before the rise of modern feminism. That is because she was among the most important followers of Caravaggio, adopting his innovations of a shallow space for composition, dramatic use of light and shadow and the portrayal of people in extremes of emotion, and helping spread them throughout the international artistic community.

Like most female artists, Gentileschi was the daughter of a painter. Orazio Gentileschi was also an important follower of Caravaggio, although he used a lighter palette and less use of light and shadow than either his master or his daughter. Orazio spotted Artemisia's talent early and began to train her to paint. Thus far her story follows the typical pattern for women artists, but in 1611, when she was 17, it took an unusual turn. Her father hired a fellow painter, Agostino Tassi, to teach her perspective. Tassi raped her and then promised her marriage – a promise he could not keep because he already had a wife. In 1612 Orazio Gentileschi took Tassi to court. The latter used the classic rapist's defence: he accused his victim of leading him on. The trial testimony shows Tassi as swaggering, boastful and thoroughly unreliable, spinning story after story, while Artemisia comes across as innocent and truthful.[9] It also shows how secluded marriageable maidens were in southern Europe: a walk or a journey in a carriage was a rare treat for Artemisia and for the rape Tassi got her alone only by getting rid of her hired chaperone. Despite the fact that Artemisia successfully maintained her innocence under torture (by cords binding her fingers – terrible for a painter!), her reputation was ruined. A marriage arranged the next year did not work, either as a marriage (her husband soon left her) or as a restorer of her reputation.

Thus Artemisia was left alone, the first woman artist to make a career by herself, without a male protector to negotiate with clients and protect her from insults. Undoubtedly, this hurt her. Much less famous and wealthy than male artists of similar talent, she lived on the edge of poverty and drifted from court to court in search of commissions. She learned to read and write so that she could negotiate with clients and understand the contracts she signed. Her letters to clients reveal the defensiveness she developed as she made her way alone in the world. To Don Antonio Ruffo, who repeatedly tried to pay her less than the agreed price, she wrote that she understood 'because a woman's name raises doubts until her work is seen' but also, triumphantly, 'I will show your Most Illustrious Lordship what a woman can do'. She warned him that she would keep fighting for what was due her: 'You will find the spirit of Caesar in the soul of this woman.'[10]

If her life experiences made Gentileschi defensive and even bitter, they also gave her subject matter: the female hero or *femme forte* (see Chapter 1). She almost always painted the heroic females of the Bible or antiquity: Lucretia, Cleopatra, Judith slaying Holofernes. These were also favourite subjects of Caravaggio and other male painters of the period, but Artemisia gave them a feminist twist: she portrayed them not as 'manly women', women reluctantly playing men's roles, but as *women*, showing a shrewd grasp of female psychology. This is obvious even to those untrained in art history. Compare Artemisia's versions of *Judith Slaying Holofernes*, in which Judith and her maid work together efficiently to get the job done (Plate 2) with male artists' Judiths, who tend to be either passive or seductive (Plate 3).

By the time of Artemisia's death in 1652, women artists had become the established and accepted norm instead of the rare exception. A major reason for this was the development of a new, middle-class art market in the Dutch Republic. Prosperous Dutch merchants had little taste for the grandiose history paintings that pleased Italian courts; what they wanted were relatively small and simple paintings – genre scenes and examples of a newly invented type of painting, the still life – to decorate their comfortable homes. This new market was tailor-made for women artists; no one minded if a woman painted a naked flower. Female painters flourished in seventeenth-century Holland, notably Clara Peeters (1594–1657?), probably one of the inventors of the still life, and Judith Leyster (1609–1660), mistress of the genre scene and probably the best female painter of the period after Gentileschi.

Although her subject matter differed from Artemisia's, Leyster too portrayed her female subjects sympathetically and shrewdly. Respectably married to a fellow painter, Leyster was not notorious like Gentileschi. But her marriage and the childbearing and housekeeping responsibilities that came with it slowed her career. Leyster was famous in her lifetime, but until recently art historians dismissed her as a mere copyist of her great colleague Franz Hals and attributed her best paintings to him.[11]

Leyster's career shows that even at the end of our period the careers of women artists were more difficult than those of men. Talented women still had problems getting training and they were still concentrated in the less prestigious genres. Female artists still were more successful if they fitted the court lady stereotype: young, attractive, witty, well educated. They still needed a spotless sexual reputation and they were expected to put aside their careers to fulfil wifely duties. They were still either extravagantly praised or harshly criticized and both their contemporaries and later art historians tended to attribute their masterpieces to their painter fathers or husbands or their male teachers. Nonetheless, by the middle of the eighteenth century, painting was an accepted career for women. Even the moderately talented could support themselves as artists. In Paris 130 of 4500 members of the artists' guild, the Academy of St Luc, were women.[12] And the outstandingly talented – the still-life painter Rachel Ruysch (1664–1750), the neo-classical history painter Angelica Kauffman (1741–1807), Rosalba Carriera (1675–1757), inventor of the pastel portrait, and the French portraitists Adélaïde Labille-Guiard (1749–1803) and Elizabeth Vigée-Lebrun (1755–1842) – received the same high fees, fame and honours (especially election to the new academies which dominated and organized the burgeoning art markets of the eighteenth century) as their male peers. Thus between 1550 and 1700 a new sort of 'women's work' had been born.

CAREERS FOR WOMEN IN MUSIC

Like the first women artists, the first female professional musicians appeared at the very end of the Renaissance, around 1550, although, again similarly to art, the foundations for their emergence had been laid in the Middle Ages, when three different types of woman participated in the creation of music. Peasant women have throughout history invented and sung folksongs, most of which are, unfortunately, lost to us. And in the Middle Ages nuns composed and performed sacred music in convents, often for public audiences; the music of the twelfth-century abbess Hildegard of Bingen is well known today. Finally, in the courts of southern France, both noblewomen and hired female troubadours, called *trobaritz*, composed and sang, often accompanying themselves on lutes and other musical instruments, songs of courtly love which gave rise to that genre of poetry.[13]

These *trobaritz* were the most direct ancestors of the female professional musicians and composers of the Renaissance. During the Renaissance peasant women continued to generate folk music and nuns continued to make music in their convents. Indeed, music took on a larger role in convent life, especially in Italy, with the invention during the Renaissance of polyphonic sacred music to supplement the earlier plain chant. This new and challenging musical style forced many convents to upgrade their musical performances by hiring lay music masters to teach the nuns and by developing orchestras to accompany the singers. Convents like San Vito in Ferrara grew famous for their choruses and orchestras, drawing visitors from all over Europe. To enrich their repertoires, many nuns began composing. The first printed collection of sacred music composed by a woman, the *Sacrae cantiones* printed in 1593, was the work of Raffaella Alcotti, a nun of San Vito. Over half the women composers whose works were published in Italy between 1566 and 1700 were nuns.[14] By the latter year, however, convent music had been severely curtailed. During the Counterreformation the decrees of the Council of Trent tried to impose enclosure on convents. This meant that the public could no longer attend performances and that convents could no longer hire lay music teachers. The decrees of Trent also forbade nuns to sing or play polyphonic music. The enforcement of these decrees depended on the local bishop and was therefore erratic, but by 1700 most bishops had acted. In 1647, for example, the bishop of Milan forbade nuns to use polyphony, hire outside teachers and play any instruments except the clavichord and organ. Similar decrees in other cities and towns gradually ended the tradition of music in convents.[15]

Thus music making by women, like female artistic endeavours, shifted from convent to court. The troubadours and *trobaritz* had made the appreciation and performance of music skills expected of both male and female court attendants. They had to be able to sing, to play at least one musical instrument and to improvise compositions to showcase these talents. They also were expected to display a knowledgeable appreciation of the performances of others. Many princes and nobles were excellent musicians. England's King Henry VIII was quite a good composer and his daughters Mary Tudor and Elizabeth I could both play a variety of instruments. Elizabeth's mother Anne Boleyn composed at least one song, 'O Death, Rock me Asleepe', aptly named considering her fate.[16] Because musical skills were so valued, the quality of what was called in Italian Renaissance courts the *musica privata* or *musica secreta* of the ruler – the private, often improvised chamber music courtiers performed nightly for their prince's entertainment – was often very high and having fine music at court brought a prince the same prestige as having his portrait painted by a famous artist.

This is how professional musicians found a place at court: rulers seeking prestige began hiring them to flesh out and improve the performances of their amateur courtiers.[17] Most of those hired were men, who were often professionally trained as composers as well as singers or musicians. It was only after Duke Alfonso II of Ferrara (as we saw, a city famous for its musical nuns) established his *concerto delle donne* in 1580 that female professional musicians became common at court. The *concerto delle donne* was an ensemble of women singers expected to perform almost nightly for Duke Alfonso. They embellished their songs with trills and cadenzas to show off their magnificent voices; these flourishes were improvised and then memorized. The *donne* were very well paid. One received a salary of 300 *scudi* a year (the Duke paid his male musicians only 135), plus a large dowry, an apartment in the palace and pensions for her husband and mother. For the Duke these were good investments: the *concerti delle donne* made his court famous.[18]

Soon envious rulers throughout Italy had their own female choruses and by the seventeenth century courts throughout Europe employed female musicians. Elizabeth-Claude Jacquet de la Guerre, a child prodigy singer, harpsichord player and composer, worked for Louis XIV at Versailles and in Vienna the very musical Hapsburgs commissioned works by female composers.[19]

The *concerti delle donne* were noblewomen trained for court service, but most of their successors – Elizabeth de la Guerre, for example – were daughters of musicians, just as most female artists were daughters of artists, and for the same reason: their fathers recognized their talent early and could give them the training they needed – a training that was almost impossible for an ordinary woman to gain. For women who were not daughters of musicians there were only two paths to a musical career: private tutoring within the home or winning a scholarship to one of the four *ospedali* (hospitals) in Venice, which were the only music conservatories that trained women.

The *ospedali* were charitable institutions caring for orphans and the incurably ill. They relied on donations for funding. Early on they discovered that public performances of sacred choral music by pathetic, angelic-looking female orphans greatly increased their intake in a city that took music seriously. So they hired famous musicians like the composer Antonio Vivaldi to train their orphans to sing and play. By the early seventeenth century, each hospital had its own all-female orchestra and chorus whose public performances were major tourist attractions. And the lessons had developed into rigorous 10-year courses that accepted fee-paying pupils from all over Europe and even had a few scholarships for poor but talented girls. After completing the course, the best students were offered positions as teachers – yet another new employment opportunity for women. Some accepted, but many left to make independent careers. Most of the famous female musicians of the eighteenth century, like the violin *virtuosa* Maddalena Lombardini Sirmin, were trained at the Venetian *ospedali*. Their course programme became the model for a new institution, the music conservatory, in all but one aspect: none of the conservatories founded in the seventeenth and eighteenth centuries on the Venetian model accepted women students. Thus training remained a problem for aspiring female musicians.[20]

WOMEN COMPOSERS

Training was an especially acute problem for female composers. As we have seen, at the beginning of the Renaissance performance and composition were almost identical because individual singers and instrumentalists improvised their material. These 'compositions', mostly madrigals, motets and solo instrumental pieces, were rarely written down and even more rarely printed. It was the growth of large ensembles – multimember choruses and instrumental groups – that led to composition in our sense of the word. Music for big groups could not be improvised: it had to be written down. This is the point at which women began to fall behind. These large-scale works were performed by *capella*, large groups of singers employed by the Church, rulers or town governments to perform in public on ceremonial occasions. These performances created a sophisticated audience with a thirst for music who proved willing to pay to hear such performances when, in the seventeenth century, they were moved into theatres and the public concert was born. But women could not be members, let alone leaders, of such choruses or the instrumental ensembles that accompanied them. This was for reasons of decorum. We have seen how the notion that respectable women did not gad about in public or gaze on male nudes restricted the training and opportunities of women artists. But artists exposed only their work to the public gaze; singers and musicians exposed *themselves* – their bodies – something no respectable woman could do. Women could perform within the confines of a court (a household, woman's natural place) or a religious institution like a convent or hospital, but not in public and especially not in public for pay. That was equivalent to prostitution. These notions not only limited employment opportunities for female musicians, they also limited their potential as composers. Chapel masters of large choirs were often entitled to free training in composition and even when they weren't they at least gained much experience in composing large-scale works: concertos, oratorios and that new art form which grew out of the oratorio, the opera. These were the most prestigious types of composition and, because of their technical complexities, the most challenging. It was in these genres that the great composers of the period broke through the boundaries of convention and took music in new directions.[21]

This meant that there were no great female composers. Although female artists were able to infiltrate male genres and become as technically accomplished as men, in music the barring of women from large-scale works and their challenges meant that female composers rarely produced more than pleasant melodies to be sung or played by solo musicians or small groups. Nonetheless, women did compose. Musicologists have found over 40 women whose musical compositions were printed between 1566 and 1700.[22] The first woman to have her compositions published, and the first woman to make her living as a composer, was Maddelena Casulana (c. 1540–c. 1590). Little is known about her life or training. She spent most of her career in Venice, where she may have played the lute and taught music. But she supported herself primarily by her compositions. She wrote only madrigals, four of which were published in a collection in 1566. They were so well received that a year later she published a book of her own works. Two more followed. Like the male composers of the period, Casulana apparently lived off the publishers' fees from these works plus gifts from the noble patrons to whom they were dedicated. In one of these dedications, to Isabella de Medici, herself a talented composer, Casulana showed the same touchy pride at being a woman in a man's field that Gentileschi showed in her letters:

I truly know, most illustrious and excellent lady, that these first fruits of mine, because of their weakness, cannot produce the effect I would like, which would be . . . to show the world . . . the vain error of men, who so believe themselves to be the possessors of the high arts of the intellect that they cannot believe themselves to have the least thing in common with women.[23]

Probably the best of the women composers who followed Casulana was Barbara Strozzi, another Venetian. She, however, was so restrained by the decorum expected of a woman of her background (she was the adopted daughter of a famous poet) that she never reached her full potential. Although a talented singer, she did not perform in public and while trained in composition by a male opera composer, she never attempted a large-scale composition but composed only *cantatas* (songs), eight volumes of which were published.[24]

The first woman to trespass into male realms and compose an opera was Francesa Caccini (1587–1640?). As might be expected, her background was different than Strozzi's. She came from a family of professional musicians; her father, mother, stepmother, brother, sister and niece all made their livings in that field and she married a musician as well. Under the chaperonage of father and husband she could perform in public; a talented singer, she first did so at age 13. Appointed court musicians to the Medicis, she and her husband were so sought after by other rulers that to satisfy them they invented the concert tour, going from court to court performing for high fees. Caccini composed as well as performed, publishing both sacred and secular choral music, as well as her opera *La liberazioni di Ruggiera dell' isola d'Alcuna*. The opera had a pronounced feminist flavour. Commissioned by two Medici princesses, it told the well-known story of the love affair of the knight Ruggiero and the sorceress Alcuna from *her* point of view, not his, as was usual in earlier versions and it had parts for an unprecedentedly large number of women's voices.[25]

WOMEN ON STAGE

By the time Caccini composed her opera, female performers were appearing on public stages in increasing numbers. In doing so, they had overcome formidable obstacles: not just the threat to their own reputations if they appeared in the public gaze but also their supposed threat to public order, for it was thought that seeing women on stage would incite men to lewd remarks, rowdy behaviour, fornication and rape. This led the pope to ban women on stages in the papal domains in 1588.[26] But such measures to keep women off stages ran into a powerful countervailing force: the desire of composers to use the full range of the human voice. In their oratorios and operas composers included parts for female voices. In the sixteenth and early seventeenth centuries, to protect public order, these were sung by countertenors and *castrati* – castrated men whose voices remained high. But their voices differed in quality and timbre from true female voices, which both audiences and composers knew from court and convent performances, and gradually in the seventeenth century female singers were allowed to take the stage. By 1700 female parts were usually sung by women, and during the eighteenth century the best female opera singers were as wealthy, famous and admired as great *divas* are today.[27]

These women opera singers paved the way for other female performers. By 1700 there were female instrumentalists performing in concerts held in public theatres both as soloists and as members of orchestras.[28] And when Louis XIV hired professional dancers to supplement the efforts of his courtiers in the ballets staged at Versailles, he hired women as well as men. Thus women were members of professional dance companies from their beginning.

ACTRESSES AND PLAYWRIGHTS

One more type of female performer appeared on public stages thanks to the opera singers: the actress. Actually, in her case it was a reappearance, for actresses had performed in plays as far back as ancient Greece. Unfortunately for the later reputation of their profession, these ancient actresses were slaves and prostitutes. The shady reputation of actresses continued during the Middle Ages. While respectable women might take the female roles in the religious mystery plays staged by medieval guilds and nuns played both men's and women's roles in the religious plays staged in convents, there were also women in the less respectable troupes of players who wandered from fair to fair and town to town, juggling, fortune-telling and performing plays, mostly bawdy comedies. Their material, their marginal lifestyle and what they did – in essence, fooling people by pretending to be what they were not – combined to give these players a very bad reputation. Male as well as female players were denied burial in consecrated ground.

It was from these ill-regarded wandering players that the first modern theatre, the *commedia dell'arte*, evolved in fifteenth-century Italy, performing comedies with risqué jokes and stock characters like Harlequin and Columbine. Women played the female parts. But when in the early sixteenth century the theatre turned serious and history plays and tragedies entered the repertoire, concerns for respectability and public morality forced actresses from the stage temporarily.[29] They were replaced by teenage boys. Women reappeared on stage at different times in different countries, first in comedies and later in the more respectable history plays and tragedies. By 1600 there were French actresses in the provinces; the first actress appeared on a Parisian stage in 1616. By then there were actresses in Spain as well. The last holdout against the female actress was England; not until 1660, when Margaret Hughes played Desdemona, did a woman take the stage.[30] Thus Shakespeare's great female parts were written to be played by actors. His numerous heroines like Viola who disguised themselves as men were played by men playing women pretending to be men and therefore had layers of sexual ambiguity lost to modern audiences.

The reappearance of women on its stages in the seventeenth century did not bring the theatre respectability; neither did the efforts to banish bawdy comedy to the fairs and popular 'boulevard' theatres and reserve playhouses for respectable dramas. The theatre retained such a bad reputation that pious women like the French queen Anne of Austria consulted their confessors before attending plays. Actors and actresses too remained beyond the bounds of respectability, despite a decree by Anne's husband King Louis XIII that they should not be 'blamed' for exercising their profession if they lived 'well'.[31] Actresses could not marry into respectable society. If they married, they married within their own milieu, wedding actors or theatre managers. Most remained single, often becoming the mistresses of noblemen or rich merchants or bankers.[32] One, La Calderona, was the mistress of Spain's King Philip IV and bore him an illegitimate son.

The continued dubious reputation of actresses meant that acting, unlike painting or music making, did not become an employment opportunity for respectable women. But for those willing to leave respectable society behind, acting was one of the most attractive sorts of women's work. The marginal world of the theatre was a meritocracy where men and women were equal and only talent counted. Many successful actresses founded and directed their own theatre companies; Molière's great love, the French actress Madeleine Béjart, is an example.[33] And even within companies founded and directed by men, actresses had power and influence. Many companies, like France's royally sponsored Comédie Française, were democracies in which the players voted on which new members to accept and which new plays to perform. In such companies actresses had equal votes with actors.[34]

Some of the freedom and equality of the marginal world of the theatre was reflected in the plays performed. Early modern playwrights seem to have found the unsavoury reputation of the theatre liberating: it gave them a licence to explore and criticize the traditional moral and gender assumptions of their audiences. Consequently, they filled the stage with female characters who challenged accepted behaviour and mores: provocative prostitutes, sympathetically portrayed adulteresses and resourceful wives and maidens who disguised themselves and took on masculine roles to get or help their men.[35]

Many of these plays were written by actors and actresses, for in the theatre, as in music, performers often composed their own material. Therefore it is not surprising that the first woman since Christine de Pisan to earn her living as a writer was the English actress Aphra Behn, who began her literary career by writing plays before she branched out into poetry and novels.[36] Little is known about Behn's life. She was probably born Aphra Johnson, the daughter of a poor English country gentleman, in 1640. In her early twenties she married the otherwise unknown Mr Behn, who quickly faded away, leaving his wife to support herself. How is not clear. She apparently spent some time in the Dutch colony of Surinam in South America. She also spied for King Charles II in the Netherlands before becoming an actress and playwright in London. Her first play was published in 1670. She wrote a total of 19, averaging one a year in the period from 1670 to the early 1680s, when they were performed in London to great acclaim and she could live off the fees paid by theatre owners for her works, mostly risqué, witty and cynical comedies like *The Rover* (1677). But by the 1680s the London theatre scene had contracted, making it harder for playwrights to live off their fees and therefore Behn branched out, publishing translations from French and Latin, poetry which discussed love and sex frankly from a woman's point of view (one of her poems, 'The Disappointment', deals with male impotence; another with a lesbian love affair), short stories and three examples of that new literary form, the novel. Of these, the most interesting is *Oroonoko*, published in 1688, which is set in Surinam and thus offers one of the earliest female accounts of the colonial experience. Its story of the noble Oroonoko, an enslaved African prince, told by a generally admiring white woman, also offers one of the earliest attacks on slavery and implied equations of slaves and women as victims of European patriarchy. Behn's poetry and fiction were successful and well regarded but not as profitable as her plays. She probably died in poverty in 1689.

WOMEN WRITERS AND 'LEARNED LADIES'

Aphra Behn was the first woman to support herself by writing for a modern mass-market audience, but she was not the first woman writer or even the first woman to support herself by her pen. As we have already seen, that distinction belonged to the famous Christine de Pisan (1369–1429), author of the anti-misogynist *Book of the City of Ladies* and initiator of the *querelle des femmes*.

As Pisan's dates suggest, the professional woman writer appeared earlier than the female artist and musician, at the dawn of the Renaissance rather than at its end. In part because of this timing, the pioneer women writers had an even harder time of it than the other female professionals. As with art and music, getting the right training was a formidable problem, the training in this case being a humanistic education in Latin and even Greek so that one could read the ancient classics that set the standards of literary excellence. As we have seen, education in the classics was deemed suitable only for royal and noble women who might have to play a role in the public sphere. Otherwise, the only women suitably educated for careers as writers and intellectuals in this early stage were daughters of humanists trained by their fathers, who saw the commercial potential of learned female prodigies. Pisan herself fitted this pattern. The daughter of an Italian humanist employed as royal astrologer in the French court, Pisan was educated by her father and succeeded to his royal patronage, indiscriminately supplying whatever her royal clients wanted: courtly love poetry, flattering royal biographies, theological and philosophical speculations and even a military manual for knights. Pisan's successors found it more difficult to make a career. Cassandra Fedele, for example, was the daughter of a Venetian humanist and state bureaucrat who had her trained in Latin, Greek, rhetoric, history and philosophy and orchestrated her career as a female prodigy giving public orations in Padua and Venice. This back-fired, however. When Isabella of Spain invited Fedele to court, the Venetian senate refused to let her leave, declaring her a national treasure. It did not, however, vote her a pension and she died in poverty.[37] So too did the once promising Laura Cereta, daughter of a learned physician. Attacked by the Church for her outspokenness, she stopped publishing at age 18 and withdrew into lady-like silence.[38]

Cereta's withdrawal is not surprising. Another major barrier to the emergence of the woman writer was the fact that if she went public – published her work or, as was the custom in Italy, entered public rhetorical contests and gave public recitations – her chastity was inevitably attacked. The equation public (published) woman = prostitute was even more likely to be made for these early humanists than for other female professionals, because they were early pioneers and people were not yet used to women in the public sphere, because the male humanists with whom they competed were acutely conscious that they had to prostitute their talent by flattering noble patrons to get publication and pensions and because, as we have seen, some female writers of the period actually *were* prostitutes; the famous Venetian courtesan Veronica Franco is an example. At any rate, attacks on the virtue of women humanists were frequent and vicious. Fifteenth-century noblewoman Isotta Nogarola was accused of not just promiscuity but incest:

> Before she made her body generally available for promiscuous intercourse, she had first permitted, and indeed even earnestly desired, that the seal of her virginity be broken by none other than her brother . . . she who sets herself no limit in this filthy lust dares to engage so deeply in the finest literary studies.[39]

Not surprisingly, after this attack Nogarola withdrew from the public literary world at age 23 and thereafter lived the life of a secular nun, seeing no one but women so her virtue could not be doubted. Also not surprisingly, she adopted a pose of cringing deference toward the male scholars with whom she competed:

> It should be little wondered at . . . if . . . a fearful tremor run through my bones . . . when I realize that I was born a woman, who breaks words rather than pronounces them, and since I write to you, whose eloquence and force of sweetness of style are so great . . .[40]

This self-deprecation was typical of early women writers. One of the few to follow Christine de Pisan, secure in her royal patronage, and defend women and their worth in the *querelle des femmes* was the Venetian Modesta da Pozzo, author of *Women's Worth* (1600), who had both a pseudonym (Moderata Fonte, 'moderate fountain' of words) and a husband to protect her.[41]

By the time *Women's Worth* was published, the Reformation and the Catholic response to it had transformed the world of the woman writer (see Chapters 9 and 10). First, they gave women a marvellous excuse to write about a hitherto 'masculine' subject: religion. They could say that although they were mere women, God was using them as His instrument and they were writing at His dictation. The English Quakeress Susannah Blandford wrote that she was 'incouraged by the Immortal God to Print this'.[42] Further, the Protestant wish that everyone, even women, be able to read the Bible themselves greatly widened the pool of female readers and potential writers. Finally, the Reformation and Counterreformation encouraged writing in the vernacular and therefore took literature from the rarified realm of Greek, Latin and high classical culture, simplified its style and turned it toward matters of daily life – in other words, toward areas familiar to women that they could write about with some expertise.

This split into two what had formerly been one: the 'learned lady' and the woman writer. Knowledge of Latin, Greek and classical culture continued to be important in the sixteenth and seventeenth centuries and a few women continued to acquire these 'masculine' attributes and even, by the seventeenth century, to use them to support themselves as intellectuals, as we shall see later in this chapter. But knowledge of classical culture was no longer a prerequisite for a writer and by the end of the seventeenth century hundreds of ordinary women were taking up their pens and making literary careers.

We can trace these changes best in England, where women writers and the market they wrote for have been carefully studied. England shows, first of all, the typical growth of women readers and writers, although it happened only in the last half of the seventeenth century. In the 1640s around 10 percent of Englishwomen could read and write; by 1700 the figure was probably 30 percent. Publishers responded to this new market by printing more books specifically targeted for women readers. From 1475 to 1570, 24 such books were published; from 1570 to 1640, the total was 139 and after that it rose substantially. And with the growth of women readers came more women writers. From 1616 to 1640, only 0.5 percent of the books published in England were authored by women, but from 1640 to 1700 the figure more than doubled, to 1.2 percent.[43]

What did these female authors write about? Above all, their religious beliefs and experiences. Nearly half (46 percent) of the works published by women in the seventeenth century were religious.[44] This total is unusually high because England had many Quakeresses who published religious testimonies; in other countries, especially Catholic ones like Spain and France, the percentage of women's works dealing with religion is smaller but still forms the largest single category of women's writings.

Women also published secular works, especially in areas deemed suitable for women. They frequently wrote on 'female' subjects like housewifery, child-rearing, and female medicine. Such 'how-to' books were as much a staple of the publishing industry then as today, and women writers could fill this lucrative niche with no loss of decorum. In 1609 the French royal midwife Louise Bourgeois published a handbook for her fellow practitioners; later in the century English midwives like Jane Sharp followed her example. Sharp not only gave practical advice, she also defended her fellow midwives, whom she called 'sisters', against the incursion of male doctors into that traditionally female profession. Male doctors might have book learning, she argued, but midwives had practical experience, which they carefully passed on to their successors.[45] Female healer Mary Trye took a similar stance in defending empirics, both men and women (she was the daughter of a male chemist and empirical healer), against attacks by the Royal College of Physicians in her *Medicatrix, Or, The Woman-Physician* (1675).[46] Defending their profession was not the only motive that inspired women medical practitioners to take up the pen: personal gain was also involved. Two female healers, Sarah Jinner and Mary Holden, supported themselves by invading one of the most lucrative areas of publishing: the almanac market.[47] Almanacs were extremely popular (and therefore profitable for publishers, who paid high fees to their authors) because they combined stories and folk proverbs with practical advice for farming, housekeeping and medical treatment and with predictions and prophesies. As such, they were tailor-made for a woman healer who often was, as Mary Holden advertised herself in the title page of her *The Woman's Almanack*, both 'midwife . . . and student in physic and astrology'.[48] Jinner and Holden both blatantly boasted about their medical and astrological successes in their almanacs. Thus they profited from their pens both directly, through publishers' fees for their writings, and indirectly, through the publicity their almanacs gave to their medical and astrological careers. This tactic was also adopted by Hannah Wolley, the first Englishwoman to invade another lucrative but hitherto masculine genre, that of the household advice book. In 1661 Wolley, who had worked as a domestic servant before marrying a schoolteacher, published *The Ladies Directory*, the first of a long line of domestic manuals with titles like *The Cooks Guide*, *The Compleat Servant-Maid*, and *The Gentlewomans Companion*. In them, between recipes, medical remedies, and advice on hiring servants, she plugged herself as a trainer of housewives, offering a seven-year apprenticeship in that difficult art.[49] Similarly, writers of educational treatises and childrearing manuals were usually governesses or schoolmistresses like Bathsua Makin (see Chapter 2); again their books themselves made money, but they also advertised their authors' educational services.[50]

Not all educational treatises and childrearing manuals were written for profit. Elizabeth Grymeston, Dorothy Leigh and Elizabeth Joceline authored childrearing manuals published in 1604, 1616 and 1624 respectively and in 1622 the Countess of Lincoln wrote to persuade mothers to breastfeed their babies. Gentlewomen all, these women wrote to express themselves, not support themselves.[51] In fact, writing as a mother advising other mothers or her children was a convenient excuse for women to produce all sorts of works otherwise prohibited to them. Histories are an example; they were considered masculine not only in subject matter (wars and affairs of state) but also in form (the best models were ancient and required a knowledge of the classics). Yet many women wrote histories under the guise of preserving the glories of their families for their children. Lucy Hutchinson, for one, produced the best chronicle of the English Civil War at the local level in her *Memoirs of the Life of Colonel Hutchinson*; as the title suggests, her excuse for writing was to preserve the brave deeds of her husband for her children.

Writing for the edification of children also provided an excuse for women to write autobiographies; Ann Fanshawe, for example, produced her *Memoirs* ostensibly for the edification of her eldest son. She described her book as being about 'the most remarkable accidents of your family as well as those more eminent ones of your father and my life'; in fact, it was about the last.[52]

Women were not supposed to write, let alone publish, autobiographies. Their petty domestically oriented lives were not thought of interest to anyone but their immediate families. Yet increasing numbers did so in the seventeenth century. More and more women also recorded the events of their lives in diaries and in long letters to friends. These two genres were permissible for women because they were thought to be written in spontaneous speech, the sort of language for which everyone, even women and children, had the necessary facility, as opposed to the consciously shaped language of the learned genres of writing, which could only be mastered by men.[53] But of course no writing is spontaneous. All writing is shaped by an author and long letter sequences like Madame de Sévigné's were carefully crafted in anticipation that they would be circulated among friends and maybe even published after their author was safely dead. In England, gentlewoman Dorothy Osborne despised the notorious Duchess of Newcastle for seeking to publish her writings:

> Sure the poor woman is a little distracted, she could never be so ridiculous else as to venture at writing books.[54]

Yet Osborne herself carefully crafted her letters to her suitor and later husband William Temple with an eye to posthumous publication. At any rate, autobiographies, diaries and letters gave women writers practice in shaping meaningful and coherent narratives of the events of daily life and of their own emotions and their familiarity with these two subjects would allow them to triumph in that new genre, the novel, when it appeared on the literary scene.

That scene was different from the modern one. For one thing, genres and the boundaries between them were not as fixed as they are today. Fiction and non-fiction mingled, each sharing some characteristics of the other. Fictional stories were often couched in non-fictional forms (many early novels, like *Robinson Crusoe*, were fake autobiographies), while fictional events and speeches clogged supposedly factual histories.[55]

Similarly tenuous was the border between poetry and prose. Much of the poetry of the early modern period took the form of the Petrarchan love sonnet, which women wrote from a female point of view. In sonnets by men they were objects of male desire, but in their own they were loving mistresses (Isabella Whitney, fl. 1567–1578), disillusioned courtesans (Veronica Franco,

1546–1591), lesbian lovers (Katherine Philips, 1632–1664), brides of Christ (Juana de la Cruz, 1648–1695) and devoted Puritan wives (Ann Bradstreet, 1612–1672). The other favoured form of poetry was the romance, which was also found in prose. The romance was characterized by exotic settings and unbelievable turns of plot which highlighted the fact that it was fiction and by characters with strange, exotic-sounding names impelled by high ideals to perform almost impossible deeds. The best known poetic romance written by a woman is *Urania* (1621), whose author, Lady Mary Wroth, niece of the famous writer of poetic romance, Sir Philip Sidney, hoped to avoid debtors' prison by its profits.[56] She didn't. Even male poets could not support themselves by their poetry alone in the early seventeenth century. Only when the other type of the romance, that in prose, evolved into the novel did female creative writers have a vehicle to support their careers.

Many authorities begin the story of the evolution of the romance into the novel with Boccaccio's *Decameron* (1348–1351), a collection of short romances set into a narrative frame: they were supposedly stories told by young aristocrats to ease their boredom while in the country avoiding the plague. This device of the short story (called *novella* in Italian, *nouvelle* in French, and *novela* in Spanish) set in a narrative frame was widely adopted by other writers, including women, notably the French royal 'learned lady' Marguerite de Navarre. Her *Heptameron* of 1558 was a set of linked stories about sacred and profane love told from a woman's point of view.[57] By the seventeenth century, a group of women writers in Spain had turned the *novela* into a vehicle for presenting criticisms of the way society treated women. For example, Maria de Zaya's *Disenchantments of Love* (1647) was deliberately written to 'change the world'. It highlighted the issue of violence against women, found even more frequently in male-authored romances than in real life. In six of its 10 stories, all written from the woman's point of view, innocent women are murdered by their supposed patriarchal protectors, fathers, brothers and husbands, to guard masculine honour; in the other four, they endure domestic violence before finding havens in convents.[58]

Meanwhile, Spain also produced what most authorities label the first novel, when Zaya's master and model Cervantes wrote his *Don Quixote* (1605, 1615). Although it contained a series of romance-plotted tales, it was a novel, not a *novela* (which Cervantes also wrote) because it was long, the narrative frame was more prominent than the individual stories and the fantastic elements of the romance were played down in favour of an accurate depiction of contemporary reality. In fact, the plot of *Don Quixote* turns on the impossibility of living the high ideals of romance in the unromantic contemporary world.

Plate 1 *The Four Humours.* As this shows, the humours were thought to determine a person's sexual identity as well as his or her personality (Topfoto/The British Library/HIP).

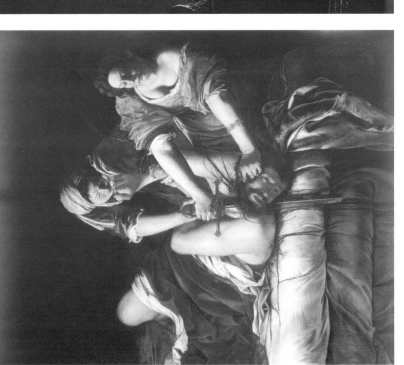

Plates 2A and B Plate 2A: *Judith Slaying Holofernes*, Artemisia Gentileschi. Plate 2B: *Judith and Her Maidservant with the Head of Holofernes*, Artemisia Gentileschi. Judith slaying Holofernes, as depicted by a female artist, the great Artemisia Gentileschi (Plate 2A: Corbis/Summerfield Press; Plate 2B: The Detroit Institute of Arts, USA/Bridgeman Art Library).

Plates 3A and B Plate 3A: *Judith Slaying Holofernes*, Niccolo Renieri. Plate 3B: *Judith with the Head of Holofernes*, Cristofano Allori. The slaying of Holofernes, as depicted by male artists (Plate 3A: AKG Images/Cameraphoto/Galleria dell'Accademia; Plate 3B: Corbis/Arte & Immagini sri)

Plate 4 *The Virgin and Saint Anne*, school of Caravaggio. This depiction of mother and child shows the central role a mother played in educating her daughter. It also shows that this 'education' was not booklearning but, rather, practical training for the girl's future role in life – in this case, the spinning and lace making of a competent housewife (Fratelli Alinari).

Plate 5 *Sor Juana de la Cruz*, Miguel Cabrera. This portrait of a nun, the South American feminist Sor Juana de la Cruz, in her cell, shows how comfortable life in a convent could be. Note Sor Juana's books and elegant clock and inkstand (Mexico City: Instituto Nacional de Antropologia e Historia, Museo Nacional de Historia Topfoto/Topham Picture Point).

LA FOLIE DES HOMMES.

La Femme porte Le Fuzi l.v. mari porte L'enfan sot ses Genou

Plates 6A and B   Plate 6A (top): *The World Right Side Up*. Plate 6B (bottom): *The World Turned Upside Down*. These cheap popular woodcuts show the expected gender roles of husband and wife. In the world as it should be, the husband leaves the house for the masculine world of the hunt, while the wife stays home and spins. In the world turned upside down, the wife leaves home in the masculine role of warrior and it is the husband who spins and tends the swaddled baby (Plate 6A: Mary Evans Picture Library).

Rofegarten
Das vierd Capitelfagt wie

fich ein yede fraw/un/vo:/vnd nach der geburt halte foll
vnd wie man ir in harter geburt zü hilff kommen foll.

Plate 7 A woman in labour. A mother-to-be sits on a birthing chair and is assisted, as most women were, by a midwife and a female neighbour (from: *Alte Meister der Medezin und Natur-Kunde in Facsimile – Ausgaben und Neudrucken nach Werken der 15.–18. Jahrhunderts* (Munich, 1910)).

Plate 8 The widow of Martin Luther in mourning, Lucas Cranach the Elder. We do not know if widows actually bound their mouth as shown here. Nonetheless, the image symbolizes the quiet lives, withdrawn from the world, that widows were expected to lead (Gotha: Schlossmuseum).

Plate 9 *Old Woman Saying Grace ('The Prayer Without End')*, Nicolaes Maes. Elderly women were usually not portrayed as individuals. Instead, as here, they were used as generic symbols of decay and death (AKG Images/ Rijksmuseum, Amsterdam).

Plate 10 *The Fish Vendor*, Adriaen van Ostade. One of the few areas of the economy dominated by women was petty retailing. Most market stallholders, like this fish-seller, and door-to-door pedlars were female (Szepmuvesz eti Museum, Budapest).

Plate 11 *Devil Seducing Witch*. This illustrates how witch beliefs grew from
deep-seated fears of female sexuality (illustration for Ulrich Muller
(Molitoris), *Von den Unholden und Hexen* (Konstanz, [1489?]/Mary Evans
Picture Library).

Plate 12   *The Birth of Louis XIII*, Peter Paul Rubens. Marie de Medici, like all queens who ruled as regents for their sons, exercised power because of their motherhood. In this painting she commissioned, that is celebrated. She is portrayed as Ceres, goddess of the earth and its abundance, and not only is her son Louis XIII shown but also, in the flowers to her right, the faces of her other children (Giraudon, Louvre, Paris, France/Bridgeman Art Library).

Cervantes' invention was refined and perfected in France by a group of noble 'learned ladies' and *femmes fortes* who turned from political activism to literary endeavours after the defeat of the Fronde.[59] In 1649 Madeleine de Scudéry produced the first volumes of her enormously long novel *Artamène*. While it retained the fantastic names and setting (the court of the ancient Persian emperor Cyrus) of the romance, the politics of the book were contemporary and the action was clogged with dialogue in which the characters debated contemporary ideas. In her *Clélie* (1654–1660), Scudéry completely abandoned the elements of romance. This novel had a contemporary setting in the literary *salons* Scudéry frequented; the characters were modelled on her friends and dialogue and character sketches replaced action. Finally, in 1667 another *salonnière*, Madame de Lafayette, produced what critics agree is the first modern novel, *La Princesse de Clèves*, a short, tightly constructed account of a doomed love affair focusing on the characters' psychology.

By the early eighteenth century the novel was flourishing in England, Spain and the German states and many of its writers were women. In France, for example, one-third of the novels published between 1687 and 1699 had female authors.[60] With the emergence of the periodical press (the first modern magazine, *The Spectator*, began publication in 1711 and was soon imitated throughout Europe), a female author could easily piece together a living by selling her novels and short story collections to publishers and by writing essays and book reviews for periodicals. Women might even edit the new journals. Eliza Haywood founded *The Female Spectator*, aimed at women readers, in 1744, and its French counterpart, the *Journal des Dames*, had two women editors.[61]

FEMALE TRANSLATORS AND LINGUISTS

By the early eighteenth century such literary hackwork also supported the remnants of the Renaissance 'learned ladies' who had been split from creative writers by the Reformation. These women, distinguished by their knowledge of Latin, Greek and classical culture, were now linguists, not writers; they studied the languages for their own sakes, not for the fine points of literary style. As such, they could make a living teaching, writing essays and, above all, by doing translations. This was one more type of literary work traditionally permitted to women. As a sixteenth-century male translator sadly noted, 'all mens conceipts . . . are their owne' but 'all translations are reputed femalls, delivered at second hand'; in other words, original works needed 'male' creativity, but translations were, like women themselves, mere copies of originals and therefore could be done by women.[62]

Female linguists could not, however, make a career as male linguists did by winning a post at a university, an institution which, in this period when knowledge was increasingly professionalized, became the centre of higher learning. Since their founding by churchmen in the Middle Ages, universities had been what historian David Noble calls 'worlds without women'.[63] A Dutchwoman, Anna Maria van Schurman (1607–1678), was widely acknowledged to be the foremost expert on ancient languages in seventeenth-century Europe. In addition to Latin and Greek, she knew Hebrew, Chaldean, Arabic and Syrian, which she had studied at the University of Utrecht – safely out of sight of the male students. But she never held a university post and she kept the respect of male scholars only by displaying a proper female modesty, living chastely, never criticizing her male rivals and cultivating 'feminine' accomplishments like art, music and needlework as well as her languages.[64] Similarly, another woman linguist, the Venetian noblewoman Elena Cornaro Piscopia, studied Hebrew, Arabic and Chaldean at a university and became the first woman to receive a PhD, which was granted by the University of Padua in 1678. But she too never held a university post and she too had to display the requisite female modesty, living in a convent and saying as she rose for her PhD oral, 'This I cannot do, because after all I am only a woman.' Despite her modesty, and despite the rumour that 20,000 people had come to Padua to see her receive her degree, the university rectors resolved never again to award one to a woman.[65]

Thus by 1700 women's scholarly achievements were widely recognized, but only if they showed appropriate female modesty. And while women could support themselves by their scholarship, their career paths were different from and less lucrative than those of men.

WOMEN SCIENTISTS

This was also true of female scientists. To us science and mathematics are the fields thought least hospitable to women, those where, despite decades of affirmative action, female scholars are still scarce. This was not true in the early modern period. From 1500 to 1700 it was the humanities and the classical languages that were thought unsuitable for women because they prepared one for a career in the public sphere. Science, by way of contrast, was an acceptable field of study for women. The main thrust of the biology, geology and astronomy of the period was toward observation and classification and these required not 'masculine' original thought but only the 'feminine' qualities of patience and care over details. Similarly, the crude experiments of the chemists and physicists were thought akin to the preparing of remedies in medicine and the transformation of food in cookery (often called 'kitchen physick'), both acceptably female endeavours.[66]

The early modern period was the heyday of the amateur scientist, usually noble, who collected ostrich eggs, mineral ores and fossils for his 'cabinet of curiosities', peered at insects through the newly invented microscope and tracked planetary orbits through the newly invented telescope. Many of these noble scientific 'virtuosi' were women. The French baroness Martine de Beausoleil was the first woman geologist; she studied mathematics, chemistry, mechanics and hydraulics and published in 1632 a sound handbook on mining and metallurgy. The Italian Isabella Cortese was a skilled herbalist and practical chemist who published her recipes for medicines and cosmetics in 1561.[67] Another Frenchwoman, Marie Meurdrac, published a basic chemistry text for women in 1666. In its forward she showed that blend of female diffidence and confidence in her own talents that typified the female practitioners of these new careers in the arts and sciences:

> When I began this little treatise, it was solely for my own satisfaction . . . upon seeing it completed better than I dared to hope, I was tempted to publish it: but . . . I objected to myself that it was not the profession of a lady to teach; that she should remain silent, listen and learn . . . that it is above her station to offer a work to the public and that . . . men always scorn and blame the products of a woman's wit . . . On the other hand, I flattered myself that I am not the first lady to have had something published; that minds have no sex and that if the minds of women were cultivated like those of men . . . they would equal those of the latter.[68]

The vogue for scientific study allowed women to support themselves as scientists. An example is the Dutchwoman Maria Sybilla Merian (1647–1717). The daughter and stepdaughter of artists, she was trained as an artist herself, and soon specialized in careful, scientifically correct drawings and prints of flowers and plants. Fascinated by the insects on her models, she became one of Europe's best entomologists, the first to trace and illustrate the stages of life of moths and butterflies. Merian eventually converted to a radical Protestant sect, left her husband and took her two daughters with her to the Dutch South American colony of Surinam, where they collected plant and insect specimens. Back in Holland she supported herself by selling these and the illustrations she made of them.[69]

Note the artisanal, family-centred, pieced-together nature of Merian's career. This was the standard career pattern for female scientists. Women astronomers, for example (of whom there were a great many in the seventeenth century, when scientists were fascinated by the new Copernican solar system), usually could make a career only as part of a family and only by doing hackwork publishing. Maria Winckelmann Kirch (1670–1720) is the standard example. Trained in astronomy as a girl, she married astronomer Gottfried Kirch and helped him with his work, while also producing, with the assistance of his sisters, the astrological tables for almanacs which provided most of the family income even after Kirch was appointed Royal Astronomer to the Prussian court in 1700. It was soon obvious that Winkelmann was a better astronomer than her husband. She discovered a comet in 1702 and published the standard works on the conjunction of the planets and the aurora borealis. When her husband died in 1710, there was some talk of appointing Winkelmann in his place, but the Prussian Academy thought Prussia would be the laughing-stock of Europe with a female Royal Astronomer. Eventually her son, whom she had trained, was appointed, with the proviso that his mother stay in his household and help him in his work. She did, while continuing with the almanac tables that were still the family's main income.[70]

The fuss over Winkelmann shows the limits of female careers in the sciences. While women could support themselves by scientific hackwork, the prizes of the profession – court and university appointments – eluded them. Only one female scientist held a university chair in the first half of the eighteenth century. This was the Italian physicist Laura Bassi, the second woman to receive a PhD. She was appointed to the faculty of the University of Bologna in 1732, largely through luck: Bologna's reputation was declining and it wanted to catch people's attention by appointing a woman. At first Bassi gave only lectures open to the public and was not allowed to teach regular classes, but gradually, through her learning and tact (she always displayed the proper female modesty), she gained regular faculty status.[71] But she was the exception; the rule was a distinct female career pattern of scientific hackwork.

Yet women could make careers in the sciences – and in the arts – in the early modern period. This significantly improved their status. Not only did it provide a respectable alternative to marriage, especially for middle-class women, it also changed gender stereotypes by showing that intelligence and creativity 'had no sex'; they were traits of individuals, not genders. This provides the best evidence against Clark's thesis. Clark assumed that women's competence in traditional women's work had earned them respect and high status, in the Middle Ages, both lost when these jobs were lost. As we have seen, this was not true. Only these new careers in the arts and sciences, which Clark did not discuss, brought women status and respect.

Part IV

WOMEN AND RELIGION

The second sphere into which the women of early modern Europe fitted uneasily was religion. That was because the teachings about women in all three of Europe's great religions, the minority faiths of Judaism and Islam as well as the Christianity of the vast majority of Europe's inhabitants, were ambivalent and contradictory. All three taught that women were men's spiritual equals, equally capable with men of living righteous lives and, in the case of Muslims and Christians, attaining a place in paradise, yet all three also taught that women were less intelligent and self-controlled than men and more inclined to sin and therefore needed male guidance. All taught that women were created men's temporal equals and given equally with men dominance over the earth and its creatures, yet all three also taught that women were created to be the helpmeets of men and that a God-ordained society was one which confined them to the domestic sphere and familial roles as wives and mothers. Therefore all barred them from any formal role in their all-male priesthoods, yet all realized that the future success of their religions depended on their female adherents, for it was they who gave birth to future believers and gave them their earliest lessons in religion.

This role of women in what is called the 'social reproduction' of religion – the preserving and passing down of religious traditions from generation to generation – was especially important to the minority faiths, Judaism and Islam. Muslims, of course, could practise their faith openly in the parts of eastern and central Europe controlled by the Ottoman Empire, but in Spain after the fall of the last Muslim stronghold in Granada in 1492, they had to convert to Catholicism or leave. From 1502 until the remaining 30,000 of them were expelled in 1609, Spain's Muslims, called *moriscos*, were not only forbidden to practise their religion but also to continue the many cultural practices – the veiling and seclusion of women, polygamy, dietary prohibitions against alcohol and pork, etc. – associated with it and they were required to live among Christians, raise their children as Christians and marry them to Christians and bury their dead in Christian cemeteries. Breaking these laws could lead to arrest and trial by the dread Inquisition, the Church court entrusted with investigating and rooting out heresy. In these circumstances it was above all the devotion of the *moriscas*, the Muslim women, that kept their faith alive. This was facilitated by their traditional seclusion within the home. There they could quietly observe the Muslim dietary laws and the fast of Ramadan, lay out their dead in the Muslim manner, circumcise their male babies and teach their children Muslim prayers and practices.[1] It was the persistence of Islam among the *moriscos*, largely through such efforts by women, that led the Spanish government to recognize that its attempts at conversion had failed and to expel the *moriscos* in 1609.

Women were also important to the survival and growth of Judaism and Jewish culture in early modern Europe. Like the *moriscos*, the Jews in Spain and Portugal were forced to convert to Christianity (thus becoming *conversos*) or leave. This initiated a new phase in the history of European Jewry, as the centre of Jewish life shifted from Spain and Portugal to those areas where the Sephardim (the Spanish and Portuguese Jews) found refuge – Italy, the German states and Poland. In the latter the number of Jews went from a few thousand in the Middle Ages to 150,000 in 1660 and 750,000 in 1764.[2] In central and eastern Europe, Jews lived in those cities and towns that allowed them to settle in return for hefty payments. Often in these cities they were confined to *ghettos*, privileged neighbourhoods where, so long as they paid their fees and obeyed laws forbidding them to employ Christian servants, profane the Christian sabbath and enter the army, the legal profession and the guilds, they were allowed to govern themselves. The first *ghetto* was established in Venice in 1516; the word means foundry, because Venice's *ghetto* was near its famous foundry. Within the *ghettos* men dominated the elected governing councils and ran the synagogues and it was they who kept alive the tradition of rabbinical scholarship in Hebrew, the written language of male Jews throughout Europe. But it was the women who perpetuated Jewish popular culture: it was they who saw to it that the dietary and other regulations making a Jewish home were kept and it was they who passed on to their children the rich accumulation of proverbs and folktales in Yiddish, known as the 'woman's language' in this period.[3]

Women also contributed to the 'social reproduction' of Christianity, but because it was the faith of the vast majority of Europeans, it was in no danger of dying out. The major theme of the history of Christianity in the years from 1500 to 1700 is not survival but schism. Even in 1500 Christianity was a divided faith, with two basic branches, the Latin Church of western Europe led by the pope in Rome and the Greek, Ukrainian and Russian Orthodox Churches in the east. In the two centuries after 1500, both these branches would experience further bitter divisions. In Russia around 1650 Czar Alexei, attempting to open his isolated country to outside intellectual influences, encouraged Archbishop Nikon, head of the Russian Orthodox Church, to reinterpret religious texts in the light of the best recent Greek and Ukrainian scholarship and to remake the Russian church service, substituting the three-fingered Greek sign of the cross for the traditional two-fingered Russian one. Nikon's reforms brought a wave of protest from the so-called Old Believers, who clung to traditional practices despite government prosecution. By the 1670s, thousands of peasants had fled to the Cossack lands of the east, out of reach of the government, and thousands more had set themselves on fire to protest against the arrest and execution of Old Believers. Women played prominent roles in the Old Believer movement, from the nuns from elite families who protected and sheltered Old Believers in their convents to peasants like the widow Katerina Palitsyna, who stated at her trial that she:

> accepted and held to the Christian faith into which she was baptised as a baby and in which she had been instructed since babyhood. But she did not hold with the present teachings on the faith . . . And she knew the cross which she had been taught since babyhood, but did not recognise or honour the four-pointed cross.[4]

The death and disruption which came in the wake of the Old Believer movement pale into insignificance, however, in comparison with the effects of the schism in the western Latin church, the Protestant Reformation. Beginning in 1517, the Reformation created two centuries of turmoil in western Christendom, permanently splitting the Church into two warring branches, Catholic and Protestant, and inaugurating 150 years of religious warfare that would transform the balance of power in Europe. The Reformation also transformed women's lives. Not only did they play prominent roles on both sides of the conflict, but the Reformation prompted a rethinking of the nature of women and their proper roles in society – a rethinking that would bring some losses but more gains and end in raising the status of women, Protestant and Catholic alike. Because the Reformation was such a landmark in women's history, we will devote the bulk of this part to it.

Chapter 9

◆

WIVES, PREACHERS, MARTYRS: WOMEN IN THE PROTESTANT REFORMATION

When in 1517 a German monk, Brother Martin Luther, nailed 95 theses about sin and salvation to the door of his parish church in Wittenberg and started the Reformation, he did not intend to change the lives of women. He did not even intend to leave the Catholic Church and found a new one. All he wanted to do was to end abuses in the sale of indulgences, a money-making device the Church advertised as a means of absolving sinners of the penalties for their sins and shortening their time in Purgatory. Long tormented by a sense of his own sinfulness and utter unworthiness of salvation, Luther had, through careful study of the Bible and the writings of the founder of his order, St Augustine, concluded that human beings were so sunk in sin that nothing they could do, no amount of prayer and pleading, repentance and good works – and certainly not the purchase of an indulgence – could cancel it out. But God in His infinite mercy had taken pity on fallen mankind and, through Jesus' sacrifice on the cross, opened up the possibility of salvation. All that was necessary to be saved was to have faith. This doctrine, which formed the basis of both Luther's 95 theses and Protestantism, was not by itself heretical. But the Church's overreaction to Luther's challenge and Luther's own stubborn refusal to acknowledge the Church's authority soon pushed Luther over the line into heresy. Relying on the Bible as the Word of God and therefore the sole source of authority in religious matters, Luther soon broke with Catholicism. He then redefined the nature and organization of the Church, its relationship to lay society, how that society should be organized and women's proper role within it.

PROTESTANT TEACHINGS ON WOMEN AND SEX

The main tenet of Protestantism was reliance on the scriptures, because the Bible embodied Christianity as it was in its early days, as God intended it to be, before the Church's lust for power and money distorted it. For women, going back to the scriptures meant that Protestants rediscovered the spiritual equality of men and women in early Christianity: 'There is neither Jew nor Greek, there is neither slave nor free, there is neither male nor female, for you are all one in Christ Jesus.' Men and women were equal in the sight of God and could equally attain salvation. To restore this spiritual equality, Luther had to reinterpret the text that lay behind the notion that women were spiritually inferior to men: the story of Eve. In Luther's interpretation of Genesis, Eve was neither an afterthought nor was she created just to be a companion to man. She had her own vital role to play in God's scheme: she would give birth to the human beings who would rule the land and creatures of His creation. Eve was created the spiritual equal of Adam; indeed, before the Fall she was his equal in every way: 'She was in no respect inferior to Adam, whether you count the qualities of the body or those of the mind.'[1] Eve lost what might be termed her temporal equality through her sin; part of her punishment was that she be ruled by her husband. But she never lost her spiritual equality and she never lost the possibility of salvation:

> Thus in the natural life . . . the woman experiences the punishments which the Lord here inflicts because of sin . . . But all these things pertain only to the natural life or to the flesh itself, and meanwhile the hope of a spiritual and eternal life after this life endures.[2]

Luther pointed out that if Eve sinned, so too did Adam, to an equal degree. He also carefully redefined the nature of their sin. It was *not* sexual, not concupiscence; instead, it was loss of faith, a turning away from the Word of God.[3] This redefinition was important for two reasons. First of all, it allowed Luther to rehabilitate women by doing away with the notion of Eve as a sexual temptress, using her sexual wiles to lure Adam into sin. No longer would women be defined, as they were in traditional misogyny, as primarily sexual beings; no longer would any and all manifestations of female sexuality be seen as sinful. Sexually active women as well as virgins would be able to attain salvation. Although Protestantism improved the position of women in other ways, this alone would mark it as a major change for the better in women's history.

Luther's redefinition of original sin also allowed him to rehabilitate sex – at least within marriage. Although he agreed with the medieval Church's teaching that after the Fall sex was tainted with sin, Luther nonetheless viewed it as a gift of God to humankind. The Ten Commandments showed that God intended mankind to marry and have children and why else, Luther asked, had God given human beings genitals and a strong sex drive?[4] He rejected as having no foundation in scripture traditional Catholic teachings that sex even within marriage was sinful and only to be undertaken as a remedy for lust or for the procreation of children and that enjoying sex with one's spouse was a venial sin. Luther was certain that marriage, the foundation of human society, was the state God intended for mankind and that the basis of marriage was the loving sexual union between husband and wife.

These convictions led him to attack the celibacy of priests, monks and, especially, nuns. Luther agreed with Catholics that celibacy was a virtue, but he thought that it was rarely attainable, especially by nuns, who had often been put into convents by their families against their will. 'Daughters and sisters', Luther wrote:

> are enticed and indeed pushed into nunneries whether or not they want to go, only to avoid the distraction and impoverishment of families and estates . . . the majority of young women in nunneries are robust and healthy, created by God to be wives and bear children . . . a young woman can do without a man as little as she can do without eating, drinking, sleeping, or other natural requirements . . . The reason for this is that to conceive children is as deeply implanted in nature as eating and drinking are. That is why God gave us and implanted into our bodies genitals, blood vessels, fluids, and everything else necessary to accomplish it . . . Thus I conclude that these nuns in the convents are forced to be chaste against their will; they dislike not having men . . . they lose in this life and the next; they are forced into hell on earth and hell in the other world . . . So if you have a daughter or a friend who has fallen into such a state, you should help her out of it.[5]

Many Protestants took Luther's advice, invading convents and urging the nuns to leave. The best known is Leonhard Koppe, a Lutheran who regularly delivered herring to a convent where his daughter was a nun. On Easter in

1523 he smuggled out of the convent in empty herring barrels 12 nuns, converts to Protestantism; they included his daughter and Katherine von Bora, who later married Martin Luther.[6]

When a city or town converted to Protestantism, the new town government usually closed down the convents and dispersed the nuns. Often they were eager to go. Florentina Ober of Weimar, for example, had been put into a convent as a child. At age 14 she realized she had no true vocation, but her mother superior intimidated her into staying and taking her vows. When she converted to Protestantism she was publicly shamed, beaten and sentenced to perpetual solitary confinement in the convent's punishment cell. She endured two years of that until one day her 'parole officer', as she called the nun assigned to guard her, forgot to lock her cell door and she escaped.[7] Most nuns, however, were reluctant to leave and some fought long and hard to keep their convents open. One was the aristocratic German abbess Charitas Pirckheimer, who ignored insults, starvation, threats of arson and required attendance at Protestant services as she bargained with the authorities to keep her convent functioning until the last of her nuns died.[8]

Historians have taken the reluctance of nuns to leave their convents as evidence that their closure was a blow to women. Convents after all provided the only honourable alternative to marriage: a materially secure life free from the sexual demands of a husband and the dangers of childbirth. Convents also gave women a chance to be educated and to devote their lives to serious spiritual and intellectual concerns. As we saw in the last chapter, much of women's writing in this period was done behind convent walls, as were painting and musical composition. Convents also allowed women to use their skills as administrators as they filled posts like mistress of novices and abbess, and in the Holy Roman Empire many abbesses had temporal as well as spiritual power, appointing judges and town councillors in the lands owned by their convents. And, above all, convents gave women a female space in which they could live together as sisters free from direct male control. Protestantism, historians say, deprived women of all this, leaving them no alternative but marriage and motherhood and perpetual control by their patriarchal husbands.

All this is true, yet we should not get too sentimental over the loss of the convents. The monastic life was an alternative open only to the wealthy. Many girls had, like Florentina Ober, taken the veil against their will and not all convents were hotbeds of intellectual endeavour. Most women probably preferred marriage to life as a nun and Luther reinterpreted marriage in a way that made it much more attractive.

PROTESTANT TEACHINGS ON MARRIAGE

To Luther and his fellow Protestants, marriage was the foundation of human society. Individual families were the basic building blocks of larger social units like states. Families were also schools of righteousness, places where fallen mankind could earn salvation. Protestants rejected the Catholic doctrine that 'good works' – prayer, charity, etc. – could bring salvation, but not good works themselves. Luther thought they should be performed spontaneously and unselfishly in everyday life. All Christians should accept the vocation or calling in life God allotted them, however humble, and strive to perform its duties well, for this would be doing God's will. Being a husband or wife was the first and most important vocation or calling and one's family were the 'nearest neighbours' whom God enjoined people to love, those most deserving of charity and the other good works.[9]

Apart from these lofty purposes, marriage also had a more mundane one: it made people happy. As one Protestant, Martin Bucer, wrote: 'Now the proper and ultimate end of marriage is not copulation or children . . . but the full and proper and main end of marriage is the communicating of all duties, both human and divine, each to the other with utmost benevolence and affection.'[10] In other words, the true end of marriage was the love and companionship without which human life is meaningless. Luther himself found such love in his own match with Katherine von Bora, whom he called his 'Lord Katie', the 'best of wives' whom he 'would not trade for France or Venice'. Luther wrote movingly about the joys of married love:

> Man has strange thoughts the first year of marriage. While sitting at the table, he suddenly thinks, 'Before you were alone, now you are two'. Or, in bed, when he awakens, he sees a pair of pigtails lying next to him. . . . The greatest gift of grace a man can have is a pious, God-fearing, home-loving wife, whom he can trust with all his goods, body, and life itself, as well as having her the mother of his children . . . Katie, you have a good man who loves you.[11]

If love were central to marriage, people should marry for love. The Protestant redefinition of marriage required that they rethink how marriages should begin. As we saw in Chapter 3, before the Reformation many marriages were arranged by the parents of the prospective spouses to advance the social, political and financial interests of their families. Luther realized the benefits of such alliances to families and thought that children should not disobey their parents and selfishly refuse such marriages for reasons of personal happiness. But since marriage rested on love, a young person should not be forced into a match with someone he or she found repugnant. Thus

Luther's position was a complicated one, probably best summed up in the title of a pamphlet he wrote in 1524: *That Parents Should Not Compel or Hinder Their Children's Marriages and That Children Should Not Marry Without Their Parents' Consent*. In it, Luther argued that because the Ten Commandments required that children obey their parents, young people should follow their parents' wishes – or at least obtain their consent – when taking a spouse. But he also argued that parents should be very careful when they made matches for their offspring. They should not force their children in marriage. And when making matches, their primary concern should not be wealth, social status or family advantage but instead their child's future happiness. Every father was 'duty bound to get a child a mate who will be just right for him'. If a child fell in love and wished to marry, the parents should consent so long as the match did not threaten the child's moral welfare, even if it did not bring material and social advantages and even if they themselves disliked their future in-law. Luther thought that if the parents explained their objections to the child but he or she persisted in the match, they should give in: 'In the case of young people who are attached to each other by mutual love (which is the basis of marriage), there should be no opposition without grave cause.'[12] It is not surprising that by the eighteenth century marriage for love had become widespread and accepted in Protestant countries, while arranged matches remained the rule in Catholic areas.

If love were the basis of marriage, couples should be able to end their marriage when love died – that is, they should be able to divorce. Unlike Catholics, Protestants permitted divorce despite the biblical injunctions against it ('Those whom God hath joined together, let no man put asunder'). Protestants did not think God joined couples in marriage. Despite its importance, to them marriage was not a sacrament (they accepted only two, baptism and communion), neither was it part of the natural order dictated by God. Instead, it was part of the civil order. It was the state that joined couples in marriage and that meant marriages could be dissolved. Grounds for divorce varied within Protestant churches and even from town to town within one denomination. In Switzerland, for example, grounds for divorce were different in Zurich and Basel. In Zurich, divorces were granted for adultery, impotence, desertion, grave incompatibility, sexually incapacitating illness and deception, while in Basel the grounds were adultery, impotence, desertion, capital crimes, leprosy and life-threatening abuse.[13] The presence of impotence, adultery and especially incompatibility on these lists underlines the Protestant belief that mutual love and fidelity made a marriage and, when they failed, the marriage had failed. The Protestant theologian Martin Bucer said a marriage was not valid if there was not 'continual cohabitation, and living together' with 'benevolence and affection'.[14] Protestant civil authorities, patriarchal household heads themselves, very conscious of the importance of marriage to their society, were initially reluctant to grant divorces, especially on the grounds of incompatibility, instead counselling the unhappy couple to stay together and try again to love one another. Yet eventually people accepted the notion that if marriage were based on love, divorce for incompatibility should be possible, as they had the notion that if marriage were based on love, young people should choose their own mates. In eighteenth-century Neufchatel around 40 percent of divorces were granted for incompatibility.[15]

Protestant notions that mutual love made a marriage transformed not only how people entered and left that state but also how they behaved within it. Like everyone in early modern Europe, women as well as men, Protestants envisioned the relationship between husband and wife as essentially patriarchal. Eve's punishment for her sin was to lose her equality with man. Henceforth she was banished from the public sphere and forced to remain at home, where she had to obey her husband. As Luther explained:

> This punishment . . . springs from original sin . . . The rule remains with the husband, and the wife is compelled to obey him by God's command. He rules the home and the state, wages wars, defends his possessions, tills the soil, builds, plants, etc. The woman, on the other hand, is like a nail driven into the wall. She sits at home . . . In the household the wife is a partner in the management and has a common interest in the children and the property, and yet there is a great difference between the sexes. The male is like the sun in heaven, the female like the moon . . . For as the sun is more excellent than the moon (although the moon, too, is a very excellent body), so the woman, although she was a most beautiful work of God, nevertheless was not the equal of the male in glory and prestige.[16]

Thus men were superior in intellect and will and were allotted the more important duties in the world. But Luther thought the female responsibilities of keeping house and rearing children were dignified vocations that took as much talent and dedication and were as vital to society as the ruling and fighting done by men:

> Without women the household and everything else that belongs to it would quickly fall apart. The collapse of the civil government, the towns and the police would soon follow. In short, the world could not do without women.[17]

And if the world could not do without women, a husband could not do without his wife. Not only did she run his house and bear and raise his children. She was also his lover and closest companion, flesh of his flesh, privy to his most intimate thoughts, partner in his hopes and dreams. This made her position in the household unique. Unlike the other subordinates under the control of the patriarch, his wife was his 'near equal', supreme authority in her own spheres of housewifery and childcare, second in authority to her husband in all other matters. As an English Puritan explained:

> For of all degrees wherein there is any difference betwixt person and person, there is least disparity betwixt man and wife. Though the man be as the head, yet is the woman as the heart.[18]

This meant that husbands should exercise their duty of guiding and correcting their wives cautiously and with the utmost tact. Luther advised husbands:

> Things will not go the way you want them to. See to it, therefore, that you play the man and act all the more reasonably to make up for your wife's behaviour. Remember that sometimes you must look through your fingers in lenience and moderation, as well as giving her the honour she deserves.[19]

Above all, husbands should not beat their wives. Traditionally, as we have seen, men were allowed to use corporal punishment to correct their spouses; only when the physical force was so excessive as to be life threatening was it frowned on. But Protestants disapproved of wifebeating. The English Puritan William Gouge summed up their position:

> Can it be thought reasonable that she who is the man's perpetual bedfellow, who hath power over his body, who is a joint parent of the children, a joint governor of the family, should be beaten by his hands? . . . The wife is as a man's selfe . . . No man but a frantic, furious, desperate wretch will beat himself.[20]

In many Protestant areas excessive abuse was grounds for divorce and it was also a crime. Wifebeaters could be hauled before the consistory, the church court which regulated behaviour, or a local secular court and punished for their actions. In Calvinist Geneva from 1542 to 1544, the consistory admonished 21 men (and four women!) for violence against their spouses; in 1572, six men were fined and jailed for wifebeating.[21] As with marriage for love and divorce, change in this area came gradually; the husbands who manned the consistories and the courts tempered the new teachings with respect for traditional patriarchal prerogatives. For example, in 1542 Claude Soutiez, a lumberjack, was summoned before Geneva's consistory because he had beaten his wife so severely that he put out one of her eyes. He was not jailed but only admonished to be more gentle with his wife; she was told to obey her husband and not provoke him.[22] Although they were not always fully implemented, the new teachings at least warned husbands to be more cautious in their behaviour and eventually this bore fruit. By the eighteenth century wifebeating was considered shameful and was done only behind closed doors.

PROTESTANT TEACHINGS ON SEX
OUTSIDE MARRIAGE

Wifebeaters were not the only people punished by the consistories. If Protestants rehabilitated sex, it was only within marriage. They regarded all sex outside marriage as sinful and treated offenders more harshly than the Catholic Church had done in earlier centuries, when couples often lived together without being married, bastardy and unwed motherhood were not considered disgraceful and prostitution and homosexuality flourished openly in most cities and towns. In Protestant communities serious sexual offences like rape and child abuse earned sentences of life imprisonment and homosexuality, considered a crime against nature, was punished by burning at the stake. Adultery was redefined as *any* sexual activity outside marriage, including even the seduction of maidservants and the visits to prostitutes previously viewed as a husband's prerogatives, and it too was severely punished, for Protestants thought adultery attacked the very basis of marriage, the loving sexual union of the couple. In Calvinist Geneva in the 1560s and 1570s adultery between a married and unmarried person was punished by the whipping and banishment from the city of both parties; adultery between married people was punished by death. In 1562, five men and two women were banished for adultery. Even consensual sex between unmarried adults was illegal in Protestant cities; defined as the crime of fornication, it was punishable in Geneva by three days' imprisonment on bread and water. Second offences doubled the jail time and habitual offenders were whipped and banished.[23]

The Protestant crackdown on sex outside marriage spelled the end of legalized prostitution. As we have seen, in the late Middle Ages cities governments tolerated and even often themselves ran brothels, arguing that they provided a safe outlet for the sexual urges of the young bachelors of the town, who otherwise would be seducing respectable maidens and ruining their marriage prospects or luring married women into adultery and imperilling the legitimate descent of property. Brothels thus preserved the social order. But Protestants found these arguments ridiculous:

> If the authorities have the power to allow a brothel and do not sin in this, where not only single men (who sin heavily) but also married men may go, and say this does no harm ... Why do they not also permit a women's brothel, where women who are old and weak and have no husbands may go?[24]

After all, Johannes Brenz continued, tongue-in-cheek, women were the lustier sex, while men had greater self-control; logic therefore demanded houses of pretty boys, not houses of female whores. By thus reducing to absurdity the argument that brothels served a public purpose, Protestants showed it to be fallacious. They thought brothels promoted rather than prevented sin: 'Some say one must have public brothels to prevent greater evil – but what if these brothels are schools in which one learns more wickedness than before?'[25]

On these grounds, Protestant city councils shut down municipal brothels. This was done in Zwichau, for example, in 1526 and in Augsburg by 1532.[26] The closing of the brothels did not, of course, instantly wipe out prostitution. Instead, the licensed 'professional' of the brothel was soon replaced by the unlicensed 'amateur'. The peddler who did not sell anything that day, the seduced servant, pregnant, fired and desperate: such women prostituted themselves occasionally when they could find no other means of staying alive.

This change in the nature of prostitution brought a change in public attitudes toward prostitutes. In the Middle Ages they had occupied a recognized if marginal and unrespectable place in the community, because they were deemed to perform an unpleasant but necessary community service. In some medieval German towns prostitutes were overseen by the same government officials who supervised those other unsavoury but necessary public servants, the gravediggers.[27] Prostitutes were clearly separated from respectable women by laws that placed brothels on the outskirts of the city and required prostitutes to wear distinctive clothing. But with the Reformation prostitution ceased to be a necessary evil and became a school for sin. And the prostitute ceased to be distinctive and marginal to the community; instead, any woman might be a prostitute.

This redefinition of the prostitute had both good and bad consequences for women. On the bad side, it brought back with a vengeance the old stereotype of woman as eternal Eve, the sexual temptress luring men into sin, which Protestant teachings on sexuality had begun to dissipate. Many Protestants, including Luther himself, viewed prostitutes as utterly lost to goodness and as dangerous sources of sin and pollution in the community. Luther called them 'dreadful, shabby, stinking, loathsome and syphilitic',[28] worse than murderers because the latter usually killed only one person but prostitutes could infect hundreds with their diseases and sinfulness. And now any woman might be such a creature. This meant that any female suspected of unchaste behaviour, even types like seduced maidservants earlier viewed sympathetically by society, might be branded as a whore and ostracized by her neighbours.[29]

On the good side, the redefinition of the prostitute also brought a new understanding of and sympathy for her plight. At least some Protestant theologians, Jorg Preu among them, recognized that poverty, not sinfulness, often drove women to prostitution. And consistories and morals courts in

Protestant towns tended to view prostitutes as relatively innocent victims of other, guiltier types. First among these were their parents, who failed in their basic duty of providing for the material needs and moral educations of their daughters. Town councils often hauled in the parents of wayward girls. Thus when Appolonia Strobel was suspected of prostitution, the town council of Augsburg questioned her parents. Her father was asked, 'why he had allowed her to leave his house and be outside it day and night' and 'why he had not punished her indiscipline in a fitting manner'?[30] Next were the procurers and pimps who lured young girls into the trade and profited from them. They were routinely punished more severely – with heavy fines, whippings and jail sentences – than the prostitutes themselves. Also punished, usually with heavy fines, were the prostitutes' male clients. After all, prostitution would not exist if men were not willing to pay for sex.

Prosecuting prostitutes' clients was a major departure from past practice. Protestants not only took a very hard line on sexual misbehaviour; they also held men and women equally to their high expectations, deliberately repudiating the traditional double standard, which demanded absolute chastity from women but rarely persecuted male sexual sins. To Protestants their doctrine of the spiritual equality of men and women meant that what was sinful for a woman was sinful for a man as well and that both should be equally punished. In Calvin's Geneva in the sixteenth century, roughly equal numbers of men and women were charged with fornication. And if bearing an illegitimate child now brought public disgrace and punishment, so did siring one; 17 men were prosecuted for that in Geneva in the two years between 1542 and 1544. In the same period more men (19) than women (seven) were charged with adultery, a dramatic reversal of the traditional pattern where absolute fidelity was demanded of wives but husbands were allowed their extramarital flings.[31] And those who were punished were not just the poor and obscure but also the rich and outwardly respectable. In Protestant Augsburg in the 1540s a civic notary, a prominent humanist and a patrician doctor were all prosecuted for visiting prostitutes, while patrician Laux Ravenspurger was fined £100 and put in irons for trying to rape his maid.[32] In Zwickau, Nichel Elbel, the head of a foundling home, was imprisoned, flogged and banished for raping and impregnating one of his 9-year-old charges.[33]

Elbel's victim was also banished, although the magistrates arranged for a place for her to live and gave her an ell and a half of cloth to sell. This shows how difficult it was for the men of a patriarchal society to rid themselves of the traditional gender stereotype of women – even a 9-year-old girl – as sexual temptresses luring men into sin. Male magistrates also were reluctant to enforce the new standards of behaviour that demanded chastity in men as well as women. In 1574 Geneva's pastors had to threaten to resign en masse to get the consistory to punish a prominent male citizen for adultery and in the seventeenth century, when the early determination of the Calvinists to make Geneva a truly godly community had long since faded, the equal and harsh adultery laws were repealed and replaced by unequal penalties. Unfaithful wives might still be publicly whipped and banished, but unfaithful husbands were merely fined and excommunicated. The consistory also gradually stopped prosecuting men for fornication and in the 1760s those laws were also repealed.[34] Thus Protestants failed to wipe out the double standard. That is not surprising, given the strength of patriarchy in their society. What is surprising is that, impelled by their doctrine of the spiritual equality of men and women, they were actually willing to try.

WOMEN'S ROLE IN PROTESTANT CHURCHES

Another area in which their conviction of the spiritual equality of men and women led Protestants to reinterpret traditional notions concerned women's role in the Church. Actually Protestants reinterpreted the role of men in the church as well. Some historians have called the Reformation a revolt of the laity that gave ordinary worshippers more active roles in church services and governance. Luther and later Protestants allowed the laity to partake of both the bread and the wine in communion, reorganized church services so that they centred not on the mass performed by the priest but on sermons for the edification of the congregation and on prayers and hymn singing in which they shared, and remodelled church government so that power rested not in the pope but in the laity, either government officials or the congregations themselves. Above all, Luther replaced the celibate, separate priesthood with what he termed 'the priesthood of all believers'. The Church and its rituals were no longer necessary for salvation; instead, salvation was by faith alone. Each lay person had to deepen his or her faith through reading the scriptures and to encourage the faith of their families and neighbours.

But was this truly a 'priesthood of *all* believers'? Could women read and interpret the scriptures for themselves and foster faith in others equally with men? What role, if any, should women have in governing the new churches? Here again, as with their reinterpretation of women's nature, Luther and his fellow Protestants had to resolve the contradictions between their basic conviction of the spiritual equality of men and women and a biblical text that seemed to deny it, in this case St Paul's injunction that women be silent in churches and ask their husbands if they had any questions about doctrine. This text, plus the fact that Jesus and all his disciples were men, were the grounds on which the Catholic Church had long excluded women from the priesthood.

As they did in the case of Eve and original sin, Luther and his fellow Protestants reinterpreted St Paul so that his words conformed more closely to their doctrine of the spiritual equality of the sexes. Luther as usual evoked the doctrine of the two kingdoms. Women's silence in church was part of the man-made laws and customs of the world, not part of the God-ordained natural order. Therefore, it could be changed according to circumstances. In fact, it had been. Luther pointed out that in Old Testament times women like Huldah, Deborah and Jael had exercised religious authority over men. Luther also suggested that St Paul wrote about the special case of the Greek Church, whose women were more 'ingenious and clever' than others, and did not intend his words as a rule for all. So while in ordinary circumstances women should be guided by male authorities in matters of religion, that was not inevitable.[35] Calvin went even further, pointing out that not only were there women prophets and religious leaders in the Old Testament but also that women had played major roles in the early Church. After His resurrection, Christ had appeared first to a woman, Mary Magdalene, and women like Phoebe and Priscilla had preached and converted many to the new faith. The order of nature ordained that women be under male authority, but God was capable of overturning that natural order to punish sinful mankind. He had done so in the past, when female prophets had led the Chosen People, and He would probably do so in the future.[36]

What did all this mean for the actual organization of the new churches? It did *not* mean that there should be female pastors. Luther argued against them not only on the philosophical grounds that it went against the God-ordained natural order for women to exercise authority over men but also on the practical grounds that pastors were primarily preachers who needed a strong voice and other qualities more likely to be found in men than women. Neither did it mean that women were to have a voice in running the Church. This was a crucial issue in Calvinism, where councils of elected elders chose pastors and ran the congregations. In some Calvinist churches women were allowed to vote for elders, but they never could become elders themselves.

If women could not be pastors or elders, what was their role in the Church? Protestants, of course, denied them the role of nun and they also rejected proposals to revive the role of deaconess – women, usually elderly widows, who in the early Christian Church had supervised the care of the poor and sick and catechized and baptized the women of the congregations. They did, however, create one new religious role for women: that of the pastor's wife. Usually middle class and well educated, often in the early days of the Reformation ex-nuns like Luther's Katherine von Bora, pastors' wives were influential members of Protestant communities. In a sense, they replaced the female Virgin Mary and the female saints as role models for Protestant women.

Veneration of Mary and the saints was banned by Protestants because they found no mention of it in the scriptures. Historians think this was felt as a loss by women; in Calvin's Geneva in the 1540s more women than men were called before the consistory for offences like keeping their rosaries and praying to the Virgin and the saints and keeping their relics and images.[37] Mary and the saints had not only provided role models for women; they also helped them through the hazards of the female lifecycle. Prayers to Saint Margaret helped women through childbirth; Saint Appollonia could cure a child's toothache and Saint Anne protected elderly widows. Protestants rejected all of this, leaving women with only an all-male trinity to pray to and their pastor's wife to emulate. Fortunately, hers was a positive and powerful example. Pastors' wives epitomized the new Protestant version of womanhood: they were loving mothers, efficient managers of households that, in the early days of the Reformation, often included pupils of the husband and religious refugees, all of whom had to be fed on their husband's miniscule salary, and 'near equals' and intellectual companions of their spouses. Pastors' wives often shared their husbands' intellectual concerns. Martin Luther consulted his Katie on theological issues and Katherine Zell, wife of Matthew Zell, a pastor in Strasbourg, published a pamphlet on religious doctrine and even conducted a public funeral.

Many Protestant women followed these models and were both 'near equal' wives and committed believers. If Protestants did not allow women positions of *authority* within the church, they did grant them *equality* within 'the priesthood of all believers'. Although they were to follow the guidance of male authority figures – their ruler, their pastor, their father, their husband – women, like men, were as individuals ultimately responsible for their own behaviour. Like men, they were to read the scriptures and apply the lessons learned there not just to their own lives and faith but also those of their family, friends and neighbours.

This doctrine brought a number of advantages to women. One was increased literacy. Protestants had to be literate to read the Bible. In 1524 Luther mandated that all towns provide schools to teach at least basic literacy to all children, boys and girls alike. The civil authorities of Protestant territories usually followed this injunction and established schools. Württemberg had 89 schools in 1520 but over 400 by 1600.[38] Thus Protestantism boosted female literacy. The Protestant commitment to and impact on female education should not be exaggerated, however. As we saw, female literacy was growing even before the Reformation for reasons unconnected with religion. And increased female literacy did not close the gap in learning between men and women — neither did Protestants intend this. Like almost everyone else in the early modern period, they thought that all women needed to fulfil their intended roles as wife and mother was basic literacy plus some instruction in household skills. Men, however (at least those of the elite), needed a human-istic education in the classics and they, unlike women, were urged to pursue their intellectual interests and eventually make their own contributions to the world of learning. Yet if Protestants did not encourage women to do this, when they taught them to read and write they nonetheless gave them the tools to do so and, as we have seen, many women used these tools to pursue their intellectual interests and become writers, scientists and philosophers. And even if they did not, the fact that they could read and write like their husbands must have given their self-confidence a boost. So the Protestant commitment to female literacy contributed to the growing equality of men and women in ways church leaders had not intended.

So too did other aspects of women's role in the priesthood of all believers. Protestant leaders envisioned women's reading and interpreting the scrip-tures as done under the guidance of fathers and husbands within the proper female sphere of the household. Its primary purpose was to enable mothers to teach the rudiments of religion to their children. None of this challenged the proper gender order of society. But what happened if a wife reading and interpreting the scripture saw its meaning more clearly than her husband did? Should she then *teach* her husband, even though that would reverse the natural order of authority within the family? This posed a real dilemma for Protestant theologians, because women were (not surprisingly, considering the advantages Protestantism offered them) often the first members of their families to convert to the new faith. Should they then try to convert their fathers and husbands? What should a Protestant wife do if her non-Protestant husband forbade her to practise her religion? Should she obey her natural superior or the dictates of her conscience? Should she try to convert him? Leave him? Divorce him? Here the various Protestant sects differed. Radical sects like the Hutterites and the Anabaptists required that believers separate from (although not divorce) spouses who did not embrace their doctrines. But neither Luther nor Calvin regarded religious differences as adequate grounds to break up a marriage. They counselled Protestant wives to stick with their husbands and try to convert them. But if their husbands tried to prevent them from worshipping as they chose, they should leave.[39] Both Luther and Calvin eagerly accepted the aid of queens and noble-women who defied their Catholic husbands to help the Protestant cause. The Lutheran Elizabeth of Brandenburg not only helped Protestants but also separated from her Catholic husband and lived in exile rather than renounce her faith. Her daughter Elizabeth of Braunschweig actively proselytized among her Catholic husband's subjects and raised her son as a Lutheran. Noblewoman Arugula von Grumbach corresponded with Luther and publicly debated the scriptures with Catholic theologians. Calvinism, too, profited from the support of female queens and noblewomen. Jeanne d'Albret, queen of Navarre, converted her kingdom to Protestantism. Renée de France, Duchess of Ferrara, sheltered Calvin and other religious refugees in defiance of her Catholic husband and the Comtesse de Roze not only converted many other French nobles, men and women alike, but also negotiated with German Protestant princes for aid in the French religious wars and helped write the peace treaty which ended one of them.[40]

Noblewomen were not the only ones to overstep the boundaries of proper female behaviour to help the Protestant cause. Middle- and lower-class women did so as well. In most areas the new religious doctrines caused conflict between Catholics and Protestants and in these battles many women actively supported their new faith. Some forms of their support remained within acceptable female roles. For example, Protestant women ostentatiously bought and ate meat on Catholic fast days and they sat in their windows spinning on holy days when Catholics were idle. In childbirth they called on God, not Saint Margaret, to help them.[41]

But women's support of the new doctrines also took forms which led them out of the proper female domain of the household onto the streets and into the masculine realms of politics and print. They marched through their towns singing hymns and they fought with Catholic women in the squares and markets. They also often led the crowds that broke into churches and destroyed religious images. In the Netherlands in 1566, a woman named Neel Spaens was arrested for such activities. She carried tools for breaking down church doors with her everywhere and stood on street corners urging crowds to attack Catholic churches. After her arrest she escaped from prison and fled into exile.[42]

Even more shockingly, women spoke out about religious doctrines in public – in effect, they preached. Informally, in the streets, they might explain the basic tenets of their faith. One such informal preacher was Claudine Levet, an apothecary's wife who lived in Geneva in the 1530s: 'When she found herself in a gathering where there was no minister present, those assembled had her explain the Scripture, for one could not find a person more gifted with the graces of the Lord.'[43] Women preaching and acting as ministers in the absence of a pastor or other men were quite common. As late as 1572 in France women went up to pulpits and read from the Bible to Protestant congregations while waiting for the minister to arrive.[44]

Mainstream Protestant churches were uneasy about such helpful women. In Zwickau in 1528, the Lutheran city council arrested four women for public preaching, including the wife of Caspar Teucher. Of her they said that she 'can never keep quiet, her influence must . . . be removed'.[45] But the more radical Protestant sects like the Anabaptists and the Quakers required a 'conversion experience' (a feeling of being overwhelmed by the power and love of God, which cleansed away sin and gave one a new start as a joyous believer) of their members and this made them more tolerant of female preachers. They believed the spirit of the Lord visited men and women alike and those who experienced His presence should make public testimony to that fact. Indeed, the radical seventeenth-century English sects required that everyone, male or female, who wished to become a member write down their conversion experience. Not surprisingly, these accounts varied by gender. Men's conversion narratives usually emphasized self-help; they were stories of manly struggles against worldly temptations like riches and drink. Women's narratives, contrariwise, emphasized passivity; they were full of dreams and visions, in which the Lord overcame their weak selves and gave them strength for the struggle. Their central theme was the Lord speaking or working through His weak and unworthy vessel. Typical was Dorothy White's explanation of her daring to speak out on religious matters: 'And the Lord God hath spoken, and therefore I will speak.'[46]

Because it was the Lord rather than the woman speaking, radical sects allowed women to preach, although not to administer the sacraments or exercise any authority over men. The English Baptists, for example, not only permitted women to organize and preach in separate women's meetings but also to testify to their religious experiences in the regular mixed-sex Baptist congregations. In 1654 a London Baptist congregation debated allowing women to preach and decided that 'a Weoman (Mayd, Wife or Widdow) being a Prophetess (I Cor: II) may speake, Prophesie, Pray, with a Vayl. Others may not.'[47] Other Baptist congregations also debated the issue and concluded that women could speak when confessing their faith, admonishing or making a public repentance, if they acknowledged the inferiority of their sex and did not challenge the authority of men.

The most radical of the Protestant sects, the Quakers, whose services consisted of testimony of the spirit of the Lord at work in each believer, gave the widest scope to 'she-preachers'. In a pamphlet published in 1674, George Keith defended the right of women to preach, so long as they were not proud, vain, sinful or unruly and did not advocate usurping authority from men. In her pamphlet *Womens Speaking Justified*, the Quakeress Margaret Fell Fox, who had been speaking out in public on religious issues since the day when, as a child of eight, she had stood up in church and announced to her Anglican minister, 'Lampitt, the plagues of God shall fall upon thee', swept aside most of these qualifications. While disclaiming any desire to put women into authority over men, she stated that if women had 'the Spirit of the Lord poured upon them', they had not only the right but the duty to speak out, as had the numerous female preachers and prophets in the Bible.[48] And Quaker women did speak out, in female-run congregations, in the regular Quaker meetings and as missionaries. The elderly widow Elizabeth Hooton undertook a mission to New England, where she was often stripped and whipped from town to town. Sarah Cheevers left her husband to go with another female Quaker on a mission to Malta, where they were imprisoned by the Inquisition for four years. Sixteen-year-old Elizabeth Fletcher preached in Ireland and Mary Fisher, a missionary in Turkey, walked 500 miles to meet and try to convert the sultan himself.[49]

Quakers and other less radical Protestant women also testified to their faith in print and tried to make converts through their writings. Besides her pamphlet defending women's right to preach, Margaret Fell Fox published 23 other religious works. Elizabeth Hooton published six and young Elizabeth Fletcher one. The self-proclaimed prophetess Lady Elinor Davis, regularly visited by angels and the prophet Daniel, published no fewer than 66, making her the most prolific female author in seventeenth-century England.[50] And Englishwomen of the radical sects were not alone in venturing into print. As we have seen, even mainstream Lutheran and Calvinist women like Katherine Zell published religious works. In doing so, they were very conscious that, like the pulpit, the realm of print was a masculine sphere. Female religious writers, like most female writers, usually prefaced their works with apologies for abandoning the modest silence expected of virtuous females (Elizabeth Warren admitted that by venturing into print she had lost her hitherto prized 'silent modestie') and for lacking the masculine intellectual training (what English prophetess Anna Trapnell enviously called 'deep speech gathered up and fetcht from both Cambridge and Oxford') to do justice to their subjects. Nonetheless, they wrote, the Lord had revealed the truth to them and they felt a duty to spread it to others. As Quaker Dorothy White explained: 'The word of the Lord came unto me, saying write.'[51] Because they were publishing not their own opinions but revelations of the Lord, religious writings were, like a mother's advice to her children and a woman's memorial to illustrious male relatives, a genre in which women could argue that it was appropriate for them to write and publish, especially if their work was intended primarily for their fellow women. The Genevan Calvinist Marie Dentière, who published not only religious writings but also a defence of herself and other women for doing so, made the argument best:

> Although it is not permitted to us [women] to preach in public assemblies and churches, it is nonetheless not forbidden to write and admonish one another, in all love . . . If God then has given graces to some good women, revealing to them by his Holy Scriptures something holy and good, will they not dare to write, speak, or declare it, one to another? . . . Ah! It would be too audacious to wish to stop them from doing it. As for us, it would be too foolish to hide the talent which God has given us.[52]

Dentière's quiet confidence that she had something worthwhile to say and the right to say it soon spread to other women. As we have seen, by 1700 female writers were publishing regularly without apology and they could support themselves by their writings.

This pattern of women using religious justifications to invade a masculine sphere and then claiming it as their own also occurred in the realm of politics. Protestant women took political action to further their cause. Queens and noblewomen raised armies and brokered treaties, while lower-class women attacked churches and rioted in the streets. As we shall see in Chapter 13, these were forms of political action traditionally permitted to women. But religion impelled one group of women – England's radical Protestants – to undertake a form of political action traditionally considered a right of English *men* only: the right to petition Parliament. During the English Civil War there were scores of petitions presented to Parliament by women, demanding action on economic, political and, above all, religious issues. The petitioners usually acknowledged that they were mere women, the 'weaker sex' trespassing in the realm of men: 'They acted not out of any Self-conceit or Pride of Heart, as *seeking to equal ourselves with Men, either in Authority or Wisdom*', but merely because as good Christians they were concerned with the future of their religion.[53] And as usual they made the argument that they were doing the will of the Lord. A petition against church tithes signed by 7000 Quaker women, 'Hand-Maids and Daughters of the Lord', in 1659, stated that:

It may seem strange to some that women should appear in so publick a manner, in a matter of so great concernment as this of Tithes . . . But let such know, that this is the work of the Lord . . . even by weak means to bring to pass his mighty Work . . . Behold our God is . . . choosing the foolish things of the world to confound the wise, weak things to confound the Mighty.[54]

Yet the very experience of making their opinions known seems to have been empowering, for women also justified their petitioning in more forthright and self-confident terms. For example, in a petition of 1642 women used their presumed spiritual equality to men to argue that they were equally members of the Church and therefore had an equal 'Right and Interest' to petition in matters concerning it: 'Because in the free Enjoying of . . . a flourishing Estate of the Church . . . consisteth the Happiness of Women as well as Men . . . [and] women are Sharers in the common calamities . . . when Oppression is exercised over the Church', they had the right and duty to petition on religious matters.[55] Some women even transferred this 'equal members' argument to the realm of politics, arguing that as citizens of the English Commonwealth they had what they called 'our undoubted right' of petitioning:

That since we are assured of our Creation in the image of God, and of an interest in Christ, equal unto men, as also of a proportionable share in the Freedoms of this Commonwealth, we cannot but wonder and grieve that we should appear so despicable in your eyes, as to be thought unworthy to Petition or represent our Grievances to this Honourable House. Have we not an equal interest with the men of this Nation in those liberties and securities contained in . . . [the] good laws of the land? Are any of our lives, limbs, liberties, or goods to be taken from us more than from men, but by due process of law . . . ? And can you imagine us to be so sottish or stupid as not to perceive, or not to be sencible when daily those strong defences of our pease and wellfare are broken down . . . are we Christians, and yet must we sit still and keep at home?[56]

This is the first collective demand for political rights by women, but it is notable also for its challenge to standard gender stereotypes and roles: its assertion that women are not 'sottish' and 'stupid' and should not be expected to 'sit still and keep at home'.

We can see a similar challenge to traditional gender roles in the most drastic step that Protestant women took to defend their faith: publicly defying the authorities of Church and state and enduring arrest, torture and execution as religious martyrs. There were numerous executions of Protestants in England under the Catholic Queen Mary – that was why she got her nickname Bloody Mary – and in the Netherlands under Spanish rule. Most of the martyrs were men, both because men were more likely to defy their rulers and speak out in public and because the authorities for that reason found male heresy more threatening than that of women. But about 20 percent of such martyrs were women.[57] Some were simply good wives and mothers arrested as part of a Protestant family; the only way they defied gender stereotypes was to display a 'manly' courage at their ghastly deaths – usually burning at the stake. But others had abandoned their husbands, children and domestic duties to preach and proselytize publicly and they seemed to relish duelling intellectually with learned male churchmen and judges during their interrogations.

Typical of this sort of martyr who defied gender stereotypes as well as religious prohibitions was the notorious Anne Askew. A gentleman's daughter forced into an arranged marriage against her will, she converted to Protestantism, abandoned her Catholic husband and children and went off to London to get a divorce. There she came to the attention of the religious authorities, who twice arrested, interrogated and tortured her before finally burning her at the stake. Askew more than held her own with her learned male interrogators, getting them to make damaging admissions and she also wrote up an account of her trials in which she portrayed herself as a 'poore woman' cleverly triumphing over the learned bullying of men and had it smuggled out of the prison and published.[58]

Anne Askew was not the only female Protestant to get the best of her male interrogators. Another was the Dutch martyr Weynken Claes, burned at the stake in 1527:

> Question: 'What do you hold concerning the sacrament?'
> Answer: 'I hold your sacrament to be bread and flour.'
> Question: 'What do you hold concerning the saints?'
> Answer: 'I know no other Mediator than Christ (1 John 2:19).'
> Question: 'What do you hold concerning the holy oil?'
> Answer: 'Oil is good for salad, or to oil your shoes with.'[59]

Elizabeth Young also matched scriptural quotations with her questioners, maddening them in the process. Said one:

> Why thou art a woman of fair years, why shouldst thou meddle with the Scriptures? It is necessary for thee to believe, and that is enough . . . Thou hast read a little in the Bible or Testament, and thou thinkest that thou art able to reason with a doctor that hath gone to school thirty years.[60]

Another was so shocked that a woman could hold her own in a theological debate that he was willing to wager that she was not a woman at all: 'Twenty pounds, it is a man in woman's clothes!'[61]

Luckily for them, most Protestant women were not called on to outwit their male interrogators and die a 'manly' death. By the mid-sixteenth century the persecution of martyrs was largely over and most Protestant women could relax into the major role Protestantism allotted to them: that of wife, housewife and mother. But this was a role transformed not only by the new Protestant teachings on the nature of women and marriage but also by the examples of the heroic female martyrs. For while the martyrs disappeared, their stories lived on. Second only to the Bible in popularity as reading matter in most Protestant countries were martyrologies, collections of life stories of martyrs like the Englishman John Foxe's *Acts and Monuments*, first published in 1563, and Thieleman van Braght's *Martyr's Mirror*, detailing the sufferings of the Dutch Anabaptists, first published in 1660. Women martyrs were overly represented in these collections intended to provide Protestants with role models to replace the traditional saints. About 20 percent of the martyrs were female, but one-third of van Braght's martyrs are women.[62] And while van Braght and Foxe were most comfortable praising traditional wives like John Marbeck's, who came to the attention of the authorities only when she begged to be allowed to visit her imprisoned husband, they also praised women like Mrs Prest, who left her husband to seek martyrdom, and even the uppity Anne Askew, whom Foxe called 'a singular example of Christian constancy for all men to follow'.[63] To Protestants, before they were dutiful and 'near equal' wives, women were Christians, equal to men in the sight of God and justified in acting in unfemale ways in defence of their faith. Thus the Protestant resurrection of the spiritual equality of men and women inherent in early Christianity was one of the most important forces for change in gender stereotypes and roles in early modern Europe. And because the Catholic Church in self-defence was forced to rework its own teachings on women, marriage and female spirituality, it affected Catholics as well as Protestants. It is to the Catholic side of the story that we now turn.

Chapter 10

◆

MOTHERS, NUNS, NURSES, TEACHERS: WOMEN IN THE CATHOLIC REFORMATION

During the Reformation, Catholic women defended their faith as zealously as Protestant women attacked it. For every nun like Katherine von Bora, who ran away from her convent and married Martin Luther, there was a Mathilde Willen, a German abbess who kept her convent open in Protestant territory for 40 years, at one time driving out a Protestant preacher with smoke bombs. For every Protestant martyr like Elizabeth Dirks, there was an Anne Line, hanged in England in 1601 for illegally hiding and assisting priests.[1]

Women's zeal in defending their faith was not initially welcomed by the Catholic Church. Women who wanted to play active roles in defending and spreading their faith posed greater problems to the male hierarchy of the Catholic Church than they did to Protestants. Protestants had remade the church structure to give greater authority to the laity and during this restructuring it was relatively easy for them to redefine their view of women and allot them new roles in the new churches. But the Catholic Church's main goal during the Reformation was to preserve its traditional structure and (all-male) hierarchy intact. And that entailed traditional and limited roles for women: they could be nuns in convents or devout wives guided by their husbands and their priests. Even before the Reformation women had found these alternatives constricting and carved out more active and satisfying roles for themselves as tertiaries, beguines, *béatas*, and other independent holy women. The challenge of Protestantism increased women's determination to take on new, more active roles in their Church. At first the Church resisted their efforts, but the women persisted and eventually the Church accepted their new organizational structures and remade its view of women and their roles in Church and society. Thus Catholicism eventually developed many of the same new roles for women and more favourable definitions of female nature as Protestants and within Catholicism even more than among Protestants this came about through the efforts of women themselves.

REFORMING WOMEN TO REFORM THE CHURCH

The Church's response to the Protestant challenge was slow in coming. Martin Luther posted his theses in 1517 but it was only in 1545, when the great Church Council at Trent opened, that the Church really began reforming itself to counteract Protestantism. The Council of Trent lasted until 1563, the task of reform even longer. In France, for example, the Church was not thoroughly reformed until 1700. Thus while the story of the Protestant Reformation centres on the first half of the sixteenth century, that of the Catholic Reformation spans the period from 1550 to 1700.

In its reform, the Church had two objectives: first, to stem the tide of Protestantism and win its adherents back to the True Faith and, second, to make sure that all Catholics understood the basic doctrines of their faith and practised it properly. To accomplish these goals, the Church began by defining its doctrines at the Council of Trent. Trent also implemented internal reforms to get rid of uneducated, corrupt and unchaste priests and to create a vigorous, dedicated, disciplined organization capable of undertaking the vast programme of proselytization necessary to meet its goals. Once the reforms were in place, the proselytization began. Protestants were reconverted and the excesses of popular religion like the worship of images and relics and dubious local saints attacked. Again the purpose was twofold: to deprive Protestants of ammunition (they made much of Catholics' 'superstitious' practices) and make sure Catholics understood the doctrines of their faith and practised it correctly.

What role would women play in these efforts? Initially, they were more the targets of the reform programme than participants in it. The male hierarchy of the Church could envisage no religious roles for women other than chaste, cloistered nun and devout, obedient wife. One of their first reform efforts was to eliminate religious women who did not fit either of these models – the tertiaries, *béatas* and other women who wished to dedicate themselves to religion yet did not choose to enter convents, because their family responsibilities prevented this, they could not afford the dowry or they simply preferred to remain in the world to minister to the poor and needy. First to go were the tertiaries (laypeople who joined a 'third order' of monks or nuns in which they did not take solemn vows or live cloistered lives), who in 1566 were required to take solemn vows and enter cloistered convents – in effect, to become nuns.[2] Men could continue to be tertiaries.

Next to go were the *béatas*, holy women who appeared to lead saintly lives and even perform miracles. Before the Reformation the uncanny prophesying, dramatic mortifications of the flesh and unstinting charity to the poor of such women had won them devoted followers among not only their fellow laymen but also priests and prelates. Some *béatas*, like Catherine of Siena, even received the Church's ultimate seal of approval, sainthood. During the Counterreformation, however, churchmen were much more reluctant to accept these unofficial holy women as truly inspired by God. Instead, the Church now considered them dangerous. The often theologically dubious practices of their followers were part of the superstitious popular religious practices the Church was determined to stamp out. And their public preaching, prophesying and instruction of their priestly followers reversed not only the principle of clerical control over the laity so central to the reforms of the Counterreformation but also the accepted gender order of society. Laypeople should not instruct priests; women should not instruct men. Therefore the Church viewed these holy women very suspiciously. They were convinced that their mortifications of the flesh and signs of divine approval like the stigmata were faked and that their prophetic dreams and visions were the work not of God but the Devil. After all, these were women, weaker in understanding than men and therefore easy prey for the Evil One. As one Spanish priest put it:

> More credit should be given to the revelations of men than those of women: because that feminine sex is weaker in the head, and they mistake natural things or diabolic illusions for those of heaven and God; . . . They are more imaginative than men, and thus less judicious and reasonable and still less prudent, and so the Devil is more likely to deceive women.[3]

To sort the fake from the real, the Church relied on the Inquisition. This Church court, charged with investigating possible cases of heresy, had been active against witches in Switzerland and the German states in the late Middle Ages and against Jews and Muslims in the Spain of Ferdinand and Isabella. The Reformation gave it a new lease on life. Along with the newly established index of prohibited books, it became a major weapon in the fight against

Protestantism. The Inquisition found relatively few Protestants in Spain, Portugal and Italy, where it was most active. In these countries, most people charged before the Inquisition were Catholics who transgressed the Church's new, stricter standards of behaviour.

Prominent among them were *béatas*. In Seville, Spain, for example, between 1559 and 1645, no fewer than 13 *béatas* were tried by the Inquisition. The most famous was Catalina de Jesus, a peasant woman who wore the habit of the Carmelite order but was not a nun. She wrote, preached, prophesied and (according to her 700 followers, including a priest) performed miracles. She was called 'Santa Catalina' and her clothes and hair were cherished as relics. The Inquisition found her guilty of believing she was divinely inspired by God and therefore exempt from the discipline of the Church and sentenced her to six years' confinement in a convent.[4] In Venice in 1664 the Inquisition tried Maria Janis, another peasant woman who wore a holy habit and numbered a priest among her following. Janis was popularly venerated because she seemed to go without food, living off the heavenly host she received at daily communion. The Inquisition pronounced her a fake and sentenced her to seven years in jail.[5] Another of the Inquisition's famous female victims was the Spaniard Lucrecia de León, who had dared to criticize publicly both her Church and king on the basis of over 400 dreams, which, she claimed, gave her divinely inspired prophetic visions of the future. She too was found guilty and sentenced to a public confession of her sins, 100 lashes and two years' confinement in a convent.[6]

NUNS AND CONVENTS

The punishments allotted to *béatas* underscore the Church's position that convents were the only possible place for holy women and nun their only possible role. This role also changed as a result of the Counterreformation. Protestants had criticized the nuns of the pre-Reformation Church as unchaste, worldly and lacking true religious vocations. All too often this was true. Therefore the Council of Trent rewrote the rules about joining a religious order. After Trent, no nun could take her final vows (of poverty, chastity and obedience) before age 16 and all were to be asked if they did so of their own free will. It was hoped this would end the use of convents as dumping grounds for the unmarriageable daughters of upper-class families and guarantee that every nun truly had a religious vocation. To prevent scandals, every convent was to be strictly cloistered, that is, cut off from the world. Laypeople were not to enter and the nuns were not to leave. To see that these rules were enforced, convents were put under the supervision of their local bishops and often of a male religious order as well.[7]

Thus the Church's reform of convents was reform from above, imposed on the nuns, and it was defensive in nature, intended to end the irregularities that had provided ammunition for Protestant attacks on the Church. As such, it was only partially successful. Even after Trent many convents were still dumping grounds for unmarriageable aristocratic girls more concerned with their lapdogs, servants and socializing than their supposed religious vocation. Some convents were reformed in the late sixteenth and seventeenth centuries into models of piety. But usually this was done by reform from below, through the efforts of the nuns themselves and for offensive rather than defensive purposes: the reforming nuns envisioned their lives of prayer and mortification as weapons the Church could use in the struggle against heresy.

The main inspiration for this reform from below was the Spanish nun Saint Theresa of Avila.[8] She was born Dona Theresa de Alumada in 1515, to a Jewish family only recently ennobled and converted to Christianity. Even as a girl, Saint Theresa dreamed of taking part in the Church's apostolic mission: she and her brother planned to run away to Muslim territory and convert the heathen. A brief stay in a convent as a teenager, ordered by her father when she fell in love with an ineligible man, gave her a taste for the monastic life and in 1535 she entered the largest and most fashionable convent in her home town of Avila, a Carmelite establishment. There she led the life of a typical upper-class nun before the reforms took hold: fashionable clothes, private quarters, long periods of leave from the convent to nurse her father or go on pilgrimages, endless spats with other nuns over family, lineage and who had precedence. But Saint Theresa became increasingly dissatisfied with this life, especially after she undertook a programme of systematic meditation and prayer and began to have visions that seemed to criticize the convent's worldliness.

As her visions continued and deepened, they aroused in her male spiritual advisors the deep suspicions that women's visions and prophecies always aroused in churchmen in this period. Her spiritual director was convinced they were delusions of the Devil. Indeed, throughout her career churchmen remained suspicious of Saint Theresa. The Inquisition accused her of acting as confessor to her nuns and therefore usurping the male priestly role and at one point she was forbidden to read theological books. The end of her life was darkened by the suspicions of the male vicar-general of her order, who accused her of sleeping with 'both black and white men' and having an affair (at age 60!) with her confessor.

Luckily Saint Theresa also found male churchmen who believed in and encouraged her mystical experiences. Often they were Jesuits, whose founder, St Ignatius Loyola, had laid out a series of systematic 'spiritual exercises' to enable his followers to have visions leading eventually to a mystical union with God. For Loyola and his Jesuits, such spiritual experiences were only a prelude to practical work in the world to further the Church's mission of converting the unconverted and this was true of Saint Theresa as well. In 1561 she had a vision of her own future in hell and, obsessed with the success of Protestantism, especially in France, where war between the two faiths had just broken out, she thought about how much worse the fate of heretics would be and resolved to do something to help them and the Church. As her niece put it: 'Being a woman and prevented from benefiting them as she would have liked, she determined to undertake this work in order to make war on the heretics with her prayers and life and with the prayers and lives of her nuns.'[9]

How would she do this? Her visions provided the answer: by reforming her convent and eventually the whole Carmelite order to conform to God's intentions for the monastic life. This meant, first, living in poverty. Not only were the nuns to renounce their personal property but also the order itself was to own nothing and depend on the earnings of the nuns and donations from the faithful for survival. This devotion to poverty gave her reformed order its name, the Discalced Carmelites; 'discalced' meant 'sandalless' or 'barefoot'. Another element in her reform was complete claustration and a complete cutting of ties with the outside world. Symbolizing this was the practice of the nun choosing a new religious name, leaving behind her family name and family pride. Carmelite nuns were to be equal; unusually for this period, the order accepted poor women and did not discriminate against them.* The final element of her reform was complete, unquestioning obedience to ecclesiastical superiors.

Thus Saint Theresa's reforms coincided with those of Trent – that is why she was allowed to carry them out. But the two reforms differed in purpose. Churchmen thought of obedience and claustration as defensive measures, protecting both the Church and individual nuns. Saint Theresa thought of them more positively. They freed the nun from the cares of the world and worries about the theological correctness of her beliefs and acts and allowed her to concentrate on the important thing: preparing herself, through systematic

---

* This was true at least while Saint Theresa was alive. Later, family pride reasserted itself and the order fell short of her ideal.

prayer and moderate mortification of the flesh, for a mystical union with God, which would deepen the effectiveness of her prayers for the conversion of heretics and success of the Church's apostolic mission. As a modern historian has written:

> The more strictly her nuns could fortify themselves behind their walls, the more effectively could they send their spirit soaring to heaven or out across the globe. Enclosure and silence, discipline and mental prayer, were intended to train the nun as a militant participant in the Christianizing mission.[10]

That this was the goal of Saint Theresa's reforms is shown by how they spread. The first barefoot Carmelite houses outside Spain were founded in northern Italy, France and Poland between 1590 and 1610. All were areas where Protestants had recently gained ground.

Saint Theresa's Carmelites were not the only nuns to undertake the Church's apostolic mission. In the sixteenth and seventeenth centuries order after order – the Cistercians, the Clarisses, the Recollects – reformed themselves and numerous new orders, like the Daughters of the Calvary, established in France in 1617, were founded. They too adopted programmes of systematic prayer and mortification of the flesh and they emphasized devotions like the Sacred Heart and the Immaculate Conception that separated Catholics from Protestants. Their nuns too dreamed of helping the Church. The French nun Marie de Valence had a vision of the souls who depended on her prayers. They ran the gamut of human society from popes and kings to lowly peasant and they included 50,000 sinners to convert, 30,000 penitents to guide and 15,000 just and 12,000 saints to maintain and increase![11] With nuns like Marie de Valence fighting the Church's battles from within their cloisters, how could Catholicism lose?

NEW FEMALE RELIGIOUS ORGANIZATIONS

There were, however, Catholic women who wanted to help their Church but could not do it within a cloister. In Protestant countries, for example, nunneries were closed; there, women could enter convents only by fleeing abroad. Most preferred to remain at home and help their Church as lay women, for in many Protestant areas the Catholic Church was outlawed, priests were few and forced to live in hiding and only the laity could keep the Church alive. England was one country where these conditions existed. Nunneries were closed in 1534 and after 1559 Anglicanism was the only legal religion. From about 1570 to 1610 Catholics were severely prosecuted. During this period, lay women kept the Church alive in England. They risked their lives to shelter the priests, mostly Jesuits, who ministered to the illegal underground Catholic congregations. And when no priest was available, the women had to assume some priestly duties, like leading the prayers, themselves.[12]

The same thing happened in the Protestant Dutch Republic. There the Church survived thanks to women who called themselves *geestilijke maagden*, 'spiritual virgins', although Protestants derisively called them *kloppen*, 'castrated men', a name Catholics affectionately shortened to *klopjes*. *Kloppen* was in some ways appropriate, because these women performed some of the functions of male priests. Living as lay women, alone or in groups, but wearing religious habits and often affiliated as tertiaries with male religious orders, the *klopjes* not only sheltered priests and cared for the poor and sick but also catechized, taught religious doctrine and preached in public. The Church's reaction was mixed. Some churchmen, especially the priests with whom they worked, admired their sanctity and courage and compared them to the female missionaries and deaconesses of the early Church. But most churchmen, especially the hierarchy in Rome, saw them only as *béatas* to be disciplined.[13]

Similarly mixed reaction greeted the numerous proposals by Catholic women, often directly inspired by these examples of female activism, for new sorts of religious organizations in which women could play an active role in the Church while remaining outside the cloister. The most famous of these was the Institutes of the Blessed Virgin Mary founded by Mary Ward. Ward was English and, as she explained, the English situation directly inspired her plan:

> As the sadly afflicted state of England, our native country, stands greatly in need of spiritual labourers . . . it seems that the female sex should and can . . . undertake something more than ordinary . . . we . . . desire . . . to embrace the religious state and at the same time to devote ourselves according to our slender capacity to the performance of those works . . . that cannot be undertaken in convents. We therefore propose to follow a mixed kind of life [that is, religious while uncloistered].[14]

Mary Ward had once been a nun, fleeing her native England to join a convent of Poor Clares in Belgium. But she found them too worldly. Wanting to help the Church's proselytizing, she and 10 like-minded nuns opened a charity school that taught poor girls reading, writing and religion. This was so successful that they soon did the same thing in England, where, because Catholicism was outlawed, they had to wear lay clothes and move about in public. As Ward wrote, her English experiences prompted her to propose a series of such schools, to be called Institutes of the Blessed Virgin Mary, all over Europe. They were innovative because of the 'mixed life' of the teachers, who would observe the nuns' vows of poverty, chastity and obedience but not take their final solemn vows, wear religious habits or observe claustration. They were also innovative in their administrative structure, copied from the Jesuits whom Ward worked with and admired. The institutes would not be controlled by bishops or a male religious order; instead they would be run by an elected mother superior responsible only to the pope. All of this worried the Church, but Ward's lobbying was so persuasive that Pope Paul V allowed her to establish her institutes for a trial period. They proved remarkably successful. By 1631 there were 10 schools in major cities from Liège to Prague, and some had over 500 pupils.

Sadly, the very success of the institutes proved their undoing. They expanded so fast that there were not enough trained teachers and administrators and problems arose. Other orders of nuns jealously attacked them. And, above all, the Church found it hard to accept this uncloistered, independent group of women. In 1621 English priests succeeded in having the institutes there suppressed, charging that, 'It was never heard in the Church that women should discharge the Apostolic Office', and that 'the members arrogate to themselves the power to speak of spiritual things before grave men and priests'.[15] In 1625 the institutes in Italian cities were also shut. Finally, in 1631, Ward was arrested by the Inquisition and imprisoned for a year. The remaining institutes were disbanded and their members sent home. The Bill of Suppression expressed the Church's discomfort with independent, uncloistered holy women. Ward's nuns were called 'noxious weeds' who lived as men:

> They went freely everywhere, without submitting to the laws of *clausura*, under the pretext of working for the salvation of souls; they undertook and exercised many other works unsuitable to their sex and their capacity, their feminine modesty, and, above all, their virginal shame.[16]

Ward could probably have kept her institutes going if she had shaped them in conformity to the Church's ideal of a female religious order, especially if she had accepted some form of enclosure. But this she refused to do. Ward would today probably be called a feminist: she was very conscious of being a woman and was eager to defend women's abilities. In an address to her nuns, she said:

> There is no such difference between men and women that women may not do great things . . . I confess wives are to be subject to their husbands, men are head of the Church, women are not to administer the Sacraments, nor preach in public places; but in all other things, wherein are we so inferior to other creatures that they should term us 'but women'? I would to God that all men understood this truth, that women . . . if they would not make us believe that we can do nothing and that we are but women might do great matters.[17]

Mary Ward was the most outspoken but far from the only Catholic woman who wanted her sex to play a more active part in the Church and tried to create new orders to make this possible. Another was an illiterate lower-class Italian woman, Angela Merici of Brescia, who wished to reach out to the poor who needed both material and spiritual help, especially poor girls in danger of losing their virtue. She wanted both to save them and make it possible for them to save others. This meant that she could not found an order of nuns, where the poor had no place but that of servant. Instead she envisaged a loose organization of women who took private vows of chastity but lived in their own homes, wore their own clothes and moved freely among the poor of the city. Her organization, the Company of Saint Ursula, took a more formal shape in 1534, when it was divided into two tiers: young virgins who did the actual work with the poor and older matrons who supervised them. Both were under a mother superior responsible only to the pope. This group was very successful. When Merici died in 1540, one-quarter of the households in Brescia included an Ursuline.[18]

With success came expansion but also pressure to turn the Ursulines into a normal cloistered order. In 1568 the great reforming bishop St Charles Borromeo invited them to Milan, but only on condition that they accept his authority and live together in communities. In this form they spread to France, where again they were remarkably successful. Between 1600 and 1610, 29 Ursuline communities were founded in southern France alone. There their major activity was catechizing the poor, men and women alike. One Ursuline, Anne de Vesvres, made missionary journeys from village to village: 'She would invite the priests of the villages that she visited to teach the children their catechisms, and when they excused themselves, saying that they did not know how, she readily and modestly showed them the method.'[19] Another Ursuline became the spiritual director of both men and women and yet another preached so effectively that she drew crowds too big for the churches to hold.

Inevitably, such female activism worried male churchmen, who pressured the Ursulines to turn themselves into a normal religious order with final vows and claustration. This was done in 1658. After this the Ursulines did not leave their convents to reach the poor but instead taught female students, mostly upper-class girls, in schools within the convent walls. These were very successful. By 1700 the Ursulines were the leading educational order in France, with 10,000 to 12,000 nuns teaching hundreds of thousands of girls. But this was not what Angela Merici had envisioned. Merici was eventually canonized as the founder of a new and successful order of nuns – the last thing she had intended.

The transformation of the Ursulines from a flexible organization with a multifaceted mission to a single-purpose cloistered order was paralleled by another new female religious group, the Visitadines. They were founded in 1607 by Jeanne de Chantal, a young French noble widow with four children. Chantal wanted to devote herself to religion but thought her family obligations precluded full enclosure. Therefore she founded a religious congregation where women like her could live together but take only simple vows, practise the minimum of physical mortification and be only partially enclosed. The Visitadines were forbidden contact with men, but they could leave the cloister for family emergencies and to visit the poor and sick. Their name came from the Virgin Mary's visit, while pregnant, to her cousin Saint Elizabeth: the mixture of practical and spiritual help Elizabeth had provided was the model for the half-active, half-contemplative congregation Chantal envisioned.

But like the institutes and the Ursulines, the Visitadines were opposed by male churchmen. The Archbishop of Lyons wrote in 1615:

> In the first place he did not approve of the sisters visiting the poor; in France, nuns were not allowed by their rules to walk in the streets . . . On one hand, those who see a nun in the world occupied with business affairs, will be scandalized; on another, the Monasteries which we are trying to enclose in obedience to the Council, will have something to say and good reason to complain.[20]

So the Visitadines too were forced to accept solemn vows, full enclosure, and the reduction of their outreach to the poor to charity dispensed to pious invalids and widows housed on the convent grounds.

The only new women's congregation to escape the seemingly inevitable evolution into a cloistered order was another French group, the Filles de Charité (Daughters of Charity). This was due to two factors: first, they were founded later than the other groups (1629–1645) and could therefore learn from their examples and, second, although their organizational plan was invented by a woman, an illiterate cowherd at that, their founder was a man, a churchman who had the confidence of his brother clergy, understood their prejudices against independent holy women and had enough knowledge of canon law and church politics to get around them.[21]

This man was one of the great saints of the Counterreformation, St Vincent de Paul. Chaplain to a French noble family, he began preaching to the poor at the request of his noble patroness. Appalled by their poverty, he resolved to give them material as well as spiritual help. He therefore organized *charités* in the various French parishes. These were groups of mostly upper-class women like his patroness who provided the poor of the parishes with food, medicine and religious instruction. Although they spread rapidly, the *charités* had two problems. First, while in theory sympathetic toward the poor, the noblewomen of the *charités* were not tactful in dealing with them or experienced in the cooking, nursing and other dirty tasks their mission required. Second, the *charités*, like the parishes in which they were organized, were mostly urban; they left the rural poor untouched.

These problems were solved by the illiterate cowherd, a young peasant woman, Marguerite Naseau. She had heard of the *charités* and she recruited some friends and offered to do the hard, dirty work unsuitable for the *charités'* ladies. This gave St Vincent the model for his new organization. The Daughters of Charity would be lower-class women who took religious vows and lived communally but uncloistered, going out to country villages to aid the poor. To prevent the seemingly inevitable claustration, St Vincent avoided anything that would suggest they were an order of nuns. They took private, simple vows, wore not a nun's habit but instead the simple skirt, bodice and headkerchief of the poor and their communal houses had no bells or grilles like convents. St Vincent told them:

> Your monastery is the house of the sick . . . your cell is your rented room . . . For cloister, the city streets, where you go in the service of your patients.[22]

These tactics worked. The Daughters of Charity were never cloistered and they proved so popular among both poor women, who finally had their own religious organization, and the Church, which finally had a means to reach the rural poor, that by 1789 15 percent of the women in religious orders in France were Daughters of Charity.[23] Yet even they saw their mission narrow. Originally they provided food, medicine and religious instruction for the poor, cared for the sick and taught reading, writing and the catechism to young girls. They also nursed soldiers on battlefields and sent missions to convert Protestants. But gradually they began to specialize in nursing the sick, at first in their homes and then in hospitals. Because they were uncloistered, they could go out to work in the hospitals, workhouses and orphanages where the poor were increasingly confined. As these institutions multiplied in the seventeenth century, the period of the Great Confinement of the poor, so too did the Daughters of Charity. And while they never forgot their mission to bring the poor to the 'True Faith' – indeed, the doctors they worked with complained that they were more concerned that their patients receive the last rites and make a 'good death' than that they get well – they became increasingly skilled and professional nurses.

By the nineteenth century the majority of nuns in most Catholic countries were members not of the traditional contemplative orders but instead of the new orders of the Counterreformation. These new orders had transformed and 'professionalized' the nun. Her life of service to God was now achieved through service to mankind; her virginity was now less important than her skills as teacher or nurse. In her new professional persona the nun made her mark on women's history. She pioneered in and set the standards for teaching and nursing. Countless girls' schools copied those of the Ursulines and Florence Nightingale modelled her nurses on the Daughters of Charity. These two 'caring professions', teaching and nursing, would eventually, in the nineteenth century, employ hundreds of thousands of women, mostly young and single, allowing them to support themselves and therefore giving them an alternative to marriage that did not require that they leave the world and renounce their sexuality.

NEW TEACHINGS ON WOMEN,
SEX AND MARRIAGE

If the Counterreformation thus ultimately produced a new alternative to marriage for women, it also made this alternative less necessary by improving the married state. For during the Counterreformation the Church, alarmed by the appeal of Protestantism to women, rethought its teachings on the lay life, marriage, sexuality and women's nature in ways favourable to women. The Church's main spokesman for the new doctrine was St François de Sales, who had been bishop of the Calvinist stronghold, Geneva, from 1602 to 1622 and therefore had first-hand experience of the Protestant challenge.

As we have seen, the pre-Reformation Church denigrated lay life and especially the married state as spiritually inferior to a life of monastic celibacy, while the Protestants maintained that the lay life was the one God intended for mankind and was fully compatible with Christian devotion: one worshipped God by obeying his commandments in daily life and by working hard at one's calling. St François agreed:

> It is not only erroneous but a heresy to hold that life in the army, the workshop, the court or the home is incompatible with devotion . . . At the creation God commanded the plants to bear fruit each according to its kind and he likewise commands Christians . . . to bear fruit by practising devotion according to their state in life. The practice of devotion must differ for the gentleman and the artisan, the servant and the prince, for widow, young girl or wife.[24]

As with Protestants, the rehabilitation of the lay life brought with it a rehabilitation of the married state, although Catholics, of course, never renounced celibacy. But celibacy was increasingly regarded as possible and necessary only for the exceptional few, primarily the clergy. Most of mankind was to be married. 'Marriage', de Sales stated, 'must be held in honour. It must be held in honour by everyone, even, with humility, by virgins . . . for its origin, its end, its advantages, and its matter and form – all are holy.'[25] One sign of this upgrading of marriage was that the Council of Trent mandated, for the first time, that a priest must be present and perform the ceremony for a marriage to be valid. Another was the encouragement by the Church of the celebration of wedding anniversaries.

For Catholics, like Protestants, the basis of marriage was the mutual love of husband and wife, invariably compared to the love of Christ for the Church. The Council of Trent therefore rewrote the Church's teachings on marriage to emphasize this. Admittedly the new requirement that marriages be celebrated publicly ended clandestine marriages, which had allowed young people to avoid arranged matches and marry for love. Yet Trent kept the doctrine that consent was necessary for a valid marriage and, although young people were urged to seek their parents' approval of the match, that was not required. While churchmen clearly expected that parents would arrange the matches of their children, they increasingly emphasized that children should not be forced into marriage against their will or made to marry someone they abhorred.[26]

This was the theme of many of the 47 novels written by a follower of St François, Bishop Jean-Pierre Camus. Camus, like de Sales bishop of a heavily Protestant diocese, thought novels would help him reach out to the laity. He was able to write so many because he blithely stole other authors' plots, but he added his own theological message and this often was to not to force young people into arranged marriages. In *Elise, or Guilty Innocence*, for example, Philippin, the young heir to a French noble family, was forced to marry the wealthy but unattractive Elise even though he was in love with Isabelle, the beautiful daughter of one of his father's servants. Elise was pregnant when Isabelle reappeared; Philippin sent his wife away and seduced Isabelle. He was therefore murdered by her outraged father and brother, but the luck-less Elise and a young man, Andronic, who loved her, were blamed for the crime and arrested and executed. Then the real murderers were also caught and killed and Isabelle ended up entering the convent. Camus' moral: the whole bloody mess could have been avoided if Philippin had been allowed to marry Isabelle.[27] The constant emphasis on love as the only proper basis of marriage eventually had an effect. Arranged marriages lasted longer in Catholic than Protestant countries (in some segments of the nobility and upper bour-geoisie in Spain, France and Italy they lasted well into the twentieth century), but from the seventeenth century on, children usually could veto potential spouses totally abhorrent to them.

This new emphasis on love as the foundation of marriage brought with it a rehabilitation of sex – at least in the marriage bed. Once again the Catholic Church did not go as far as the Protestants, who celebrated sex as God's gift for human happiness. But post-Reformation Catholic theologians viewed it more favourably than had the churchmen of the Middle Ages. For the latter the only justification for sex had been procreation; the sex act was to be performed reluctantly, as a duty to one's spouse, and to enjoy it was a venial sin. They counselled married couples to abstain whenever possible. In contrast, St François de Sales compared sex to eating: a physical action necessary for the preservation of life but also pleasurable. Sex not for procreation but 'to promote the mutual friendship and concord' of husband and wife was permissible and should be undertaken 'freely, without constraint, and with some show of appetite', although St François did caution against 'immoderate and excessive' sex and against 'wallow[ing] in the remembered pleasures' afterward.[28]

As with Protestants, this newly positive view of sex extended only to that within lawful marriage. Extramarital sex of any kind was to be firmly suppressed. This meant that popular behaviour and attitudes had to be transformed, because many forms of extramarital sex, while defined in theory as sinful, had been tolerated in practice by the pre-Reformation Church. As in Protestant countries, this transformation was achieved in part through education from the pulpit and in part through repression by the courts. In most Catholic countries, the latter was done not by local magistrates and consistories but by the Inquisition, the Church court charged with stamping out heresy. Naturally the bulk of the Inquisition's cases concerned actual heretics: converted Jews or Muslims who continued to practise their old religions, Protestants, witches. But after Trent an increasing proportion of its cases – over 25 percent of those tried in Valencia, Spain, from 1554 to 1820, for example – concerned sexual sin.[29] In these cases what brought defendants before the Inquisition was not the sin itself but denying it *was* a sin – that is, false doctrine or heresy. Thus acting according to traditionally accepted standards and maintaining that such actions were acceptable could, in the stricter atmosphere of the Counterreformation, get you hauled before the Inquisition.

Three examples of this are bigamous marriages, engaged couples living together and casual sexual affairs. Although illegal, bigamy had been widely tolerated in the Middle Ages. It was the only way that couples too poor for expensive annulments could get out of unhappy marriages. If a husband deserted his wife and she found someone else to marry, the Church traditionally had not worried too much about whether the first husband was still alive. After Trent, it did. Similarly, in the Middle Ages engaged couples had often lived together. Their community considered them as good as married, because consent made a marriage and they had given that in their betrothal. But after Trent only a ceremony performed by a priest made a marriage and engaged couples who lived together were hauled before the local bishop and told to regularize their union.

The aspect of popular mores most difficult to modify was the attitude toward casual sex – simple fornication in canon law. As Alonso de Meixide stated indignantly when he was brought before the Inquisition for that crime: 'in his village it had never been a sin to have carnal intercourse between men and women' – but now, alas, it was and it was increasingly prosecuted by the Inquisition.[30] In Toledo, Spain, simple fornication accounted for one-fifth of the Inquisition's cases in 1566–1570 but one-third in 1581–1585.[31] These included prosecutions for patronizing prostitutes, something that had been not only tolerated but encouraged in the Middle Ages. Prostitution was no longer viewed as a necessary evil. Now that men were actually expected to remain chaste outside marriage and to keep their marriage vows, it was viewed as providing an occasion to sin. After Trent the Church struggled to close municipal brothels and make prostitution illegal. In 1623, for example, it succeeded in closing all the legal brothels in Spain.[32]

Most of the people brought before the Inquisition for sexual offences were men.[33] This suggests that another change in sexual attitudes brought by the Counterreformation was a tendency to apply the same high standards of sexual conduct to men as had traditionally been applied to women. Of course, in theory, this had always been the case. The Church propounded a single standard of sexual conduct: virginity before and fidelity after marriage were expected of men as well as women. But before Trent, only women were held to this high standard. After Trent, it applied to men as well and at least the most blatant, notorious and unrepentant male sexual offenders were denounced and hauled before the Inquisition, although the married man who exhorted an occasional sexual favour from his servant or discreetly kept a mistress was unlikely to be bothered. Again, typically, Catholics were less extreme than Protestants in their prosecution of male sexual offenders, but at least they recognized that men might be as sinful as the daughters of Eve.

The flipside of this reinterpretation of men's potential for sin was a more favourable view of women's nature and this too came to the Church with the Counterreformation. We can see it in the Church's new attitude toward prostitutes, who were no longer portrayed as wantons luring men into sin but instead as innocents corrupted by immoral men – or at least as victims of economic circumstances, forced into prostitution by poverty. This prompted the founding of a new type of charitable institution characteristic of the Catholic Reformation: shelters for poor girls in danger of falling into prostitution. The Conservatorio delle Zitelle Periclitanti (Conservatory for Single Females in Peril) was founded in Venice in the 1530s. Naples acquired a similar institution in the 1560s, two opened in Milan in the 1570s and Florence eventually had five. These houses of refuge spread in Spain and Portugal and their overseas colonies as well.[34]

If sinful prostitutes were now seen as merely weak, respectable married women were now viewed as moral and virtuous, possibly even more moral and virtuous than their husbands. This led to a drastic reinterpretation of the roles of husband and wife within marriage. Traditionally, husbands had been the moral guides of those 'weaker vessels', their wives. It was a husband's duty to guide his wife and correct and even chastise her when she did wrong. This view of marriage still lingered in the Counterreformation. St François de Sales admonished wives to view their husbands with 'reverence and respect', for they were members of 'the more vigorous and dominant sex'. 'A wife', he stated, is 'subject to his [her husband's] guiding hand.' But in the Counterreformation this traditional advice to wives was accompanied by admonitions to husbands to exercise their moral authority with, as St François put it, 'love, tenderness, and gentleness'.[35] The Jesuit Jean Benedicti reminded a husband forced to correct his wife that 'even though she is inferior, nevertheless she is not the slave or the chambermaid but the companion and flesh ... of her husband'.[36] Catholics did not punish wifebeaters as Protestants did, but they did provide a new saint, Saint Rita, as patroness of abused wives.

The Church not only urged husbands to be tactful in correcting their wives; it also envisioned situations where wives might actually be morally superior to and the moral and spiritual guides of their husbands. This new view of gender roles in marriage was articulated in a letter from that archetypal figure of the Counterreformation, St Ignatius Loyola, to Joanna Colonna, a noblewoman who had quarrelled with her spouse. St Ignatius advised her to give in to him, because 'it will be more in conformity with the laws which God's majesty has laid down for holy matrimony'. So far, so traditional. But St Ignatius went on to say that by humbling herself even though she was in the right, Colonna would 'derive excellent merit before God' and she might also shame her husband into repenting and behaving better in the future, and might therefore 'bring him back to a state more secure for his salvation'.

Thus, St Ignatius stated, 'Sir Ascanio [the husband] is given into your hands and will now be your slave' [!][37]

This letter reflects the realization of churchmen like Loyola that wives were more likely to be good, pious and faithful Catholics than their husbands and that they might moralize their families, reforming their husbands and raising their children to be good Catholics. This new appreciation of female piety and its importance to the Church stemmed from what historians term the 'feminization' of Catholicism after the Counterreformation. This happened not because women were increasingly drawn to the religion but because men began to desert the Church. The Church's drive to end popular superstitions and teach everyone the rudiments of the faith often brought conflict with lay *men* – the members of town councils or communal governments in peasant villages who wanted to preserve traditional shrines and celebrations. And, as we have seen, most of the people arrested for not adhering to the new moral standards were men. Further, because they were more likely to be literate than women, it was men who were more exposed to the new ideas of the scientific revolution and the Enlightenment, which often led them to question the teachings of the Church. Therefore men, especially elite men, began by the end of the seventeenth century to desert Catholicism and, as this happened, churchmen began to appreciate women. Pious wives and mothers raising their children in the true faith seemed the Church's best hope for the future.

Of course, because they were but women, of weak understanding, these pious wives and mothers could not be relied on to moralize their families by themselves. They needed male guidance. But despite the Church's rhetoric about marriage, this would not be the guidance of their husbands, whose faith might be dubious. Instead, it would be that of their spiritual advisors and confessors. The piety of the Counterreformation, focused not on external ritual but on the inward state of the believer, promoted the practice of confession and this became the means by which the Church controlled and influenced its newly valued female members. Unfortunately, it also, briefly, became the occasion for much priestly misbehaviour. The reforms of the Counterreformation banished the priest's 'wife', his 'nieces' and 'nephews' and attractive young servants from priestly households, but they could not completely obliterate the desires of the flesh. In the early years of the Counterreformation some priests used the intimacy of confession to solicit sex from and make lewd remarks and advances to their female penitents. Such misdeeds, called 'solicitation' by the Church, formed 3 percent of the cases brought before the Inquisition in Spain from 1540 to 1700.[38]

Solicitation gradually disappeared with the better training of priests and the spread of the confessional stall, which separated priest and penitent and guarded the latter's anonymity. Purged of its sexual overtones, the relationship of confessor and female penitent would remain the Church's main tool for moralizing lay society into the twentieth century.

Thus the newly moral wife and mother took her place beside the refigured nun as a pillar of the post-Reformation Catholic Church. The Reformation prompted the Catholic Church to redefine traditional roles and images of women rather than create new ones, as the more radical Protestants did, but the end result was similar. Both Protestants and Catholics discarded much of Christianity's traditional misogyny and newly recognized and emphasized the spiritual equality and worth of women.

The equality we enjoy today would have been impossible without this vital change.

Chapter 11

♦

WITCHES

In the previous chapters I have argued that both the Reformation and the Counterreformation had many favourable consequences for women, from divorce to marriage for love to new careers as teachers and nurses to better treatment for wives. But of these none was more important than the abandonment of the misogynist tradition of early Christianity which painted women as daughters of Eve, the more sinful sex. Just how important this was can be seen when we examine the witch craze of the early modern period. The Catholics and Protestants who labelled each other heretics in the sixteenth and seventeenth centuries were united in fearing an even more frightening group of heretics in their midst: witches, who deliberately chose evil over good, rejected God and worshipped the Devil, and used the evil powers he gave them to harm friends and neighbours. From 1450 to 1750 about 110,000 people were officially tried for witchcraft and of these about 60,000 were executed. Over three-quarters of those tried for witchcraft were women.[1] Some radical feminists have suggested that the witchcraft prosecutions were a sort of genocide against women, prompted by virulent misogyny, a deep-seated, visceral fear and hatred of the female sex.[2] That is an immense oversimplification of a complex historical reality. But it is undeniable that the misogyny so deeply embodied in traditional Christianity – the conviction that women were sinful daughters of Eve and therefore easy prey for the Devil – was a major factor making women vulnerable to prosecution as witches.

WHY PEOPLE BELIEVED IN WITCHCRAFT

Of the aspects of the lives of early modern women, probably the one most difficult for us today to understand is that fact that almost all of them believed in the possibility of witchcraft and feared both being harmed by a witch and being accused of practising witchcraft. Why women believed in witchcraft is simple. Witchcraft was defined as *maleficia*, harmful magic, and before the scientific revolution of the late seventeenth century everyone believed in magic. They lived in an enchanted universe where the physical and the spiritual were intertwined and acted on one another. The four elements, earth, air, fire and water, each had spiritual qualities emanating from it, as did the four humours – blood, phlegm, yellow bile, black bile. Melancholy came from an excess of black bile, for example. Ordinarily both the human body and the physical universe operated under natural law: predictable rules ordained by God Himself governing their physical functioning. But these laws could be suspended or contravened by the manipulation of the spiritual forces in the universe – that is, by magic. The miracles performed by God and, with His assistance, by the saints, were magical and holy words and objects had magical properties. Prayers were often used as magic spells and the Church feared that communicants would not swallow the Host but instead use it in magical rites. There was also non-religious magic, performed by professional sorcerers, 'wise women' and 'cunning men'. Peasants seeking cures for illnesses went to the local wise woman, who gave them magical herbs and told them the spells to say to make them work. Wise women and cunning men also sold love potions and charms to ward off the evil eye and to protect travellers on journeys and they could find lost objects through conjuration. Even educated and sophisticated aristocrats bought magical herbs, charms and love potions and consulted astrologers, sorcerers and cunning men. Magician Richard Napier made his fortune consoling the lovelorn and bereaved of Tudor London; his method, which consisted mostly of listening to his clients as they told their stories, was rather like modern psychoanalysis.[3]

All of this was white magic, good magic, and in most places it was perfectly legal – indeed, it was the routine way to deal with the problems and uncertainties of life. But white magic had its opposite – black magic, harmful magic, *maleficia* – and practitioners of white magic were suspected of performing *maleficia* as well. He who could find lost objects might be able to make them disappear; she who could cure illness could also cause it. Accusations of witchcraft usually started with suspicions of *maleficia*, and naturally suspicion fell on known practitioners of magic. This explains many of the cases of *men* accused of witchcraft. Table 11.1 summarizes the sex of accused witches. In most areas they are overwhelmingly female. But in some places – Iceland, Estonia, Russia – most people tried for witchcraft were male. This was because in such areas, significantly on the fringes rather than in the heartland of Europe,

Table 11.1 Sex of accused witches

Region	Years	Male	Female	% Female
Southwestern Germany	1562–1684	238	1050	82
Bishopric of Basel	1571–1670	9	181	95
Franche Comté	1559–1667	49	153	76
Geneva	1537–1662	34	240	76
Pays de Vaud	1581–1620	325	624	66
County of Namur	1509–1646	29	337	92
Luxembourg	1519–1623	130	417	76
City of Toul	1584–1623	14	53	79
Dept of the Nord, France	1542–1679	54	232	81
Castile	1540–1685	132	324	71
Aragon	1600–1650	69	90	57
Venice	1550–1650	224	490	69
Finland	1520–1699	316	325	51
Estonia	1520–1729	116	77	40
Russia	1622–1700	93	43	32
Hungary	1520–1777	160	1482	90
County of Essex, England	1560–1675	23	290	93
New England	1620–1725	35	267	78

Source: B. Levack, *The Witch-Hunt in Early Modern Europe* (Harlow, 1995).

most magicians were men, like Tereshka Malakurov, the local cunning man in the Russian village of Lukh tried for witchcraft in 1656. Malakurov was the village healer, treating even the local priest with charms, herbs and talismans. When accused, he confessed that a horse doctor named Oska had taught him to bewitch people by scattering salt on the road and chanting spells and that he had done so for the last three years so that his victims would come to him for cures.[4] Where most practitioners of magic were men like Malakurov and where the practice of harmful magic was what made witchcraft a crime, witches were gendered male. As a historian of witchcraft in Iceland explained, a magician had to be learned in chants and spells and knowledge was a male prerogative; therefore Iceland's witches were usually men.[5]

WHO WERE THE WITCHES?

But in most of Europe folk medicine and white magic were in the hands of women, so not surprisingly those accused of witchcraft were usually women too. Often they were well-known practitioners of folk medicine like Clara

Botzi, the first woman to be tried for witchcraft in Hungary, or midwives like Walpurga Hausmänin of Dillingen, Germany, charged in 1587 with causing the deaths of over 40 babies, two women in childbirth, eight cows and a horse, plus miscellaneous geese and pigs. She was also charged with causing three adults to languish to the point of death and raising a damaging hailstorm.[6] Female healers like Hausmänin were so likely to be accused that some early feminist historians of witchcraft argued that the persecution of witches was a plot by male doctors to rid themselves of their female rivals (see Chapter 7). This was soon disproved. Sometimes professional rivalries *did* trigger accusations. In Hungary, for example, rival midwives accused each other, as did rival cunning men.[7] But it was far more typical for female healers to be denounced not by their male professional rivals but by their female clients or potential clients – in other words, by their female neighbours in their villages. Furthermore, female healers formed only a small portion of the women accused of being witches. In Scotland, for example, only about 6 percent of those accused were midwives and/or healers. The vast majority were simply wives or widows of tenant farmers, as were most women in rural Scotland.[8]

Elsewhere as well, most of the women accused of witchcraft were just ordinary women. But they shared three important characteristics. First, they were usually relatively poor. Sometimes wealthy and prominent women (and men) were accused of witchcraft. In Scotland, two wives of lairds (landowners), 16 noblewomen, 14 wives of local government officials and 14 wives of teachers or ministers were among the 192 accused whose social status is known.[9] But such cases were quite rare. Neither were the accused drawn from the very lowest ranks of society. Only in England were beggars, vagabonds and the utterly destitute victims of accusations. Instead, accused witches were usually, in rural areas, settled members of their communities with a cottage and a small plot of land they owned or rented. In towns they tended to be the wives or widows of craftsmen who themselves worked as laundresses, petty retailers and the like. Thus they were not destitute, but they were nonetheless poorer than many of their neighbours. This was often due to the other two characteristics accused witches shared: their age and their marital state. As Table 11.2 shows, in most places most women accused of witchcraft were old by the standards of their time and, simply because they were old, they were often widows living alone.

Why were such women accused of witchcraft? Historians have come up with two explanations, one based on the socioeconomic circumstances of the 'witch' and one based on the psychology of her accuser.

Table 11.2 Ages of accused witches

Region	Years	Witches of known age	Number over 50	% over 50
Geneva	1537–1662	95	71	75
Dept of the Nord, France	1542–1679	47	24	51
County of Essex, England	1645 only	15	13	87
Württemberg	1560–1701	29	16	55
Salem, MA	1692–1693	118	49	42

Source: B. Levack, *The Witch-Hunt in Early Modern Europe* (Harlow, 1995).

The latter has its roots in a theme running consistently through the denunciations of witches: motherhood. Often a baby's illness and/or death triggered an accusation of witchcraft. This, not professional jealousy, prompted the denunciation of midwives. As we saw, Walpurga Hausmänin was accused of killing over 40 babies plus two women in childbed. Midwives were not the only women associated with birth and babycare to be targeted as witches. Lying-in maids, the women hired to look after the mother and newborn during her extended 'lying-in' period, were also routinely accused. In fact, they were accused so often that one German suspect asked plaintively: 'Why must it always be the lying-in maid who is to blame?'[10] An example is 67-year-old Anna Ebeler of Augsburg, accused of killing a new mother by giving her poisoned soup and also a baby who starved to death, another who was unable to nurse and two others who died covered in red splotches and blisters. Ebeler confessed after being threatened with torture and she was executed.[11] Even the neighbour women invited to assist at and celebrate births were vulnerable to witchcraft accusations. In Scotland, Rosina McGhie accused her sister-in-law, Elspeth Thomson, of causing the death of her child in revenge for not being invited to the birth or baptism. When her baby could not nurse, Rosina tried to counteract the evil spell she thought Elspeth had cast on the child. She got a neighbour to steal thatch from Elspeth's roof and burn it; burning something owned by a witch would supposedly end a spell. She also went to Elspeth and persuaded her to say 'God send all folks good of their milk', after which her milk began to flow. But the baby remained ill and Rosina remained convinced that Elspeth was determined to kill it. One day Elspeth visited Rosina to borrow a loom. Because it was near the baby's bed, she touched the bed. That made Rosina afraid to lay the baby there. Instead she put a puppy in the bed; it promptly fell sick and died. When the baby died too, Rosina accused Elspeth of witchcraft.[12]

It is easy to see what prompted such accusations of witchcraft. As we have seen, in early modern Europe pregnancy and childbirth were fraught with danger and newborns were likely to die within days or weeks of birth. Yet motherhood was increasingly regarded as woman's main purpose in life, the essence of her female identity, and mothers were blamed – and sometimes arrested and punished – for 'bad mothering'. Therefore how guilty a mother like Rosina would feel if, despite all her efforts, her baby died, and how tempting it would be to shift the blame to someone else. It was especially tempting if that someone was someone the accuser subconsciously resented, and probably new mothers often felt that way towards the midwives, lying-in maids and neighbours whom they accused. Remember that new mothers were forced to remain idle during their long lyings-in. How they must have resented the lying-in maid bustling about *their* house, taking *their* place, doing *their* jobs – and doing them wrong! Remember too that midwives and lying-in maids were usually old, old enough to be the mothers of the new mothers who employed them. We have seen that the elderly were generally resented in early modern Europe, and I have suggested that grown daughters might have subconsciously hated their mothers because they were the ones who socialized them into their subservient female roles (see Chapter 4). It seems quite likely that young new mothers would see the older women who helped them through childbirth as substitute mothers and displace the hatred and resentment they bore their own mothers onto them.

Thus it is easy for us to find fairly plausible psychological explanations for young mothers accusing elderly women of witchcraft. The people of the time, however, found what they regarded as plausible psychological explanations for elderly witches harming young mothers: envy and spite. These old women could no longer have children; they envied the young mothers their babies. And spite prompted the slighted neighbours and relatives like Elspeth Thomson to take their revenge.

Envy and spite were also thought to lay behind another common scenario of witchcraft, one which we might call 'charity refused'. The case of Janet Macmurdoch, wife of James Hendrie, a Scotswoman accused of witchcraft in 1671, typifies this. Janet's first accuser was John Moor, the agent of her landlord, who had seized her livestock for unpaid rent. Janet had yelled at him and 'promised him an evil turn'; shortly after, his cattle and his child had died. Janet was also accused by three other men, substantial farmers who had chased her cattle off their land. She had yelled at them and sworn revenge and, soon after, their cattle and family members had sickened and died. John Murray also accused her. He had accidentally tripped her and six weeks later two of his cattle and a horse fell ill. Not all Janet's accusers were men. Margaret Maclellan had employed Janet's daughter as a servant and scolded her for laziness, saying that both she and her mother were witches; a month later Maclellan's husband fell sick. Jean Sprot had refused Janet a meal; the next day she felt ill.[13]

These accusations reveal a common pattern. Janet was clearly fairly old – she had a grown daughter – and she was also clearly poorer than her accusers. Her daughter worked as a servant and she herself was behind in her rent. As we have seen, it was usual for poor elderly women to be given help by their neighbours; widows and old women were thought to have a priority on charity. Janet seems to have tried to take advantage of this, demanding meals and pasturing her cattle on other people's land. But her neighbours were not charitable toward her. This probably made them feel guilty and, like the guilt-ridden mothers, they relieved their consciences by projecting their guilt onto the person who had caused it. This pattern of a poor elderly woman demanding charity, being refused and then being accused of witchcraft by the refuser is very common in witchcraft cases.

Projecting guilt onto Janet was probably made easier by the fact that she seems to have been rather disliked. Certainly she was assertive and quarrelsome, traits seen as negative and threatening in women (see Chapter 3). This too was common in witchcraft accusations. Meek, quiet, accommodating women were rarely accused, at least at the beginning of a witchhunt; instead, accusations pursued the assertive and aggressive. This is yet another reason why widows were so often accused. Living on their own, with no husband to protect them and handle negotiations with the outside world, they had to be assertive and aggressive. So too did wives of poor men. Their economic activities were vital for their families' survival, but to succeed in scrounging odd jobs and petty charities they too needed an assertiveness and aggressiveness that could give them bad reputations.[14]

In addition to being contentious, women accused of witchcraft also often had reputations for sexual misconduct. This was not true of Janet, but it was true of the English witches Elizabeth Frauncis, rumored to have aborted an illegitimate pregnancy; Ursley Kempe and Annys Herd, bastard bearers; Ales Newman, accused by her son of luring him into incestuous relations; and Elizabeth Bennet, suspected of a lesbian relationship with a neighbour's wife. Of 42 women accused of witchcraft in Essex in the sixteenth and seventeenth centuries, 12 had reputations for sexual deviance of one kind or another.[15]

A final characteristic of accused women is that they already had a long-standing reputation as a witch before the official charge was lodged. This is yet another reason why suspected witches were old: they needed time to acquire a reputation. What gave a woman such a reputation? She might be related to a suspect (witchcraft was thought to run in families) or she might earn suspicion on her own. Constantly at odds with her neighbours, in the heat of a quarrel she may have cursed someone who sickened or died. Doctors tell us that worry or depression can suppress the immune system, making us more susceptible to disease. A believer in magic and witchcraft would worry if cursed and might well fall ill. A few such cases and a woman's reputation as a witch was made.

Thus we can draw a profile of the typical woman accused of witchcraft. She was usually old and poor, she often worked as a wise woman or lying-in maid and she had, either through quarrelsomeness or sexual misconduct, lost her good reputation among her neighbours – something which made it easier for them to project their guilt feelings onto her. Notice that misogyny seems to play little role in these scenarios of witchcraft accusations. Most of the accusers as well as the accused were women and the accusations grew out of the ordinary circumstances of women's lives. Admittedly, these were shaped by the gender stereotypes and gender role expectations of a patriarchal society which we today would consider demeaning to women, especially the suspicion of and contempt for the post-menopausal woman and the popular disapproval of women who were noisy, assertive and sexually aggressive. But there are few signs of true misogyny, a true hatred of women, in these stories of witchcraft at the village level and there is little evidence that, as some historians have asserted, men used the threat of witchcraft accusations to keep assertive and uppity women in line. Mere assertiveness alone did not get you accused of witchcraft. Misogyny is an important factor behind the prosecution of witches, but not at the village level. Where misogyny – and the Devil, for that matter – can be found is in a second set of beliefs about witches, those held by the learned elite.

LEARNED BELIEFS ABOUT WITCHCRAFT

What most villagers feared about witches was the harm they could do, destroying crops and causing illness and death in animals and people. These acts of *maleficia* were to them the essence of witchcraft and it was for such crimes that peasants denounced their neighbours. But to the learned authorities who received these denunciations the essence of witchcraft was different. To them it was the pact with the Devil, who supposedly gave the witch her magical powers in return for her soul, that made witchcraft a crime, specifically the religious crime of heresy, the worship of the Devil over God. It was as heretics that most witches were tried (in Catholic countries by the same court, the Inquisition, that tried other heretics) and executed (by burning at the stake, the standard method of executing heretics).

The belief that witchcraft was heresy had developed slowly over the centuries. Christian beliefs about the Devil had their source in the New Testament, where Satan is depicted as commanding a host of subordinate demons (theologians spent endless hours trying to discover just how many; one came up with the figure of 133,306,668)[16] and engaged in a titanic struggle to lure men and women away from Christ and His teachings. As Christianity spread, theologians identified the Devil's Kingdom of Darkness with the religions with which Christianity competed – paganism, Judaism, Islam – and endowed the Devil with characteristics of the competing gods. For example, the Devil's cloven hooves were derived from the Roman god Pan. Thus, gradually, worshipping the Devil was equated with worshipping a false god. This was a violation of the first of the Ten Commandments and therefore heresy.

The Devil enticed people to worship him through gifts like wealth, political power and magical control over nature. This last 'gift' was carefully defined by theologians, who did not want to make the Devil equal in power to God, Who alone could suspend natural laws, perform miracles and create new life. The Devil could do none of these things. But he did have the power to move around the elements of physical reality and he used this power to create a physical body in which to appear to potential followers, since he was a pure spirit with no body of his own. He and his demons also often borrowed the body of a person or animal. These cases of possession are quite common among witchcraft cases. Both the Catholic and Protestant churches had special rituals to exorcise or drive out evil demons. The Devil could also use his power to move physical substances around to create illusions: to make people think they were flying or had been turned into animals or made impotent. Finally, the Devil's power to move the physical elements of reality allowed him to perform harmful magic: to raise storms or make people and animals sicken and die.[17]

According to learned writers on witchcraft, the Devil bestowed his power of *maleficia* on witches in return for worship. That usually took place at a *sabbat*, a gathering of witches, held as a rule in a clearing in a wood at night. There the Devil appeared to his followers, usually as a big black man, although sometimes as a goat or toad. They did homage to him by kissing his ass and worshipped him in ceremonies that included obscene parodies of the Christian mass. At the *sabbat* they also feasted, indulged in naked dancing and promiscuous sexual intercourse, both heterosexual and homosexual, and killed infants, whose flesh they either ate or boiled down to make 'devil's grease', a magical salve that enabled them to squeeze through cracks and keyholes and fly at night.[18]

What was the source of these ideas? An early scholar of witchcraft, folklorist Margaret Murray, thought they might have had an actual basis in fact. Murray had studied the ancient pagan fertility cults of the Great Goddess and was convinced that they survived in secret among the peasantry throughout the centuries of Christianity. Because these cults involved gatherings of women in open-air services, Murray thought that rumours and glimpses of gatherings to worship the Great Goddess gave rise to belief in the *sabbat*.[19] Scholars today reject this hypothesis; there is no evidence of the survival of goddess worship. Instead they believe that elements of the *sabbat* originated in the early days of the Church. Gathering in secret at night and indulging in promiscuous sexual intercourse and cannibalism were accusations levelled by their opponents at early Christians and recorded as such in the writings of the Church Fathers. They had some basis in fact. When Christianity was still illegal, Christians met at night to worship and their 'love feasts' could easily be misinterpreted as promiscuous sex. At any rate, during the Middle Ages churchmen found these accusations in holy writings and levelled them against groups they defined as heretics.[20] Thus when witchcraft became a heresy, witches acquired the *sabbat*. Scholars have even found the first appearances of the *sabbat* in witchcraft trials. In 1324 Dame Alice Kytler, an Irish noblewoman, and her friends were accused of *maleficia* and also of meeting at night, having sex with demons and using devil's grease.[21]

Witches supposedly flew to the *sabbat*. Beliefs about night-flying women formed another cluster of learned ideas about witchcraft. Unlike those about the *sabbat*, these had roots in popular as well as learned culture. Most peoples of the world believe in some sort of night witch, a woman who could transform herself into a bird and fly and do evil deeds. Europeans are no exception. Both the ancient Romans and the Germanic peoples who overthrew them believed in *strigae*, women who at night transformed themselves into flying screech owls and seized and devoured infants. A second popular source of belief in night-flying witches were the 'wild hunts', the nocturnal processions organized to honour fertility goddesses like the Roman Diana or the Germanic Holda. These goddesses were both nurturing and terrifying. Diana brought fertility, but as a virgin she killed her would-be lovers or turned them into animals. Holda was beneficent on earth but led a 'Furious Horde' of angry souls who had died prematurely across the sky. Beliefs in these nightly processions were widespread in European culture. As late as the sixteenth century peasants in northern Italy had delusions that they were *benandanti* who went out at night in processions, armed with stalks of sorghum to fight off witches and demons and ensure fertility in the fields. Learned culture fused the *strigae* and the *benandanti* into night-flying witches who attended *sabbats*, practised harmful magic and worshipped the Devil.[22]

These popular contributions to witchcraft beliefs are important because they helped gender the witch as feminine; in earlier periods, those seduced by the Devil's offers of wealth, power and control of nature had usually been men, often learned magicians. But the permanent and deeply misogynist identification of the witch as a woman came not from popular beliefs but from a learned treatise about witchcraft published in 1487: the *Malleus Maleficarum*, or *Hammer of Witches*.[23] The *Malleus*, one of the most misogynistic books ever written, added to the learned view of witchcraft as Devil worship four new and important propositions: that most witches were women, that their pact with the Devil was sexual in nature, that their aim was nothing less than overthrowing the proper gender order of society and that there was a vast conspiracy of witches posed to take over the world that should be uncovered and destroyed by killing them all.[24]

The *Malleus* was written by two German Dominican monks, Heinrich Kramer (1430–1505) and Jakob Sprenger (1436–1495), who were members of the papal Inquisition for southern Germany. As learned monks they were familiar with the writings on women and female sexuality by the early Church Fathers and medieval churchmen. These appear to be the major source of their misogyny. But it was deepened by their own experiences. Sprenger apparently never actually took part in a witchcraft trial. Instead he spent his career reforming the monasteries of his order. This meant trying to make monks live up to the ideal of clerical celibacy. Therefore it is not surprising that Sprenger viewed female sexuality as seductive and dangerous. Unlike Sprenger, Kramer actually tried witches. In 1485 he was involved in a trial in Innsbruck. The original accusations concerned only the usual illnesses caused by *maleficia*, but in his interrogations of suspects Kramer tried to elicit details of what to him was the essence of witchcraft: the witch's sexual relations with the Devil. His questions about their sex lives were so detailed and obscene that the female suspects threatened to sue for slander and the local bishop stopped the trial. Kramer then sat down with Sprenger to write the *Malleus* to educate people in the true nature of witchcraft.[25]

For women's history, the most important section of the *Malleus* is that entitled 'Concerning Witches who copulate with Devils. Why is it that Women are chiefly addicted to Evil Superstitions?' in which the authors explain why women are more likely to be witches. Here they repeated all the traditional arguments about women's inferiority. Women are 'feebler in both mind and body' than men. Because they are 'intellectually like children', their grasp of the fundamentals of Christianity is less sure than men's; '*Femina* comes from *Fe* (Faith) and *Minus*, since she [woman] is ever weaker to hold and preserve the faith.' Women's bodies are more impressionable than men's and thus it is easier for the Devil to take possession of them. Women are more vain, passionate and vengeful than men, so when they are insulted they are more apt to seek revenge through witchcraft. Above all, women are lustier than men. Female sexuality is by definition both insatiable and sinful, as Eve shows; when women lose their virginity, they lose the possibility of salvation (!). It is through their sexuality that women are seduced into evil by the Devil; the pact between witch and Devil is sealed by sexual intercourse. 'All witchcraft comes from carnal lust, which is in women insatiable.'[26] (See Plate 11.)

According to Sprenger and Kramer, their sexuality not only made women easy prey for the Devil, it also drove them to try to dominate men. Their ultimate goal was to invert the proper gender order of society. Wives often used witchcraft to get the upper hand in their households or to punish their husbands. The *Malleus* has long passages on the miseries of marriage and the problems of dealing with shrewish wives. Witches attacked the very essence of masculinity by 'tying the knot' and making men impotent. They also destroyed men's hopes of gaining immortality through their children by promoting contraception, abortion and infanticide. Their supposed connivance in such practices made midwives especially likely to be witches. Also likely to be witches were what Sprenger and Kramer called 'the concubines of the great': the mistresses of kings. They inverted the proper gender order of society not only by dominating their infatuated lovers but also by using that dominance to achieve that ultimate forbidden fruit for women: power in the public sphere.[27]

Thus the *Malleus* presented a new and profoundly gendered version of witchcraft. Unfortunately for women, it was a very popular book, reprinted 13 times before 1520. It was from the *Malleus* that the European elite, the doctors and theologians who wrote about witchcraft, the magistrates and judges who arrested and tried witches, derived their ideas about the phenomenon. Not all of Sprenger's and Kramer's notions were widely adopted. Neither midwives nor royal mistresses were specifically targeted in witchcraft accusations and shrewish wives weren't either. But Sprenger's and Kramer's convictions that most witches were women, that the Devil tempted witches sexually and sealed his pact with them through sexual intercourse, did become part of the learned lore of witchcraft. And along with notions about the *sabbat*, they also began to show up in popular beliefs. This transfer of ideas from learned to popular culture occurred because of the way witchhunts were conducted during the high point of witchcraft prosecutions from around 1560 to 1680.

WITCHHUNTS

A witchhunt usually began at the village level with the standard suspicions of *maleficia*: someone, or someone's livestock, had fallen ill and a witch was suspected. The suspect usually fitted the standard profile: she was female, elderly, poorer than her accuser, with whom she was involved in a 'new mother' or 'charity refused' situation, and she had a bad reputation among her neighbours. Often she had a reputation as a witch as well. Usually the first reaction of the bewitched party was to try to get the curse lifted, through pleas, bribery or threats. In sixteenth-century Lorraine, a poor elderly woman, Laurence Viney, hired for haymaking, was publicly accused by her employer's young wife of causing a hailstorm that ruined the crop. The wife fell ill and the husband sent for Laurence on the pretext of hiring her to work flax. Laurence said she knew the real reason she had been summoned and she crossed the wife's forehead five times with her thumb. The wife recovered.[28]

If the witch refused to cooperate, the afflicted parties had four more options. They could hire a wise woman or cunning man to lift the curse or try to lift it themselves by stealing and destroying something from the witch's house: bread, salt, ashes from the hearth, thatch from the roof. They could also beat the witch until she gave in. Often these beatings ended in the witch's death. How often we do not know, but it is probable that many more women than appear in the official 60,000 death toll died because they were suspected of witchcraft.

If all these methods failed, the final resort of the afflicted was to denounce the witch to the local authorities. This set in motion a process which usually resulted not only in a full-blown witchhunt with many accusations and arrests but also an infusion of the learned concepts of witchcraft into local witch beliefs. That happened because the judges as they prepared their cases asked leading questions shaped by their learned ideas about witchcraft: did you make a pact with the Devil? did you have sex with him? did you attend a *sabbat*? Accused witches usually confessed to whatever they were asked, elaborating details to please their questioners. And these confessions usually became public. They were spread by gossip from the spectators at trials, public readings of charges before executions and by printed pamphlets and books like *The Apprehension and confession of three notorious Witches, Arreigned and by Justice condemned and executed at Chelms-forde*, printed in London in 1589.[29] Once witches confessed, people naturally believed what they confessed to and thus the pact with the Devil and the *sabbat* gradually passed into popular lore. The most famous example of how this happened concerns the *benandanti* of northern Italy, the men and women who thought they had marched off to the fields at night to fight off witches and protect the crops. They were tried by the Venetian Inquisition, whose judges asked them questions shaped by the learned concept of witchcraft and got most of them to confess that they were witches, not *benandanti*. Within 50 years the *benandanti* disappeared from the popular culture of the area, displaced by more orthodox witch beliefs.[30]

Why did accused witches confess? The most obvious answer is because they were tortured. Everywhere but in England, torture was a standard part of the investigation of not just witchcraft but all serious crimes. To protect defendants, standards of proof in crimes like robbery and murder were very high. Circumstantial evidence could not convict; instead, either the testimony of two eyewitnesses or a confession was necessary. Since crimes were rarely committed in front of two witnesses, courts relied on confessions and it was to encourage these that torture was used during investigations. Because it was recognized that most people would say anything to stop torture, its use was hedged with restrictions. Torture could be employed only when there was strong circumstantial evidence of guilt. Children and pregnant women could not be tortured. Torture could last only one day and the methods used could not be severe enough to cause death. Interrogators could not ask leading questions and the testimony taken during torture could not be used as evidence; the defendant had to repeat his or her confession voluntarily afterwards.

Unfortunately for accused witches, these safeguards could be suspended in cases of especially dangerous crimes like treason or heresy or for 'hidden' crimes that left little evidence. Witchcraft fitted both categories, so witches were routinely tortured. In fact, they were tortured more severely than other suspects, for it was thought that the Devil gave witches the power to withstand pain, and enduring torture without confessing, in other crimes a sign of innocence, was taken as a sign of guilt. So witches were subjected to thumbscrews, leg screws and head clamps; to the rack; to the *strappado*, in which they were lifted off the floor by a pulley and suspended by their wrists, with weights of from 40 to 660 pounds attached to their feet; to the 'witches' chair', suspended above fire; to the water torture, in which water is dripped on rags stuffed up the nose and down the throat until the subject can't breathe; and to what their interrogators considered the worst of all, prolonged sleep deprivation (it was claimed that 98 percent of its victims confessed).[31]

Thus it is not surprising that accused witches usually confessed and that, as Table 11.3 shows, conviction and therefore execution rates were higher in areas where torture was employed. What is surprising is that some accused witches endured torture without confessing. Probably the record for endurance was held by a woman of Nördlingen who refused to confess through 56 torture sessions; she was finally released.

Sometimes suspects withdrew their confessions after the torture stopped, as did Mengeatte des Woirelz. She said that she was:

> tired of being in prison, and of the pain of the torture, joined with the fear of the evil reputation she had been falsely given in the town, she had chosen to die rather than live in such anguish. She had reckoned that in saying what she did . . . copying the confessions of a woman executed at Crecy, and the suspicions held by various witnesses used against her, we [the judges] would have enough reason to put her to death.[32]

This suggests that people confessed not only to stop the torture but also because they were shocked to learn how much their neighbours feared and hated them and didn't see how they could go on living in such an atmosphere. As Barbelline Chaperey explained: 'She had not reckoned there would be so many people hostile to her, after thinking about which, she had been led to make such confessions.'[33] Judges were aware of this possibility; those in Lorraine rejected the voluntary admission of an elderly widow, Claudon

Table 11.3 Regional execution rates in witchcraft trials

Region	Years	Persons tried (fates known)	Executions	% executed
Fribourg	1607–83	162	53	33T
Geneva	1537–1662	318	68	21T
Neuchâtel	1568–1677	341	214	63T
Pays de Vaud	1537–1630	102	90	90T
Luxembourg	1509–1687	547	358	69T
County of Namur	1509–1646	270	144	54T
Isle of Guernsey	1563–1634	78	33	46T
Dept of the Nord, France	1542–1679	187	90	48T
Finland	1520–1699	710	115	16
Norway	1551–1760	730	280	38
County of Essex, England	1560–1672	291	74	24
Scotland	1563–1727	402	216	54T
Hungary	1520–1777	932	449	48T

Source: B. Levack, *The Witch-Hunt in Early Modern Europe* (Harlow, 1995).
'T' indicates torture used.

Wannier, that she was a witch who had killed two people with powder given to her by the Devil:

> [I]t is difficult for us to believe in this, because there is no sign that the powder was real, rather that tired of life and seeing herself to have become old and crippled, poor and needy, without relatives or friends to sustain her, she was trying to achieve the aim of her own death.[34]

Other sorts of despair also prompted confessions. In Lorraine many self-proclaimed witches said that they had succumbed to the Devil's blandishments when grieving over the death of a child. Today they would be diagnosed with clinical depression. People also confessed because of guilt feelings. In 1608 Catherine La Rondelatte voluntarily stated:

> I am a witch. Ten years ago last St Laurence's day I was coming back from visiting my sister ... walking alone through the woods all dreaming and thoughtful that I had been so long a childless widow, and that my relatives discouraged me from remarrying, which I would have liked to do. When I arrived at the place of the round oak ... I was astonished and very frightened by the sight of a great black man ... although I quickly recommended myself to St Nicholas, he then suddenly threw me down, had intercourse with me, and at the same time pinched me roughly on the forehead. After this he said, 'You are mine. Have no regret; I will make you a lady and give you great wealth', I knew in the same hour it was the evil spirit, but could not retract because he had instantly made me renounce God.[35]

Clearly the long-time widow La Rondelatte did not have sex with the Devil, but she probably had sex with *someone* or at least felt troubled and guilty about her sexual desires. Franceatte Charier confessed out of guilt of a different sort, hatred of an abusive husband:

> [S]he was extremely angry and miserable because her husband did her much harm, while she saw herself reduced to poverty; desolated as she was by this situation, one day behind the house she was overcome by several evil thoughts which blew in her ears, and at that moment she saw a man of middling size dressed in black climb down from a tree.[36]

A final reason for voluntary confessions was that the suspects actually believed they *were* witches and so they confessed to what they thought they had actually experienced. They may have dreamed that they had flown through the air or attended a *sabbat*; many voluntary confessions have a dream-like quality. They also may have confessed to drug-induced delusions. Witches supposedly flew by applying magical ointments to their bodies or broomsticks. Recipes for some of these have survived and while most are harmless (and ineffective), some contain atrophines, which can have hallucinogenic or mind-altering effects.[37] The delusions they confessed to may also have been caused by senility or insanity. Clearly some accused witches, especially the elderly, were either insane or senile. Even some of her neighbours wondered whether Alice Whittle, described as 'a very old, withered, spent and decrepit creature, her sight almost gone . . . Her lips ever chattering and talking, but no man knew what',[38] was only senile, not evil. Finally, perfectly sane people may have confessed because they actually believed they had supernatural powers. Accused witches were usually poor, powerless and ostracized by their neighbours. They may have deliberately cultivated a reputation for witchcraft to gain money, power and attention. Edward Fairfax noted that the witch who tormented his children:

> had so powerful a hand over the wealthiest neighbours that none of them refused to do anything she required; yea, they provided her with fire, and meat from their own tables, and did what else they thought to please her.[39]

As we have seen, the people they cursed may well have sickened and when this happened, such women may have become convinced they actually had supernatural powers.

Whatever the reasons behind them, witches' confessions were usually believed, and thus the pact with the Devil, the *sabbat*, and a strong dose of misogyny passed from learned culture into local folklore. Confessions also guaranteed that the witchhunt would continue, because the accused were asked to name names: whom did you see at the *sabbat*? Usually they simply named women who already had reputations as witches. When all were named, the hunt ended. Most witches were prosecuted in small-scale local hunts involving 10 people or fewer.

Sometimes, however, the hunt continued, with scores and even hundreds of people tried. The largest known witchhunt took place in the Basque country in 1610; over 2000 people were prosecuted. But most of these large hunts (indeed, three-quarters of all witchcraft trials), took place within the borders of the Holy Roman Empire, especially in southern and western Germany, Switzerland, Lorraine, the Franche-Comté and Savoy.[40]

These areas had all the ingredients necessary for large-scale witchhunts. They had, first of all, a law which defined witchcraft as heresy, not *maleficium*, and proscribed the death penalty, the famous *lex Carolina* of 1532. Second, their legal procedures allowed the use of torture. Third, and most importantly, witchcraft cases were tried in local courts with no appeal to higher jurisdictions. Local judges and magistrates had the final say. This was important because it was the attitude of the judges and magistrates that determined whether a witchhunt would continue and spread. Everywhere in Europe the common people believed in the possibility of witchcraft and local judges and magistrates reflected the attitudes of their neighbours. They were determined to root out the entire witch conspiracy and cleanse their home town of heresy. But higher court judges, with no ties to the area and often more sophisticated attitudes toward witchcraft – or at least more knowledge of the law and more determination to stick to proper legal procedures – might well call a halt to the proceedings.[41]

We can see the importance of these factors when we examine witchhunts in areas such as Spain, Portugal and Italy where witchcraft came under the jurisdiction not of local magistrates but of the Inquisition. The late medieval Inquisitions had harboured enthusiastic witchhunters like Kramer and Sprenger, but the judges in the Inquisitions of the sixteenth and seventeenth centuries, the era of the great witchhunts, were more sceptical – or at least more concerned with rooting out Protestants and suppressing 'superstitious' practices among Catholics than they were with witches. Therefore popular healers were often called before the Inquisition, but witches rarely; in Portugal, for example, only 2.5 percent of the Inquisition's cases concerned witchcraft.[42] And when witches *were* tried by the Inquisition, they were likely to be acquitted, for despite its fearsome reputation, the Inquisition had the most procedural safeguards to protect defendants of any court in early modern Europe. The accused was allowed a lawyer and the court paid the travel expenses of witnesses testifying for the defence. Defendants could submit lists of their enemies so the court could judge if the accusation grew from spite and physicians were called in to see if the victim had died of natural causes. Torture was rarely used and judges were sceptical of witches' confessions. In Bologna, Maria di Gentili confessed to murder by witchcraft, but she was sentenced only to banishment because a judge thought 'there are too many contradictory elements in her confession which do not agree with the evidence presented at the trial'.[43]

If you were accused of witchcraft and could not be tried by the Inquisition, your next best bet was to be tried in an area where appeal to a higher court was possible. In Denmark every witchcraft case was subject to review; lower courts convicted 90 percent of the defendants brought before them, but the higher court overturned half the convictions.[44] In France the highest court of appeal, the Paris Parlement, overturned convictions in 36 percent of the witchcraft cases brought before it; unlike the lower courts, the Parlement did not accept confessions obtained under torture as proof of guilt. In Scotland, too, higher courts were much more lenient than lower courts, which usually convicted almost all the defendants brought before them.[45]

Lower court judges too tried to be scrupulous about evidence, but unfortunately this often resulted in higher conviction rates. If they found confessions obtained under torture doubtful, they might look for corroborating evidence. They might, for example, enquire into the local reputation of the accused – which usually was that she was a witch. They might search for the devil's mark – a protuberance or flaw – on her body, something all too easy to find on elderly women covered with age spots, moles, warts and goitres. In England, even then apparently pet obsessed, corroborating evidence often took the form of a witch's familiar, a small animal – a cat, dog, rat or toad, usually – the Devil gave her to help her cast her spells. Many a lonely old woman who talked incessantly to her cat condemned herself in the eyes of her neighbours. Finally, if they still felt uncertain, local officials might consult outside experts. The laws of the Holy Roman Empire suggested they consult university professors, who might be sceptics, but all too often they consulted professional witchfinders, who were paid for their efforts and therefore had professional and financial interests in having the hunt continue. Two professional witchhunters, Matthew Hopkins and John Stearne, were personally responsible for England's largest witchhunt, in which over 200 people were executed.[46]

For all these reasons local witchhunts might move forward, growing until there were no more poor elderly women left to accuse. Suspects arrested in the later stages of large witchhunts, when asked to identify others at the *sabbat*, had to name young women, men, even children. Often they said the first name that popped into their heads, perhaps the mayor's or a prominent town councillor's. These accusations sowed the first seeds of doubt among the local people.[47] Clearly anyone could be accused – even members of their own families! Why, they themselves might even fall under suspicion! Also encouraging doubt was the fact that in large-scale hunts accusations seemed to follow lines of the economic, social or political divisions in the village – that is, people seemed to be using witchcraft accusations to strike at their enemies. Thus in the famous outbreak in Salem, Massachusetts, in 1692, accusations mirrored rivalries between economically declining Salem Village and economically thriving Salem Town. Similarly, in Winnigen, Germany from 1640 to the 1660s, many family members of the local elite were arrested; their accusers were younger, poorer men tired of being kept out of power.[48] Such patterns were as obvious to contemporaries as they are to historians and they encouraged people to be sceptical about accusations. At any rate, most large-scale hunts ended very abruptly. Accusations suddenly stopped and often those convicted but not yet executed were freed.

THE END OF THE WITCHHUNTS

Most witch trials took place between 1560 and 1680, peaking in the 1620s. The beginning date of 1560 and the peak in the 1620s are easy to explain. The great hunts could not have occurred until the intellectual and legal changes which made them possible – the spread of the learned concept of witchcraft, its legal definition as heresy, the use of torture in witch trials – were in place. That happened only during the first half of the sixteenth century. But that period saw few witch trials, because people were preoccupied with the religious conflicts and changes of the Reformation. By the early years of the seventeenth century, the religious conflicts had died down, yet they had made everyone conscious of the dangers of heresy. And the adverse economic situation (most European economies declined from the 1590s through to the 1620s) and constant warfare made people anxious and eager for scapegoats. Witches provided these.

The disappearance of witchhunts at the end of the seventeenth century has a more complex explanation. They did not end because peasants stopped blaming witchcraft for their misfortunes. Ethnographers have found that belief in witchcraft lingered in rural areas well into the twentieth century. Instead, it was the learned elite who ceased to believe in witchcraft. After around 1690, villagers continued to denounce their neighbours, but officials refused to prosecute.

Why? In part, because of the witchhunts that had gone before. Judges had always been dubious about their illegal procedures and questionable evidence and the more hunts there were, the more dubious they became. They were especially doubtful about evidence produced by torture, not just in witch cases but for all crimes. Many countries banned or severely restricted torture after 1680.[49] Eventually these legal concerns filtered down to local judges and magistrates.

The numerous trials and confessions also strengthened doubts about the very existence of witches and witchcraft. Even in the heyday of witch beliefs, there had always been sceptics who wondered if witchcraft really existed. As early as 1509, the Renaissance humanist and champion of women Henricus Cornelius Agrippa attacked witch beliefs on the grounds that the spiritual elements of the world could be manipulated by human reason; the Devil was not necessary to cast spells. In the 1560s and 1580s Agrippa's disciple Johann Weyer argued that most cases of 'witchcraft' had natural causes. The illnesses and deaths were due to disease, not spells. For Weyer, disease even explained witches' confessions. Those who confessed suffered from *melancholia*, the female disease of 'wandering womb' that made them vulnerable to delusions. Even more sceptical was the Englishman Reginald Scot, who, as a good Protestant lumped witchcraft with 'popish miracles' as an outmoded superstition and published case after case of fraud like that of witchfinder Mother Baker, consulted by the relatives of a sick girl. When they named a suspect, Mother Baker said that she was indeed a witch, 'the very party that wrought the maiden's destruction by making a heart of hay and pricking the same with pins and needles'. Mother Baker was discovered planting just such a heart on the suspect's property.[50]

As Scot's dismissal of witchcraft as 'popish superstition' suggests, sceptics' doubts were strengthened by the religious trends of the period. In some ways the Reformation and Counterreformation encouraged the prosecution of witches. Both the Protestant and the Catholic churches officially believed in the possibility of witchcraft and demonic possession, and, as we said, their conflicts made everyone conscious of the dangers posed by heretics – including witches – hidden in the midst of godly communities. But the Reformation and Counterreformation also helped to end witchhunts by promoting a new view of the physical universe. Protestants believed that God could suspend the natural laws through which the physical universe functioned and perform miracles, but that He did so only rarely. Thus Protestants drew a sharp line between the spiritual and material worlds and suggested that usually only natural causes worked in the latter. And the Counterreformation's repudiation of the traditional miracle-working saints in favour of a more inward-looking, intellectual and theologically correct religion encouraged Catholics too to adopt this new worldview.

The final triumph of this newly 'disenchanted universe' came with the scientific revolution of the late seventeenth century. The new science convinced the elites that the universe was totally material and that matter was inert, without spiritual properties. This totally material universe, from which spiritual forces were banished, functioned according to fixed laws discoverable by human reason, which could not be suspended. This meant that phenomena formerly blamed on witchcraft must instead have natural causes.

There is one more cause for the end of witchhunts, one more way in which the new religious ideas contributed to their demise: the end of the stereotype of woman as sinful Eve. Historians find it significant that in many countries the last witchhunts – the 1669 outbreak in Sweden, the 1692 Salem, Massachusetts witch craze and the 1723 accusations in Augsberg, Germany – did not involve the adult females of the standard stereotype but instead large numbers of children possessed by the Devil.[51] Why this shift? As we have seen, witches had been gendered female because of the long misogynistic tradition in Christianity, elaborating on the frailty of sinful Eve. Protestantism had attacked this tradition; to Protestants women were the spiritual equals of men, equally liable to sin but equally eligible for salvation. Protestants said less about the sinfulness of women than about their private and public virtues as wives and mothers, and during the Counterreformation Catholics too promoted a new, more favourable image of women. Witchhunts can therefore be seen as the last stands of traditional misogyny as these new ideas spread. When they triumphed, the traditional witch disappeared.

In her place came the evil child. When the elites of the late seventeenth and eighteenth centuries thought about original sin, they found it embodied not in the daughters of Eve but in children of both sexes, born tainted with mankind's tendency to sin and not yet having developed the moral sense to control it. The sexual games and rebellions against adult authority of the 'possessed' children embodied their parents' deepest fears about childhood sinfulness, fears that would last until the scientific revolution destroyed revealed religion and its idea of original sin and gave rise to the notion of childhood innocence. With that the witch craze would finally end.

Part V

♦

WOMEN AND THE STATE

The final area of the public sphere into which women fitted only partially and uncomfortably was the state. In early modern Europe, it was taken for granted that women's interests were confined to the domestic sphere of the household and that they should play no role in public affairs. The sixteenth-century French political theorist Jean Bodin wrote a 300-page treatise touching on almost every aspect of politics, but he mentioned women only in a brief (for Bodin) sentence explaining why he need not discuss them further:

> Now as to the order and degree of women, I meddle not with it; only I think it meet them to be kept far off from all magistracies, places of command, public assemblies, and counsels; so to be attentive only unto their womanly and domestical business.[1]

This assumption that women had no place in the state was echoed by the English political theorist Sir Thomas Smith, author of *De Republica Anglorum* (1565):

> We do reject women [from public office], as those whom nature had made to keepe home and to nourish their familie and children, and not to medle in matters abroade, nor to beare office in a citie or common wealth no more than children or infants.[2]

Yet in the same work Smith ardently defended the right of his queen, Elizabeth I, to rule. Elizabeth was heir of the blood, and:

> These I say have the same authoritie although they be women or children . . . as they should have if they had bin men of full age. For the right and honour of the blood, and the quietnes and sueritie [security] of the realme, is more to be considered than . . . [the fact that they are of] the sex not accustomed (otherwise) to intermeddle in publicke affairs.[3]

Smith's emphasis on 'the honour of the blood', the right of the true heir, gives the clue to the paradoxical position of women in the public realm. For despite their gendering as masculine domains, women did have roles in early modern states. Like men, they were citizens, subject to the state's laws and taxes. Like men, they were protected by a state's administration and endangered by its wars. And like men, a surprising number of them exercised political power, either informally through pressure and influence or, like Elizabeth I, formally through the holding of public office. This presence of women in public affairs was possible because the state was less masculine than patriarchal. In early modern Europe, society was envisioned as a collection of patriarchal house-holds, in which the father provided protection and guidance to the house-hold members and they, in turn, owed him obedience and deference. The state was simply a household writ large, with a ruler as its patriarchal head, the father of his people. As Erasmus explained:

> The good prince ought to have the same attitude toward his subjects as a good *pater-familias* toward his household – for what else is a kingdom but a great family? What is the king if not the father to a great multitude?[4]

In this vision of politics, women were present in the public sphere just as they were present in the patriarchal household, and, as in the household, their roles there were shaped and legitimated by their relationship to the male patriarch. Thus women could exercise political power as wives, daughters and widows of, and as stand-ins for, male patriarchal kings or citizens, although their own rights were severely limited.

QUEENS REGNANT: STAND-INS FOR MALE HEIRS

The most powerful women in the public sphere were queens regnant, those like Elizabeth I who ruled in their own right as legitimate heirs to male kings. Their rule was always controversial because it was considered unnatural – that is, a reversal of the proper order of nature – that a woman would rule over men. This was the argument made by John Knox, a Protestant Scot galled by having to obey his Catholic ruler, Mary Queen of Scots, in his *First Blast of the Trumpet Against the Monstrous Regiment of Women*, published in 1558. Knox argued that 'nature hath in all beastes printed a certein mark of domination in the male, and a certein subjection in the female'. Knox also argued that a woman ruling men contravened the laws of God (the Bible clearly stated 'that woman in her greatest perfection was made to serve and obey man, not to rule and command him') and public peace and order ('experience hath declared [women] to be unconstant, variable, cruell, and lacking in the spirit of counsel and regiment [rule]').[1] Most people probably shared these convictions. Yet in early modern Europe the claims of patriarchy and patrilineal descent overrode these objections and of the major states only France barred daughters from inheriting the throne in the absence of a legitimate male heir. And because the male line failed in a number of major states, Europe in the sixteenth and seventeenth centuries had a slew of 'unnatural' female sovereigns, including Mary Queen of Scots, Mary Tudor and Elizabeth I in England, Isabella in Castile and Christina of Sweden.

These women playing a male role faced a formidable challenge, although their task was made easier by the nature of kingship in the early modern period. By 1500 a king was no longer expected personally to lead his troops into battle, as medieval kings had done; neither was he expected to be what Frederick the Great would later term 'the first servant of the state', the head administrator of a vast impersonal government bureaucracy, as eighteenth-century sovereigns would be. Both of these roles were difficult for women to fill. Instead, early modern kings functioned primarily as ceremonial figures in the ever-growing public rituals of rule and as patrons of the arts and dispensers of favours in their ever-growing courts. Both were roles which women could perform; indeed, some women, queen consorts, the wives of kings, already did so. They were also roles which, when performed with skill, female rulers could use to overcome the disadvantages of their gender.

Take court ritual. In their coronations, their carefully choreographed royal entries into the chief cities of their realms and in other public ceremonies, queens could surround themselves with the symbols of legitimate – that is, male – rule. Of course, they had to do this tactfully and not present themselves to their subjects as more masculine than feminine, more king than queen. That would open them to the attacks that early modern society launched against any woman who tried to go 'beyond her sex'. Queen Christina of Sweden forgot that simple rule. Because it was obvious immediately after her birth that she would be her parents' only child and would one day inherit the throne, Christina was given the education of a male prince and taught Latin, philosophy, fencing, riding and hunting, not feminine accomplishments. She often wore men's clothes and she took her coronation oath as king, not queen. She never married and had a number of close relationships with women. It is not surprising that Christina was attacked as a 'tribate' (lesbian) and, quite unpopular among her people, she eventually abdicated the throne.[2]

Elizabeth I of England was much cleverer at manipulating the masculine symbols of kingship. She usually referred to herself as a prince and she assumed male kingly roles in public ceremonies, but she was always careful to acknowledge that she was a woman playing a man's role – a queen, not a king. For example, when England was threatened by invasion by the Spanish Armada in 1588, Elizabeth reviewed her troops as a male king would, marching 'King-like', 'with a Leader's Truncheon in her Hand' – but wearing a dress. She had herself depicted wearing a breastplate and helmet – but never in full masculine armor. Her famous Armada speech showed a similar artful claim to masculine roles while acknowledging her femaleness:

[I am] resolved, in the midst and heat of battle, [to] lay down for my God, and my kingdom, and for my people, my honour and my blood, even in the dust. I know I have the body of a weak and feeble woman, but I have the heart and stomach of a king, and of a king of England too . . . rather than any Dishonour shall grow by me, I myself will take up Armes, I myself will be your General.[3]

She showed equal tact when assuming the masculine roles growing out of the religious aspects of kingship. She carried out the religious rituals associated with the English monarchy, applying the royal touch to cure scrofula and washing the feet of the poor on Maundy Thursday. The latter ceremony allowed her to assume three masculine identities simultaneously – king, priest and Christ Himself – for English kings had traditionally done this in imitation of priests, who in turn followed the lead of Christ, Who had washed the feet of the poor before His crucifixion. Yet when Elizabeth became head of the Anglican Church (as English monarchs were since 1534 and are today), she did not call herself that because she did not wish to remind churchmen that they had to obey a woman. Instead she called herself governor, which in the sixteenth century meant simply 'administrator', with fewer connotations of rule.[4]

If Elizabeth was careful in presenting herself to her subjects in the male guises of kingship, she was equally careful in presenting herself as a woman. She was especially successful in avoiding the major pitfall of her womanhood: marriage. Elizabeth was of course the Virgin Queen; she never married. Doubtless she had a personal distaste for the wedded state (she once told the Spanish ambassador that marriage was 'a thing for which I have never had any inclination')[5] derived from what happened to her mother, Anne Boleyn and her various stepmothers, Henry VIII's wives, famously dead, divorced or beheaded. But political motives also lay behind her refusal to wed. Marriage was the Achilles' heel of queens regnant in our period. Their subjects expected them to marry, both because marriage was the only acceptable state for an adult woman (apart from being a nun in Catholic countries) and because only through marriage could they produce legitimate heirs for their thrones.

But marriage created problems for reigning queens. As rulers they were supreme in their realms, but as wives they would have to obey their husbands. And since a sovereign could not easily obey one of her subjects, their husbands were usually foreign princes who might sacrifice the interest of their wives' countries to advance those of their own. It was this fear of the influence of foreign princes, not worries about women's incapacity to rule, which made France bar women from the throne and led Russian czars to leave their sisters and daughters unmarried. In Russia, only foreign princes were of suitable rank as husbands for royal women, but not only did they bring the threat of foreign influence, they were also not of the Russian Orthodox faith, and that church forbade interfaith marriages.[6]

It was possible for a queen regnant to marry and still rule effectively. The prime example is Isabella of Castile, Elizabeth's major challenger for the title of most successful female ruler in our period. Isabella picked the right husband, Ferdinand of neighbouring Aragon. The marriage united the two countries to form a powerful new state, Spain, but their administrations remained autonomous. Within her own state, Isabella kept the reins of power firmly in her own hands and while she was always careful to appear the dutiful, deferential, devout and modestly clad wife in public, in private she indulged in an inordinate passion for clothes and jewels and did as she pleased.[7] But more common was the experience of Mary Tudor, whose proper wifely deference to her husband, Philip II of Spain, a classic foreign prince who put the interests of his own country first, led her to try to reconvert England to Catholicism and to intervene in the French religious wars on the side of the Catholic League. Both policies were disastrous (England lost Calais) and made her widely unpopular.

Apart from deference to a foreign prince, marriage set another trap for a queen regnant: it reminded her subjects that she was a woman and like all women, supposedly prey to insatiable lust. As with any woman, a queen's honour and public reputation depended on her sexual propriety and if this was vulnerable to attack, political disaster could result. Elizabeth's arch rival, Mary Queen of Scots, provides a striking example. Thrice wed, Mary Stuart was called by her many enemies a wanton who took lovers and chose her young and handsome second husband Lord Darnley for his looks, had him murdered when he no longer pleased her and then married his murderer, the Earl of Bothwell. Modern historians paint Mary differently, as an innocent victim, guilty in the Darnley affair of no more than misjudgement and possibly raped into marriage by the politically ambitious Bothwell.[8] Elizabeth managed her sexual reputation more wisely than Mary, probably taking lovers but keeping her public reputation intact by avoiding marriage and proclaiming herself often and loudly the Virgin Queen.

This most famous of Elizabeth's public images not only protected her sexual reputation but also coupled her in the public mind with the most admired of women, the Virgin Mary. Apparently this was a deliberate ploy of the queen and her advisors, who saw veneration of the queen as a way to ease the transition of her subjects from Catholicism, with its veneration of Mary, to Protestantism. Elizabeth's Ascension Day and her birthday, which by lucky coincidence fell on the feast of Mary's nativity, were celebrated publicly as the Marian feasts had been. Artists often painted the queen with symbols, like the rose, stars, the moon and ermines, associated with Mary, and pictures of the queen replaced images of the Virgin in many English homes.[9]

Elizabeth also presented herself to her subjects in other female guises. She was portrayed as various classical goddesses, especially chaste Diana, and as the longed for lady of courtly love lyrics.[10] The queen also appeared in the more prosaic female roles of wife and mother, simultaneously married to her kingdom and mother to its people. She said in a speech to Parliament:

> I have already joyned my selfe in mariage to an husband, namely the kingdome of England . . . and doe not upbraid me with miserable lacke of children, for everyone of you, and as many as are Englishmen, are children . . . to me.[11]

The queen's role as mother of her people was reinforced by her acting as godmother to many of her subjects and by pictures of her with bared breasts, protruding belly and cornucopias spewing forth bounty for her kingdom.[12] In having herself portrayed as wife and mother, Elizabeth drew on well-established and generally non-threatening female roles.

FEMALE REGENTS: STAND-INS FOR MALE RULERS

Apart from queens regnant, other royal women also exercised political power as stand-ins for male rulers. These were the regents, the sisters, daughters and wives of kings appointed by their menfolk to rule in their place when they had to be absent. The appointment of relatives, both male and female, as regents, was common in early modern Europe; the Hapsburgs, an immense family controlling vast, usually geographically separate and socially and politically diverse territories, were especially likely to do this. Indeed, it was one of the secrets of their success. The power of the Hapsburgs is usually credited to their successful marriage strategies (the Hapsburg motto was 'Let others fight; you, happy Austria, will marry'). But they also owed their success to their willingness to make full use of the political skills of all their family members, female as well as male. Thus Charles V's aunt Margaret of Austria ruled the Netherlands in the early sixteenth century, as did his sister Mary of Hungary and illegitimate daughter Margaret of Parma and he entrusted the government of his huge empire to his wife when he set sail for Tunis in 1535. His son Philip II appointed his sister Juana as regent of Spain when he went to

England to marry Mary Tudor and he made his daughter Isabel joint ruler of the Spanish Netherlands along with her husband; when the husband died she ruled alone for 12 years.[13] These examples could be multiplied indefinitely. Because these appointments were temporary and the female rulers in theory at least wielded their power under the direction of their male relatives, they tended to be relatively uncontroversial. The major exception to this was the rule in Muscovy of Sophia Alekseevna, daughter of Czar Aleksei, as regent for her two underage brothers, the mentally incompetent Fedor and Peter, later Peter the Great. This was controversial because in this period Muscovite royal women played no public part in politics. Doomed to remain unmarried because no foreign prince worthy of their rank was willing to convert to the Orthodox faith, they, like other elite women, spent their lives confined to the *terem*. Yet Sophia wielded political power. Unfortunately, she did so tactlessly, having herself portrayed with crown and sceptre and her likeness stamped on coins as if she were the czar. When she planned a public coronation for herself, she was overthrown.[14]

QUEEN MOTHERS: STAND-INS FOR CHILD KINGS

It was unusual for a sister to act as regent when a male king was not old enough to rule on his own. That position was usually filled by the boy's mother, the widow of the late king. This type of female rule was justified by notions about mother love, the same notions that justified a non-royal widow's legal guardianship of her children. In France the very law of 1407 that barred daughters from inheriting the throne specified that queen mothers be chosen over male relatives as regents for underage kings because mothers were the natural guardians and tutors of their children. Their devotion to their child's welfare would outweigh their feminine inability to understand affairs of state. Ruling instinctively to promote the happiness of her child, a queen mother would promote the welfare of his realm.[15]

France was ruled by three queen mothers during our period: Catherine de Medici, regent successively for her three unpopular sons during the religious wars between Catholic and Protestant; her niece Marie de Medici, wife of the popular Henri IV and regent for her son, Louis XIII; and Anne of Austria, wife of Louis XIII and regent for the young Louis XIV. All had troubled reigns. Catherine had to protect royal power against both Catholic and Protestant nobles during the religious wars; Marie faced revolt by her own son; and Anne had to crush the potentially revolutionary revolt of the Fronde. This points up the public distrust of this sort of regency, perceived as more dangerous than the other type for two reasons. First, although a regent was enjoined to take the advice of the royal council on policy decisions just as non-royal mothers given guardianship of their children were often required to consult male advisors, ultimately power rested with her; advisors could not overrule a queen mother as male royal relatives could overrule an ordinary female regent. Second, a queen mother was usually a princess of a foreign royal house, whose interests might conflict with those of her husband's country, leaving her vulnerable to charges of divided loyalties. This was, for example, a problem for Anne of Austria. Despite her name, she was the daughter of the Spanish King Philip III and she ruled France while France and Spain were at war.

Because they were so vulnerable to attack, queen mothers consistently emphasized in their ceremonial public appearances the source of their power: their motherhood. Marie de Medici commissioned the great artist Peter Paul Rubens to paint a series of pictures commemorating the major moments of her life. The episodes chosen, including the consummation of her marriage (depicted allegorically, not literally, of course), the birth of her son and the proclamation of her regency, emphasized the linked themes of her maternity and rule. The paintings are full of references to the greatest of mothers, the Virgin Mary, and to Cybele, mother of the gods. In Plate 12, an allegorical figure representing fertility holds a cornucopia in which the rosy, tousled heads of Marie's five children appear alongside flowers and fruit.[16] Catherine de Medici also celebrated her fertility and motherhood. During her ceremonial entry into the city of Lyons in 1548, cornucopias and flowering laurel branches decorated the triumphal arch under which she passed and on the arch verses in Latin proclaimed:

> It is to your wisdom that our age owes the fact that peace and concord flourish and war has been tamed. To the King thou gavest birth, and his Spectre [rules] by thy counsel.[17]

Although the actual rule of queen mothers ended when their sons came of age, they often tried to continue to exercise power informally through advice and counsel to their offspring. If their sons loved them, this worked; if they didn't, it did not. Both Marie de Medici and Anne of Austria had little influence over their adult offspring, but Marianna of Austria, widow of Philip IV of Spain and regent for Charles II, continued to advise her son throughout her life. When attacked by Charles's other chief advisor, his illegitimate half-brother Don José, all she had to do to retain her influence was to remind Charles 'that I love you more than he does'.[18]

QUEEN CONSORTS: WIVES OF KINGS

If the power of the queen mother depended on her motherhood, that of the queen consort, wife of the king, grew from her position as wife. Unlike the royal women discussed so far, queen consorts did not directly rule states. Although they were crowned and had important roles in the ceremonies and rituals of monarchy, they could wield power only indirectly, through their husband and his advisors; their major weapon was what the English called the 'bolster lecture', the intimate influence of a wife over her husband. Unfortunately, royal marriages rarely developed much intimacy. Entered into for reasons of state, they were even less likely to be love matches than ordinary marriages were. The only king who married for love in this period was England's Henry VIII; the fate of his wives, two of whom he had judicially murdered when he tired of them, suggests that this was perhaps a good thing. And only one royal arranged marriage grew into a close and loving relationship, that of Marguerite de Valois and Emmanuel Philibert of Savoy.[19] Usually a royal couple lived in separate households and led separate lives. But if a queen performed her public duties well, she might gain the trust and confidence of her husband and his advisors and thus influence public policy. She might also become popular among her subjects and her popularity would give her advice on public issues added weight.

The most important duty of a queen consort was to produce an heir to the throne. Kings needed heirs even more than ordinary patriarchs. When his niece Marie de Medici married Henry IV, the Grand Duke of Tuscany had just two words of advice, 'Get pregnant!'[20] Failure to do so could make a queen's life miserable; witness Catherine of Aragon, divorced by Henry VIII, and her niece Anne of Austria, who spent the first 20 childless years of her marriage traipsing from shrine to shrine, praying to conceive. By the same token, successful fulfilment of her maternal duties could earn a queen the affection, respect and trust of her husband. Margaret of Austria arrived in Spain as the 14-year-old bride of Philip III, who at first ignored her, but her prompt production of first a male heir and eventually seven other royal infants gave her prestige and she soon was Philip's trusted advisor.[21]

Queens had other weapons apart from their maternity. One was the power and prestige of their own royal family. Of course, this was a two-edged sword. As we have seen, when her father's country and her new home were at odds, a queen might be accused of disloyally favouring her native land. A queen of Spain had to swear during her coronation oath 'to forget her people and her father's house'.[22] Yet subjects were often proud of having a princess of a great royal house as their queen; this accounted in part for the popularity of Catherine of Aragon, daughter of Ferdinand and Isabella, princess of Spain, the greatest power in the early sixteenth-century world, when she was queen of England. Also, queens were often used as unofficial go-betweens between their old and new countries. The Austrian emperor Rudolf II asked Margaret of Austria to press her husband Philip III to ally Spain with Austria in war against the Turks, and the Spanish ambassador to the Austrian Hapsburgs always consulted with the widowed Empress Maria, a Spanish princess once married to the Austrian Emperor Maximilian II, about the best way to present Spanish demands at the Hapsburg court.[23] Sometimes queens were even given official diplomatic duties. The treaty ending the Italian wars of the French king François I and the Hapsburg emperor Charles V was known as the Ladies' Peace because it was negotiated by two royal women, François's mother Louise of Savoy and her sister-in-law, the Hapsburg Archduchess Margaret, Charles's aunt.[24]

Another source of popularity and prestige for queens was a reputation for religious piety and charity. These were virtues expected of all Christians but thought especially suitable for women: piety to restrain their sinful natures and charity to express their motherly love and compassion. How a reputation for piety and charity could strengthen a queen's position is illustrated by the career of Anne Boleyn. Initially disliked because of the irregularity of her marriage to Henry VIII and her displacement of the respected Catherine of Aragon, Anne gained popularity by a forthright public championing of the Protestant cause and by bountiful charity. An intellectual herself, Anne donated money to Oxford and Cambridge colleges and to poor scholars. She also gave to mothers and to families 'overcharged with children'. Anne's charitable giving was so substantial that a treatise on poor relief was dedicated to her.[25]

A final source of power for a queen consort was her position as mistress of a household. Like all wives, she gained respect if her household ran smoothly and her servants were pious, obedient and well behaved. Of course a queen's household contained more than just domestic servants. Often numbering hundreds of people, it included numerous noble attendants both male and female, plus musicians, singers, dancers, playwrights, poets and artists. The talents of the artists, writers and performers she could attract to her household enhanced a queen's prestige and they busily churned out poems and pictures presenting a favourable image of their royal mistress to the world.

A queen's noble household attendants were useful politically in other ways as well. In early modern Europe, service in a royal household was the road to political power. There was no clear division between the royal household and the government bureaucracy. Most government ministers also held posts in the king's household and their power derived less from the prerogatives of their official position than from their intimate daily contact with the ruler. The queen's household was often the entryway into government service for ambitious young men, who learned the ways of the court there and then moved into the king's household and high government office.[26] The great Cardinal Richelieu, chief minister of Louis XIII, got his start as chaplain in the household of Louis's mother Marie de Medici. Queens who picked their protégés shrewdly therefore could hope that they would further their interests as they moved into higher office. Queens could also turn their whole household into a political weapon, making it a centre of opposition to their husbands' policies. That is what Anne of Denmark, wife of England's unpopular James I, did. Intellectual, sophisticated and politically savvy, Anne attracted to her household respectable playwrights, poets and politicians who would have felt uncomfortable in the service of her dirty, vulgar-tongued husband. In the queen's service they produced a steady stream of poems, pamphlets, plays and masques articulating an alternate vision of politics and society to James's intensely absolutist and patriarchal rule.[27]

EQUIVALENTS OF QUEEN CONSORTS: THE VENETIAN DOGARESSE

The roles of a queen consort – dutiful spouse, devout matron, efficient housewife, family mediator, mother of an heir – were simply those of normal wives writ large. Therefore queen consorts served as role models for the women of their realms and also as symbolic representations of the importance of wives in the patriarchal households which were the foundations of the social order. By celebrating the various roles of the queen in public rituals, monarchs assured their subjects that these roles were being filled and all was functioning smoothly in both the patriarchal households composing the realm and the king's own patriarchal household which was their symbolic embodiment. So important was this reassurance to the stability and well-being of early modern states that even states with elected governments rather than hereditary kings often made a public figure of the wife of their head of government, endowing her with many of the ritual and representational duties of the queen consort.

The prime example of this is the republic of Venice. A city-state, Venice was governed by an elected official called the *doge*, chosen by his fellow noblemen from a small group of elite families whose members were eligible to elect and serve as the head of the Venetian state. Like kings, *doges* were crowned in public coronations, performed official state rituals and were buried in public funerals. While in monarchies such rituals exalted the king and his dynasty, in Venice public rites emphasized that power lay not with individual *doges* and their families, but with the collective entity of the state. Each *doge* had to sign a pledge called the *permissione ducale* which severely restricted his freedom of action, especially to benefit and perpetuate in power his own family.

If the *doge* were the Venetian equivalent of a king, his wife, called the *dogaressa*, was the Venetian equivalent of a queen consort.[28] Usually from one of the great noble families, she too had to swear publicly to uphold the *permissione ducale* and not further the interests of her family. Because *doge* was not a hereditary office that needed an heir, the *dogaressa*'s motherhood was not emphasized as a queen's was. In fact, because *doges* were usually elected quite late in life, when *dogaresse* took office their days of active maternity were usually behind them. Otherwise their roles and rituals were very similar to those of queens. Like queens, *dogaresse* were publicly crowned and buried; in the seventeenth century their coronations were more elaborate than the *doges*'. Rituals centring on the *dogaressa* emphasized her role as mediator between families (at her coronation Morosina Grimani passed under a triumphal arch portraying the offices and honours of her family and those of her husband's), pious and charitable matron (the religious institutions and guilds she patronized gave the *dogaressa* banquets at her coronation) and role model for women (although respectable Venetian matrons were expected to remain indoors out of the public eye, delegations of women accompanied the *dogaressa* at her coronation and funeral). The presence of the dignified *dogaressa* in public ceremonies signified the presence of the dutiful wife in Venetian households and therefore the dignity and stability of the Venetian state.

EQUIVALENTS OF QUEEN CONSORTS: THE HAREM WOMEN OF THE OTTOMAN EMPIRE

If the importance of the wife to the smooth functioning of the patriarchal household necessitated the presence of a queen consort or her equivalent in the states of western Europe, the very different nature of the household, marriage and gender roles in Islamic society precluded the presence of any such figure in the Ottoman Empire. The lack of a queenly figure there was always commented on by western observers. Many attributed it to thrift. Islamic marriage laws required that a wife get back her dowry on widowhood and returning the magnificent dowries of foreign princesses would periodically bankrupt the state. In reality, other factors were at work. Because succession to the throne was not through primogeniture, as in western monarchies, a sultan did not need a wife to provide a legitimate heir. Also, the practice of polygamy and the seclusion of women precluded the public display of a single wifely consort. Finally, such a display would have gone against Ottoman notions of political power as undivided and residing in the male sultan alone. The sultan himself, hidden from public view in the sacred space of the harem, embodied the might of the Ottoman state and it was his seclusion from the public view, rather than his ceremonial public appearances, as in western monarchies, that enhanced the mystique surrounding him.[29]

In the early years of their empire, the Ottomans did not use royal women for the strategic marriage alliances that were so important to the success of western monarchies. Only rarely did they marry off their daughters or sisters to neighbouring rulers and only rarely did they marry the daughters or sisters of such rulers. These foreign wives never became queen consorts. They were not even allowed to fill the one role open to women in the Ottoman political landscape: mother of a potential future sultan.[30] Instead this role was given to the concubines in the sultan's harem, mostly slave women from the Christian portions of the empire. Usually each concubine was allowed to bear only one son, who, if he had potential, was sent as a teenager to be a governor in the provinces to learn how to rule. His mother accompanied him to run his household and give advice. When the sultan died, these princes competed for the throne in a Darwinian struggle for the survival of the fittest; the winner had his half-brothers executed so they would pose no threat to his rule.[31]

In 1520 the great sultan Suleiman the Magnificent changed this pattern, inaugurating what Ottoman historians call the Age of the Women, which lasted until 1656. Suleiman had fallen in love with his concubine Hurrem, born Roxelana in Polish Ukraine. He freed her, married her and remained faithful to her. She had five sons, not one, and did not go to the provinces with them, but remained with Suleiman, who relied on her political advice.[32]

Roxelana was the nearest thing to a queen consort the Ottoman Empire ever had and Suleiman's shrewd political sense as well as his love made her so. Engaged in a battle with western powers over control of the Mediterranean fought by diplomacy and display as well as war, Suleiman adopted many aspects of western monarchies, including public ceremonial, the wearing of a crown and having his portrait painted to impress western diplomats. The elevation of Roxelana fitted this pattern. While it may have been effective abroad, it was too shocking an innovation to be popular at home and no later harem favourite came so close to being a queen.

Nonetheless harem women continued to exercise political power. After Suleiman, the succession was decided by the less murderous policy of primogeniture and a series of young and/or incompetent heirs elevated their mothers to the position of *valide sultan*, mother of the sultan, equivalent to the western queen mother who acted as regent for her son. Like her, a *valide sultan* ruled in her son's stead, meeting, veiled and behind a curtain, with ministers to decide state policy. And as with the queen mother, it was thought that the *valide sultan*'s maternal instincts would lead her to make the right choices despite her feeble female intellect.[33]

While the *valide sultan*'s power was based on her motherhood, she also had some characteristics of a queen consort. Allowed, like all Muslim women past menopause, to appear in public if properly veiled and chaperoned, she was formally crowned and took part in public ceremonies like the greeting of victorious generals and the coming of age of royal heirs. She was a role model of the piety and charity expected of Muslim as well as Christian matrons, endowing mosques, hospitals and charities, especially those focused on women. She also ran the royal household, in this case the imperial harem. Because that included the slaves who manned the bureaucracy, she ran the government as well, building networks of loyal servants and advancing her protégés to the highest positions. She also chose and trained her successor, picking from among the young concubines the one she thought most capable of both pleasing her son and running the government.[34] Thus during the Age of the Women the Ottoman Empire was partially governed by a self-selected succession of *valide sultans* running parallel to the official Ottoman dynasty. Little wonder that in 1599 Sunullah Efendi, guardian of the holy law of Islam, lamented in terms reminiscent of John Knox's *Trumpet Blast* that women had too much influence in 'matters of government and sovereignty'.[35]

FEMALE SERVANTS IN ROYAL HOUSEHOLDS

However grudgingly, the exercise of political power by the women discussed so far was considered legitimate because they either filled an accepted female public role, that of queen consort or her equivalent, or they were royal women standing in for their male relatives. But there were also other, non-royal, women who exercised political power in early modern Europe. Theirs, however, was not considered legitimate because it was not exercised through an accepted public role but instead informally: they were powerful because they were intimate with and could influence the decisions of the sovereign. These women fall into two categories: the ladies-in-waiting and other female attendants in royal households and the mistresses of male rulers.

As we have seen, queens had separate households which could number in the hundreds: stewards, chamberlains, ladies-in-waiting, keeper of the wardrobe, keeper of the linen, etc. These positions were usually filled by noblemen ambitious for high public office. But because gender stereotypes dictated that royal children be cared for by women when young, and decorum dictated that a queen's personal attendants be female, many positions in royal households were filled by women. In the households of the women and children of the French royal family in our period, about 20 percent of the noble attendants were female.[36]

Noblewomen entered royal households for a variety of reasons. Some came for an education, following the medieval tradition in which noble girls were sent to the households of great ladies to learn household management and courtly graces. Others came in hopes of marrying well. Royal courts drew the wealthiest, most prestigious and most ambitious nobles in the realm and they might need a bride for a son or nephew if not for themselves and might be willing to overlook a less than impressive pedigree and dowry if they got a pretty face, lively wit and courtly skills. Therefore, courts were the singles bars of early modern Europe and flirtation a constant pastime. Anne Boleyn is an example of a noble girl sent to court to marry well and she did, of course, capturing the king himself. Most noblewomen, however, entered household service because their marriage prospects were bleak and household service was the only career open to them apart from taking the veil or because their marriages had failed and household service was the only venue in which they could live respectably apart from their husbands. Their goal was to amass wealth and patronage for themselves and their families. An example from seventeenth-century France is Magdeleine de Venel, unhappily married to a very poor and minor noble. Mme de Venel left her husband to enter the household of a niece of Cardinal Mazarin, chief advisor to Anne of Austria. She ended her career in service as lady-in-waiting to Louis XIV's queen, Marie-Thérèse. Along the way she acquired a yearly salary of 1200 *livres* plus 3600 *livres* for living expenses and a free apartment in Versailles, a 6000 *livre* pension when she retired, a 30,000 *livre* legacy and a large diamond. She also managed to place no fewer than 16 of her relatives in royal households![37]

Mme de Venel seems to have used her intimacy with the powerful solely to advance herself and her relatives. But other household servants used their positions as confidantes and advisors of the great to exercise political power and influence public policy. This was expected of courtiers both male and female; the major justification of teaching noblewomen the 'masculine' subjects of Latin and Greek was that in reading the classics they would absorb their lessons in civic virtue and therefore be able to advise their royal mistresses wisely. One household servant who actually did so was the Princesse des Ursins, a French noblewoman who was in fact if not in title the chief minister of Spain in the early eighteenth century. The country was nominally ruled by its 15-year-old king Philip V, but he was strongly influenced by his 12-year-old wife, who was in turn guided by her lady-in-waiting, Mme des Ursins. It was Mme des Ursins who met with the ministers and decided government policy.[38]

ROYAL MISTRESSES

One final type of woman could exercise political power through her relationship with a royal personage. This was a ruler's mistress. Often they were household servants as well, for while some rulers like France's Henri IV, *le roi gallant*, democratically spread their sexual favours among peasants and barmaids, most chose their mistresses from the women at court, who were, after all, those they could most easily meet and seduce. England's Henry VIII successively took as his mistress Bessie Blount, Mary Boleyn and her sister Anne; all were ladies-in-waiting to his queen, Catherine of Aragon. Louis XIV fell in love with Mme de Maintenon while she was governess to his illegitimate children by his previous mistress, Mme de Montespan. If they were not members of the royal household when they caught the king's eye, royal mistresses were usually appointed to such posts soon after, for that kept them conveniently nearby. Thus the French king Henry II made his mistress Diane de Poitiers governess to his children, much to the indignation of their mother Catherine de Medici.[39]

Royal mistresses had unparalleled opportunities to accumulate wealth, advance the careers of relatives and protégés and influence affairs of state. Henri II made Diane de Poitiers a duchess and loaded her with lands, *chateaux*, pensions, titles and even the crown jewels. Louis XIV gave Mme de Maintenon her heart's desire, a girls' school, the famous St Cyr. Louis also regularly discussed politics with her and many of his wisest decisions are attributed to her influence. Besides wealth and political power, mistresses could dream of the grandest prize of all: a crown. Henry VIII married and crowned his mistresses Anne Boleyn and Catherine Howard and Henri IV planned to make his mistress Gabrielle d'Estrées his queen; she died in childbirth before they could be married. Louis XIV married Mme de Maintenon but kept the marriage a secret; by her own wish she was never crowned queen.[40]

Mme de Maintenon realized that despite all their power, royal mistresses were very vulnerable to public criticism, on two counts: they exercised power illegitimately and their power was based on that fearsome force, female sexuality. As we have seen, any woman who was thought to overstep the bounds of proper female behaviour and go 'beyond her sex' was automatically accused of sexual immorality. This was true of women artists, writers and preachers. It was even true of legitimate queens. Mary Queen of Scots was regularly called a whore and Anne of Austria was the subject of pornographic pamphlets about her supposed relationship with her chief advisor, Cardinal Mazarin, while she was regent. Even the popular Elizabeth was rumoured to have had illegitimate children.[41] Mistresses faced even more fearsome charges than these royal women: they were labelled not just whores but witches, the most potentially dangerous thing that could be said about any woman. Royal mistresses may have been accused of witchcraft because it absolved their kingly lovers of the sin of adultery; they could not have helped straying from their marriage vows if they were bewitched. At any rate, witchcraft was closely associated with royal mistresses. The book that shaped standard notions of witchcraft in our period, the *Malleus Maleficarum*, listed royal concubines among the women most likely to be witches.[42] Diane de Poitiers was accused of bewitching Henri II; although she was extremely intelligent and very beautiful, people thought her hold on the affections of the king, 20 years her junior, could not otherwise be explained. Mme de Montespan was also accused of using witchcraft and love potions to retain the affections of Louis XIV and of poisoning her rivals, accusations that could have brought a death sentence had the king not quashed them.[43]

These truly dangerous attacks on the royal mistresses, whose power was considered illegitimate, contrast with the general acceptance of the legitimate political role of lawful queens. Although only a few women could fill such a role, its existence was important for women in general. Female rulers, like the other women who stepped 'beyond their sex' and filled male roles capably, helped break down popular stereotypes about gender and the abilities and proper roles of men and women. During Elizabeth I's long reign, the English people got so used to being ruled by a woman that many forgetfully referred to her successor James I as 'queen'. Women functioning ably in the public sphere challenged learned theories about gender and gender roles. Defending the right of Elizabeth and other lawful queens to rule, John Aylmer had to abandon the deeply entrenched notion that nature dictated certain roles for men and for women. Nature, Aylmer argued, produced too many variations and exceptions to be taken as a guide. Most men were more capable of ruling than most women, but some superior women were more capable than some inferior men.[44] This rejection of rigidly defined gender roles dictated by nature was necessary if new ideas about the essential similarity and equality of men and women were to emerge. Thus female rulers served their subjects well, especially the women among them.

Chapter 13

◆

CITIZENS

In one of the very few legal cases in early modern Europe concerning the political status of women, France's highest court ruled in 1565 that Marie Mabile was indeed a French citizen. What had made Mabile's citizenship a matter of dispute was not her gender; instead it was her place of birth. Although the daughter of a Parisian master goldsmith, Mabile had been born in London and lived in England most of her life, moving back to France and claiming French citizenship only when her English husband died. Mabile argued that while she did not meet the primary criterion of citizenship in early modern Europe, native birth, she was French by descent and by choice. The court agreed.[1]

As this case suggests, women were routinely considered citizens of early modern states. In the Ottoman Empire Muslim women were citizens by virtue of their religion.[2] In western European states, women were citizens if they were born within the country's borders. The only people of native birth who were not citizens and had no legal standing in courts were slaves and, as the famous French political theorist Jean Bodin pointed out, that term did not apply to 'men's wives and children, who are free from all servitude and bondage'. Yet Bodin, who, like all early modern political theorists, thought of society as a series of patriarchal households, also maintained that the male head of such a household was the only true citizen:

> Now when the maister of the Familie goeth out of his owne house where he commandeth, to entreat and trafficke with other heads of Families, of that which concerneth them all in generale, he then loseth the title of master . . . and in stead of a lord calleth himselfe a Citizen.

Aware of this contradiction, Bodin argued that the citizenship of women and children differed from that of male patriarchs in that, for the former, 'their rights and liberties, and power to dispose of their owne goods, be from them in some sort cut off by the domesticall power' of the male household head.[3] And this was true. Women's roles in the public sphere depended on their relationships with patriarchal household heads. As we saw in the last chapter, in early modern Europe, membership in a patriarchal household gave royal women political power. Yet it also confined non-royal women to a sort of second-class citizenship, with their relationship to the state and the law and their legal rights and duties different from and more restricted than those of male patriarchs.

WOMEN'S LEGAL RIGHTS AND DISABILITIES

The differences between male and female citizenship are most obvious in the area of legal rights. The differences between male and female citizenship for Muslims in the Ottoman Empire were limited and straightforward compared to those in the Christian west. Muslim women could own property, enter into business contracts, make wills and bring cases in court. Girls as well as boys inherited property from their relatives, although they were entitled to only half the share of a male heir. Similarly, women could be witnesses in court cases, but it took the testimony of two female witnesses to outweigh that of a man.[4]

In Christian western Europe, the situation was more complex. There the legal status of men and women was derived mostly from ancient Roman law, which formed the basis of the law codes of Spain, Portugal and southern France and Italy and was highly influential even in northern Europe, where Germanic customary law prevailed. In Roman law, only the patriarchal household head (the *paterfamilias*) was a full legal person who could represent himself at law and exercise control over others. Women, as free but subordinate members of patriarchal households, were legal persons too, but they were incapable of exercising authority over others and even their ability to represent themselves at law was limited by what one Roman legal commentator termed the 'fragility, imbecility, irresponsibility and ignorance' of the female sex.[5] Thus a woman's legal rights were limited by her gender and by her subordinate position in a patriarchal household; furthermore, they varied over the course of her life, as her position in the household and relationship to its patriarchal head changed.

We can see this when we examine the most crucial legal right in early modern Europe, the right to own and administer property, especially landed property. Because land usually formed the economic base of the household and of the patriliny, most law codes tried to keep it out of the hands of women, whose inheritance rights were generally more limited than men's. Further, these rights varied by life stage. They were generally greatest when a woman was still unmarried, especially after she legally came of age. In Roman law areas, daughters were entitled to inherit from their fathers equally with sons, although, as we have seen, elite families got around these provisions by giving daughters their portion in the form of a cash dowry instead of land or by setting up entails which passed the family estate intact to the eldest son. In the customary law areas of northern and western Europe, the right of daughters to inherit was in theory even more restricted, because these law codes derived from the laws of the ancient Germanic tribes, where land was held in common by the male warriors. Thus in some customary law codes, daughters were totally barred from inheriting land and could only inherit 'moveables', that is, non-landed property. In others – English common law, for example – daughters inherited only in the absence of sons. But these theoretical restrictions were often ignored in practice. In England fathers got around the common law provisions by giving daughters substantial 'portions' and by writing wills naming them as heirs. Thus daughters did often inherit substantial property and if they were of age and still unmarried they had complete control over their property and could administer it as they pleased.[6] Only the law code of Florence took the doctrine of female imbecility seriously enough to require that adult spinsters have male guardians to administer their property and act for them at law.[7]

Widows too had broad legal rights, although they were generally more restricted than those of spinsters. As we saw in Chapter 5, families were even more anxious to keep patrilineal property out of the hands of widows than of daughters. Therefore many law codes allowed a widow to inherit only a share (in English common law, for example, one-third) of her husband's estate and she did not own it outright but got only the use of it during her lifetime; after her death, it passed to her husband's children. Nonetheless many widows inherited substantial estates and they were free to administer them as they pleased. Often they acted as executors of their husbands' estates and legal guardians of their underage children and administrators of their properties as well. Again, only Florence required that a widow have a male guardian to represent her at law and only a few law codes required that mothers acting as their children's guardians consult with a male relative or family council before taking legal action.[8]

Thus both daughters and widows enjoyed fairly broad property rights, although these rights were never equal to those of men. It was in the stage of life between maidenhood and widowhood – that is, wifehood – that a woman's legal rights were most restricted. This was because marriage fused husband and wife into a single legal entity, whose sole representative at law was the husband. A married woman was, in the legal phrase, a *feme couvert*; her legal personhood was 'covered' by and submerged in that of her husband. Englishman Thomas Edgar compared the legal situation of a woman at marriage to that of a stream joining a mighty river and losing its identity within it. 'By this a married woman perhaps may either doubt whether she be either none or no more than half a person [in law].'[9] In practice, this meant that in most European law codes husbands had the right to administer all property the wife brought into the marriage and inherited during it, as well as the right to administer all communal property acquired by the couple during their union. The only ways to avoid this were to declare in the marriage contract that the wife's property was 'lineage property' of her family which, while it might be administered by the husband, would pass intact to her children or to specify in the contract that part of her property would remain a 'separate estate' from her husband's.[10]

Property owning was not the only area where wives' legal rights were restricted. The doctrine of *feme couvert* deprived wives not only of the right to administer their property but also of the right to transmit it by a will. In English common law, wives could not make wills separately from their husbands; other, more lenient law codes required that they get their husbands' permission before doing so.[11] Wives were also limited in their ability to sign legally binding business contracts. In English common law, they could not. In most French law codes wives could sign contracts only with their husbands' permission. In Spain, wives were not only denied the ability to make legal contracts, they also, in theory at least, could not buy anything apart from daily necessities without their husbands' permission. A husband could disavow his wife's purchases of jewellery, furniture and the like if he wanted to.[12] The German city-states also allowed husbands to disavow their wives' financial dealings. And, through the doctrine of *weibliche Freiheit* (female freedom), they allowed wives to disavow any contracts they had signed if they had been pressured by their husbands or had not understood the contract's provisions. (Here the Roman law assumption of woman's 'imbecility' was at work.[13])

In fact, the legal position of wives was not as limited as it seems because these restrictions were widely ignored. Commerce could not function without the sanctity of contract and women, especially wives, were so deeply involved in commerce that they had to be allowed to sign valid contracts. Therefore English married women often had themselves declared *femes soles*, thereby acquiring the right to sign contracts. In the German city-states, women who made their living selling goods or loaning or borrowing money could not claim *weibliche Freiheit*. In fact, there were so many exemptions to *weibliche Freiheit* that it was largely a dead letter.[14] And the French found the laws against wives signing contracts such a hindrance to commerce that they abolished most of them in 1606.[15]

Similarly inconvenient were laws restricting women from witnessing wills or being called as witnesses in court cases. In the customary law areas of France and Spain, married women could not be witnesses in court cases and in the German city-states all women, married or unmarried, were called to testify only if there were no male witnesses.[16] These restrictions did not stem, as we might expect, from the notion of female 'imbecility', the conviction that women were too stupid and flighty to be reliable witnesses. In fact, early modern courts recognized women's intelligence and frequently called on women as expert witnesses in cases where feminine expertise was vital, like pregnancy, rape and witchcraft. Instead the ban on women as witnesses stemmed, like the limits on their signing of contracts, from the fact that a husband's and wife's property was legally inseparable. In early Germanic law witnesses stood surety for (that is, pledged their property in support of) those they testified about and married women could not do this because they did not control their own property. Like women's other legal disabilities, the ban on female witnesses functioned more in theory than in practice. Often women were the only witnesses to crimes and therefore their testimony had to be heard. In Hertfordshire, England, from 1610 to 1619, 36 women testified as witnesses in felony cases, while 572 men did so.[17]

Another legal limitation on women frequently ignored was that preventing them from acting as executors of wills or guardians of minor children. Unlike the prohibition of women witnesses, this grew out of the Roman law notion that, as subordinate members of a patriarchal household, women could not exercise authority over others. In practice, these restrictions were often flouted. For example, according to English common law, women could not be executors of wills. But in England, wills were probated in church courts, which, unlike the common law courts, regarded women as full legal persons and husbands routinely named their wives executors, either as sole executor or jointly with someone else. Figures from various areas of England from 1280 to 1690 range from a low of 46 percent to a high of 96 percent of husbands naming their wives executors; most are in the 70 to 80 percent range.[18] If they didn't name their wives executors, Englishmen tended to name their daughters, even if they had sons. In fact, women were so often made executors that solicitors, used to writing the feminine form of the word, *executrix*, sometimes wrote that even if the executor was a man.[19] Similarly, husbands often ignored the legal prohibition on naming women the guardians of minor children and entrusted their offspring to their wives. As we saw in Chapter 4, this happened even in Florence, where women themselves were supposed to need male legal guardians. These examples of husbands entrusting their property and offspring to their wives testify not only to the fact that women's legal disabilities were far fewer in practice than they were in theory; they also support our conclusions about the nature of early modern marriage in Chapter 3. Clearly, despite all rhetoric about husbandly dominance and wifely subordination, many husbands loved and respected their wives and treated them as capable adults.

Apart from their inability to sign contracts, testify as witnesses and execute wills, women were legally disadvantaged in one other area: according to many law codes, they could not initiate legal cases to protect their honour and punish offences against it. This disability grew not only from principle of *feme couvert* but also from the widespread conviction that a woman's honour – always, as we have seen, defined as her sexual reputation, her chastity – was not so much hers as the property of her menfolk. It was the duty of fathers to guard and defend the chastity of their daughters, of husbands, that of their wives. When a woman's honour was publicly insulted, that of her menfolk was too, and it was thought natural that they would be the ones seeking legal redress. Thus English common law barred married women from suing for slander, and, as we have seen, when Artemisia Gentileschi was raped, it was her father who took the rapist to court; *he* was the injured party.

Yet, like the others, this disability was widely ignored in practice. While many civil courts barred women, especially married women, from bringing suits, church courts allowed them to do so and their jurisdiction over sexual offences could be stretched to cover slander cases. During the early modern period, women increasingly took advantage of this, an indication perhaps that they viewed their honour as their own property, theirs to defend. After all, a woman's reputation determined her social standing among her neighbours and even, as we have seen, her opportunities for employment. At any rate, London's principal church court, the consistory court of St Paul's, found its docket increasingly dominated by cases of sexual defamation brought by women. By 1633, 70 percent of the court's cases were defamation suits, and 85 percent of them were initiated by women; approximately 230 women brought suits each year.[20] Even in Russia women increasingly used church courts to defend their honour. In 1687, for example, Mavrutka Ventsyleeva sued the nobleman who raped her. (He had asked his servant to find him a woman and the servant lured Mavrutka to his room by saying that he was taking her to her mother.) The court awarded Ventsyleeva a 500-rouble dowry in recompense for her lost honour.[21]

Ventsyleeva won her case not only because courts everywhere increasingly recognized a woman's honour as her own to defend but also because they increasingly defined rape as a serious violent crime against the woman herself. Rape was endemic in early modern Europe. As we saw in Chapters 6 and 7, masters routinely raped their servants; as we will see in the next chapter, soldiers routinely raped the women of the towns they conquered. And gang rape was one of the major activities of the youth groups most urban males joined in adolescence. Yet the number of rapes in official crime statistics was very low. Amsterdam had only two rape cases reported in the entire seventeenth century, as did Frankfurt in the years from 1540 to 1692.[22] Obviously, rape was vastly underreported. In part this was because, then as today, rape victims were reluctant to go to the authorities for fear that their 'shame' would be publicized and that they would be accused of leading their attacker on.* In fact, 'blaming the victim' was even more likely to occur in the early modern period than today because everyone believed that women were uncontrollably lusty. This made it hard for any adult woman to bring rape charges. And if the attack resulted in pregnancy, bringing charges was impossible because medical science said that a female did not secrete eggs unless she had achieved orgasm and orgasm meant that she had enjoyed, and thus consented to, the sexual act. Therefore pregnancy proved consent: 'Rape is the forcible ravishment of a woman, but if she conceive it is not rape, for she cannot conceive unless she consent',[23] as one seventeenth-century legal scholar explained. As a result, adult rape victims were vastly underrepresented in official rape statistics and many official cases had underage, clearly non-pregnant and therefore innocent, victims. One-third of the 49 reported rapes in Florence from 1495 to 1515 concerned girls six to 12 years old.[24]

There was, however, another reason for the low level of reported rapes and that was the way the law defined the crime. Many rapes did not fit its narrow legal definition. For example, prostitutes and inn servants (thought little better than prostitutes) could not bring rape cases and it was very difficult for domestic servants to do so. This was because laws were made and enforced by elite men and they regarded the sexual exploitation of their servants as

---

* Financial considerations also kept official statistics low. In most European countries, the state prosecuted only the most serious crimes; for all others, the victims initiated the court cases and paid the hefty court costs.

their right. The only type of rape that concerned them was that of their daughters, especially if it was done by a man of lesser social status who hoped to use the fact of sexual intercourse to force a marriage. Therefore in the Middle Ages rape was synonymous with abduction; the same Latin term, *raptus*, was used for both. And both were considered theft perpetrated against the victim's family, for both robbed them of her 'honour' and therefore of the chance to marry her off profitably.[25] Thus a fine paid to the girl's family or a dowry paid to the girl herself were the usual punishments. In some places, if the perpetrator could not afford these, he had to marry the girl himself. The victim's wishes were not consulted. But in the early modern period some countries rewrote their statutes on rape, defining it as a violent crime against the woman herself, allowing her to initiate prosecution and decreeing harsh penalties for the rapist, especially if his victim was underage or excessive force was used. The Dutch Republic, for example, revised its rape statutes in the seventeenth century, allowing victims to bring suit and decreeing penalties of whipping, banishment and even death.[26] Similarly, England redefined rape in 1576 and deprived rapists of the benefit of clergy (immunity from arrest if they remained on church property) they had earlier enjoyed.[27]

These changes in the laws about rape typified the broader changes in women's position at law from 1500 to 1700. Women, especially married women, were not true persons in the eyes of the law and they experienced various legal disabilities not inflicted on men. But over the two centuries the general trend was to eliminate these disabilities and to treat women, even married women, not as members of a patriarchal household subsumed under the legal identity of the patriarch but as legal persons in their own right. Thus in this aspect of women's lives, as in so many others, the early modern period saw improvement – one more bit of evidence that the Clark thesis was unfounded.

FEMALE CRIMINALITY

The growing tendency to treat women as legal persons in their own right rather than subordinates in a patriarchal household was not totally favourable for women, however. For the flipside of the legal disabilities which arose from their subordinate position was the notion that, as subordinates, they were not completely responsible for criminal actions they committed. This assumption that women were not responsible for their criminal acts because they were acting under the orders of their menfolk, as good wives and daughters should, was not embodied in any criminal code in early modern Europe. Even those like English common law which denied the personhood of married women in civil cases treated them as distinct legal persons responsible for their own actions in criminal matters. As Thomas Edgar explained:

> [Although by] the near conjunction which is between man and wife . . . they be by intent and wise fiction of law, one person, yet in nature and in some other cases by the law of God and man, they remain diverse . . . so in criminal and other special cases our law argues them several persons.[28]

In criminal law, the only legal advantages women enjoyed because of their sex was that pregnant felons could 'plead their belly' and avoid execution until their baby was born and that when executed they were usually, to prevent their bodies being indecently exposed to the public gaze, drowned, buried alive or beheaded, not hanged, as men were.[29]

But if they were not actually written into law, the assumptions that women were more impulsive and less intelligent than men (as a German legal manual put it, 'long dresses, short minds'[30]) and that they acted under men's orders and were therefore not really responsible for their crimes nonetheless permeated early modern legal systems, making magistrates reluctant to charge them with crimes and judges and juries reluctant to convict them. Female felons often played on this to win clemency. Natalie Davis has examined pleas for pardons in sixteenth-century France. She found that women often emphasized their ignorance and stupidity and asserted that they were reluctant criminals acting under male guidance. Jeanne Domecourt, for example, a servant who impersonated an heiress to gain her fortune, stated that she had done so under the orders of her master, who had seduced her; she even mentioned the 'fragility of the female sex'. If they could not portray themselves as mere tools of men – if, for example, they killed their abusive husbands, as Bonne Goberde did – they presented themselves as 'good wives'. Bonne stated that she was slaughtering a chicken for her husband's dinner when he struck her with a board, thus not only showing that her husband's abuse was unjustified but also subtly reminding officials of the diminished responsibility of wives at law.[31] Similarly, female felons in German courts got lesser sentences if they repented and displayed, by crying, the typical female inability to control their emotions and, by falling to their knees and begging, the proper female deference to male authority.[32]

The assumption of women's diminished responsibility accounts partially – but only partially – for the low numbers of women charged with crimes compared to men. In France and England from the thirteenth through the eighteenth centuries, if the almost exclusively female crime of infanticide is omitted, women were charged with less than 10 percent of the homicides. In

Arras in the sixteenth century, women were indicted in just 15 percent of *all* crimes and in seventeenth-century Chesire women were charged in just one-quarter of the crimes against property.[33] But because this disparity between male and female criminality prevails throughout western history (indeed, it still exists, although the gap is narrowing), the medieval and early modern assumptions of diminished female responsibility cannot completely explain it. Early historians of female criminality postulated that relatively few women showed up in criminal statistics because women internalized the subordination, meekness and timidity expected of them by society and were afraid to break the law.[34] But later research discredited this hypothesis and today historians believe that women were just as criminally inclined as men; the gender differences in criminal behaviour were shaped by what was possible and familiar to each sex.

What were these differences? While men predominated in most crimes, the most distinctly masculine crimes were crimes of violence, the most prevalent offence in the Middle Ages. That men were more likely to commit violent crimes than women is not surprising. Most violent crimes were assaults, where men attacked strangers who had impugned their honour. Women were not likely to commit such crimes, both because their honour was not theirs to defend and because, given their weaker physiques, violence was not an effective female weapon. When women defended themselves, they did so with words (and witchcraft).[35] Hence the importance of gossip and slander and of women's access to the courts to file defamation suits.

The most distinctly female crimes were infanticide (see Chapter 4), witchcraft (Chapter 11) and, when and where they were criminalized, bastard bearing, prostitution and adultery. Because these *were* female crimes, and because they all grew from what society feared most about women, their unbridled sexuality, women who committed them were not treated leniently. Quite the contrary. For example, in early modern Germany, male murderers might, if their crime were committed in the course of an argument, be charged only with manslaughter (an unpremeditated killing in self-defence or in the grip of strong emotion) and get away with a small fine, but unwed mothers who killed their infants were almost inevitably charged with murder and executed, although their crime fitted the criteria for manslaughter.[36] Indeed, because infanticide was considered 'unnatural', denying women's inborn maternal instincts, it was punished more severely than ordinary murder. In late seventeenth-century Württemberg some women who had killed their babies were burned with red-hot pincers before they died.[37]

Women also committed a larger than expected number of crimes against property, the fastest growing category of offences in early modern Europe, although the majority of such crimes were committed by men. Here again patterns of criminality varied by gender. Men were more likely to commit the more serious thefts: breaking and entering, armed robbery, highway robbery and horse theft. This was not because women were timid and fearful of committing serious felonies; instead it was because they were less likely than men to have the freedom of movement and access to weapons such crimes entailed. Women, by contrast, tended to dominate petty thievery, especially the theft of cloth, clothing and household goods. The reasons are obvious. As we have seen, the making and selling of clothing were traditionally women's work and women had unparalleled knowledge of and access to household goods. Women also dominated the second-hand trade, which allowed them to dispose of their stolen property easily.[38]

Many female thieves were poor wives and mothers, perhaps out of work and hungry, desperate to feed their children, who embezzled thread from a putting-out contractor, snatched a mirror from a market stall or grabbed a sheet from a clothesline when the opportunity presented itself. Such women, like 31-year-old seamstress Anna Acker, with two sons and an aged mother to provide for, were often treated leniently. While male thieves who stole valuable goods and used violence were usually executed, women like Acker, who stole because she 'would have died of hunger' otherwise and was convinced God would forgive her, were often just publicly shamed and banished.[39]

Like the needy and desperate wives and mothers, domestic servants were also prominent among female thieves. Their motives were different. Much servant theft was not theft at all in their eyes, for, as we have seen, servants were often paid in kind, especially clothing, and employers were often reluctant to cough up what they owed. Thus it is not surprising that servants often 'appropriated' their employers' clothing or household goods. Servants also stole in revenge for ill-treatment and to get cash (since they were paid so irregularly) to buy themselves little luxuries, save for a dowry or pay for a feast or a round of drinks for their friends. German servant Barbara Jager, for example, routinely stole 'salt, lard, bread, flour and sausages' from her employers; she sold them to buy herself 'caps and bodices' and to pay for drinks for the journeymen and soldiers with whom she flirted.[40] Whatever its motive, theft by servants was regarded more seriously than other kinds of thievery (in France it was a distinct crime, *vol domestique*) because it brought danger into the one place a master and mistress ought to feel secure, their household, and exemplified betrayal by the one person they ought to be able to trust, their servant. Therefore it was often harshly punished. Parisian law specified that thieving servants be hanged in their masters' doorways.[41]

A final group of female thieves were, unlike the others, professional criminals. Every town and city had its resident thieves like Margaretha Riechler of Memmingen, who lived by breaking into houses and shops when their occupants were away, and Barbara Meyer of Esslingen, who sewed a 'thief's bag' under her apron to hide the things she stole from market stalls.[42] They were also plagued by criminal gangs, often 20 strong, who roamed from town to town to keep out of reach of the police. Such gangs also terrorized the countryside. Usually they were mixed sex, with gender roles clearly divided. The men led the gangs and did the actual robbing, while the women scouted possible victims, disposed of the stolen goods and provided sex for the male gangsters. Occasionally, however, there were gangs headed by women. One headed by Marie Lescalier operated in Brittany in the 1730s; she had 10 children by three different male gang members.[43] Professional thieves were treated harshly by the authorities; they were often branded or otherwise disfigured so that people would recognize them as criminals. Margaretha Riechler, for example, had her ears cut off in 1564.[44]

WOMEN IN POLITICAL RIOTS AND DEMONSTRATIONS

A final category of crimes in which women were strongly represented was political offences. Throughout early modern Europe public order was periodically punctuated by riots: crowds in the streets shouting slogans, attacking and looting shops, roughing up and often killing government officials. Some of these demonstrations were food riots, provoked in times of dearth by the scarcity and high price of bread. Taxes, especially new ones, also provoked riots, as did military recruiting and unpopular ministers and policies in general. In these cases, people's assumptions about how their government and society should function had been outraged and they rioted to make the authorities abandon the policies they considered illegitimate and restore the acceptable, natural, social and political order. In food riots, for example, crowds often invaded bakers' shops and sold the bread at what they considered a fair price. They did not object to bakers making a profit, but they thought it unfair that bread be priced out of the reach of poor families in times of scarcity. Similarly, in tax riots crowds often proclaimed their loyalty to the sovereign and their willingness to pay old, established taxes; it was only the newly decreed ones they considered illegitimate and refused to pay. Thus riots were the major way the lower classes brought their beliefs and needs to the attention of their rulers. Indeed, where there were no elected representative bodies, these riots were the only form of political action open to the lower classes.

Therefore it is surprising that women were heavily involved in rioting, given the gendering of the public sphere as masculine and the assumption that politics were men's business. A partial explanation for the predominance of women in riots involves the food riot. Buying the bread to feed their families *was* women's work, and therefore both the authorities and the people thought it natural that women would know the price of bread and protest when it rose. Historians have traced the gender of the crowds in 12 food riots in the Netherlands in the seventeenth and early eighteenth centuries; of these, 10 were predominantly female. The problem with this argument is that women were also prominent in more purely political riots. In 10 out of the 38 tax riots in the Netherlands, the majority of the crowd was female. One tax riot of 1616 was even called 'the Women's Revolt of Delft'.[45]

Another possible explanation for the prominence of women in riots is the legal notion of female irresponsibility. Historians have not investigated whether it was actually true, but it was widely assumed that female rioters would be treated more leniently than men. Who could punish a mother desperate to feed her child – or a foolish creature whose very nature made her prone to uncontrolled, riotous behaviour? Both men and women played on this assumption by putting women in the forefront of political crowds. In the Netherlands in 1691, the women of a village freed from the police a man arrested for tax evasion; they yelled to their husbands: 'Let us do it. We cannot be prosecuted.' But in a 1616 riot it had worked the other way: women were urged by their menfolk to free an arrested man. The men shouted 'that they should freely attack, that women are not legally answerable for their actions'.[46] So prevalent was the assumption that female rioters were not to be prosecuted that men often donned women's clothes for political demonstrations. In Edinburgh in 1736 'Madge Wildfire' led a large crowd of men in women's clothing protesting against English customs laws. While this might be an attempt at disguise, it seems unlikely that a man in a dress actually fooled anyone into thinking that he was a woman; probably the major purpose of donning a dress was to remind officials of the legitimacy of riot.[47]

A final reason why women were so prominent in riots is the simplest and most probable: that they were interested in and concerned about political issues. Admittedly few lower-class women could read the newspapers, books and pamphlets that shaped the political opinions of the elite, but this was also true of lower-class men. Yet women as well as men could view the political cartoons and hear the rumours about the doings of the great that shaped lower-class political opinion. And the prominence of women in riot suggests that they were expected to be interested in politics, to contribute to the discussions of political matters in the marketplace and tavern and to be in the forefront of the crowds in political demonstrations. Thus while politics were 'men's business' in early modern Europe, their gendering was, like that of work, multilayered and complex, and women clearly had a place in political rioting, the major form of political action of the lower classes. Unfortunately for the future of women in politics, from 1500 to 1700 the elites grew increasingly worried about the disruptive and indeed revolutionary potential of street riots and, with the growth of the absolutist state with its large and efficient bureaucracy, police force and army, increasingly able to repress them. Therefore this major form of political expression became less available to lower-class people of either sex.

WOMEN IN GOVERNMENT ADMINISTRATION

Ironically, the very vehicle of repression of political riot, the state, was itself another forum for women's participation in the masculine sphere of politics, at least at the beginning of our period. Around 1500 women often held appointive office in government bureaucracies. The same principle of a female relative standing in for a male patriarch that allowed queens to rule allowed women to fill government offices. For example, it was customary for kings to appoint close relatives or important nobles to major posts – cabinet offices, governorships of provinces – to signify the importance of such positions, although the actual work involved was usually done by lower ranking male bureaucrats. The appointees were often women. In France Marie de Medici was governor of the provinces of Normandy and Anjou and the Duchesse d'Aiguillon governor of the city of Le Havre. Anne of Austria, believe it or not, was Superintendent of Navigation and Commerce![48] In England, Henry VII appointed his mother Margaret Beaufort, Countess of Richmond, High Commissioner to the Council of the North when that region's loyalty was uncertain, and noblewomen often inherited the important local administrative post of sheriff, as Lady Anne Clifford did in the seventeenth century. There may even have been a woman justice of the peace, the key local government position in England. Inconclusive evidence suggests that Mary Tudor appointed a Lady Bartlet as justice of the peace after she argued that since the queen herself was the chief justice of the realm, lesser judicial posts could be filled by women too.[49]

Certainly numerous women were found in the lower ranks of government bureaucracies, where offices were often sold to raise money for the government. France and Spain were notorious for this. Such offices were viewed by their possessors as akin to land or a mastership (in French law that is how they were classified). Thus they were the property that supported a patriarchal family and could be passed on to the officeholder's heirs. In France, for example, judgeships in the Parlements, the nation's highest courts, were for sale. A widow could inherit this office and sell it, but she could not fill it herself, because the law was thought to require the masculine qualities of rationality and calm, mature judgement.[50] But widows of minor officials – tax collectors, inspectors of weights and measures and the like – helped their husbands with their work when they were alive and sometimes took over their posts when they died. They might even be appointed to such offices on their own merit, especially in the German city-states. There minor posts like jailer, keeper of the city gates, grain measurer and salt weigher were mixed-sex positions held by both men and women. For example, Catharina Vihllieberin was in the seventeenth century the official mail carrier between Constance and Innsbruck.[51] There were even some government offices reserved for women only. These included administrative posts in hospitals, orphanages and other charitable organizations, especially those dealing with women and children, and positions as inspectors and supervisors of midwives. And in almost every country women were appointed by the state to examine suspected witches, victims of rape and incest and female criminals who tried to avoid execution by claiming to be pregnant.

Thus women had a greater presence in early modern states than we might have expected. But they were more apt to be found in the sixteenth than the seventeenth century, in minor, not major, offices and in small city-states rather than the emerging great powers. From 1500 to 1700 two factors were squeezing women out of government bureaucracies. One was the male onslaught on lucrative types of 'women's work' we saw in Chapter 7. Just as men invaded and colonized brewing and midwifery, so too did they take over positions as hospital and charity administrators and inspectors of weights and measures. The other factor was the major political trend of the period: the emergence of the great powers, centralized states with large efficient bureaucracies manned by professional bureaucrats trained in the law and public administration – *cameralism*, as it was then called. As these bureaucrats replaced local nobles and members of the royal family as administrators, women, who could not attend universities for the requisite training, were shut out of government. By 1700 state bureaucracies were totally masculine.

FEMALE CITIZENS AND VOTING RIGHTS

The third and final way in which people could participate in politics in early modern Europe was to vote and hold elective office. No state was a modern democracy, but there were many opportunities for at least male citizens to vote and be elected to office. Most cities were governed by elected mayors and town councils and even peasant villages were often run by assemblies of all the male landowners. Most countries had elected representative bodies, either at the provincial level, like Spain's Cortes of Castille, or at the national level, like England's Parliament. France, with its provincial estates and its national Estates-General, had both.

The right to vote for representatives usually derived from property owner-ship or from being the citizen of a town. Therefore many women were tech-nically qualified to vote and hold public office. This was especially true in cities governed by elected officials – many of those in Germany, for example. There the right to vote for and sit on the elected city councils came with citizenship, which was theoretically required of all those who lived within the city's walls. As with national citizenship, its main requirement was native birth; all those, men and women, born in the town of citizen parents were citizens. Citizenship brought duties as well as rights: citizens had to swear an oath of loyalty, renewed yearly in an outdoor ceremony, and they had to serve in the militia or pay for a substitute. Male newcomers to the city could become citizens if they could prove they were of legitimate birth and 'honourable reputation' and that they could perform or pay for someone to perform their military duty. As always, a wife took the citizenship of her husband, but single women and widows could become citizens if they met the same criteria as men: legitimate birth, 'honourable reputation' and the ability to pay for a soldier.[52] Nonetheless, female citizenship was different from that of the full citizen, the male household head. For one thing, cities were increasingly reluctant to grant women citizenship over the course of our period. In Nuremberg, women were 13 percent of the new citizens in the 1460s but less than 1 percent by the 1550s.[53] And women citizens were increasingly hemmed in by restrictions – against marrying for-eigners or men of a different religion, for example – that did not apply to male citizens. But the most fundamental distinction between male and female citizens was political. In most German towns and villages, female citizens met together publicly to elect the municipal midwife, but they did not vote for or sit on the town councils, even though they were technically qualified to do so. They did not even take part in the yearly civic oath taking. This exclusion of women was not mandated by any law. Both men and women simply seem to have accepted the fact that female citizenship was different from men's and that choosing a midwife was women's work but running a city was not.[54]

This was true everywhere in Europe. In England, for example, women may have voted in elections for churchwarden and sexton (the evidence is unclear), but those were religious rather than political positions.[55] Although some women were technically qualified to vote for members of Parliament, there is no evidence that they did so. They accepted the notion that public elections and assemblies were no place for women, even though they might be very influential in politics behind the scenes. Before the English Civil War some members of Parliament were not elected but instead were appointed by the local lord of the manor, a position women could inherit. At least two women are known to have chosen members of Parliament in the seventeenth century.[56] Once in Westminister, members of Parliament often split into factions that did the bidding of the biggest landowner in their district – again a position a woman might inherit. Historians have found no fewer than five peeresses heading political factions in the seventeenth century.[57] Yet no woman voted for or sat in Parliament.

This same split between informal, behind-the-scenes political activity and formal voting is visible in France. There politics on the national level were played out among the nobles at court; their intrigues often culminated in outright rebellion against the king. Noblewomen played active roles in these intrigues; they even led troops during the rebellion of the Fronde. At the local level factions tied to great nobles by patronage struggled against each other and the crown, often in the provincial representative bodies, the estates, which collected taxes and dealt with other local administrative matters. Noblewomen often headed these factions, yet they took no part in formal politics. Many were eligible to sit in the provincial estates, because every fief-owning noble was, yet there is no evidence that any did, although many took part in the social events surrounding the meetings. Two estates, Brittany and Languedoc, specifically forbade women from sitting. Fief-owning noblewomen were also eligible to vote for representatives to the Estates-General, the national body that met when summoned by the king to advise him in times of crisis. Noblewomen were actually summoned to attend the election meetings for the Estates-General of 1614, but there is no evidence that they did so.[58]

Why didn't qualified women exercise their right to vote? Hilda Smith, an expert on English political thought in this period, has argued that in a sense they weren't really qualified, because the qualifications were stated in what she calls 'false universals': 'citizen', 'householder', 'fief owner' were used when really 'male citizen', 'male householder', 'male fief owner' were meant.[59] But this just leads to another question: why was it automatically assumed that just men were meant? Why was the world of elective politics exclusively male?

Perhaps the best answer is that it had simply always been so. The roots of Europe's representative institutions lay in the legislatures of the city-states of ancient Greece and Rome and in the *committus* of the barbarian tribes that overthrew the Roman Empire. Both were totally masculine institutions. And when Renaissance political theorists wrote about how politics should work, they drew on these ancient models, assigning to the ideal citizen qualities – property ownership, willingness to defend the country militarily, knowledge of and good judgement in public affairs, a shunning of 'luxury' and material goods and a willingness to sacrifice one's own interests for the good of the state – which seemed to be found only or at least largely in men.

Thus in early modern Europe, there were two levels of citizenship and only men were full citizens, citizens in the modern sense of the term: those who had the rights as well as the duties of citizenship. The partial citizenship of women created many contradictions and problems, but it was challenged only once, during the English Civil War, when English women demanded the traditional 'right of Englishmen' to petition Parliament on important issues. As we saw in Chapter 9, religious concerns first emboldened these women to speak out and the Protestant doctrine of the spiritual equality of men and women provided their major justification. A petition against church tithes signed by 7000 Quaker women stated that:

> It may seem strange to some that women should appear in so publick a manner, in a matter of so great concernment as this of Tithes . . . But let such know, that this is the work of the Lord . . . Behold our God is . . . choosing the foolish things of the world to confound the wise, weak things to confound the Mighty.[60]

As this passage suggests, at first the women were careful to acknowledge that they were mere foolish women trespassing in the realm of men; one petition stated: 'They acted not out of any Self-conceit or Pride of Heart, as *seeking to equal ourselves with Men, either in Authority or Wisdom*.'[61] But eventually they abandoned this acknowledgement of the separate spheres and instead based their claim on their citizenship:

> That since we are assured of our Creation in the image of God, and of an interest in Christ, equal unto men, as also of a proportionable share in the Freedoms of this Commonwealth, we cannot but wonder and grieve that we should appear so despicable in your eyes, as to be thought unworthy to Petition or represent our Grievances to this Honourable House. Have we not an equal interest with the men of this Nation in those liberties and securities contained [in] . . . [the] good laws of the land? Are any of our lives, limbs, liberties, or goods to be taken from us more than from men, but

by due process of law ...? And can you imagine us to be so sottish or stupid as not to perceive, or not to be sencible when daily those strong defences of our pease and wellfare are broken down ... are we Christians, and yet must we sit still and keep at home?[62]

Here the female petitioners not only assert that their citizenship is full citizenship, equal to that of men (aren't they too, like men, protected by the good laws of the land and due process of law?), they also attack the clichés of the separate sphere argument (women are not so 'sottish and stupid' as to just 'sit still and keep at home' in a time of national danger). But it was with precisely these clichés that Parliament and public opinion answered these women's demands. The members of the House of Commons told female petitioners in 1649:

> That the matter you petition about, is of higher concernment then you understand, that the House gave an answer to your Husbands; and therefore you are desired to goe home, and looke after your owne business, and meddle with your huswiferey.[63]

A contemporary newspaper echoed this, telling women: 'It is fitter for you to be washing your dishes, and meddle with the [spinning] wheele and distaffe.' Another wrote: 'We shall have things brought to a fine passe, if women came to teach Parliament how to make Lawes.'[64]

When their demands were rebuffed, the female petitioners gave up; the end of the war and the settlement of religious matters made their participation in politics less urgent. So the differing levels of citizenship remained throughout the early modern period. In law, except for women's property rights, the gap between male and female citizenship narrowed and the contradictions lessened, but in politics, as women were squeezed out of government bureaucracies and riot was increasingly repressed, the gap widened. It would take another major war, the French Revolution of 1789, and a long struggle in the nineteenth and twentieth centuries before women would lose their second-class status and become citizens equal in rights and duties to men.

Chapter 14

◆

WARRIORS AND EMPIRE BUILDERS

In 1600 14-year-old Catalina de Erauso, who had been put in a convent by her father, a Spanish army officer, decided that she was 'displeased with that enclosed life' and did not wish to be a nun. So she ran away, taking along scissors, a needle and thread, with which she cut her hair and turned her habit into a man's breeches and doublet. Dressed as a man to avoid detection and sexual overtures, she worked for three years as a manservant. In 1603 she decided that she was 'naturally inclined to arms and to seeing the world' and sailed off to the Spanish colonies in America, where she joined the army. She spent the next 17 years as a *conquistador*, fighting Indians and brawling in taverns. In 1620 she was arrested during one of these brawls and her sex was discovered. But by proving she had remained a virgin and been a brave and honourable soldier, she persuaded both the king of Spain and the pope to exempt her from the laws against cross-dressing and allow her to continue to live as a man. In old age she wrote – or at least 'told to' a professional writer – the story of her life, which fascinated the reading public, serving as the basis for novels and plays and making her famous as the 'Lieutenant Nun'.[1]

During her life the Lieutenant Nun crossed many gender boundaries. Not only did she dress in men's clothes and work at 'male' occupations, she also joined the army and sailed off to the Indies. In doing so she invaded arenas that were, even more than the rest of the public sphere, considered quintessentially masculine. Indeed, war, and its most daring early modern offshoot, overseas empire building, were thought to define masculinity in the period. Men proved their manhood in battle or by sailing bravely off into the unknown. Conversely, women were thought to have an inborn aversion to warfare. Their detractors traced this to women's innate physical weakness and cowardice, while women's defenders cited their maternal compassion for suffering. Christine de Pisan wrote proudly of her sex:

> They neither kill nor wound, nor lop off limbs. They do not plot, or plunder and persecute.[2]

But de Pisan was wrong. Women did take part in war, some, like the Lieutenant Nun, dressed as men and playing men's roles, but most as women. And while no women sailed with Columbus in 1492, 30 women accompanied him on his third voyage to America in 1497 and from then on women played an important role in overseas colonization.[3] In fact, as we shall see, it was largely due to women that European social and cultural practices were transferred to and replicated in the colonies. In this chapter, we will explore the central roles of women in those two most 'masculine' of state enterprises, war and empire building.

WOMEN AND WAR: FEMALE VICTIMS OF WARFARE

War was endemic in early modern Europe; in the 100 years from 1600 to 1700 there were only seven in which there was no war anywhere on the European continent. The sixteenth century saw religious warfare between Catholic and Protestant in Germany, France, the Low Countries and eastern Europe, plus Spain's attempted invasion of England in 1588, the French–Spanish duel for hegemony in Italy and the great struggle between the Christian states of Europe and the Ottoman Empire for control of the Mediterranean. The first half of the seventeenth century was dominated by the terrible Thirty Years' War and the second by the four wars of France's ambitious king Louis XIV. This ubiquity of war was one reason why, although it was considered 'men's' work, war affected women. In the years from 1500 to 1700 there were few families that did not find themselves in the path of an enemy army or have their menfolk called for military service. And everyone paid heavier taxes, often at the cost of deepening poverty, to support the wars of their sovereigns.

As always throughout history, women's main role in war was to send their loved ones off to battle and to bear the lonely months and years worrying about them until they returned – if they did return. This was not easy, as this poignant letter from Susan Rodway, the wife of a soldier in Cromwell's army during the English Civil War, makes clear:

> Most dear and loving husband, my king love. I remember me unto you hoping that you are in good health, as I am in the writing hereof. My little Willie have been sick

this fortnight. I pray you to come home, if you can come safely. I do marvel that I cannot hear from you as other neighbors do. I do desire to hear from you as soon as you can. I pray you to send me word when you do think you shall return. You do not consider I am a lone woman; I thought you would never leave me thus long together, so I rest ever praying for your safest return.

Your loving wife,
Susan Rodway[4]

Because most people depended on family economies in which the labour of both husband and wife was necessary for survival, women had more to worry about than loneliness and having to cope with little Willie's illness on their own. They had somehow to replace their husband's labour in the shop or field. Therefore the departure of men for war could suddenly plunge their families into destitution. And because often half of the men who went off to war never returned (most due to disease or desertion, not battlefield wounds) women stood a good chance of facing not only grief at the loss of a loved one (Margaret Eure, another Englishwoman whose husband fought in the Civil War, described his death as 'the greatest misfortune that could ever happen to me in this world'[5]), but also permanent poverty. State archives are full of letters of war widows begging for a small pension to relieve their destitution. Alice Stonier was the widow of a drover who took her to Ireland hoping to make their fortune. Instead, he was drafted into Cromwell's army and promptly killed, leaving her with five children and no means of support. She petitioned to be shipped back to her home parish in England, which granted her 8d a week and placed her three eldest children 'in good service'.[6] The loss of the family head could spell poverty even for upper-class women. When Sir Edmund Verney was killed in the English Civil War, his five unmarried daughters saw their prospects for substantial dowries – and therefore respectable marriages – vanish.[7]

Women were victimized by war in more direct ways as well, especially if they found themselves in the path of an advancing army – a likely occurrence when war was so widespread. If this happened, the best thing to do was to abandon your home and flee. During the Thirty Years' War the family of Hans Heberle, a shoemaker in the village of Neenstetten, packed up their possessions and fled to safety within the nearby walled city of Ulm no fewer than 30 times.[8] People fled oncoming armies, even their own, because in this period troops were quartered on the civilian population. Early modern armies were not like our citizen armies raised and supplied by the state. Instead they were composed of companies of troops, often foreigners, raised by private entrepreneurs and hired by rulers for the campaigning season, usually spring and summer.

The entrepreneurs supplied the troops by buying food and shelter from the civilian population in the areas through which they campaigned. In theory they paid a 'reasonable price', but in practice they often simply commandeered what they needed. And their needs were so great that they might leave food shortages and starvation in their wake. When a French peasant woman was offered money for bread taken by English soldiers in 1544, she said scornfully, 'God in heaven, what should I do with money, or anything else but bread'?[9]

Armies also left epidemic diseases in their wake. Usually the villages and towns through which they passed were too small to house them adequately. In the Thirty Years' War, for example, troops were quartered 10 to 20 a house in the towns of Hesse-Darmstadt. They brought the plague with them. Not surprisingly, it spread rapidly through the army and to the civilian population. Such things happened repeatedly in this period. It has been estimated that in 1627–1628 the diseases spread as they marched and camped by one French army of just 6000 men led to the deaths of over 1 million civilians![10]

Apart from starvation and disease, there was always the danger that the troops quartered on you would be especially vicious and steal your valuables, beat you up and abuse your womenfolk. The chances of this happening were infinitely multiplied if the army passing through was not your own troops but your opponent's. According to the laws of war, civilians and their property were not to be harmed unless they aided the enemy. But in hostile territory everyone seemed to support the enemy. How could soldiers separate the guilty from the innocent? Was anyone, except for very small children, truly innocent? Luis de Molina, a Spanish jurist, stated that: 'Grown women who march with the enemy or are beside them in a besieged town are usually not free of blame, but are as a rule helping the enemy. For this reason they are not to be considered as having the same degree of innocence as children.'[11] In other words, they could be killed if necessary. And usually it was considered necessary. Armies of this period made frequent use of the scorched earth policy, destroying everything and killing everyone in their paths to deny their opponents provisions and terrorize the civilian population into submission. In 1593 Sir Arthur Chicester reported on the actions of his English troops in Ireland:

> We have killed, burnt and spoiled all along the lough . . . in which journeys we have killed above one hundred people of all sorts, besides such as were burnt, how many I know not. We spare none of what quality or sex so ever, and it has bred much terror in the people.[12]

Carrying out such policies was easier when the victims were peasants, for soldiers, like the rest of early modern society, regarded peasants with contempt, as little better than animals. This was as true of common soldiers, often peasants themselves who had run away from their dull villages in search of adventure, as it was of their upper-class officers. A soldiers' proverb during the Thirty Years' War maintained that, 'Every soldier needs three peasants, one to give up his lodging, one to provide his wife, and one to take his place in hell.'[13]

As this suggests, peasant women were often sexually victimized by enemy armies. In 1634, again during the Thirty Years' War, 20 Swedish soldiers entered the little village of Linden, near the German city of Rothenburg. They demanded food and wine and searched the village for valuables. Two of them, 'a fat soldier from East Finland and his friend the white-haired young soldier', entered the cottage of Georg Rösch, beat him up and raped his wife, who then ran screaming through the village. This case was unusual only in that the villagers caught one of the rapists, who was eventually tried and punished.[14] In theory most armies forbade the raping of civilian women, not to protect the women but because it was bad for discipline. But, in practice, these rules were usually ignored. Not only was rape an integral part of the scorched earth policy, it was deemed a soldier's reward for risking his life.

Usually townspeople fared better in war, both because town walls protected them (that was the reason Hans Heberle's family fled so often to Ulm) and because they were not regarded with the contempt that peasants evoked. But there was one major exception to this: the siege. According to the rules of war, when an army came to a walled castle or town, it should first demand its peaceful surrender. If this were forthcoming, the civilian population was not to be harmed. But if surrender were refused, all the inhabitants, men, women and children, were considered guilty of aiding the enemy and therefore fair game. Sieges were long-drawn-out affairs; the Spanish siege of Ostend, for example, lasted over three years. Food often ran out. Thirteen thousand people starved to death during Henri IV's siege of Paris in 1590. Stray bullets killed civilians as well as soldiers. As the castles and towns fell, they were looted and their inhabitants, soldiers and civilians alike, often massacred. Seven thousand people died when Antwerp fell in 1576.[15] Men were usually killed, while women were raped or otherwise sexually humiliated. If they survived, raped women were usually too ashamed to lodge a complaint, although one Irishwoman raped by English soldiers did so, stating that she 'thought she would never be well or in her right mind again the fact was so foul and grievous unto her'.[16] But women did lodge complaints about being stripped naked by the invading troops. Such complaints are so frequent that they suggest this, if nothing worse, was standard treatment for women when a castle or town fell.

WOMEN AND WAR: FEMALE WARRIORS

Not surprisingly, considering what they could expect if the siege were successful, women often actively participated in the defence of their castle or town. Royalist Lady Bankes, for example, defended her home, Corfe Castle, against a parliamentary army of 500 to 600 men during the English Civil War. Lady Bankes's troops consisted of five men plus her daughters and maidservants. They threw stones and hot embers down on the soldiers who tried to scale the castle walls.[17] Lady Dowdall defended her Irish castle against 3000 rebels; she had a garrison of 80 men trained by a soldier she hired.[18] Noblewomen were not the only ones to defend their homes against besieging armies. When the Spanish laid siege to Marseilles in 1524, the city's women worked with spades and shovels to keep the walls repaired and when Siena was besieged for 18 months in 1552–1553, every woman, noble and commoner alike, was issued a basket, shovel and pick, assigned to a labour gang and ordered to drop everything and report to the walls when the church bells rang.[19]

Such women were admired and praised for displaying a 'courage beyond their sex'. They were not criticized for taking part in the quintessentially masculine occupation of warfare because they acted in self-defence – they were thought to have had no choice. But there were also many women who voluntarily *chose* to take part in warfare out of conviction. Many of the wars of the period were religious conflicts or patriotic risings and women felt as passionately about the issues involved as men did. Society was more ambivalent about these female volunteers. They were generally admired only if they helped their cause in ways that did not overstep gender boundaries. For example, it was acceptable for women to raise money for their cause. Cromwell's army included the 'Virgin' and 'Maiden' Troops, so called because funds raised by women paid for their equipment.[20] It was also acceptable for women to nurse the wounded; indeed, if women did not nurse them, casualties got little care. Paradoxically, spying too was an acceptable female role; the very unlikelihood that women would engage in such dangerous work made them effective spies – no one suspected them. Again in the English Civil War, Jane Whorwood repeatedly talked her way past the king's guards in futile attempts to free the captive Charles I and Anne Murray actually managed to free Charles's son James Duke of York by smuggling women's clothes past the sentries and dressing the young prince in them.[21] Both women were hailed as heroines by English royalists.

Public opinion was more ambivalent about the lower-class women who voluntarily followed armies – soldiers' wives and sweethearts, prostitutes, plus the homeless and uprooted who had nowhere else to go. Their numbers were enormous. Sixteenth- and early seventeenth-century armies were like villages on the move. A small core of actual soldiers was accompanied by large numbers of what were called 'mouths' (to be fed): wives, children, officers' servants, prostitutes and suppliers of all sorts. In 1577 a Spanish force in the Netherlands consisted of 5300 soldiers, 2000 servants and 20,000 other 'mouths'.[22] In 1646, a Bavarian regiment fighting in the Thirty Years' War numbered 480 infantrymen, 74 servants, 314 women and children, three sutlers (sellers of provisions to armies) and 160 horses.[23] Officials were ambivalent about the many prostitutes who followed the troops. Some governments – the English, for example – tried to ban them on the grounds that they made the soldiers even more lascivious than they naturally were and distracted them from their duties. Other states, however, tolerated them, believing that if prostitutes were available the troops would be less likely to molest female civilians.

All governments were enthusiastic about the soldiers' wives who accompanied armies. English officer Sir James Turner noted that 'the married souldiers fared better, looked more vigorously and were able to do more duty than bachelors'.[24] Wives provided a steadying influence on the troops and they also performed many important services for their husbands and for the army as a whole. These are nicely summed up in *Simplicissimus*, the famous picaresque novel depicting the horrors of the Thirty Years' War in Germany:

> In their misery, a few troopers took on wives (some of these formerly two-bit sluts) who could increase their income by such work as sewing, washing, spinning, or by selling second-hand clothing or other junk, or even by stealing. Among the women was a female ensign who drew her pay like a corporal! Another was a midwife, and she was given many a good meal for herself and her husband. Another took in laundry and ironing: she washed shirts, socks, nightshirts, and other apparel for the bachelors among the officers and men, and she had quite a reputation. Others sold tobacco and furnished pipes for those who needed them. Still others sold brandy; it was generally thought that they were adulterating it with water distilled by their own bodies – but that didn't change the color of the liquor in the least! Another was a seamstress who was able to earn money through hemstitching and embroidery. Still another could pick a living off the field: in the winter she dug up snails, in spring she picked salad herbs, in summer she took the young out of birds' nests, and in fall she would gather hundreds of other little tidbits. Some sold kindling wood, which they carried to market like donkeys; others peddled still other merchandise.[25]

Note how these occupations paralleled 'women's work' in civilian life; in effect, the soldier husband and his wife formed the standard family economy, the husband doing 'men's work', the wife 'women's work'. Both were vital to the family – and to the army. As Sir James Turner put it: 'As woman was created to be a helper to man, so women are great helpers to armies.'[26]

Despite their usefulness, armies lost most of their female 'mouths' by 1700. The military revolution of the seventeenth century was responsible for this. The military revolution was in part tactical. In the infantry, the musket replaced the pike and with the invention of the salvo, in which advancing troops fired when ordered to, all at once, generals finally figured out how to use guns effectively on the battlefield. The military revolution also changed how armies were organized. The salvo needed discipline, so armies were no longer disbanded once the summer campaigning season was over. Instead they remained in being and used the winter months for drill. But this made it harder for these now 'standing' (that is, permanent) armies to live off the land, so states increasingly took responsibility for raising and supplying their troops. As they did so, armies became increasingly regularized and disciplined; the spread of uniforms and ranks for officers and men reflected this.

As armies changed, the relationship of women to military life changed too. By the late seventeenth century, war was increasingly the business of the professional men of the military services. The new, better supplied and disciplined armies were more isolated from civilian life and inflicted fewer civilian – and therefore fewer female – casualties. The new supply systems and discipline also meant that fewer 'mouths' were allowed to accompany the troops. States now contracted out the work that army wives had previously done and family life was seen as incompatible with the new military discipline. Wives did not completely disappear from armies until about 1850, but from 1650 on their numbers steadily shrank, as armies began to require men to get their officer's permission before marrying and allowed only a small number of wives to accompany the troops. Their duties, now largely reduced to sewing and washing, were strictly regulated and they were often entered on the official troop rosters.[27]

Paradoxically, as the number of women in an army's civilian tail fell, the number of those who, like Catalina de Erauso, donned men's clothes and served in its ranks, grew dramatically. In fact, the late seventeenth, eighteenth and early nineteenth centuries were the heyday of cross-dressing women serving in the ranks of Europe's armed forces. Between 1606 and 1811, 83 women disguised as men served in the army and navy of the Netherlands; in the late eighteenth century at least 44 women served in the ranks of the French revolutionary army, two of them as aides-de-camp to a general.[28] Other countries show similar figures.

Women donned men's clothing and joined the armed forces for a number of reasons. Some, like Catalina de Erauso, chafed at the confinement of traditional women's roles and longed for adventure. Others felt ambivalent about their sexual identity and were more comfortable as men. Still others simply wanted to be with their lovers or husbands and could no longer do this as part of an army's civilian tail. That was what motivated the seventeenth-century Englishwoman Mrs Christian Davies, who joined the army to search for her soldier husband.[29] A few were moved by patriotism; the Dutchwoman Maria van Spanjen declared that she had joined the navy because of 'a great desire to serve her country as a sailor'.[30] But the most common motivating factor was probably simple poverty. As we have seen, in the seventeenth century lower-class women often disguised themselves as men so that they could get higher paying male jobs; cross-dressing was a response to the shrinking employment opportunities for women. To someone like Maria van der Gijsse, reduced to begging for food from farmhouse to farmhouse, soldiering (a job with relatively high pay, food, clothing and shelter provided and not much more hardship and danger than life on the road) must have seemed an attractive option. When a kind soul gave her some men's clothes and advised her to join the army, she did.[31]

Living as a man was probably more difficult in the armed forces than in civilian life, although the difficulties did not stem from the fighting itself. Thanks to the military revolution, which replaced the long and cumbersome pike with the musket, an army's weapons were not beyond the physical capacities of most women. And often female soldiers were sheltered by their comrades from the worst of the fighting. This was especially likely to be true of the women who joined armies to be with their husbands or lovers. Their menfolk of course knew their true sexual identity and often they and their friends contrived to protect the women not only from discovery but also from the most brutal aspects of army life. Even lone women soldiers were often protected by their comrades. Cross-dressing women usually passed themselves off as very young men to explain their lack of beards, and their 'youth' and frailty often aroused the protective instincts of grizzled veterans. Their 'youth' was also a convenient excuse for avoiding the drinking and debauchery that characterized most activities recreations. Yet these soldiers could not be avoided entirely. Catalina de Erauso was not the only woman whose disguise was penetrated when she was enjoying herself with her fellow soldiers: the female soldier forced to reveal her sexual identity when accused by a pregnant tavern servant of fathering her child is a standard motif of stories and ballads about women warriors. Others were undone by the forced intimacies of barrack life. To prevent discovery cross-dressing women had to hide the rags they used for their menstrual periods and to contrive always to be alone when they undressed or relieved themselves. All this was difficult in a crowded barracks.

Wounds posed another hazard: many female soldiers were unmasked when they were wounded and undressed for treatment.[32]

These hazards were multiplied in the navy. In the era of sail, ships were powered less by wind than by heavy physical labour, difficult for women to perform. And on ships there was literally no privacy. Sailors slept side by side in hammocks and relieved themselves publicly over the ship's side. Therefore it is not surprising that there were far fewer female sailors than soldiers and that most of them lived aboard ships as women, not men. Hannah Snell survived for five years as James Grey, common seaman, cook and assistant steward on British naval vessels, but the two best-known female sailors, the pirate shipmates Mary Read and Anne Bonny, wore trousers and men's jackets only when fighting. Otherwise, they wore women's clothes and their fellow crewmembers knew their sexual identity.

The stories of Mary Read and Anne Bonny in many ways typified those of women who joined the army or navy. Mary Read was the daughter of a poor mother, soon widowed, who dressed her in boys' clothing and pretended that Mary was her dead son to get money from her late husband's family. When she was old enough to work, Mary continued to wear masculine attire to gain higher paying jobs. She worked as a male servant and sailor and finally entered the army, where she met and married a fellow soldier. When he died and left her a poor widow, she abandoned the tavern they had been running and joined the army again in masculine attire. She was on a troop ship sailing to the West Indies when it was captured by pirates. She, like many captured soldiers and sailors, decided she liked the democracy of pirate life, where officers were elected and booty evenly shared. When the governor of the West Indies called for privateers to fight the Spanish, she volunteered to join a ship.[33]

Anne Bonny came from a higher social class; she was the acknowledged illegitimate daughter of a prominent Irish lawyer turned Virginia planter. She spurned the proper suitors her father found for her, and eventually she ran off to marry a penniless sailor, who brought her to the West Indies. There she met and fell in love with the pirate captain Calico Jack Rackam and left her husband to join Rackam's ship. On board she met and unmasked Mary Read, whose masculine disguise had fooled Rackam and his crew.[34]

Both Read and Bonny showed much physical courage, an important trait in the egalitarian pirate society where a man's status depended on bravery, not birth. Anne Bonny beat up a man who tried to rape her and Mary Read fought a duel to defend her lover. When their ship was captured, Rackam and most of his men fled below. Only Bonny, Read and one other sailor were left on deck to face the enemy:

upon which, she, Mary Read, called to those under Deck, to come up and fight like Men, and finding they did not stir, fired her Arms down the Hold amongst them, killing one, and wounding others.[35]

Anne Bonny also shamed the men who were more cowardly than she, including her former lover:

> The Day that Rackam was executed, by special Favour, he was admitted to see her; but all the Comfort she gave him, was that she was sorry to see him there, but if he had fought like a Man, he need not have been hang'd like a Dog.[36]

Were women like Mary Read and Anne Bonny known and admired? Did the fact that they and countless other women warriors 'fought like men' and 'displayed manly courage and valour' change popular gender stereotypes? Probably. The exploits of women like Catalina de Erauso, Mary Read and Anne Bonny were well known. Women warriors were a staple of popular plays, poems and ballads in the early modern period. Although Catalina de Erauso's autobiography was not published until 1829, a number of plays based on her life were performed in the seventeenth century. More than 30 popular ballads with cross-dressing heroines dating from the early modern period have been found in the Netherlands, and in England over 120 ballads featuring women warriors were published between 1600 and 1815.[37] Most of these ballads presented the woman warrior in the guise least threatening to traditional gender stereotypes: that of lovesick woman who put on men's clothing and joined the army to be with the man she loved. They inevitably ended with marriage – and with the bride back in women's attire. But many of these ballads praised their heroines for showing the 'manly' qualities of intelligence, ambition, physical courage, steadfastness, and gallantry. 'Few men might compare with her, her actions were so gallant':[38]

> I'm a girl that fears no danger
> I'll boldly fight with sword in hand

sang one woman warrior, while another:

> said she was determined to follow the sea
> And in a short time Commander she would be[39]

Thus the woman warrior of popular culture was what her contemporaries would have called a manly woman, endowed with both masculine and feminine qualities. As such, she, like those other 'manly' women of the period, the learned lady and the female ruler, helped break down the patriarchal paradigm with its notions of inborn gender traits and naturally dictated gender roles. Therefore the growing 'professionalization' of war had mixed effects on women:

while it saved the lives of many potential female victims of marauding armies, it also, when it closed the ranks of the military to the woman warrior, put an end to an important factor in challenging traditional notions of gender and improving the status of women.

WOMEN IN OVERSEAS COLONIZATION: THE PORTUGUESE EMPIRE

Mary Read, Anne Bonny and Catalina de Erauso were not only women warriors; they were also female colonizers. All spent important parts of their lives in European colonies in the New World. In the early modern period, colonization, like war, was considered a masculine enterprise requiring masculine qualities like physical courage. So strongly were conquest and empire identified with masculinity that the lands Europeans colonized were usually personified in maps and prints as female; they were 'virgin lands' which, like women, needed the male to make them fruitful.[40]

Yet women were a part of Europe's attempts at colonization from their outset and their role in colonization was vital to its success. Men may have done the exploration and conquest and established political and economic dominance over non-European peoples, but it was the women colonists, drawing on inherited traditions as they made their homes in the colonies, who established European cultural hegemony. The degree to which the manners and mores of colonial societies matched those of the mother country was directly related to the proportion of women in the settler population.

We can see this in the experience of the first European country to explore and colonize other lands, Portugal. Portugal's empire was not only the first, it was also the most far flung, with colonies in Madeira, the Azores, along both coasts of Africa, India, Ceylon, the Spice Islands, Macao and Brazil. Except for Madeira, the Azores, Brazil and Zambesia in East Africa, Portuguese settlements were trading posts rather than permanent colonies. The Portuguese usually did not try to displace native rulers or control and cultivate lands beyond the small hinterland of their coastal settlement. This determined the numbers and roles of women in the Portuguese colonies. Because their colonies were simply trading posts that did not need a large population to control vast stretches of land, the Portuguese sent to their colonies soldiers, sailors, merchants and administrators like judges and customs inspectors – in other words, men. Accurate statistics on the sex of Portuguese colonial emigrants are lacking, but it seems probable that the ratio of European-born or descended women to European-born or descended men was lower in

Portuguese possessions than in those of any other colonial power. There was only one white woman in the Portuguese colony of Muscat in 1553 and only one in Macao in 1636. On Mozambique there were only six white families in 1822, despite the fact that the Portuguese had been there 300 years.[41]

Because there were so few European women in their colonies, Portuguese men satisfied their sexual needs with native-born women – Africans in Angola, Indians, Malays and Indonesians in Goa, Chinese and Japanese in Macao. The different sexual mores of these areas, plus the fact that many of these women were slaves, encouraged sexual licence. Some Portuguese slaveowners had virtual harems. The more common practice was to take a native-born woman as a mistress or, more rarely, a legal wife (Portugal and its colonies had no laws against miscegenation). The children of such liaisons, both legitimate and illegitimate, were usually acknowledged and raised by their fathers and inherited their property. Thus the elite of the Portuguese colonies was of mixed blood. Wealthy and prominent colonial families intermarried and incoming Portuguese merchants and administrators married colonial heiresses rather than importing brides from Portugal. Lower-class men in the colonies could not aspire to a mixed-blood bride and married or had liaisons with black, Indian or Chinese women.

This mixing of races led to a mixing of cultures. Mixed-blood or native-born wives and mistresses ran their households in their own languages and according to their own customs. Therefore lifestyles in the colonies gradually diverged from the Portuguese model. This alarmed the Portuguese government enough to prompt it to send Portuguese women to the colonies. The government rightly believed that female colonists would run their households and raise their children using the Portuguese language and customs. This points up the major contribution of women to European colonization: they were the transmitters of European culture to the colonies. The extent to which the manners and mores of these colonial societies lined up with those of the colonizing country was in direct proportion to the number of women in the settler population.

The Portuguese government seems to have realized this. In 1545 it inaugurated a programme of sending 'orphans of the king', respectably born young women from the orphanages of Lisbon and Oporto, to Goa as prospective brides for the colonists. Usually between five and 15 girls were sent out every year, although in 1560 a record-high 54 were transported. Unfortunately, the programme did not work; prospective bridegrooms preferred their native-born mistresses. In 1583 the government tried to make the orphans more attractive by giving them offices in the colonial government bureaucracies as dowries. Any man who married an orphan could fill the office; he also received a hefty cash bonus. Later, land grants giving the holder the right to exploit the labour of the natives in specified villages were added as well. But even this did not make the orphans attractive as brides.

Despite their failure, orphans of the king were also sent to Angola beginning in 1593. And in Portuguese East Africa – Zambesia – a variant on the land grant programme was tried, in which women of Portuguese birth or descent were granted rights to *prazeros*, enormous ranches carved from Bantu lands, provided they married a Portuguese man.[42] In Brazil, Portugal's last colony and the one it was most determined to make a permanent colony of settlement, even more was done to encourage female migration and marriage between whites. Added to the usual orphans of the king and land grants and government offices reserved for male migrants who married white women were bounties for married migrants who brought their wives and children with them. In 1732 white women were even forbidden to leave Brazil without government permission.[43]

Despite these efforts, which eventually evened out the sex ratio, white men continued to marry and have liaisons with women of other races. Brazil became a truly multiracial and multicultural society. Within this society, white women enjoyed more power and status than would have been the case had they stayed in Portugal. If the role of women in colonization was the basically conservative one of replicating the culture of the mother country, the effect of colonization on women was more radical: they gained power and status in comparison to the situation in the mother country. These gains did not come through changes in the legal position of women; usually the laws of the mother country were transferred intact to the colonies. Instead they came from the way the laws were applied in the very different circumstances overseas.

For example, women of Portuguese descent in Brazil owned substantial amounts of property. Portuguese law allowed daughters to inherit equally with sons, but in Portugal daughters were usually fobbed off with dowries while sons were favoured. In Brazil, however, fathers tended to skimp on their sons' portions, both because sons could easily make fortunes in the gold or diamond mines or the vast ranches of the interior and because, once independently wealthy, they could ignore their parents' wishes and take a non-white mistress rather than marry. Instead of favouring sons, fathers of the colonial elite of São Paolo gave their daughters enormous dowries so that they might have the pick of the ambitious bachelor migrants as husbands; daughters, not sons, perpetuated family honour and prestige. Daughters often also inherited from male bachelor relatives. In Portugal such men left their money to their nephews, but in Brazil that might mean that it would end up in the hands of an Indian or 'negro' mistress, while leaving it to a niece kept it in the family.[44] Once married, a Brazilian wife was more likely to keep control of her property. Portuguese law allowed husbands to administer their wives' property and in Portugal they did. But in Brazil wives not only often administered their own property; with their menfolk away in the interior for months or even years, they administered the family holdings as well. In Portugal, widows were discouraged from becoming their children's guardians and from remarrying; in Brazil, they administered their children's estates – who else was there to do it? – and remarried at will.[45] Even the lives of lower-class women in Brazil differed from those of their Portuguese sisters. In Portugal, lower-class women were white; in Brazil, they were native Americans, blacks or of mixed race. In Portugal, most were married; in Brazil, most were not. In Vila Rica in 1804 only 16.6 percent of the adult population was married; this was mostly the white elite.[46] In Portugal, lower-class women did poorly paid 'women's work'; in Brazil, they might take up shopkeeping, goldmining and other 'male' occupations. Women owned 40 percent of the shops in Vila Rica and comprised one-quarter of the miners and prospectors.[47] For such women, unmarried, economically independent, heading their own households, European standards of chastity, deference to men and seclusion within the home were meaningless. In the early eighteenth century the bishop of Rio de Janeiro was rebuked by the Portuguese government for prohibiting women from leaving their homes after dark. The bishop was told that working women had to shop after dark and that Brazil was not Portugal.[48]

WOMEN IN OVERSEAS COLONIZATION: THE SPANISH EMPIRE

Portugal's major rival in the early days of colonization, Spain, was determined that such divergence between colony and mother country would not take place in *its* empire. Drawing on their experience in reconquering Spain from the moors, the Spanish aimed from the outset at establishing permanent settlements replicating the culture of the mother country, and converting the indigenous peoples to Christianity. Unfortunately, this got off to a bad start. As we have seen, no women sailed with Columbus on his first two voyages and until the 1520s very few Spanish women came to the New World. The *conquistadors* therefore formed liaisons, usually exploitative, with native women. Rape was as routine in the *conquistadors'* wars of extermination against the indigenous peoples as it was in European wars of the period and many settlers apparently thought their *encomiendas*, grants to exploit an area of land by exacting work and tribute from the natives living on it, included the right to the sexual services of native women. *Conquistadors* also entered relationships with native women for political reasons; Cuzco, Peru, came under Spanish control when one of Pizarro's lieutenants took as his mistress the sister of its last Inca ruler. But at least some of these relationships were loving consensual unions, and royal orders of 1503 and 1514 urged Spaniards to marry their native concubines and legitimize their offspring.[49] Therefore the Spanish colonies, like the Portuguese, developed a substantial mixed-blood population and an elaborate vocabulary (*casta*) of racial types: *mestizo* (Spanish and Indian); *castizo* (Spanish and *mestizo*); *mulato* (Spanish and African); *morisco* (Spanish and *mulato*); *pardo* (African and Indian); *lobo* (*pardo* and Indian).[50] But soon the large numbers of female migrants made Spanish marriages the norm not just for the ruling elite but also for lower-class settlers (although Spanish men continued to take Indian, African and mixed-blood women as their mistresses) and 'purity of blood' a prime marker of social status.

After about 1520 female migration from Spain to the New World was substantial, reaching its peak between 1560 and 1579, when 28.5 percent of the migrants were women.[51] Thereafter it declined slightly, but by then the higher male death rate (due mainly to wars against the native peoples), plus the natural increase of the population, made the number of European-born or descended women in the more settled colonies (Santo Domingo, Mexico, Peru) almost equal to that of men.

Most of the Spanish women who came to the colonies came as part of a family group; 30 to 40 percent of the female migrants were married women.[52] The government encouraged the migration of families; the easiest way to create stable families in the New World was to transplant them from the Old. Every married man who left Spain for the Indies was required either to bring his wife with him or get her written permission to leave her behind, and in the latter case men were urged to send for their wives later. Only married men were eligible for most government offices and officials were required to bring their families when they took up their posts. And the government favoured married men when granting *encomiendas*, the key to wealth and status in the Spanish empire.

If they were not married when they set sail, Spanish men could usually find Spanish-born or descended brides in the New World, because in addition to the married women, large numbers of young single girls migrated to the Indies.[53] The Spanish colonies differed from the Portuguese in attracting not just elite migrants but also a mass migration of the lower classes hoping to better themselves. Such migrants either paid for their own passage or came as indentured servants, agreeing to work for a number of years for only room and board for the person willing to pay their fare. Male lower-class migrants came from all over Spain, but because of the problems women faced travelling alone, the third of the lower-class migrants who were female came mostly from Seville, the port from which ships sailed to the Indies and its hinterland.[54] That is the reason Latin American Spanish is even today spoken with the accent of sixteenth-century Seville. For girls from Seville, migration to the New World was another employment option, like becoming a textile worker or servant in town. In the peak period of migration, from 1560–1579, one-sixth of the female migrants were domestic servants.[55]

Did these women realize their dreams of a better life in the New World? Individual circumstances varied enormously. Some migrants found only misery and even returned to Spain. But in general female migrants found the better lives they sought. Both the status of individual women and the status of the sex as a whole were higher in the colonies than in Spain.

For elite women, the improvements lay in two areas: control of property and control over love and marriage. As in the Portuguese empire, the laws about property holding were similar in Spain and its colonies, but the special circumstances of colonial life encouraged men to place the family land in the hands of women. In some areas of New Spain, women owned 30 percent of the land.[56] The special circumstances of colonial life also gave women more opportunities for marriage and for choosing their marriage partners. Because marriage with a Spanish-born or descended woman was a sign of social status, almost all of them married; in sixteenth-century Peru over 90 percent did so. So sought after were they that many married 'according to the custom of the Indies' – that is, with no dowry or with a dowry secretly provided by the smitten groom.[57] And there are indications that by the eighteenth century a determined girl might actually marry for love and pick her own husband or even live unwed with a lover and bear his children without social disgrace – behaviour impossible for respectable maidens in Spain. A study of marriage litigation in colonial Mexico suggests that many young people – certainly more than in Europe – used the Church's recognition of clandestine marriage to wed despite their parents' disapproval.[58] And petitions for the legitimization of children show that even a 'respectable' woman like Dona Maria del Carmen Lopez Nieto, daughter of a judge of the *audiencia* of Bolivia, might live openly with her lover, who was Don Ramón de Rivera, another judge. Judges were forbidden to marry people under their jurisdiction without royal permission, so the impatient lovers lived together while waiting for it. Dona Maria died in childbirth.[59]

Most lower-class migrant women also found more prosperity and freedom of choice in the Americas. At the bottom of the social hierarchy in Spain, in the New World they were part of a racial elite outranking Indians, African slaves, and persons of mixed race. In a society that valued their Spanish blood, they could pick and choose among their suitors. Most married, either for love or economic gain. Usually their bridegrooms were Spanish and of slightly higher social status. But a daring minority married across racial boundaries, presumably for love. In one parish in Mexico City from 1646 to 1746, 71 Spanish women married men of mixed blood and one married an African black.[60]

Apart from more freedom of choice in marriage, lower-class women also gained economically from settling in the Americas. In the colonies the traditional low-pay, low-prestige sorts of 'women's work' – domestic service, laundry, sewing – were filled by Indian, mixed-blood or slave women, leaving for Spanish women the better paying opportunities as shopkeepers or crafts-women. And because there were so many other paths to fortune for men, the colonies did not see the male invasion of lucrative female crafts characteristic of early modern Europe. In the colonies baking and inn and tavern keeping were still largely in women's hands. Further, because in the colonies wealth was abundant but goods to buy with it were scarce, the crafts and shop keeping were usually quite profitable. In Spain, a pewterer's wife might live on the verge of poverty, but in Peru, she might wear fine silks and have a staff of servants. In Lima, in 1546 one artisan's wife employed an African slave woman, a freed native American woman from Nicaragua and a Peruvian Indian servant. Her husband had two slaves in his workshop.[61]

In such households, women performed their primary function in colonial history: replicating the culture of the mother country. As historian James Lockhart put it:

> Spanish women made their most basic contribution . . . by educating those around them in the ways of the homeland. In their houses Spanish was spoken and learned. They taught their black and Indian maids to make beds, sew European clothes, and prepare Spanish foods in Spanish fashion . . . they taught religion to their slaves and servants, and encouraged them to form steady unions and marry.[62]

They also transplanted the values and customs of European patriarchy. But because the circumstances of colonization gave more property and freedom to women, it was a patriarchy in which women enjoyed more power and status than in the European model. It is not surprising that the most outspoken defence of women's intellectual equality and their right to learn, teach and write in the early modern period came not from a woman in Europe but from Sor Juana de la Cruz, a nun in seventeenth-century Peru.[63]

WOMEN IN OVERSEAS COLONIZATION:
THE FRENCH IN NORTH AMERICA

By the time of Sor Juana, the focus of colonization had shifted from the Spanish colonies to North America and to two new colonial powers, England and France. In their colonies, women played their usual role as cultural transmitters and individual female emigrants saw their status improve. But the differing circumstances of these later colonization efforts gave less power and freedom to women and therefore the status of women as a sex did not improve as it did in the Spanish and Portuguese colonies.

The French presence in North America dated from 1608, when Samuel de Champlain founded Quebec. From their beginnings, the French colonies had a split personality. The government intended them as permanent settlements and chartered a trading company to send expeditions to Canada on the condition that it bring over a specified number of settlers each year and encourage them to clear and farm the land. But the company's merchants wanted only a trading post where they could buy the beaver skins, brought from the interior by the Huron and Algonquin tribes, which were fashionable for men's hats in Europe. Until the 1660s the government paid little attention to Canada, so it remained merely a trading post. Its few Europeans were mostly men and they soon established relationships with indigenous women, not just for sex but also because such women were keys to the lucrative fur trade. They served as guides, cargo carriers and interpreters for the *courreurs du bois*, the Frenchmen who ventured by canoe into the vast interior of the continent to trade with the western tribes when beaver died out in the east. The *courreurs* often married their paramours, either with Christian rites or with a mixture of Christian and tribal rituals, and they dealt with the indigenous peoples, often their in-laws, on terms of equality, learning their language and adopting much of their lifestyle and dress. Thus until the 1660s French Canada was scarcely French.[64]

Louis XIV was determined to change this. From the beginning of his personal rule in 1660, he took steps to turn Canada into a true colony of settlement. The trading companies' charters were cancelled and the crown took over the colony's administration. Land was promised to men who would emigrate and a variant of Portugal's orphans of the king programme brought them French brides. These *filles du roi*, whose transportation costs were paid by the king, were either volunteers from Paris orphanages or young women of good family and reputation recruited from Normandy by the trading companies. At least 774 *filles du roi* came to Quebec in the 10 years (1663–1673) of the programme's existence. They were eagerly welcomed by the male settlers, who thronged the docks when there were rumours of a ship with women on board. Most *filles du roi* were betrothed within weeks – some within days and even hours – of arrival.[65]

The *filles du roi* and the women who followed them as individual free migrants or indentured servants had to adjust to harsh living conditions: hard winters, primitive one-room log cabins even less likely to have the basic amenities of chairs, chests and cooking utensils than the most miserable peasant cottages in France and the possibility of death or captivity at the hands of the indigenous peoples. They also had to learn how to be farm wives, for most of them came from cities, as their husbands did. But their new way of life had its compensations. Women in New France were more likely to marry (over 90 percent did so) and to marry young; in New France the average age of marriage was 20, not Europe's 25. Because they married earlier they bore more children than their French counterparts and because food was abundant (France had a famine in 1710, but Quebec had a glut of cheap wheat that year) both they and their infants were more likely to survive. In France only half the children born reached adulthood; in New France two-thirds did so. And by the 1750s living conditions had greatly improved. The large families of New France lived in large, well-built stone houses that were far more likely to have curtains, clocks, mirrors and other domestic amenities than were peasant homes in Europe. Most Canadians owned their own horses and carriages, plus sleighs for the winter – unimaginable luxuries for European peasants.[66]

With their prosperity and rapid population growth, the settlements around Quebec and Montréal evolved a distinctive lifestyle, the beginnings of what is still a separate, unique French Canadian civilization. Then, as today, it was a minority civilization in Canada. The dominant civilization was not today's Anglo-American. Instead it was *métis*: the mixture of French and native American ways that characterized the fur trade. The major theme of later Canadian history is the gradual erosion of this *métis* culture as first French and, after 1763, English ways spread west.

WOMEN IN OVERSEAS COLONIZATION: THE ENGLISH IN NORTH AMERICA

The first successful English settlement in North America was the colony founded at Jamestown on the Chesapeake Bay in Virginia in 1607. The 105 colonists were all men, mostly soldiers of gentlemanly stock. They hoped to discover gold as the Spanish had. They discovered native American women instead. Interracial marriages were legal and there were some, notably that which turned the famous Pocahontas into Mrs John Rolfe. But marriage was unusual; more typical were temporary liaisons. Yet whether because European racism had grown in the years between 1492 and 1607 or because the English from their experiences in colonizing Ireland felt the need to differentiate themselves from and feel superior to the colonized other or simply because they were Protestant, the English did not have sex with native American women as enthusiastically as did the men of the other colonial powers. John Rolfe had religious scruples about marrying a wife culturally unlike – and in his mind, inferior to – himself. He wrote of:

> the heavie displeasure which almightie God conceived against the sonnes of Levie and Israel for marrying strange wives . . . which made me look about warily . . . into the grounds . . . which thus should provoke me to be in love with one whose education hath bin rude, her manners barbarous, her generation accursed, and so discrepant in all nurtriture from myselfe.[67]

Rolfe attributed the sexual attraction he felt for her to the Devil.

The settlers wanted white wives and in 1620 the Virginia Company, which oversaw the colony, sent its first shipment of 'maids young and uncorrupt to make wifes to the inhabitants and by that means to make the men there more setled'. The cost of their passage, 120 pounds of the colony's new crop, tobacco, was paid by their future husbands. By 1624 there were 230 English women in Virginia but over 1000 English men.[68] After that date, the special importation of women was unnecessary; the profits of tobacco culture lured voluntary migrants who paid their own passage or sailed as indentured servants. England sent a larger percentage of its population to its colonies than any other colonial power. By 1700 about 120,000 English settlers had migrated to Virginia and Maryland, its sister colony on the Chesapeake Bay founded in 1630; of this figure, 95,000 had come as indentured servants. Most were young (the average age of migrants was 20), single and male; there were still two to three men for every woman in the Chesapeake.[69]

This high sex ratio meant that women were eagerly sought in marriage and that they were more likely to marry and to marry young than if they had stayed in England. The mean age of marriage in Virginia for native-born white girls was 17, for female indentured servants, 22. Rates of pre-bridal pregnancy and illegitimacy were much higher than in England. In one Maryland county, almost 40 percent of the brides were pregnant when they married and in another one-fifth of all female indentured servants bore at least one illegitimate child.[70] Some of this illicit sex was exploitative, masters seducing indentured servants;

a pregnant servant had to serve two extra years to compensate her master for her lost work time. But much of it seems to have been initiated by the women, determined to make the best possible marriage bargain for themselves, even if it meant marrying across the colour line. In one Virginia county between 1664 and 1677, five white women married free black men.[71] Sometimes this hard-headed pursuit of their own interests continued even after marriage. In Virginia in 1634 Marie Drew spent her evenings talking and drinking with two men when her husband was away. She frankly admitted she was testing them as possible second husbands should her first die.[72]

The chances of that were very high. In one Maryland county, half the marriages were cut short by the death of one of the partners within seven years, in contrast to England, where marriages usually lasted 17 to 20 years. The death rate in the Chesapeake was high; the area was extremely unhealthy. The bay's stagnant waters bred all sorts of intestinal disorders and fevers, especially the deadly 'swamp fever', malaria. About half the new migrants died within two years of their arrival.[73]

The survivors had to adjust to the usual harsh living conditions; houses in the Chesapeake were small two-room cabins with minimal furniture. They also had to adjust to changes in their traditional work patterns. Obviously there was little need for traditional housewifery and because settlers lived not in villages but on isolated plantations along the bay and its tributary rivers, the usual female by-employments like market gardening, dairying and regrating to neighbours were useless too. Instead, women had to work in the fields, because tobacco was a very labour-intensive crop; the young plants needed constant hoeing, weeding and stripping. So fieldwork alongside men became the American norm. This was such an affront to traditional gender expectations that ballads lamented it (one sang of working with axe and hoe, plough and cart and warned women to stay in England: 'For if you do come here, You all will be weary, weary, weary, O'), recruiting pamphlets lied about it (one said 'women are not [as is reported] put into the ground to worke but occupie such domestique imployments and house wifery as in England') and the canniest servants had exemptions from it written into their contracts.[74]

In the last half of the seventeenth century, this problem was solved by the importation of black slaves from Africa and the West Indies. By 1700 there were 13,000 slaves in the Chesapeake, forming 13 percent of the population.[75] Slavery brought prosperity to white female migrants, turning many indentured servants into wives of plantation owners and ladies of leisure whose sole work was supervising slaves in household tasks. But this prosperity came at a price. Slavery was codified in Virginia by a series of laws of the 1680s and

1690s that also codified racism and re-established patriarchy. By these laws the privileges of being a patriarchal household head were reserved to white males. Slaves were forbidden to marry and free blacks, while allowed legal marriages, were denied other marks of manhood like property ownership, possession of guns and service in the militia. They were also denied sexual access to white women. Interracial marriage was outlawed and illicit sex between white women and black men harshly punished. Bastard bearing and illegitimacy were also harshly treated, thus disciplining women and ending their earlier freedom of choice.[76] Patriarchy had been profoundly altered in the Portuguese and Spanish colonies, as white women gained freedom and power and the lower classes shaped new, multiracial societies offering a variety of lifestyles largely beyond the control of their superiors. For a while it had looked as though the same thing would happen in the Chesapeake, but by 1700 traditional patriarchy was secure.

Patriarchy was never in doubt in the other major English settlement in North America, the Massachusetts Bay Colony. But luckily for women, this was patriarchy of the radical Protestant variety, in which women were the spiritual equals of men and wives the 'near equals' of husbands, for Massachusetts Bay was settled in the 1620s by Puritan refugees from religious persecution.

Because they left home for religious rather than economic reasons, the Puritans migrated not as single young people but as patriarchal family groups. In one group of Massachusetts migrants, 73 percent came to the New World in nuclear families; in another the figure was 94 percent. These are not only the highest percentages of family migration for any of the European colonies; they are also the highest percentages for all subsequent migration to America.[77]

Because the Puritans came to America in family groups, Massachusetts had from the very beginning of its settlement a high ratio of white women to white men – again the highest of any of the European colonies in the New World. In seventeenth-century Massachusetts there were 150 white men for every 100 white women, while New Spain had 100 white men for every 10 white women and in Brazil the ratio was 100 to one.[78] The high numbers of white women guaranteed that English practices and folkways were successfully transplanted to the New World. What is striking about the Massachusetts Bay Colony is how strongly it duplicated the mother country. Massachusetts settlers planned their villages, built their houses and ran their households just as they had done at home. Luckily the terrain of New England was very similar to that of East Anglia, where most of the Puritans originated. Therefore they could practise the mixed arable and dairy farming with which they were familiar. This meant that men and women could perform their traditional work roles. The only change in work roles due to New World conditions was that in New England, which lacked manufactured goods, women's manufacturing by-employments and their local networks for trading goods and services were even more important to their families' prosperity than they had been in Europe.[79] This importance was reflected in women's ability to own and manage property. In New England, women could own property and make valid contracts. Daughters inherited equally with sons, although male heirs usually received land while daughters got household goods. And wives often retained control of their own property. Although these provisions seem to follow our typical pattern of New World conditions enhancing women's legal rights, they actually were similar to the common law provisions in those areas of England where the colonists had originated.[80]

Family life too duplicated English patterns. As in England, the Puritans married late and had very low levels of illegitimacy, in marked contrast to other European colonies in the New World including the Chesapeake. In Massachusetts the only modifications to traditional family patterns were, first, that because land was abundant, almost everyone could marry and, second, because food was plentiful and the climate was healthy, most of the children of such marriages survived. Therefore families were usually much larger than comparative ones in England. The average family in one Massachusetts town had nine children – an extraordinarily high figure.[81]

Otherwise family life in New England followed the standard radical Protestant pattern the Puritans brought with them from the Old World. The basis of marriage was mutual love between spouses. Therefore children were allowed to choose their marriage partners, although they were expected to get their parents' consent to the match. Massachusetts law punished both 'self-marriers' (children who disregarded their parents' wishes when marrying) and parents who withheld consent to their childrens' union for no good reason.[82]

When love died, the marriage could be dissolved. In Massachusetts, divorces were granted for desertion and adultery. A wife could also get a divorce if her husband 'failed to provide' or if he physically abused her. On the issue of spousal abuse, Massachusetts Puritans favoured women even more than English ones did. English law allowed husbands to use physical correction on wayward wives, but in Massachusetts both partners were forbidden to strike their spouse.[83]

Letters, diaries, autobiographies and court records testify that in most New England families husbands treated their 'near equal' wives with the love and respect that such provisions suggest. Thus in the Massachusetts Bay Colony women enjoyed the same enhanced property rights, ability to choose their spouses and love and respect within marriage that the women of the other European settlements enjoyed, but in New England this was not due to the special conditions of the New World; instead, the Puritans brought these laws and customs with them from England. This exception that proves the rule points up the paradox of European women's experience of colonization: while their major role as colonizers was to replicate European culture, often the special conditions of the colonies made exact duplication impossible. Instead, women's lives changed in ways that gave them enhanced freedom and status.

CONCLUSION

◆

The women of the colonies, with their freer choice of husbands, early marriage, large families and role as leisured housewives, were precursors of the women back in Europe: in the eighteenth century these changes would come to many middle- and upper-class European women. And these were not the only factors which made their lives different from those of the earlier generations of European women we have studied. The eighteenth century was the beginning of a new period of European women's history, one that would stretch throughout the nineteenth century and into the beginning of the twentieth. The main theme of this period of women's history is the struggle between two new – and opposite – paradigms of the nature of women and their proper role in society.

One of these was the vision of woman as wife, mother, and 'angel of the house'. The scientific revolution of the seventeenth century had destroyed the one-sex model of human beings, in which women were simply inferior men, and created a new two-sex model, which emphasized the supposed physical, mental and emotional differences between men and women. It was thought that these differences arose because women were destined by nature for motherhood. Therefore they were still confined to the domestic sphere and the social roles of homemaker, wife and, above all, mother. But because they had been stripped of their traditional lewdness (indeed, the two-sex model predicated that sexual desire was largely confined to males) and their confinement in the home saved them from corruption in the impure worlds of business and politics, they became 'angels in the house', preservers of society's cultural and moral values, the pure moral guides of not only their children but also their husbands and society at large.

This new vision of women, both restricting and empowering, contended with another one: that men and women were more or less the same, physically, mentally and emotionally, and that women were equal to men, entitled to the same rights and, with proper education, able to perform the same social roles. Both these new versions of women's nature, especially the latter, inspired ultimately successful battles in the eighteenth, nineteenth and twentieth centuries for better education for women, expanded employment opportunities in business and the professions and legal and political rights equal to those of men.

These new notions of women's nature and their proper roles in society were possible only because the traditional patriarchal paradigm, which saw women as sinful Eve, inevitably subordinate to man, had been destroyed. That was the major achievement of the early modern period of European women's history covered in this book. As we have seen, the destruction of the patriarchal paradigm was the work of many forces. Broad historical trends such as the Reformation and the scientific revolution, the spread of the absolutist state, exploration and colonization and the growth and trans-formation of capitalism were important factors. So too was the *querelle des femmes* and the ideas of its male and especially female contributors. But perhaps the most important force behind the destruction of the patriarchal paradigm was the millions of ordinary women who, in going about their daily lives, dis-played intelligence, virtue, steadfastness and moral strength that contradicted the traditional stereotypes about female nature and showed their menfolk that women were worthy of love and respect. All later generations of women, not just in Europe but throughout the world where, thanks to western cultural imperialism, European ideas about democracy and human rights have spread, owe them a debt of gratitude.

NOTES

———— ◆ ————

Introduction

1 Alice Clark, *The Working Life of Women in the Seventeenth Century* (London, 1919). For a debate on the continuing relevance of Clark's interpretation, see the articles by Bridget Hill and Judith Bennett in *Women's History Review* 2 (1993), pp. 5–22 and 173–84.

2 Joan Kelly, 'Did Women Have a Renaissance?' in Joan Kelly, *Women, History, and Theory* (Chicago, 1984), pp. 19–50.

Part I: The Patriarchal Paradigm

1 Ruth Kelso, *Doctrine for the Lady of the Renaissance* (Urbana, 1978), p. 12.

Chapter 1: Inferiors or Equals? Ideas about the Nature of Women

1 Elaine Pagels, *The Gnostic Gospels* (New York, 1979).

2 Printed in Julia O'Faolain and Lauro Martines, eds, *Not in God's Image* (New York, 1973), p. 132.

3 Printed in *ibid.*, p. 138.

4 Thomas Laqueur, *Making Sex: Body and Gender from the Greeks to Freud* (Cambridge, MA, 1990).

5 Printed in Lisa Di Caprio and Merry E. Wiesner, eds, *Lives and Voices: Sources in European Women's History* (Boston, 2001), pp. 62–63.

6 Margaret L. King and Albert Rabil, Jr, 'The Other Voice in Early Modern Europe', in Henricus Cornelius Agrippa, *Declamation on the Nobility and Preeminence of the Female Sex* (Chicago, 1996), p. x.

7 Quoted in *ibid.*

8 Yan Thomas, 'The Division of the Sexes in Roman Law', in P. Pantel, ed., *A History of Women in the West*, Vol. 1 (Cambridge, MA, 1992), pp. 83–137.

9 My treatment of Pisan is based on Earl Jeffrey Richards, Introduction to Christine de Pizan, *The Book of the City of Ladies* (New York, 1982), pp. xix–xlv.

10 Pizan, *Book of the City of Ladies*, pp. 3–4.

11 *Ibid.*, p. 23.

12 *Ibid.*

13 *Ibid.*, p. 24.

14 *Ibid.*, pp. 166–68; 32–43; 52–57.

15 *Ibid.*, p. 63.

16 *Ibid.*, pp. 17–20.

17 *Ibid.*, pp. 31; 26–27.

18 Kelso, *Doctrine for the Lady of the Renaissance*, pp. 17–19.

19 Leon Battista Alberti, *The Family in Renaissance Florence*, trans. Renée Neu Watkins (Prospect Park, IL, 2004); Francesco Barbaro, *On Wifely Duties*, in Benjamin Kohl and R. G. Witt, eds, *The Earthly Republic* (Philadelphia, 1978), pp. 179–228.

20 Juan Luis Vives, *The Education of a Christian Woman: A Sixteenth-Century Manual*, ed. and trans. Charles Fantazzi (Chicago, 2000).

21 Kelso, *Doctrine for the Lady of the Renaissance*, pp. 7–8; Albert Rabil, Jr, Introduction to Agrippa, *Declamation on the Nobility and Preeminence of the Female Sex*, pp. 18–27.

22 *Ibid.*, pp. 3–13.

23 Agrippa, *Declamation on the Female Sex*, pp. 44–50.

24 *Ibid.*, pp. 54–59.

25 *Ibid.*, pp. 79–94; 68–72; 62–65.

26 *Ibid.*, p. 96.

27 *Ibid.*, pp. 94–95.

28 *Ibid.*, pp. 94; 79.

29 Letizia Panizza, Introduction to Lucrezia Marinella, *The Nobility and Excellence of Women and The Defects and Vices of Men* (Chicago, 1999), pp. 15–19.

30 Manfred P. Fleischer, '"Are Women Human?" The Debate of 1595 between Valens Acidalius & Simon Gediccus', *Sixteenth Century Journal* XII, 2 (Summer, 1981), pp. 107–20.

31 Baldesar Castiglione, *The Book of the Courtier*, trans. Charles S. Singleton (New York, 1959), p. 214.

32 Printed in O'Faolain and Martines, *Not in God's Image*, pp. 196–97.

33 Londa Schiebinger, *The Mind Has No Sex? Women in the Origins of Modern Science* (Harvard, 1989), pp. 160–65; Mary D. Garrard, *Artemisia Gentileschi: The Image of the Female Hero in Italian Baroque Art* (Princeton, 1989), pp. 154–71.

34 Quoted in Margaret L. King, *Women of the Renaissance* (Chicago, 1991), p. 191.

35 Garrard, *Artemisia Gentileschi*, pp. 171–79; 211–39.

36 *Ibid.*, *passim*.

37 Joan De Jean, *Tender Geographies: Women and the Origins of the Novel in France* (New York, 1991), pp. 18–42.

38 Garrard, *Artemisia Gentileschi*, p. 170.

39 Constance Jordan, *Renaissance Feminism: Literary Texts and Political Models* (Ithaca, NY, 1990), pp. 129–32; 242–46.

40 Quoted in *ibid.*, p. 273.

41 Quoted in *ibid.*, p. 296.

42 *Ibid.*, pp. 168–69.

43 Quoted in *ibid.*, pp. 169; 170.

44 Richard Hillman, Introduction to Marie le Jars de Gournay, *Apology for the Woman Writing and Other Works* (Chicago, 2002), pp. 3–20.

45 de Gournay, *Apology for the Woman Writing*, pp. 76; 87.

46 *Ibid.*, pp. 76; 75.

47 *Ibid.*, pp. 91; 94.

48 François Poullain de La Barre, *The Woman as Good as the Man, Or, The Equality of Both Sexes*, ed. Gerald M. MacLean (Detroit, 1988), p. 103. This is a reprint of the first English translation of the work, published in 1677.

49 *Ibid.*, pp. 123; 121.

50 *Ibid.*, p. 122.

51 *Ibid.*, pp. 123–24.

52 Schiebinger, *The Mind Has No Sex?*, pp. 189–244; Laqueur, *Making Sex*, pp. 149–244.

Chapter 2: Girls and Maidens

1 Simone de Beauvoir, *The Second Sex*, trans. H. M. Parshley (New York, 1971), p. 267.

2 Michèle Longino Farrell, *Performing Motherhood: the Sévigné Correspondence* (Hanover, NH, 1991), pp. 238–40. The quote is from p. 238.

3 Joan Sherwood, *Poverty in Eighteenth-Century Spain: The Women and Children of the Inclusa* (Toronto, 1988), pp. 138; 139.

4 Linda A. Pollock, 'Parent–Child Relations', in David I. Kertzer and Marzio Barbagli, eds, *Family Life in Early Modern Times, 1500–1789* (New Haven, 2001), pp. 197; 202–203.

5 Quoted in *ibid.*, p. 202.

6 Quoted in Farrell, *Performing Motherhood*, pp. 97; 96; 105.

7 Quoted in Cornelia Niekus Moore, *The Maiden's Mirror: Reading Material for German Girls in the Sixteenth and Seventeenth Centuries* (Wiesbaden, 1987), p. 20.

8 Quoted in Farrell, *Performing Motherhood*, p. 239.

9 Ian C. Dengler, 'Turkish Women in the Ottoman Empire: The Classical Age' in Lois Beck and Nikki Keddie, eds, *Women in the Muslim World* (Cambridge, MA, 1978), pp. 230; 231.

10 Pizan, *City of Ladies*, pp. 62–64.

11 Desiderius Erasmus, *Prologue to the New Testament*.

12 R. A. Houston, *Literacy in Early Modern Europe: Culture and Education 1500–1800* (London, 2002), p. 23.

13 Quoted in Dorothy Gardiner, *English Girlhood at School* (London, 1929), p. 196.

14 Houston, *Literacy in Early Modern Europe*, p. 34.

15 *Ibid.*, p. 158.

16 *Ibid.*, pp. 147; 142.

17 *Ibid.*, p. 144; Lindsay Hughes, *Sophia: Regent of Russia 1657–1704* (New Haven, 1990), pp. 32–33.

18 Quoted in Gardiner, *English Girlhood at School*, p. 192.

19 Houston, *Literacy in Early Modern Europe*, pp. 61–72.

20 Marta V. Vicente, 'Images and Realities of Work: Women and Guilds in Early Modern Barcelona', in Magdalena S. Sanchez and Alain Saint Saëns, eds, *Spanish Women in the Golden Age* (Westport, CT, 1996), p. 131.

21 Gardiner, *English Girlhood at School*, p. 295.

22 Quoted in *ibid.*, p. 297.

23 Quoted in *ibid.*, p. 299.

24 *Ibid.*, p. 298.

25 Moore, *The Maiden's Mirror*, pp. 49–56.

26 Quoted in *ibid.*, p. 21.

27 Garrard, *Artemisia Gentileschi*, pp. 403–87.

28 Quoted in Moore, *The Maiden's Mirror*, p. 23.

29 Carol Gilligan, *In A Different Voice: Psychological Theory and Women's Development* (Cambridge, MA, 1982).

30 *The Life of Saint Theresa of Avila By Herself*, trans. J. M. Cohen (London, 1957), p. 24.

31 Lucy Hutchinson, *Memoirs of the Life of Colonel Hutchinson*, ed. James Sutherland (London, 1973).

32 Quoted in Moore, *The Maiden's Mirror*, pp. 23–24.

33 Quoted in Dengler, 'Turkish Women in the Ottoman Empire', p. 241, n. 13.

34 Moore, *The Maiden's Mirror*, pp. 51; 52.

35 Quoted in *ibid.*, p. 30.

36 Gardiner, *English Girlhood at School*, pp. 172–78. The quote is from p. 176.

37 Nancy L. Roelker, *Queen of Navarre: Jeanne d'Albret, 1528–1572* (Cambridge, MA, 1968); David P. Daniel, 'Piety, Politics, and Perversion: Noblewomen in Reformation Hungary', in Sherrin Marshall, ed., *Women in Reformation and Counter-Reformation Europe* (Bloomington, IN, 1989), pp. 68–88.

38 Moore, *The Maiden's Mirror*, pp. 44; 45.

39 Quoted in Gardiner, *English Girlhood at School*, pp. 261–62.

40 *Ibid.*, pp. 224–25.

41 Carolyn C. Lougee, *Le paradis des Femmes: Women, Salons and Social Stratification in Seventeenth-Century France* (Princeton, 1976), pp. 188–208.

42 Marie-Jeanne Phlipon Roland, *The Memoirs of Madame Roland*, trans. Evelyn Shuckburgh (New York, 1990).

Chapter 3: Wives

1 J. H. Haijnal, 'The European Marriage Pattern in Perspective', in D. V. Glass and D. E. C. Eversley, eds, *Population in History* (Chicago, 1965), pp. 101–43.

2 John L. Esposito, *Women in Muslim Family Law* (Syracuse, 1982), pp. 16–28; Judith Tucker, *In the House of the Law: Gender & Islamic Law in Ottoman Syria & Palestine* (Berkeley, 2000), pp. 37–77. The quotes are from p. 44.

3 Daniel Tollet, 'The Private Life of Polish Jews in the Vasa Period', in Antony Polonsky *et al.*, eds, *The Jews in Old Poland 1000–1795* (London, 1993), p. 52.

4 *The Memoirs of Gluckel of Hameln*, trans. Marvin Lowenthal (New York, 1977), pp. viii–ix.

5 Eve Levin, *Sex and Society in the World of the Orthodox Slavs, 900–1700* (Ithaca, 1989), pp. 80–88, 95–101.

6 Robert F. Byrnes, ed., *Communal Families in the Balkans: The Zadruga* (Notre Dame, IN, 1976).

7 Levin, *Sex and Society*, pp. 95–101. The quote is from p. 99.

8 Marie A. Thomas, 'Muscovite Convents in the Seventeenth Century', *Russian History* 10.2 (1983), pp. 230–42.

9 Susan E. Pritchett-Post, *Women in Modern Albania* (London, 1998), p. 54.

10 Gregory Hanlon, *Early Modern Italy, 1550–1800* (New York, 2000), p. 169.

11 *Ibid.*

12 Stanley Chojnacki, 'Daughters and Oligarchs: Gender and the Early Renaissance State', in Judith C. Brown and Robert C. Davis, eds, *Gender and Society in Renaissance Italy* (Harlow, 1998), pp. 71; 70.

13 Hanlon, *Early Modern Italy*, pp. 172–73.

14 My description of marriage rites is based on Sharon T. Stroccia, 'Gender and the Rites of Honour in Italian Renaissance Cities', in Brown and Davis, *Gender and Society*, pp. 43–47.

15 Renata Ago, 'Young Nobles in the Age of Absolutism: Paternal Authority and Freedom of Choice in Seventeenth-Century Italy' in Giovanni Lévi and Jean-Claude Schmitt, eds, *A History of Young People in the West*, Vol. 1 (Cambridge, MA, 1997), pp. 312–13.

16 Amy Louise Erickson, *Women and Property in Early Modern England* (London, 1993), p. 120.

17 Miriam Slater, *Family Life in the Seventeenth Century: The Verneys of Claydon House* (London, 1984), p. 63.

18 Christine Peters, *Women in Early Modern Britain 1450–1640* (Houndmills, 2004), p. 36.

19 Quoted in Christine Peters, 'Single Women in Early Modern England', *Continuity and Change* 12, 3 (1997), p. 340.

20 *The Autobiography of Mrs. Alice Thornton* (Edinburgh, 1875), p. 75.

21 *Ibid.*, pp. 77; 78–79.

22 Slater, *Family Life in the Seventeenth Century*, pp. 63–73.

23 Anthony Fletcher, *Gender, Sex, and Subordination in England 1500–1800* (New Haven, 1995), p. 155.

24 Sara Heller Mendelson, 'Stuart Women's Diaries and Occasional Memoirs', in Mary Prior, ed., *Women in English Society, 1500–1800* (London, 1985), pp. 193–94.

25 Erickson, *Women and Property in Early Modern England*, pp. 119–22.

26 David Cressy, *Birth, Marriage, and Death: Ritual and the Life Cycle in Tudor and Stuart England* (Oxford, 1997), pp. 223–97.

27 Quoted in John R. Gillis, *For Better, For Worse: British Marriages, 1600 to the Present* (Oxford, 1985), p. 22.

28 Quoted in *ibid.*, p. 36.

29 Quoted in Martine Segalen, *Love and Power in the Peasant Family* (Chicago, 1983), p. 18 and Gillis, *For Better, For Worse*, p. 60.

30 Gillis, *For Better, For Worse*, pp. 11–54; Cressy, *Birth, Marriage, and Death*, pp. 233–66.

31 Jeffrey R. Watt, *The Making of Modern Marriage: Matrimonial Control and the Rise of Sentiment in Neuchâtel, 1550–1800* (Ithaca, 1992), pp. 67–68.

32 Peters, *Women in Early Modern Britain*, pp. 9–10.

33 The following is based on Segalen, *Love and Power*, pp. 25–37; Gillis, *For Better, For Worse*, pp. 55–83; and Natalia Pushkareva, *Women in Russian History from the Tenth to the Twentieth Century*, trans. Eve Levin (New York, 1997), pp. 31–33.

34 Laura Gowing, 'Language, Power and the Law: Women's Slander Litigation in Early Modern London', in Jennifer Kermode and Garthine Walker, eds, *Women, Crime and the Courts in Early Modern England* (Chapel Hill, 1994), pp. 26–47.

35 Quoted in Segalen, *Love and Power*, p. 128.

36 Quoted in *ibid.*, pp. 156–57.

37 Printed in Joan Larsen Klein, ed., *Daughters, Wives, and Widows: Writings by Men about Women and Marriage in England, 1500–1640* (Urbana, IL, 1992), p. 16.

38 Pushkareva, *Women in Russian History*, p. 32.

39 Quoted in Segalen, *Love and Power*, p. 158.

40 Thomas Max Safley, *Let No Man Put Asunder* (Kirksville, MO, 1984), p. 175.

41 Quoted in Segalen, *Love and Power*, p. 158.

42 Lawrence Stone, *The Family, Sex, and Marriage in England 1500–1800* (New York, 1977), p. 375.

43 Quoted in Steven Ozment, *When Fathers Ruled: Family Life in Reformation Europe* (Cambridge, MA, 1983), p. 52.

44 Watt, *The Making of Modern Marriage*, pp. 150–51.

45 Esposito, *Women in Muslim Family Law*, p. 24.

46 Erickson, *Women and Property*, pp. 24–25.

47 Martha C. Howell, *The Marriage Exchange: Property, Social Place, and Gender in Cities of the Low Countries, 1300–1550* (Chicago, 1998), p. 6.

48 Julie Hardwick, *The Practice of Patriarchy: Gender and the Politics of Household Authority in Early Modern France* (University Park, PA, 1998), p. 54.

49 Jeffrey R. Watt, 'The Impact of the Reformation and Counter-Reformation' in Kertzer and Barbagli, *Family Life in Early Modern Times*, pp. 130–37.

50 Lucy A. Sponsler, 'The Status of Married Women Under the Legal System of Spain', *Journal of Legal History* 3 (1982), p. 142.

51 Heide Wunder, *He is the Sun, She is the Moon: Women in Early Modern Germany*, trans. Thomas Dunlap (Cambridge, MA, 1998), pp. 191–92.

52 Quoted in Segalen, *Love and Power*, p. 153.

53 Martin Ingram, 'Scolding Women Cucked or Washed', in Kermode and Walker, *Women, Crime and the Courts in Early Modern England*, pp. 48–80.

54 Marvin Lunenfeld, 'Isabella I of Castile and the Company of Women in Power', *Historical Reflections* 4 (1977), pp. 225–26.

55 Jeanne-Marie Bouvières de La Motte Guyon, *La Vie de Mme, J. M. B. de la Mothe-Guion, écrite par elle-même* (Cologne, 1720).

56 Fletcher, *Gender, Sex, and Subordination*, p. 164.

57 Quoted in Linda Pollock, *With Faith and Physic: The Life of a Tudor Gentlewoman, Lady Grace Mildmay 1552–1620* (London, 1993), pp. 41–42.

58 Quoted in Fletcher, *Gender, Sex, and Subordination*, pp. 161; 162.

59 Quoted in Steven Ozment, *Magdalena and Balthasar* (New York, 1986), p. 50.

60 Quoted in Ozment, *When Fathers Ruled*, pp. 69–70.

61 Quoted in Fletcher, *Gender, Sex, and Subordination*, p. 156.

62 Quoted in Ozment, *When Fathers Ruled*, p. 63.

63 Quoted in Margaret Alic, *Hypatia's Heritage: A History of Women in Science from Antiquity through the Nineteenth Century* (Boston, 1986), pp. 86; 85; 87; 199, n. 11.

64 Mendelson, 'Stuart Women's Diaries', pp. 193–94.

Chapter 4: Mothers

1 Quoted in Pushkareva, *Women in Russian History*, p. 38.

2 Quoted in Patricia Crawford, 'The Construction and Experience of Maternity in Seventeenth-Century England', in Valerie Fildes, ed., *Women as Mothers in Pre-Industrial England* (London, 1990), p. 14.

3 Pierre Darmon, *Trial by Impotence* (London, 1985).

4 Jacques Gélis, *History of Childbirth*, trans. Rosemary Morris (Boston, 1991), pp. 10–41.

5 *Ibid.*, pp. 61–63.

6 Quoted in Linda A. Pollock, 'Embarking on a Rough Passage: the Experience of Pregnancy in Early-Modern Society' in *Women as Mothers in Pre-Industrial England*, p. 39; 63 n. 52; Fletcher, *Gender, Sex and Subordination*, p. 185.

7 Roger Schofield, 'Did the Mothers Really Die?', in Lloyd Bonfield *et al.*, eds, *The World We Have Gained* (Oxford, 1986), pp. 250; 252; 231.

8 Audrey Eccles, *Obstetrics and Gynaecology in Tudor and Stuart England* (Kent, OH, 1982).

9 Pushkareva, *Women in Russian History*, p. 39.

10 Ulinka Rublack, 'Pregnancy, Childbirth and the Female Body in Early Modern Germany', *Past and Present* 150 (1996), p. 95.

11 *Ibid.*, pp. 96; 105.

12 Pushkareva, *Women in Russian History*, p. 39.

13 J. Gélis *et al.*, *Entrer dans la vie: Naissances et enfances dans la France traditionnelle* (Paris, 1978), p. 87.

14 The memoirs of one of them, Justine Siegemund, have been published recently: *The Court Midwife*, ed. and trans. Lynne Tatlock (Chicago, 2005).

15 Rublack, 'Pregnancy, Childbirth and the Female Body', pp. 88; 89.

16 Adrian Wilson, *The Making of Man-Midwifery: Childbirth in England, 1660–1770* (Cambridge, MA, 1995).

17 Adrian Wilson, 'The Ceremony of Childbirth and its Interpretation', in *Women as Mothers in Pre-Industrial England*, pp. 68–108.

18 Pollock, 'Embarking on a Rough Passage', pp. 53; 52; Rublack, 'Pregnancy, Childbirth, and the Female Body', pp. 99–100.

19 *Ibid.*, p. 91.

20 Wilson, 'The Ceremony of Childbirth'.

21 Eve Levin, 'Childbirth in Pre-Petrine Russia: Canon Law & Popular Traditions' in Barbara Evans Clements *et al.*, *Russia's Women: Accommodation, Resistance, Transformation* (Berkeley, 1991), pp. 48–49.

22 Cressy, *Birth, Marriage, and Death*, pp. 197–229.

23 Françoise Loux, *Le jeune enfant et son corps dans la médecine traditionnelle* (Paris, 1978), pp. 253–55.

24 Wunder, *He is the Sun, She is the Moon*, p. 119.

25 Maria Bogucka, 'Polish Customs in the 16th–18th Centuries', *Acta Poloniae Historica* 70 (1994), p. 32.

26 Michael W. Flinn, *The European Demographic System, 1500–1820* (Baltimore, 1981), p. 82.

27 R. W. Malcolmson, 'Infanticide in the Eighteenth Century', in J. S. Cockburn, ed., *Crime in England, 1550–1800* (London, 1977), p. 194; Keith Wrightson, 'Infanticide in European History', *Criminal Justice History* 3 (1982), p. 7.

28 Quoted in *ibid.*

29 Peters, *Women in Early Modern Britain*, pp. 9–10.

30 Wunder, *He is the Sun, She is the Moon*, p. 121.

31 Wrightson, 'Infanticide in European History', p. 8.

32 *Ibid.*, pp. 1; 10–11.

33 Olwen H. Hufton, *The Poor of Eighteenth-Century France, 1750–1789* (Oxford, 1974), p. 349.

34 Sherwood, *Poverty in Eighteenth-Century Spain*, p. 113.

35 *Ibid.*; Wrightson, 'Infanticide in European History', p. 13.

36 Rublack, 'Pregnancy, Childbirth, and the Female Body', p. 91.

37 Quoted in Valerie Fildes, 'Maternal Feelings Re-Assessed: Child Abandonment and Neglect in London and Westminster, 1550–1800', in *Women as Mothers in Pre-Industrial England*, p. 153.

38 Quoted in Linda A. Pollock, *Forgotten Children: Parent–Child Relations from 1500 to 1900* (Cambridge, 1983), p. 102.

39 Pier Paolo Viazzo, 'Mortality, Fertility, and Family', in *Family Life in Early Modern Times*, pp. 169–73.

40 Quoted in Eccles, *Obstetrics and Gynaecology in Tudor & Stuart England*, p. 70.

41 *Ibid.*, pp. 67–68.

42 Pollock, 'Embarking on a Rough Passage', p. 55.

43 Eccles, *Obstetrics and Gynaecology*, p. 70.

44 Mireille Laget, *Naissances: L'accouchement avant l'âge de la clinique* (Paris, 1982), p. 286.

45 Viazzo, 'Mortality, Fertility, and Family', pp. 165–67.

46 Wrightson, 'Infanticide in European History', p. 12.

47 Quoted in Steven Ozment, *Flesh and Spirit: Private Life in Early Modern Germany* (New York, 1999), pp. 97–98.

48 Pollock, *Forgotten Children*, pp. 212–30.

49 Quoted in Ozment, *Flesh and Spirit*, p. 105; Pollock, *Forgotten Children*, p. 226.

50 Quoted in Pollock, *Forgotten Children*, pp. 147; 146.

51 Hans Roodenberg, 'The Autobiography of Isabella de Moerloose: Sex, Childrearing, and Popular Belief in Seventeenth-Century Holland', *Journal of Social History* 18 (1985), pp. 517–40. Quotes pp. 524; 525.

52 Quoted in Pollock, *Forgotten Children*, p. 148.

53 Quoted in William H. Lazareth, *Luther on the Christian Home* (Philadelphia, 1960), p. 219.

54 Pushkareva, *Women in Russian History*, p. 45.

55 Hardwick, *The Practice of Patriarchy*, pp. 120–23.

56 Guilia Calvi, 'Widows, the State, and the Guardianship of Children in Early Modern Tuscany', in Sandra Cavallo and Lyndan Warner, eds, *Widowhood in Medieval and Early Modern Europe* (Harlow, 1999), pp. 209–19.

57 Alan Macfarlane, *The Family Life of Ralph Josselin* (New York, 1970), p. 126.

58 Quoted in Margaret Hunt, 'Wife Beating, Domesticity, and Women's Independence in Eighteenth-Century London', *Gender and History* 4, 1 (Spring, 1992), p. 22.

59 Farrell, *Performing Motherhood*.

60 Elspeth Graham *et al.*, *Her Own Life: Autobiographical Writings by Seventeenth-Century Englishwomen* (London, 1989), pp. 38–44.

61 Lyndal Roper, 'Witchcraft and Fantasy in Early Modern Germany', in Lyndal Roper, *Oedipus and the Devil* (London, 1994), pp. 210–11.

62 Hardwick, *The Practice of Patriarchy*, pp. 139–40.

63 Caroline Castiglione, 'Accounting for Affection: Battles Between Aristocratic Mothers and Sons in Eighteenth-Century Rome', *Journal of Family History* (Oct. 2000), p. 410.

64 Quoted in Sherrin Marshall, *The Dutch Gentry, 1500–1650: Family, Faith, and Fortune* (Westport, Conn., 1987), p. 18.

65 Barbara J. Harris, 'Property, Power, and Personal Relations: Elite Mothers and Sons in Yorkist and Early Tudor England', *Signs* 15, 3 (1990), pp. 614; 620.

66 Natalie Zemon Davis, *Women on the Margins* (Cambridge, MA, 1995), pp. 73; 72.

Chapter 5: Widows and Elderly Women

1 David Levine, 'The Population of Europe: Early Modern Demographic Patterns', *Encyclopedia of European Social History: From 1350 to 2000*, Vol. 2 (New York, 2001), p. 152.

2 Sherri Klassen, 'The Life Cycle', *Encyclopedia of European Social History*, Vol. 2, pp. 193–203.

3 Davis, *Women on the Margins*, pp. 65–66.

4 Epstein, *The Jewish Marriage Contract*, pp. 182; 234.

5 Levin, *Sex and Society in the World of the Orthodox Slavs*, pp. 105–12.

6 A. Burguière, 'Réticences theoriques et intrigration practique du remarriage dans la France de l'Ancien-Régime-17-18e siècles', in Jacques Dupâquier *et al.*, eds, *Marriage and Remarriage in the Populations of the Past* (London, 1981), pp. 41–42.

7 C. A. Corsini, 'Why is Remarriage a Male Affair: Some Evidence from Tuscan Villages During the 18th Century', in Dupâquier, *Marriage and Remarriage in the Populations of the Past*, p. 388.

8 Marshall, *Dutch Gentry*, p. 65.

9 *Ibid.*, p. 67.

10 Antoinette Fauve-Chamoux, 'Marriage, Widowhood, and Divorce', in Kertzer and Barbagli, *Family Life in Early Modern Times*, p. 242.

11 D. Gaunt and O. Löfgren, 'Remarriage in the Nordic Countries: the Cultural and Socio-Economic Background', in Dupâquier, *Marriage and Remarriage in the Populations of the Past*, p. 57.

12 Quoted in Barbara J. Todd, 'The Virtuous Widow in Protestant England', in Cavallo and Warner, *Widowhood in Medieval and Early Modern Europe*, p. 69.

13 *Ibid.*, p. 70.

14 Magdalena S. Sanchez, *The Empress, the Queen, and the Nun: Women and Power at the Court of Philip III of Spain* (Baltimore, 1998), p. 145 and Fig. 1 caption.

15 Richard C. Trexler, 'A Widow's Asylum of the Renaissance: the Orbatello of Florence', in Trexler, *Dependence in Context in Renaissance Florence* (Binghamton, NY, 1994), pp. 415–48.

16 Prior, *Women in English Society*, p. 7.

17 Gaunt and Löfgren, 'Remarriage in the Nordic Countries', p. 57.

18 Isabelle Chabot, 'Lineage Strategies, and the Control of Widows in Renaissance Florence', in Cavallo and Warner, *Widowhood in Medieval and Early Modern Europe*, p. 130.

19 Howell, *The Marriage Exchange*, p. 6.

20 David E. Vassberg, 'The Status of Widows in Sixteenth-Century Rural Castile', in John Henderson and Richard Wall, eds, *Poor Women and Children in the European Past* (London, 1994), p. 181.

21 Erickson, *Women and Property*, p. 178.

22 Christiane Klapisch-Zuber, 'The "Cruel Mother": Maternity, Widowhood, and Dowry in Florence in the fourteenth and fifteenth centuries', in Christiane Klapisch-Zuber, *Women, Family and Ritual in Renaissance Italy* (Chicago, 1985), pp. 117–31.

23 Marshall, *Dutch Gentry*, p. 62; Barbara Diefendorf, 'Widowhood and Remarriage in Sixteenth-Century Paris', *Journal of Family History* (Winter, 1982), p. 379.

24 Quoted in Barbara J. Todd, 'The Remarrying Widow: A Stereotype Reconsidered', in Prior, *Women in English Society*, p. 77.

25 Quoted in Lyndan Warner, 'Widows, Widowers and the Problem of "Second Marriages" in Sixteenth-Century France', in Cavallo and Warner, *Widowhood in Medieval and Early Modern Europe*, p. 94.

26 Quoted in Todd, 'The Remarrying Widow', p. 82.

27 Chabot, 'Lineage Strategies in Renaissance Florence', pp. 134–35.

28 Vera St Erlich, 'The Last Big Zadrugas: Albanian Extended Families in the Kosovo Region' in Byrnes, *Communal Families in the Balkans*, p. 247.

29 Erickson, *Women and Property*, p. 200.

30 Vassberg, 'The Status of Widows in Rural Castile', p. 186.

31 James E. Smith, 'Widowhood and Ageing in Traditional English Society', *Ageing and Society* 4 (1984), pp. 445–46.

32 Pamela Sharpe, 'Survival Strategies and Stories: Poor Widows and Widowers in Early Industrial England', in Cavallo and Warner, *Widowhood in Medieval and Early Modern Europe*, p. 226.

33 Trexler, 'A Widows' Asylum', p. 429.

34 S. Akerman, 'The Importance of Remarriage in the Seventeenth and Eighteenth Centuries', in Dupâquier, *Marriage and Remarriage in Populations of the Past*, p. 169.

35 Todd, 'The Remarrying Widow', pp. 69–71.

36 Quoted in Olwen Hufton, 'Women without Men: Widows and Spinsters in Britain and France in the Eighteenth Century', in Jan Bremmer and Lourens van den Bosch, eds, *Between Poverty and the Pyre: Moments in the History of Widowhood* (London, 1995), pp. 135–36.

37 *Ibid.*, p. 136.

38 Merry E. Weisner, *Working Women in Renaissance Germany* (New Brunswick, 1986), pp. 76–77.

39 Wendy Gibson, *Women in Seventeenth-Century France* (New York, 1989), p. 89.

40 Gaunt and Löfgren, 'Remarriage in the Nordic Countries', pp. 55–56.

41 Quoted in Todd, 'The Virtuous Widow', p. 79.

42 Quoted in Vassberg, 'The Status of Widows in Rural Castile', pp. 183–84, and Elizabeth Foyster, 'Marrying the Experienced Widow in Early Modern England: the Male Perspective', in Cavallo and Warner, eds, *Widowhood in Medieval and Early Modern Europe*, p. 111.

43 Vivian Brodsky, 'Widows in Late Elizabethan London', in Bonfield *et al.*, *The World We Have Gained*, p. 127.

44 Foyster, 'Marrying the Experienced Widow', p. 115.

45 *Ibid.*

46 Quoted in *ibid.*, pp. 120–21.
47 Georges Minois, *History of Old Age*, trans. Sarah Hanbury Tenison (Chicago, 1987), p. 295.
48 Quoted in *ibid.*, p. 250.
49 Quoted in *ibid.*, p. 251.
50 Quoted in *ibid.*, pp. 259–60.
51 St Pascu and V. Pascu, 'Le remarriage chez les orthodoxes', in Dupâquier, *Marriage and Remarriage in Populations of the Past*, p. 62.
52 Margaret Pelling, 'Old Age, Poverty and Disability in Early Modern Norwich', in Margaret Pelling and Richard M. Smith, eds, *Life, Death, and the Elderly: Historical Perspectives* (London, 1991), p. 89.
53 Quoted in Foyster, 'Marrying the Experienced Widow', p. 110.
54 Jeremy Bolton, 'London Widowhood Revisited: The Decline of Female Remarriage in the Seventeenth and Early Eighteenth Centuries', *Continuity and Change* 3 (1990), pp. 323–55.
55. Margaret Pelling, 'Finding Widowers: Men Without Women in English Towns Before 1700', in Cavallo and Warner, *Widowhood in Medieval and Early Modern Europe*, p. 50; Pelling, 'Old Age, Poverty, and Disability', p. 88.
56 Cissie Fairchilds, *Domestic Enemies: Servants and Their Masters in Old Regime France* (Baltimore, 1984), pp. 142–43.
57 Pelling, 'Old Age, Poverty, and Disability', pp. 83; 82.
58 Quoted in Erickson, *Women and Property*, p. 189.
59 Pelling, 'Old Age, Poverty, and Disability', p. 87.
60 *Ibid.*, p. 86.
61 *Ibid.*, pp. 86; 87.
62 Cissie Fairchilds, *Poverty and Charity in Aix-en-Provence, 1640–1789* (Baltimore, 1976), pp. 94–99.
63 Sherri Klassen, 'Greying in the Cloister: The Ursuline Life Course in Eighteenth-Century France', *Journal of Women's History* 12, 4 (Winter, 2001), p. 90.
64 Quoted in *ibid.*, p. 103.
65 Wayne Franits, *Paragons of Virtue: Women and Domesticity in Seventeenth-Century Dutch Art* (Cambridge, 1993), p. 43.
66 Erickson, *Women and Property*, pp. 212–21.
67 Quoted in *ibid.*, p. 217.
68 Quoted in *ibid.*, p. 209.
69 *Ibid.*
70 Gibson, *Women in Seventeenth-Century France*, p. 242.
71 Erickson, *Women and Property*, pp. 140–41.
72 Cressy, *Birth, Marriage, and Death*, pp. 389–92; 421–55.
73 *Ibid.*, p. 461; Erickson, *Women and Property*, pp. 140–41.

Part III: Women and Work

1 Mary Prior, 'Women and the Urban Economy: Oxford 1500–1800' in Prior, ed., *Women in English Society*, p. 95.

2 Sandy Bardsley, 'Women's Work Reconsidered: Gender and Wage Differentiation in Late Medieval England', *Past and Present* 165 (Nov. 1999), pp. 3–29.

Chapter 6: Housewives, Spinsters, Harvest Hands: Women's Work in the Countryside

1 Quoted in James B. Collins, 'The Economic Role of Women in Seventeenth-Century France', *French Historical Studies* 16, 2 (Fall, 1989), p. 441.

2 Thomas Tusser, 'The Points of Housewifery', in Klein, *Daughters, Wives, and Widows*, p. 212.

3 *The Domostroi: Rules for Russian Households in the Time of Ivan the Terrible*, ed. and trans. Carolyn Johnston Pouncy (Ithaca, 1994), p. 152.

4 *The Private Life of an Elizabethan Lady: the Diary of Lady Margaret Hoby 1599–1605*, ed. Joanna Moody (Thrupp, 1998), pp. 4–6; 6; 11; 13; 26; 27; 32; 40; 164; 165. I have modernized the spelling of these entries.

5 Pollock, *With Faith & Physic*, pp. 92–109.

6 Quoted in Wunder, *He is the Sun, She is the Moon*, p. 63.

7 Clark, *Working Life of Women*, pp. 42–56; 296–97; 302–8.

8 Wayne Vucinich, 'A Zadruga in Bileća Rudine', in Byrnes, *Communal Families in the Balkans: The Zadruga*, pp. 171–72.

9 Michael Roberts, 'Sickles and Scythes: Women's Work and Men's Work at Harvest Time', *History Workshop* 7 (1979), pp. 3–28.

10 Carole Shammas, 'The World Women Knew: Women Workers in the North of England During the Late Seventeenth Century', in Richard S. Dunn and Mary Maples Dunn, eds, *The World of William Penn* (Philadelphia, 1986), pp. 106–7.

11 Quoted in Sheilagh Ogilvie, *A Bitter Living: Women, Markets, and Social Capital in Early Modern Germany* (Oxford, 2003), p. 151.

12 Quoted in *ibid.*, p. 147.

13 *Ibid.*, p. 146.

14 Hufton, 'Women Without Men', p. 146.

15 Clark, *Working Life of Women*, pp. 93–149.

16 Ulrich Pfister, 'Proto-industrialization', in Kertzer and Barbagli, *Family Life in Early Modern Times*, pp. 63–84.

17 Ogilvie, *A Bitter Living*, p. 225.

18 *Ibid.*, p. 227.

19 Quoted in *ibid.*, p. 257.

20 Quoted in *ibid.*, pp. 253; 254.

21 Sheilagh Ogilvie and Jeremy Edwards, 'Women and the "Second Serfdom": Evidence from Early Modern Bohemia', *Journal of Economic History*, 60 (2000), p. 986.

22 Quoted in *ibid.*, p. 983.

23 Quoted in *ibid.*, p. 984.

24 Peters, *Women in Early Modern Britain*, p. 33.

25 Peters, 'Single Women in Early Modern England', p. 340.

26 Pamela Sharpe, 'Literally Spinsters: A New Interpretation of Local Economy and Demography in Colyton in the 17th and 18th Centuries', *Economic History Review*, xliv, 1 (1991), pp. 46–65.

27 Quoted in Ogilvie, *A Bitter Living*, p. 294.

28 Quoted in *ibid.*, p. 309.

29 *Ibid.*, pp. 103–27.

30 Quoted in *ibid.*, p. 161.

31 Quoted in Fairchilds, *Domestic Enemies*, p. 166.

32 Ann Kussmaul, *Servants in Husbandry in Early Modern England* (Cambridge, 1981), p. 44.

Chapter 7: Craftswomen, Midwives, Servants: Women's Work in Cities and Towns

1 Quoted in Vicente, 'Images and Realities of Work', p. 129.

2 Monica Chojnacka, *Working Women of Early Modern Venice* (Baltimore, 2001), p. 79.

3 *Ibid.*, pp. 125–28.

4 A. Hunt, *Governance of the Consuming Passions: A History of Sumptuary Law* (Houndmills, 1996), p. 214.

5 Ogilvie, *A Bitter Living*, p. 202.

6 Ozment, *Magdalena and Balthasar*, p. 80.

7 *Ibid.*, pp. 76; 67.

8 *Ibid.*, pp. 72–73.

9 Heiko A. Oberman, *Luther: Man Between God and the Devil* (New Haven, 1989), p. 280.

10 Mark Pattison, *Isaac Casaubon 1559–1614* (Oxford, 1892), pp. 30; 388; 419.

11 Hardwick, *The Practice of Patriarchy*, pp. 113–14.

12 Philip T. Hoffman, Gilles Postel-Vinay and Jean-Laurent Rosenthal, *Priceless Markets: The Political Economy of Credit in Paris, 1660–1870* (Chicago, 2000), pp. 11–30; 154–73.

13 Ogilvie, *A Bitter Living*, p. 153.

14 *Ibid.*, pp. 155; 148; 163.

15 Carol L. Loats, 'Gender, Guilds, and Work Identity: Perspectives from Sixteenth-Century Paris', *French Historical Studies* 20, 1 (Winter, 1997), pp. 19; 21; 22.

16 Peter Earle, 'The Female Labour Market in London in the Late Seventeenth and Early Eighteenth Centuries' in Pamela Sharpe, ed., *Women's Work: The English Experience 1650–1914* (London, 1998), p. 131.

17 King, *Women of the Renaissance*, p. 65.

18 Clare Haru Crowston, *Fabricating Women: The Seamstresses of Old Regime France 1675–1791* (Durham, NC, 2001), p. 181 *et passim*.

19 Vicente, 'Images and Realities of Work', p. 128; Ogilvie, *A Bitter Living*, pp. 96–97.

20 Martha C. Howell, *Women, Production and Patriarchy in Late Medieval Cities* (Chicago, 1986).

21 Quoted in Ogilvie, *A Bitter Living*, p. 97.

22 Quoted in *ibid.*

23 My treatment of this topic is based on Judith M. Bennett, *Ale, Beer, and Brewsters in England: Women's Work in a Changing World 1300–1600* (Oxford, 1996).

24 *Ibid.*, pp. 18–19.

25 *Ibid.*, pp. 98–121.

26 *Ibid.*, pp. 142–43.

27 Wunder, *He is the Sun, She is the Moon*, p. 170.

28 Katherine Parks, 'Medicine and Magic: The Healing Arts', in Brown and Davis, eds, *Gender and Society in Renaissance Italy*, p. 136.

29 *Ibid.*, p. 135.

30 A. L. Wyman, 'The Surgeoness: The Female Practitioner of Surgery 1400–1800', *Medical History* 28 (1984), p. 29.

31 *Ibid.*, p. 34.

32 *Ibid.*, p. 29.

33 Parks, 'Medicine and Magic', p. 140.

34 *Ibid.*, p. 143.

35 Wyman, 'The Surgeoness', p. 27.

36 Chojnacka, *Working Women of Early Modern Venice*, pp. 108–109.

37 Pollock, 'With Faith and Physic', pp. 92–109.

38 Wyman, 'The Surgeoness', pp. 25–26.

39 Ogilvie, *A Bitter Living*, p. 234.

40 Quoted in Wyman, 'The Surgeoness', pp. 36–37.

41 Earle, 'The Female Labour Market in London', pp. 144–47.

42 Crowston, *Fabricating Women*, p. 186.

43 Vicente, 'Images and Realities of Work', p. 127.

44 Crowston, *Fabricating Women*, p. 196.

45 Vicente, 'Images and Realities of Work', p. 134.

46 Crowston, *Fabricating Women*.

47 Wiesner, *Working Women in Renaissance Germany*, p. 136.

48 Marybeth Carlson, 'A Trojan Horse of Worldliness? Maidservants in the burgher household in Rotterdam at the End of the 17th Century', in Els Kloek, *et al.*, eds, *Women of the Golden Age* (Hilversum, 1994), p. 92.

49 Fairchilds, *Domestic Enemies*, p. 63.

50 Peters, *Women in Early Modern Britain*, p. 34.

51 Stone, *Family, Sex, and Marriage in England*, pp. 552–61.

52 Ulinka Rublack, *The Crimes of Women in Early Modern Germany* (Oxford, 1999), p. 141.

53 *Ibid.*, pp. 113; 121.

54 *Ibid.*, pp. 124–25.

55 Leah Lydia Otis, *Prostitution in Medieval Society* (Chicago, 1985).

56 Margaret F. Rosenthal, *The Honest Courtesan* (Chicago, 1992), p. 11.

57 *Ibid.*

58 Printed in Veronica Franco, *Poems and Selected Letters*, ed. and trans. Ann Rosalind Jones and Margaret F. Rosenthal (Chicago, 1998), pp. 37–40.

59 Rudolf M. Dekker and Lotte C. van de Pol, *The Tradition of Female Transvestism in Early Modern Europe* (New York, 1989), p. 33.

60 *Ibid.*, p. 1.

Chapter 8: Artists, Musicians, Actresses, Writers, Scholars, Scientists: New Employment Opportunities for Women

1 Quoted in Anthony Newcomb, 'Courtesans, Muses or Musicians? Professional Women Musicians in Sixteenth-Century Italy' in Jane Bowers and Judith Tick, eds, *Women Making Music: The Western Art Tradition 1150–1950* (Urbana, IL, 1986), p. 90.

2 Ann Sutherland Harris and Linda Nochlin, *Women Artists 1550–1950* (New York, 1976), pp. 13–20.

3 Germaine Greer, *The Obstacle Race* (New York, 1979), pp. 151–88.

4 Harris and Nochlin, *Women Artists*, pp. 23–27.

5 *Ibid.*, pp. 24–28; 105–10; Greer, *The Obstacle Race*, pp. 71; 72.

6 Harris and Nochlin, *Women Artists*, pp. 111–14; Greer, *The Obstacle Race*, pp. 208–14.

7 Greer, *The Obstacle Race*, pp. 214–26.

8 My treatment of Gentileschi is based on Garrard, *Artemisia Gentileschi*.

9 The trial testimony is printed in *ibid.*, pp. 403–87.

10 Printed in *ibid.*, pp. 390; 394; 397.

11 Harris and Nochlin, *Women Artists*, pp. 137–40; Greer, *The Obstacle Race*, pp. 136–41.

12 Harris and Nochlin, *Women Artists*, p. 37.

13 J. Michele Edwards, 'Women in Music to ca. 1450', in Karin Pendle, ed., *Women & Music: A History* (Bloomington, IN, 1991), pp. 8–28; Maria V. Coldwell, 'Jougleresses and Trobairitz: Secular Musicians in Medieval France' in Bowers and Tick, *Women Making Music*, pp. 39–61.

14 Jane Bowers, 'The Emergence of Women Composers in Italy, 1566–1700', in Bowers and Tick, *Women Making Music*, pp. 125–26.

15 *Ibid.*, pp. 141–43.

16 Karin Pendle, 'Women in Music, ca. 1450–1600', pp. 35; 46–47.

17 Newcomb, 'Courtesans, Muses or Musicians?', p. 93.

18 *Ibid.*, pp. 93–98.

19 Barbara Garvey Jackson, 'Musical Women of the Seventeenth and Eighteenth Centuries', in Pendle, *Women & Music*, pp. 72–74; 80.

20 Jane Baldauf-Berdes, *Women Musicians of Venice: Musical Foundations, 1525–1855* (Oxford, 1993).

21 Bowers, 'Women Composers in Italy', pp. 134–38.

22 *Ibid.*, pp. 162–67.

23 Quoted in Pendle, 'Women in Music, ca. 1450–1600', p. 48.

24 Ellen Rosand, 'The Voice of Barbara Strozzi' in Bowers and Tick, *Women Making Music*, pp. 168–87.

25 Bowers, 'Women Composers in Italy', pp. 123–25; Jackson, 'Musical Women of the Seventeenth and Eighteenth Centuries', pp. 58–61.

26 Bowers, 'Women Composers in Italy', p. 135.

27 Jackson, 'Musical Women of the Seventeenth and Eighteenth Centuries', pp. 54–91.

28 Julie Anne Sadie, '*Musiciennes* of the *Ancien Régime*', in Bowers and Tick, *Women Making Music*, pp. 191–223.

29 Eric A. Nicholson, 'The Theater', in Davis and Farge, *A History of Women*, Vol. 3, pp. 309–10.

30 Leopold Lacour, *Les premières actrices françaises* (Paris, 1921), pp. 6; 16; Nicolson, 'The Theater', pp. 310; 311.

31 Lacour, *Les premières actrices françaises*, p. 166.

32 Nicolson, 'The Theater', p. 311.

33 Lacour, *Les premières actrices françaises*, p. 208.

34 Lenard R. Berlanstein, 'Women and Power in Eighteenth-Century France: Actresses at the Comédie-Française' in Christine Adams *et al.*, *Visions and Revisions of Eighteenth-Century France* (University Park, PA, 1997), p. 156.

35 Nicolson, 'The Theater', pp. 297–309.

36 My treatment of Behn is based on Maureen Duffy, *The Passionate Shepherdess* (New York, 1977).

37 Margaret L. King and Albert Rabil, Jr, eds, *Her Immaculate Hand* (Binghamton, NY, 1983), pp. 21–23.

38 *Ibid.*, pp. 23–24.

39 Quoted in King, *Women of the Renaissance*, p. 196.

40 Quoted in *ibid.*, p. 213.

41 Moderata Fonte (Modesta Pozzo), *The Worth of Women*, ed. and trans. Virginia Cox (Chicago, 1997).

42 Quoted in Patricia Crawford, 'Women's Published Writings 1600–1700' in Prior, *Women in English Society*, p. 224.

43 *Ibid.*, p. 216; Suzanne Hull, *Chaste, Silent and Obedient* (Los Angeles, 1982), p. 7; Crawford, 'Women's Published Writings', p. 266.

44 *Ibid.*, p. 221.

45 Elaine Hobby, *Virtue of Necessity: English Women's Writing: 1649–88* (Ann Arbor, MI, 1989), pp. 185–87.

46 *Ibid.*, pp. 178–80.

47 *Ibid.*, pp. 180–82.

48 Quoted in *ibid.*, p. 182.

49 *Ibid.*, pp. 166–73.

50 *Ibid.*, pp. 199–203.

51 Crawford, 'Women's Published Writings', p. 222.

52 Quoted in Hobby, *Virtue of Necessity*, p. 78.

53 Ruth Perry, *Women, Letters and the Novel* (New York, 1980), p. 76.

54 Quoted in Paul Salzman, ed., *Early Modern Women's Writing* (Oxford, 2000), p. xxvi.

55 My treatment of the origins of the novel is largely based on Ioan Williams, *The Idea of the Novel in Europe, 1600–1800* (New York, 1979).

56 Salzman, *Early Modern Women's Writing*, pp. xviii–xx.

57 Marguerite de Navarre, *Heptameron*, trans. P. A. Chilton (New York, 1984).

58 Maria de Zayas, *The Disenchantments of Love*, trans. H. Patsy Boyer (Albany, NY, 1997).

59 My treatment of the rise of the novel in France is based on De Jean, *Tender Geographies*.

60 *Ibid.*, p. 128.

61 Nina Gelbart, *Feminine and Opposition Journalism in Old Regime France: Le Journal des Dames* (Berkeley, 1987).

62 Quoted in Jonathan Goldberg, *Desiring Women Writing: English Renaissance Examples* (Stanford, 1997), pp. 76; 75.

63 David Noble, *A World Without Women: the Christian Clerical Culture of Western Science* (New York, 1992).

64 Anna Maria Van Schurman, *'Whether a Christian Woman Should Be Educated'*, ed. Joyce L. Irwin (Chicago, 1998), pp. 1–21.

65 Paula Findlen, 'Science as a Career in Enlightenment Italy: The Strategies of Laura Bassi', *Isis* 84 (1993), p. 445; King, *Women of the Renaissance*, p. 212. The quote is from King.

66 Schiebinger, *The Mind Has No Sex?*, pp. 102–59.

67 Alic, *Hypatia's Heritage*, pp. 114; 99.

68 Quoted in *ibid.*, pp. 95–96.

69 Davis, *Women on the Margins*, pp. 140–202.

70 Schiebinger, *The Mind Has No Sex?*, pp. 79–101.

71 Findlen, 'Science as a Career in Enlightenment Italy', pp. 441–69.

Part IV: Women and Religion

1 Mary Elizabeth Perry, 'Behind the Veil: Moriscas and the Politics of Resistance and Survival', in Sanchez and Saint Saëns, *Spanish Women in the Golden Age*, pp. 37–53.

2 Jerzy Wyrozumski, 'Jews in Medieval Poland', in Antony Polonsky *et al.*, *The Jews in Old Poland 1000–1795* (London, 1993), pp. 15–16; Gershon David Hundert, *Jews in Poland–Lithuania in the Eighteenth Century* (Berkeley, 2004), p. 22.

3 Davis, *Women on the Margins*, pp. 9–11; 22–24.

4 Pushkareva, *Women in Russian History*, pp. 80–81. The quote is from Hughes, *Sophia*, p. 122.

Chapter 9: Wives, Preachers, Martyrs: Women in the Protestant Reformation

1 *Luther's Works*, ed. Jaroslav Peliken, Vol. 1 (St Louis, 1958), p. 115.

2 *Ibid.*, p. 198.

3 *Ibid.*, p. 162.

4 Quoted in Oberman, *Luther: Man Between God and the Devil*, pp. 275–76.

5 *Luther's Works*, ed. Eric W. Gritsch, Vol. 39 (Philadelphia, 1970), pp. 296–99.

6 Ozment, *When Fathers Ruled*, pp. 16–17.

7 Ozment, *When Fathers Ruled*, pp. 19–20.

8 Merry E. Wiesner, 'Nuns, Wives, and Mothers: Women and the Reformation in Germany' in Marshall, *Women in Reformation and Counter-Reformation Europe*, p. 10.

9 Lazareth, *Luther on the Christian Home*, pp. 217–34.

10 Quoted in Ozment, *When Fathers Ruled*, p. 84.

11 Quoted in Lazareth, *Luther on the Christian Home*, pp. 31; 32; 30; 32.

12 Quoted in Ozment, *When Fathers Ruled*, p. 40 and Lazareth, *Luther on the Christian Home*, p. 147.

13 Ozment, *When Fathers Ruled*, p. 93.

14 Quoted in *ibid.*, p. 84.

15 Watt, *The Making of Modern Marriage*, p. 223, Table II.

16 *Luther's Works*, Vol. 1, p. 69.

17 Quoted in Lazareth, *Luther on the Christian Home*, p. 226.

18 William Gouge, 'Of Domesticall Duties', in Joyce L. Irwin, ed., *Womanhood in Radical Protestantism 1525–1675* (New York, 1979), pp. 97–98.

19 Quoted in Lazareth, *Luther on the Christian Home*, p. 226.

20 Gouge, 'Domesticall Duties', pp. 103–4.

21 Jeffrey R. Watt, 'Women and the Consistory in Calvin's Geneva', *Sixteenth Century Journal* XXIV, 2 (1993), p. 436; E. William Monter, 'Women in Calvinist Geneva (1550–1800)', *Signs* 6, 2 (1980), p. 194.

22 Watt, 'Women and the Consistory', p. 437.

23 Monter, 'Women in Calvinist Geneva', p. 192.

24 Quoted in Lyndal Roper, *The Holy Household: Women and Morals in Reformation Augsburg* (Oxford, 1989), p. 99.

25 *Ibid.*

26 Susan C. Karant-Nunn, 'Continuity and Change: Some Effects of The Reformation on the Women of Zwickau', *Sixteenth Century Journal* XII, 2 (1982), p. 23; Roper, *Holy Household*, p. 89.

27 Wiesner, *Working Women in Renaissance Germany*, p. 99.

28 Quoted in Roper, *Holy Household*, p. 109.

29 *Ibid.*, p. 130.

30 Quoted in *ibid.*, p. 115.

31 Watt, 'Women and the Consistory', p. 438.

32 Roper, *Holy Household*, pp. 125; 199.

33 Karant-Nunn, 'Continuity and Change', pp. 31–32.

34 Monter, 'Women in Calvinist Geneva', pp. 192–93.

35 Quoted in Jane Dempsey Douglas, *Women, Freedom, and Calvin* (Philadelphia, 1985), p. 88.

36 *Ibid.*, pp. 52–56.

37 Watt, 'Women and the Consistory', p. 433.

38 R. W. Scribner and C. Scott Dixon, *The German Reformation* (Houndmills, 2003), p. 61.

39 Ozment, *When Fathers Ruled*, pp. 90–92.

40 Charmarie Jenkins Blaisdell, 'The Matrix of Reform: Women in the Lutheran and Calvinist Movements', in Richard L. Greaves, ed., *Triumph Over Silence: Women in Protestant History* (Westport, CT, 1985), pp. 24–25; 31–33.

41 Natalie Zemon Davis, 'City Women and Religious Change', in *Society and Culture in Early Modern France* (Stanford, 1975), p. 92.

42 Sherrin Marshall, 'Protestant, Catholic, and Jewish Women in the Early Modern Netherlands', in Marshall, *Women in Reformation and Counter-Reformation Europe*, p. 126.

43 Quoted in Douglass, *Women, Freedom and Calvin*, p. 102.

44 Davis, 'City Women and Religious Change', p. 83.

45 Karant-Nunn, 'Continuity and Change', p. 40.

46 Anne Laurence, 'A Priesthood of She-Believers: Women and Congregation in Mid-Seventeenth-Century England', in W. Sheils and D. Woods, eds, *Women in the Church: Studies in Church History* 27 (1990), pp. 348–49.

47 Quoted in *ibid.*, p. 351.

48 Margaret Askew Fell, 'Women Speaking Justified', in Irwin, *Womanhood in Radical Protestantism*, pp. 180–88.

49 Phyllis Mack, 'Teaching About Gender and Spirituality in Early English Quakerism', *Women's Studies* 19 (1991), pp. 223–25; Sarah Cheevers, 'Letter to Her Husband', in Irwin, *Womanhood in Radical Protestantism*, p. 235.

50 Crawford, 'Women's Published Writings', pp. 245; 247; 246; 225–6.
51 *Ibid.*, pp. 216; 224.
52 Quoted in Douglass, *Women, Freedom and Calvin*, pp. 103–104.
53 Quoted in Patricia A. Higgins, 'The Reactions of Women, with Special Reference to Women Petitioners', in Brian Manning, ed., *Politics, Religion, and the English Civil War* (New York, 1973), pp. 210–11.
54 Printed in Patricia Crawford, 'The Challenges to Patriarchalism: How Did the Revolution Affect Women?' in J. S. Morrill, *Revolution and Restoration: England in the 1650s* (London, 1992), p. 117.
55 Quoted in Higgins, 'The Reactions of Women', pp. 215–16.
56 Printed in Crawford, 'Challenges to Patriarchalism', p. 126.
57 Diane Willen, 'Women and Religion in Early Modern England', in Marshall, *Women in Reformation and Counter-Reformation Europe*, p. 146.
58 Elaine V. Beillin, ed., *The Examinations of Anne Askew* (Oxford, 1996).
59 Quoted in Keith L. Sprunger, 'God's Powerful Army of the Weak: Anabaptist Women of the Radical Reformation' in Greaves, *Triumph Over Silence*, p. 67.
60 Quoted in Carole Levin, 'Women in *The Book of Martyrs* as Models of Behavior in Tudor England', *International Journal of Women's Studies* 4 (1981), p. 204.
61 Quoted in *ibid.*
62 Willen, 'Women and Religion in Early Modern England', p. 143; Sprunger, 'God's Powerful Army of the Weak', p. 66.
63 Quoted in Levin, 'Women in *The Book of Martyrs*', p. 201.

Chapter 10: Mothers, Nuns, Nurses, Teachers: Women in the Catholic Reformation

1 Jo Ann Kay McNamara, *Sisters in Arms: Catholic Nuns through Two Millennia* (Cambridge, MA, 1996) p. 442; Marie B. Rowlands, 'Recusant Women 1560–1640', in Prior, *Women in English Society*, p. 159.
2 McNamara, *Sisters in Arms*, p. 461.
3 Quoted in *ibid.*, p. 507.
4 Mary Elizabeth Perry, *Gender and Disorder in Early Modern Seville* (Princeton, 1990), pp. 97–117.
5 Fulvio Tomizza, *Heavenly Supper: The Story of Maria Janis*, trans. Anne Schutte (Chicago, 1991).
6 Richard L. Kagan, *Lucrecia's Dreams: Politics and Prophecy in Sixteenth-Century Spain* (Berkeley, 1990).
7 *Canons and Decrees of the Council of Trent*, trans. H. J. Schroeder (St Louis, 1941), pp. 217–32.
8 My treatment of Saint Theresa is largely based on McNamara, *Sisters in Arms*, pp. 489–525 and Jodi Bilinkoff, *The Avila of St Theresa* (Ithaca, 1989), pp. 108–51.
9 Quoted in Bilinkoff, *The Avila of St Theresa*, pp. 135–36.
10 McNamara, *Sisters in Arms*, p. 515.
11 *Ibid.*, p. 518.
12 Rowlands, 'Recusant Women', especially pp. 160–66.

13 Elisja Schulte van Kessel, 'Virgins and Mothers between Heaven and Earth', in Natalie Zemon Davis and Arlette Farge, eds, *A History of Women in the West*, Vol. III (Cambridge, MA, 1993), pp. 162–63.

14 Quoted in Rowlands, 'Recusant Women', p. 169.

15 Quoted in Elizabeth Rapley, *The Dévotes: Women and Church in Seventeenth-Century France* (Montreal, 1990), pp. 31–32.

16 Quoted in *ibid.*, pp. 32–33.

17 Quoted in *ibid.*, p. 33.

18 McNamara, *Sisters in Arms*, pp. 460–61.

19 Quoted in Rapley, *The Dévotes*, p. 51.

20 Quoted in *ibid.*, p. 38.

21 *Ibid.*

22 Quoted in *ibid.*, p. 88.

23 Hufton, 'Women without Men', p. 140.

24 St François de Sales, *Introduction to the Devout Life*, trans. Michael Day (London, 1961), pp. 14; 13.

25 *Ibid.*, p. 184.

26 Jeffrey R. Watt, 'The Impact of the Reformation and Counter-Reformation', in Kertzer and Barbagli, *Family Life in Early Modern Times 1500–1789*, p. 141.

27 Pamela Brown Roberts, 'Jean Pierre Camus: A Bishop of the Early Catholic Reformation in France' (masters' thesis, Syracuse University, 1985), pp. 87–89.

28 St François de Sales, *Introduction to the Devout Life*, pp. 191–93.

29 Stephen Haliczer, *Inquisition and Society in the Kingdom of Valencia, 1478–1834* (Berkeley, 1990), p. 299.

30 Quoted in Henry Kamen, *Inquisition and Society in Spain in the Sixteenth and Seventeenth Centuries* (Bloomington, IN, 1985), p. 184.

31 *Ibid.*

32 Perry, *Gender and Disorder in Early Modern Seville*, p. 150.

33 Haliczer, *Inquisition and Society in the Kingdom of Valencia*, p. 304.

34 Chojnacka, *Working Women of Early Modern Venice*, pp. 124–27; Sherrill Cohen, *The Evolution of Women's Asylums Since 1500: From Refuges for Ex-Prostitutes to Shelters for Battered Women* (New York, 1992), pp. 20–21.

35 St François de Sales, *Introduction to the Devout Life*, p. 186.

36 Quoted in Jean-Louis Flandrin, *Families in Former Times: Kinship, Household and Sexuality*, trans. Richard Southern (Cambridge, 1976), pp. 128–29.

37 Hugo Rahner, ed., *St Ignatius Loyola: Letters to Women* (Edinburgh, 1960), pp. 141–44.

38 Kamen, *Inquisition and Society*, p. 183.

Chapter 11: Witches

1 Brian P. Levack, *The Witch-Hunt in Early Modern Europe* (Harlow, 1995), pp. 25; 133.

2 Marianne Hester, *Lewd Women and Wicked Witches* (London, 1992).

3 Michael MacDonald, *Mystical Bedlam* (Cambridge, 1979).

4 Valerie A. Kivelson, 'Through the Prism of Witchcraft: Gender and Social Change in Seventeenth-Century Muscovy', in B. E. Engel *et al.*, *Russia's Women: Accommodation, Resistance, Transformation* (Berkeley, 1991), pp. 76–78; 87; 89.

5 Kirsten Hastrup, 'Iceland: Sorcerers and Paganism', in Bengt Ankarloo and Gustav Henningsen, eds, *Early Modern European Witchdraft: Centres and Peripheries* (Oxford, 1990), p. 388.

6 Gabor Klaniczay, 'Hungary: The Accusations and the Universe of Popular Magic', in Ankarloo and Henningsen, *Early Modern European Witchcraft*, p. 255, n. 126; Anne Llewellyn Barstow, *Witchcraze: A New History of the European Witch Hunts* (New York, 1994), pp. 16–17.

7 Klaniczay, 'Hungary', p. 254.

8 Christina Larner, *Enemies of God: The Witch-Hunt in Scotland* (Baltimore, 1981), p. 89.

9 *Ibid.*

10 Quoted in Lyndal Roper, 'Witchcraft and Fantasy in Early Modern Germany' in Roper, *Oedipus and the Devil* (London, 1994), p. 214.

11 *Ibid.*, p. 199.

12 Larner, *Enemies of God*, pp. 126–27.

13 *Ibid.*, pp. 120–23.

14 *Ibid.*, p. 97.

15 Hester, *Lewd Women and Wicked Witches*, pp. 164–65.

16 Levack, *The Witchhunt in Early Modern Europe*, p. 31.

17 *Ibid.*, pp. 29–35.

18 *Ibid.*, pp. 38–44.

19 Margaret Murray, *The Witch-Cult in Western Europe* (London, 1921).

20 H. R. Trevor-Roper, *The European Witch-Craze of the Sixteenth and Seventeenth Centuries* (New York, 1969).

21 Levack, *The Witchhunt in Early Modern Europe*, p. 42.

22 Carlo Ginzburg, *The Night Battles: Witchcraft and Agrarian Cults in the Sixteenth and Seventeenth Centuries*, trans. John and Anne Tedeschi (Baltimore, 1983).

23 *The Malleus Maleficarum of Heinrich Kramer and James Sprenger*, trans. Montague Summers (New York, 1971).

24 Sigrid Brauner, *Fearless Wives and Frightened Shrews: The Construction of the Witch in Early Modern Germany* (Amherst, MA, 1995), pp. 31–49.

25 *Ibid.* Walter Stephens has recently argued in *Demon Lovers: Witchcraft, Sex, and the Crisis of Belief* (Chicago, 2002) that Sprenger and Kramer were not necessarily misogynists. Stephens suggests that their main concern in the *Malleus* was to prove the existence of demons, as one step toward proving the existence of God. Therefore they emphasized sex between demons and mortal women; if real women can have sex with demons, demons must exist. They piled on the misogyny to persuade their readers that women were depraved enough for such acts. This may well be true. But whatever the motives for their misogyny, the important point for women's history is that it permeated the *Malleus* and most later learned treatises on witchcraft.

26 Kramer and Sprenger, *Malleus Maleficarum*, pp. 44–47.

27 *Ibid.*, pp. 43; 45; 47.

28 Robin Briggs, *Witches and Neighbors: The Social Cultural Context of European Witchcraft* (New York, 1996), p. 117.

29 Hester, *Lewd Women and Wicked Witches*, pp. 187–91.

30 Ginzburg, *The Night Battles*.

31 Levack, *The Witchhunt in Early Modern Europe*, pp. 76–84.

32 Quoted in Briggs, *Witches and Neighbors*, p. 43.

33 Quoted in *ibid.*

34 Quoted in *ibid.*, pp. 156–57.

35 Quoted in *ibid.*, pp. 26–27.

36 Quoted in *ibid.*, p. 27.

37 Levack, *The Witchhunt in Early Modern Europe*, pp. 17–18.

38 Quoted in Briggs, *Witches and Neighbors*, p. 20.

39 Quoted in *ibid.*, p. 155.

40 Levack, *The Witchhunt in Early Modern Europe*, pp. 21–26; 160–67.

41 *Ibid.*, pp. 93–94.

42 Francisco Bethencourt, 'Portugal: A Scrupulous Inquisition', in Ankarloo and Henningsen, *Early Modern European Witchcraft*, p. 405.

43 John A. Tedeschi, 'Inquisitional Law and the Witch', in Ankarloo and Henningsen, *Early Modern European Witchcraft*, pp. 83–118. Quote p. 104.

44 Jens Christian v. Johansen, 'Denmark: The Sociology of Accusations', in Ankarloo and Henningsen, *Early Modern European Witchcraft*, pp. 341; 344.

45 Levack, *The Witchhunt in Early Modern Europe*, p. 97; Larner, *Enemies of God*, pp. 63; 119.

46 Hester, *Lewd Women and Wicked Witches*, pp. 187–91.

47 H. C. Erik Midelfort, *Witch Hunting in Southwestern Germany 1562–1684* (Stanford, 1972).

48 P. Boyer and S. Nissenbaum, *Salem Possessed: The Social Origins of Witchcraft* (Cambridge, MA, 1974); Briggs, *Witches and Neighbors*, pp. 344–45.

49 Levack, *The Witchhunt in Early Modern Europe*, pp. 237–38.

50 *Ibid.*, pp. 60–64; Briggs, *Witches and Neighbors*, p. 172.

51 Lyndal Roper, '"Evil Imaginings and Fantasies": Child witches and the end of the Witch Craze', in Ulinka Rublack, ed., *Gender in Early Modern German History* (Cambridge, 2002), pp. 102–30.

Part V: Women and the State

1 Quoted in Natalie Zemon Davis, 'Women in Politics', in Davis and Farge, eds, *A History of Women in the West*, Vol. III, p. 167.

2 Quoted in Constance Jordan, 'Women's Rule in Sixteenth-Century British Political Thought', *Renaissance Quarterly* 40 (1987), p. 441.

3 Quoted in *ibid.*

4 Quoted in Gordon J. Schochet, *Patriarchalism in Political Thought* (New York, 1975), p. 30.

Chapter 12: Rulers

1 Printed in Kate Aughterson, ed., *Renaissance Women: A Sourcebook* (London, 1995), pp. 138–39.

2 Sven Stolpe, *Christina of Sweden* (London, 1966).

3 Quoted in Carole Levin, *'The Heart and Stomach of a King': Elizabeth I and the Politics of Sex and Power* (Philadelphia, 1994), p. 144. The authenticity of this traditional version of the Armada speech has been questioned, but in the alternate version Elizabeth also takes on masculine kingly roles: 'I have been your Prince in peace, so will I be in warre/'. *Ibid.*

4 *Ibid.*, pp. 10–28.

5 Quoted in *ibid.*, p. 49.

6 Fanny Cosandey, 'De Lance en Quenouille: La place de la reine dans l'Etat moderne (14e–17e siécles)', *Annales: Histoire, Sciences Sociales* 52, 4 (Jul–Aug. 1997), pp. 799–820; Hughes, *Sophia Regent of Russia*, p. 16.

7 Lunenfeld, 'Isabella I of Castile'.

8 John Guy, *The True Life of Mary Stuart, Queen of Scots* (London, 2004), pp. 163–423.

9 Levin, *'The Heart and Stomach of a King'*, pp. 26–30.

10 *Ibid.*, p. 40.

11 Quoted in *ibid.*, p. 41.

12 *Ibid.*, p. 15.

13 Lisa Hopkins, *Women Who Would Be Kings: Female Rulers of the Sixteenth Century* (London, 1991), pp. 144–55; Jo Ellen Campbell, 'Women and Factionalism in the Court of Charles II of Spain', in Sanchez and Saint Saëns, *Spanish Women in the Golden Age*, p. 112.

14 Hughes, *Sophia Regent of Russia*, p. 224.

15 Cosandey, 'De Lance en Quenouille'.

16 Deborah Marrow, *The Art Patronage of Maria de Medici* (Ann Arbor, 1982), pp. 55–57; 61–65.

17 Rachel Weil, 'The Crown has Fallen to the Distaff Side: Gender and Politics in the Age of Catherine de Medici', *Critical Matrix* 1, 4 (1985), pp. 8; 9.

18 Quoted in Campbell, 'Women and Factionalism in the Court of Charles II', p. 118.

19 Hopkins, *Women Who Would Be Kings*, pp. 147–48.

20 Quoted in Simone Berthière, 'Le Metier de Reine en France aux XVIe et XVIIe Siécles', *Proceedings of the Western Society for French History* 23 (1996), p. 7.

21 Magdalena S. Sanchez, *The Empress, the Queen, and the Nun: Women and Power at the Court of Philip III of Spain* (Baltimore, 1998).

22 Quoted in Berthière, 'Le Metier de Reine en France', p. 5.

23 Sanchez, *The Empress, the Queen, and the Nun*.

24 Hopkins, *Women Who Would Be Kings*, pp. 61–62.

25 Retha M. Warnicke, *The Rise and Fall of Anne Boleyn* (Cambridge, 1989), pp. 149–51. Quote p. 150.

26 Ruth Kleinman, 'Social Dynamics of the French Court: The Household of Anne of Austria', *French Historical Studies* 16, 3 (Spring, 1990), pp. 517–21.

27 Barbara Kiefer Lewalski, *Writing Women in Jacobean England* (Cambridge, MA, 1993), pp. 15–43.

28 My treatment of the *dogaresse* is based on Holly Hurlburt, *Dogaresse of Venice 1200–1500: Wives and Icons* (London, 2006).

29 Leslie P. Peirce, *The Imperial Harem: Women and Sovereignty in the Ottoman Empire* (Oxford, 1993), pp. 3–39.

30 *Ibid.*, pp. 28–42.

31 *Ibid.*, pp. 42–50.

32 *Ibid.*, pp. 57–90.

33 *Ibid.*, pp. 248–55.

34 *Ibid.*, pp. 186–218.

35 Quoted in *ibid.*, p. vii.

36 Sharon Kettering, 'The Household Service of Early Modern French Noblewomen', *French Historical Studies* 20, 1 (Winter, 1992), p. 55.

37 *Ibid.*, pp. 69–78.

38 John Lynch, *Bourbon Spain 1700–1808* (London, 1989), pp. 46–52; 73–75.

39 Hopkins, *Women Who Would Be Kings*, p. 66.

40 *Ibid.*, p. 96; John B. Wolfe, *Louis XIV* (New York, 1968).

41 Guy, *Mary Queen of Scots*; Jeffrey Merrick, 'The Cardinal and the Queen: Sexual and Political Disorders in the Mazarinades', *French Historical Studies* 18.3 (Spring, 1994), pp. 667–99; Levin, *The Heart and Stomach of a King*, pp. 75–85.

42 Kramer and Sprenger, *Malleus Maleficarum*, p. 47.

43 Wolf, *Louis XIV*, p. 325.

44 Jordan, *Renaissance Feminism*, p. 130.

Chapter 13: Citizens

1 Charlotte C. Wells, *Law and Citizenship in Early Modern France* (Baltimore, 1995), pp. 40–41.

2 Barbara Freyer Stowasser, 'Women and Citizenship in the Qur'an', in Amira El Azhary Sonbol, ed., *Women, the Family, and Divorce Laws in Islamic History* (Syracuse, 1996), pp. 23–28.

3 Quoted in Gordon J. Schochet, *Patriarchalism in Political Thought* (New York, 1975), p. 33.

4 Svetlana Ivanova, 'The Divorce Between Zubaida Hateen and Esseid Osman Aga: Women in the 18th-Century Shari'a Court of Rumelia', in Sonbol, *Women, the Family, and Divorce Laws*, p. 124.

5 Yan Thomas, 'The Division of the Sexes in Roman Law', in *A History of Women in the West*, Vol. 1, pp. 83–137.

6 Erickson, *Women and Property*, pp. 61–78; 187–93; 204–22.

7 Thomas Kuehn, 'Person and Gender in the Laws', in Brown and Davis, *Gender and Society in Renaissance Italy*, pp. 87–106.

8 Hardwick, *The Practice of Patriarchy*, p. 133.

9 T. E. [Thomas Edgar?], *The Law's Resolutions of Women's Rights* (London, 1632), printed in Klein, *Daughters, Wives, and Widows*, p. 32.

10 Hardwick, *The Practice of Patriarchy*; Erickson, *Women and Property*, p. 103.

11 Erickson, *Women and Property*, pp. 139–40; Gibson, *Women in Seventeenth-Century France*, p. 61.

12 *Ibid.*; Sponsler, 'The Status of Married Women', p. 131.

13 Weisner, *Working Women in Renaissance Germany*, p. 26.

14 *Ibid.*, pp. 27–30.

15 Gibson, *Women in Seventeenth-Century France*, p. 60.

16 *Ibid.*; Sponsler, 'The Status of Married Women', p. 130; Weisner, *Working Women in Renaissance Germany*, p. 22.

17 Jim Sharpe, 'Women, Witchcraft, and the Legal Process', in Kermode and Walker, *Women, Crime, and the Courts in Early Modern England*, p. 112.

18 Erickson, *Women and Property*, p. 158.

19 *Ibid.*, p. 156.

20 Laura Gowing, 'Language, Power, and the Law: Women's Slander Litigation in Early Modern London', in Kermode and Walker, *Women, Crime, and the Courts in Early Modern England*, p. 27.

21 Nancy Kollmann Shields, *By Honor Bound: State and Society in Early Modern Russia*, p. 74.

22 Julius R. Ruff, *Violence in Early Modern Europe 1500–1800* (Cambridge, 2001), p. 141.

23 Quoted in *ibid.*, p. 145.

24 Michael Rocke, 'Gender and Sexual Culture in Renaissance Italy', in Brown and Davis, *Gender and Society in Renaissance Italy*, p. 163.

25 Nazife Bashar, 'Rape in England Between 1550 and 1700', in *The Sexual Dynamics of History* (London, 1983), pp. 29–30; Miranda Chaytor, 'Husband(ry): Narratives of Rape in the Seventeenth Century', *Gender and History* 7, 3 (1995), p. 384.

26 Manon van der Heijden, 'Women as Victims of Sexual and Domestic Violence in Seventeenth-Century Holland', *Journal of Social History*, 33, 3 (2000), pp. 624–28.

27 Bashar, 'Rape in England', p. 32.

28 [Edgar], *Law's Resolution*, p. 32.

29 Rublack, *Crimes of Women in Early Modern Germany*, pp. 81–83.

30 Quoted in *ibid.*, p. 60.

31 Natalie Zemon Davis, *Fiction in the Archives: Pardon Tales and their Tellers in Sixteenth-Century France* (Stanford, 1987), p. 190; pp. 93–94.

32 Rublack, *Crimes of Women in Early Modern Germany*, pp. 56–66.

33 Davis, *Fiction in the Archives*, pp. 84–85; 191, n. 21; Walker, 'Women, Theft, and the World of Stolen Goods', p. 82.

34 Carol Z. Weiner, 'Sex Roles and Crime in Late Elizabethan Hertfordshire', *Journal of Social History* 8 (1974–75), pp. 38–59.

35 Ruff, *Violence in Early Modern Europe*, pp. 117–25.

36 Rublack, *Crimes of Women in Early Modern Germany*, pp. 165–70.

37 *Ibid.*, p. 165.

38 Walker, 'Women, Theft, and the World of Stolen Goods'.

39 Rublack, *Crimes of Women in Early Modern Germany*, p. 117.

40 *Ibid.*, p. 104.

41 Fairchilds, *Domestic Enemies*, pp. 72–73.

42 Rublack, *Crimes of Women in Early Modern Germany*, pp. 113–16; 121.

43 Ruff, *Violence in Early Modern Europe*, p. 235.

44 Rublack, *Crimes of Women in Early Modern Germany*, p. 116.

45 Rudolf M. Decker, 'Popular Protest and its Social Basis in Holland in the Seventeenth and Eighteenth Centuries', *Theory and Society* 16 (1987), p. 340.

46 Quoted in *ibid.*, pp. 344; 345.

47 Ruff, *Violence in Early Modern Europe*, pp. 206–207.

48 Gibson, *Women in Seventeenth-Century France*, p. 315.

49 Pearl Hogrefe, *Tudor Women: Commoners and Queens* (Ames, IA, 1975), pp. 34; 32.

50 Gibson, *Women in Seventeenth-Century France*, p. 89.

51 Rublack, *Crimes of Women in Early Modern Germany*, p. 112.

52 Weisner, *Working Women in Renaissance Germany*, pp. 18–19.

53 Merry Weisner, 'The Holy Roman Empire', in Hilda L. Smith, *Women Writers and the Early Modern British Political Tradition* (Cambridge, 1998), pp. 316–17.

54 Wunder, *He is the Sun, She is the Moon*, pp. 165–69.

55 Hogrefe, *Tudor Women*, pp. 27–28; Hilda L. Smith, 'Women as Sextons and Electors: King's Bench and Precedents for Women's Citizenship', in Smith, *Women Writers and British Political Tradition*, pp. 324–42.

56 Mark Kishlansky, *Parliamentary Selection: Society and Political Choice in Early Modern England* (Cambridge, 1986), pp. 42–43.

57 J. K. Gruenfelder, *Influence in Early Stuart Elections, 1604–1640* (Columbus, OH, 1981), Appendix 7.

58 Gibson, *Women in Seventeenth-Century France*, pp. 159–61.

59 Hilda L. Smith, *All Men and Both Sexes: Gender, Politics, and the False Universal in England 1640–1832* (University Park, PA, 2002), pp. 1–38.

60 Printed in Crawford, 'The Challenges to Patriarchalism', p. 117.

61 Quoted in Higgins, 'The Reactions of Women', p. 211.

62 Printed in Crawford, 'The Challenges to Patriarchalism', p. 126.

63 Quoted in Higgins, 'The Reactions of Women', p. 212.

64 Quoted in *ibid.*, p. 213.

Chapter 14: Warriors and Empire Builders

1 Catalina de Erauso, *Lieutenant Nun: Memoir of a Basque Transvestite in the New World*, ed. and trans. Michele and Gabriel Step (Boston, 1995).

2 Christine de Pisan, 'L'Epistre au Dieu d'Amour'.

3 C. R. Boxer, *Women in Iberian Expansion Overseas, 1415–1815* (New York, 1975), p. 35.

4 Quoted in Antonia Fraser, *The Weaker Vessel* (New York, 1984), p. 194.

5 Quoted in *ibid.*, p. 190.

6 Mary O'Dowd, 'Women and War in Ireland in the 1640s', in Margaret MacCurtain and Mary O'Dowd, eds, *Women in Early Modern Ireland* (Edinburgh, 1991), pp. 99–100.

7 Slater, *Family Life in the Seventeenth Century*, pp. 78–104.

8 Geoffrey Parker, *The Thirty Years' War* (London, 1997), p. 192.

9 Quoted in J. R. Hale, *War and Society in Renaissance Europe 1450–1620* (New York, 1985), pp. 183–84.

10 *Ibid.*, p. 180.

11 Quoted in *ibid.*, pp. 186–87.

12 Quoted in *ibid.*, pp. 184–85.

13 Quoted in Parker, *The Thirty Years' War*, p. 179.

14 *Ibid.*, pp. 186–87; 192.

15 Hale, *War and Society in Renaissance Europe*, pp. 191–93.

16 Quoted in O'Dowd, 'Women and War in Ireland', p. 101.

17 Fraser, *The Weaker Vessel*, pp. 172–74.

18 O'Dowd, 'Women and War in Ireland', pp. 92–93.

19 Hale, *War and Society in Renaissance Europe*, p. 192.

20 Fraser, *The Weaker Vessel*, p. 185.

21 *Ibid.*, pp. 186–89.

22 Barton C. Hacker, 'Women and Military Institutions in Early Modern Europe: A Reconnaissance', *Signs* 6, 4 (1981), pp. 647–48.

23 Parker, *The Thirty Years' War*, p. 178.

24 Quoted in Hacker, 'Women and Military Institutions', pp. 653–54.

25 Quoted in *ibid.*, p. 650.

26 Quoted in *ibid.*, p. 653.

27 *Ibid.*, pp. 654–65.

28 Dekker and van de Pol, *Female Transvestism*, p. 9; Dominique Godineau, *The Women of Paris and their French Revolution*, trans. Katherine Streip (Berkeley, 1998), pp. 244–47.

29 Fraser, *The Weaker Vessel*, p. 200.

30 Dekker and van de Pol, *Female Transvestism*, p. 30.

31 *Ibid.*, pp. 32–33.

32 *Ibid.*, pp. 13–24.

33 [Daniel Defoe], *A General History of the Pyrates*, ed. Manuel Schonhorn (Columbia, SC, 1972), pp. 153–59.

34 *Ibid.*, pp. 159–65.

35 *Ibid.*, p. 156.

36 *Ibid.*, p. 165.

37 Dekker and van de Pol, *Female Transvestism*, p. 85; Dianne Dugaw, *Warrior Women and Popular Balladry 1650–1850* (Chicago, 1989), pp. 216–19.

38 Quoted in Dugaw, *Warrior Women and Popular Balladry*, p. 156.

39 Quoted in *ibid.*, pp. 154; 155.

40 Kathleen M. Brown, *Good Wives, Nasty Wenches, and Anxious Patriarchs: Gender, Race, and Power in Colonial Virginia* (Chapel Hill, NC, 1996), pp. 18–19.

41 Boxer, *Women in Iberian Expansion*, p. 68.

42 *Ibid.*, pp. 66; 23; 80–82.

43 A. J. R. Russell-Wood, 'Female and Family in the Economy and Society of Colonial Brazil' in Asuncion Lavrin, ed., *Latin American Women: Historical Perspectives* (Westport, CT, 1978), pp. 62–65.

44 Muriel Nazzari, 'Parents and Daughters: Change in the Practice of Dowry in São Paolo (1600–1770)', in Marie Beatriz Nizza da Silva, ed., *Families in the Expansion of Europe, 1500–1800* (Aldershot, 1998), pp. 1–27; Russell-Wood, 'Female and Family in Colonial Brazil', pp. 90–91.

45 *Ibid.*, pp. 82–90.

46 Donald Ramos, 'Marriage and the Family in Colonial Vila Rica', in da Silva, *Families in the Expansion of Europe*, p. 46.

47 *Ibid.*, pp. 60; 61.

48 *Ibid.*, p. 60.

49 Elinor C. Burkett, 'Indian Women and White Society: The Case of Sixteenth-Century Peru', in Lavrin, *Latin American Women*, pp. 105–6; Boxer, *Women in Iberian Expansion*, p. 36.

50 Edgar F. Love, 'Marriage Patterns of Persons of African Descent in a Colonial Mexico City Parish', in da Silva, *Families in the Expansion of Europe*, p. 281.

51 Peter Boyd-Bowman, 'Patterns of Spanish Emigration to the Indies until 1600', *Hispanic American Historical Review* 56 (Nov. 1976), p. 601.

52 *Ibid.*, pp. 597; 598.

53 James Lockhart, *Spanish Peru 1532–1560: A Social History* (Madison, WI, 1994), p. 175.

54 Boyd-Bowman, 'Spanish Emigration', p. 598.

55 Asuncion Lavrin, 'Women in Spanish American Colonial Society' in Leslie Bethell, ed., *Cambridge History of Latin America*, Vol. II: *Colonial Latin America* (Cambridge, 1984), p. 322.

56 Asuncion Lavrin, 'In Search of the Colonial Woman in Mexico: the Seventeenth and Eighteenth Centuries', in Lavrin, *Latin American Women*, p. 45, Table 1.1.

57 Lockhart, *Spanish Peru*, p. 176.

58 Patricia Seed, *To Love, Honor and Obey in Colonial Mexico: Conflicts over Marriage Choice, 1574–1821* (Stanford, 1988).

59 Ann Twinam, 'Honor, Sexuality, and Illegitimacy in Colonial Spanish America', in da Silva, ed., *Families in the Expansion of Europe*, pp. 104–5.

60 Love, 'Marriage Patterns of Persons of African Descent', p. 91.

61 Lockhart, *Spanish Peru*, pp. 179; 180.

62 *Ibid.*, pp. 184–85.

63 Sor Juana Inés de la Cruz, 'Response to the Most Illustrious Poetess Sor Filotea de la Cruz', in her *Poems, Protest, and a Dream*, trans. Margaret Sayers Peden (New York, 1997), pp. 1–75.

64 Sylvia van Kirk, *Many Tender Ties: Women in Fur-Trade Society, 1670–1870* (Norman, OK, 1980), pp. 9–52.

65 Silvio Dumas, *Les Filles du roi en Nouvelle France* (Quebec, 1972). The figure is from p. 166.

66 Allen Greer, *The People of New France* (Toronto, 1997), p. 22; Peter Moogk, *La Nouvelle France: The Making of French Canada* (East Lansing, MI, 2000), p. 219; William Eccles, *The Canadian Frontier, 1534–1760* (Albequerque, 1969), p. 96.

67 Brown, *Good Wives, Nasty Wenches, and Anxious Patriarchs*, p. 63.

68 *Ibid.*, pp. 81–82.

69 James Horn, *Adapting to a New World: English Society in the Seventeenth-Century Chesapeake* (Chapel Hill, NC, 1994), pp. 25; 31–38.

70 *Ibid.*, p. 210.

71 Brown, *Good Wives, Nasty Wenches, and Anxious Patriarchs*, p. 126.

72 *Ibid.*, p. 96.

73 Horn, *Adapting to a New World*, pp. 216; 217.

74 Brown, *Good Wives, Nasty Wenches, and Anxious Patriarchs*, pp. 87; 88.

75 *Ibid.*, p. 149.

76 *Ibid.*, pp. 188–244.

77 David Hackett Fisher, *Albion's Seed: Four British Folkways in America* (New York, 1989), p. 25.

78 *Ibid.*, p. 26.

79 Laurel Thatcher Ulrich, *Good Wives: Image and Reality in the Lives of Women in Northern New England, 1650–1750* (New York, 1980).

80 Fisher, *Albion's Seed*, pp. 173; 84.

81 *Ibid.*, pp. 75; 89; 71.

82 *Ibid.*, p. 78.

83 Mary Beth Norton, *Founding Mothers and Fathers: Gendered Power and the Forming of American Society* (New York, 1996), p. 78.

FURTHER READING

———— ◆ ————

This is not a bibliography; rather, it is suggestions for further reading. The notes following each chapter better indicate the sources I consulted.

GENERAL TEXTS

Merry E. Wiesner, *Women and Gender in Early Modern Europe*, 2nd edn. Cambridge: Cambridge University Press, 2000. Has a wonderful bibliography.

Natalie Davis and Arlette Farge, eds, *A History of Women in the West, Vol. 3: Renaissance and Enlightenment Paradoxes*. Cambridge, MA: Harvard University Press, 1993.

Olwen Hufton, *The Prospect Before Her*. New York: Alfred A. Knopf, 1996.

Renate Bridenthal *et al.*, eds, *Becoming Visible: Women in European History*, 3rd edn. Boston: Houghton Mifflin, 1998.

Marilyn J. Boxer and Jean H. Quateret, eds, *Connecting Spheres: Women in the Western World, 1500 to the Present*, 2nd edn. New York: Oxford University Press, 1999.

Margaret L. King, *Women in the Renaissance*. Chicago: University of Chicago Press, 1991.

NATIONAL SURVEYS

Mary E. Prior, ed., *Women in English Society, 1500–1800*. London: Methuen, 1985.

Sara Mendelson and Patricia Crawford, *Women in Early Modern England, 1550–1720*. New York: Oxford University Press, 1998.

Christine Peters, *Women in Early Modern Britain, 1450–1640*. Houndsmills: Palgrave Press, 2004.

Margaret MacCurtain and Mary O'Dowd, eds, *Women in Early Modern Ireland, 1500–1800*. Edinburgh: Edinburgh University Press, 1991.

R. K. Marshall, *Virgins and Viragos: A History of Women in Scotland from 1080–1980*. Chicago: University of Chicago Press, 1993.

Wendy Gibson, *Women in Seventeenth-Century France*. New York: St Martin's, 1989.

Magdalena S. Sanchez and Alain Saint Saëns, eds, *Spanish Women in the Golden Age*. Westport, CT: Greenwood Press, 1996.

Judith C. Brown and Robert C. Davis, eds, *Gender and Society in Renaissance Italy*. London: Longman, 1998.

Heide Wunder, *He is the Sun, She is the Moon: Women in Early Modern Germany*, trans. Thomas Dunlop. Cambridge, MA: Harvard University Press, 1998.

Jenny Jochens, *Women in Old Norse Society*. Ithaca: Cornell University Press, 1995. Deals with the medieval period, but good for background.

Els Kloek *et al.*, eds, *Women of the Golden Age*. Hilversum: Verloren, 1994. Primarily covers the Netherlands.

Natalia Pushkareva, *Women in Russian History: From the Tenth to the Twentieth Century*. New York: M. E. Sharpe, 1997.

Andrei Wyrobisz, 'Patterns of the Family and Woman in Old Poland', *Acta Poloniae Historica* 71 (1995), pp. 69–82.

Ian C. Dengler, 'Turkish Women in the Ottoman Empire: The Classical Age', In Lois Beck and Nikki Keddie, eds, *Women in the Muslim World*. Cambridge, MA: Harvard University Press, 1978.

WOMEN'S NATURE AND THE QUERELLE DES FEMMES

Original sources

Most of the major texts of the *querelle des femmes* have been published in modern translations and in paperback, notably in *The Other Voice* series of the University of Chicago Press.

Secondary sources

Thomas Laqueur, *Making Sex: Body and Gender from the Greeks to Freud*. Cambridge, MA: Harvard University Press, 1990. For the medieval and philosophical underpinnings of the patriarchal paradigm.

Constance Jordan, *Renaissance Feminism: Literary Texts and Political Models*. Ithaca: Cornell University Press, 1990. Difficult but rewarding analysis of the *querelle*.

Ian Maclean, *The Renaissance Notion of Women*. Cambridge: Cambridge University Press, 1980.

GIRLHOOD AND GIRLS' EDUCATION

Original sources

Juan Luis Vives, *'The Education of a Christian Woman': A Sixteenth-Century Manual*, ed. and trans. Charles Fantazzi. Chicago: University of Chicago Press, 2000. The most influential humanist treatise on women's education.

Anna Maria van Schurman, *'Whether a Christian Woman Should be Educated' and Other Writings from her Intellectual Circle*, ed. and trans. Joyce L. Irwin. Chicago: Chicago University Press, 1998. A learned lady's defence of educating women.

Secondary sources

R. A. Houston, *Literacy in Early Modern Europe 1500–1800*, 2nd edn. London: Longman, 2002. The best survey of literacy and schooling.

Cornelia Niekus Moore, *The Maiden's Mirror: Reading Material for German Girls in the Sixteenth and Seventeenth Centuries*. Wiesbaden: Harrasowitz, 1987. Broader than its title suggests; deals with girls' education and training as well as reading matter.

Dorothy Gardiner, *English Girlhood at School*. London: Macmillan, 1929. Old but still useful. Covers training outside schools as well.

COURTSHIP AND MARRIAGE

'European' and 'Non-European' Marriage Patterns

J. H. Haijnal, 'The European Marriage Pattern in Perspective', in D. V. Glass and D. E. C. Eversley, eds, *Population in History*. Chicago: University of Chicago Press, 1965.
John L. Esposito, *Women in Muslim Family Law*. Syracuse: Syracuse University Press, 1982.
Louis M. Epstein, *The Jewish Marriage Contract: A Study of the Status of Women in Jewish Law*. New York: Arno Press, 1973.
Eve Levin, *Sex and Society in the World of the Orthodox Slavs, 900–1700*. Ithaca: Cornell University Press, 1989.

Courtship and Marriage Rituals

Martine Segalen, *Love and Power in the Peasant Family*, trans. Sarah Matthews. Chicago: Chicago University Press, 1989.
David Cressy, *Birth, Marriage and Death: Ritual, Religion and the Life-Cycle in Tudor and Stuart England*. Oxford: Oxford University Press, 1983.

Legal Aspects of Marriage

Jeffrey R. Watt, *The Making of Modern Marriage: Matrimonial Control and the Rise of Sentiment in Neuchâtel, 1500–1800*. Ithaca: Cornell University Press, 1992.

Case Studies of Individual Marriages

Steven Ozment, *Magdalena and Balthasar*. New York: Simon & Schuster, 1986.
Anthony Fletcher, *Gender, Sex and Subordination in England 1500–1800*. New Haven: Yale University Press, 1995. Chapters 8–10.

MOTHERHOOD AND CHILDRAISING

Pregnancy and Childbirth

Jacques Gélis, *History of Childbirth: Fertility, Pregnancy and Birth in Early Modern Europe*, trans. Rosemary Morris. Cambridge: Polity Press, 1991.
Ulinka Rublack, 'Pregnancy, Childbirth and the Female Body in Early Modern Germany', *Past and Present* 150 (1996), pp. 84–110.

Midwifery

Hilary Marland, ed., *The Art of Midwifery: Early Modern Midwives in Europe*. London: Routledge, 1994.

Contraception, Abortion, Infanticide

Angus MacLaren, *A History of Contraception from Antiquity to the Present Day*. Oxford: Basil Blackwell, 1990.

Peter C. Hoffer and N. E. H. Hull, *Murdering Mothers: Infanticide in England and New England 1558–1803*. New York: New York University Press, 1984.

Childraising

Linda Pollock, *Forgotten Children: Parent–Child Relations from 1500 to 1900*. Cambridge: Cambridge University Press, 1983.

Hans Roodenberg, 'The Autobiography of Isabella de Moerloose: Sex, Childrearing and Popular Belief in Seventeenth-Century Holland', *Journal of Social History* 18 (1985), pp. 517–40.

Mothers and Older Children

Michele Longino-Farrel, *Performing Motherhood: The Sévigné Correspondence*. Hanover, NH: University of New England Press, 1991.

Barbara J. Harris, 'Property, Power and Personal Relations: Elite Mothers and Sons in Yorkist and Early Tudor England', *Signs* 15 (1990), pp. 606–32.

WIDOWHOOD AND OLD AGE

Widowhood and Remarriage

Sandra Cavallo and Lindsey Warner, eds, *Widowhood in Medieval and Early Modern Europe*. London: Longman, 1999. Excellent articles.

Barbara Todd, 'The Re-marrying Widow: A Stereotype Reconsidered', in Mary Prior, ed., *Women in English Society 1500–1800*. London: Methuen, 1985.

David E. Vassburg, 'The Status of Widows in Sixteenth Century Rural Castile', in John Henderson and Richard Wall, eds, *Poor Women and Children in the European Past*. London: Routledge, 1994. Poor widows.

Old Age

George Minois, *History of Old Age: From Antiquity to the Renaissance*, trans. Sarah Hanbury Tenison. Chicago: Chicago University Press, 1989. Attitudes toward the elderly in general.

Wayne E. Franits, *Paragons of Virtue: Women and Domesticity in Seventeenth-Century Dutch Art*. Cambridge: Cambridge University Press, 1995. Artistic depictions of elderly women.

Margaret Pelling, 'Old Age, Poverty and Disability in Early Modern Norwich: Work, Remarriage and Other Expedients', in Margaret Pelling and Richard M. Smith, eds, *Life, Death and the Elderly*. London: Routledge, 1991.

WOMEN AND WORK

General Surveys

Alice Clark, *Working Life of Women in the Seventeenth Century*. London: Routledge & Kegan Paul, 1919.

Sheilagh Ogilvie, *A Bitter Living: Women, Markets and Social Capital in Early Modern Germany*. Oxford: Oxford University Press, 2003. The latest and most sophisticated treatment.

Merry E. Wiesner, *Working Women in Renaissance Germany*. New Brunswick, NJ: Rutgers University Press, 1986.

Monica Chojnacka, *Working Women of Early Modern Venice*. Baltimore: Johns Hopkins University Press, 2001.

Pamela Sharpe, ed., *Women's Work: The English Experience 1650–1914*. London: Arnold, 1998.

Housewifery

Thomas Tusser, 'The Points of Housewifery', in Joan Larson Klein, ed., *Daughters, Wives and Widows: Writing by Men about Women and Marriage in England 1500–1640*. Urbana, IL: University of Illinois Press, 1992.

Agricultural Labour

Michael Roberts, 'Sickles and Scythes: Women's Work and Men's Work at Harvest Time', *History Workshop* 7 (1979), pp. 3–28.

Ann Kussmaul, *Servants in Husbandry in Early Modern England*. Cambridge: Cambridge University Press, 1981.

The Crafts and Guilds

Marta V. Vicente, 'Images and Realities of Work: Women and Guilds in Early Modern Barcelona', in Magdalena S. Sanchez and Alain Saint Saëns, eds, *Spanish Women in the Golden Age*. Westport, CT: Greenwood Press, 1996.

Carol L. Loats, 'Gender, Guilds and Work Identity: Perspectives from Sixteenth-Century Paris', *French Historical Studies* 20 (1997), pp. 15–30.

Grethe Jacobsen, 'Women's Work and Women's Role: Ideology and Reality in Danish Urban Society, 1300–1550', *Scandinavian Economic History Review* 31, 1 (1983), pp. 1–20.

The Textile Industry

Daryl M. Hafter, 'Women in the Underground Business of Eighteenth-Century Lyon', *Enterprise and Society* 2 (2001), pp. 11–40.

Domestic Service

Dennis Romano, *Housecraft and Statecraft in Renaissance Venice 1400–1600*. Baltimore: Johns Hopkins University Press, 1996.

M. Carlson, 'A Trojan Horse of Worldliness: Maidservants in the Burger Household in Rotterdam at the End of the Seventeenth Century' in Els Kloek *et al.*, eds, *Women of the Golden Age*. Hilversum: Verloren, 1994.

Crime and Prostitution

Ulinka Rublack, *The Crimes of Women in Early Modern Germany*. Oxford: Oxford University Press, 1999.

Garthine Walker, 'Women, Thrift and the World of Stolen Goods', in Jennifer Kermode and Garthine Walker, eds, *Women, Crime and the Courts in Early Modern England*. London: University College Press, 1994.

Kathryn Norberg, 'Prostitution', in Natalie Davis and Arlette Farge, eds, *A History of Women in the West, Vol. 3*. Cambridge, MA: Harvard University Press, 1993.

Veronica Franco, *Poems and Selected Letters*, ed. and trans. Ann Rosalind Jones and Margaret F. Rosenthal. Chicago: University of Chicago Press, 1998.

The Male Invasion of Women's Work

Judith M. Bennett, *Ale, Beer and Brewsters in England: Women's Work in a Changing World*. Oxford: Oxford University Press, 1996.

A. L. Wyman, 'The Surgeoness: The Female Practitioner of Surgery 1400–1800', *Medical History* 28 (1984), pp. 22–41.

WOMEN IN THE ARTS AND SCIENCES

Women Artists

Ann Sutherland Harris and Linda Nochlin, *Women Artists 1550–1950*. New York: Alfred A. Knopf, 1976.

Germaine Greer, *The Obstacle Race: The Fortunes of Women Painters and Their Work*. New York: Farrar Straus Giroux, 1979.

Mary D. Garrard, *Artemisia Gentileschi: The Image of the Female Hero in Italian Baroque Art*. Princeton: Princeton University Press, 1989.

Women Musicians

Jane Bowers and Judith Tick, eds, *Women Making Music: The Western Art Tradition, 1150–1950*. Urbana, IL: University of Illinois Press, 1986.

Jane Baldauf-Berdes, *Women Musicians of Venice: Musical Foundations, 1525–1855*. Oxford: Oxford University Press, 1993.

Actresses

Viviana Comensoli and Anne Russell, eds, *Enacting Gender on the Renaissance Stage*. Champaign-Urbana, IL: University of Illinois Press, 1999.

Women Writers

Original sources

Most of the major English women writers have now been published in paperback. A good anthology is Paul Salzman, ed., *Early Modern Women's Writing*. Oxford: Oxford University Press, 2000.

Among the continental women writers, Maria de Zayas is especially interesting for her attacks on patriarchy: Maria de Zayas, *The Disenchantments of Love*, trans. H. Patsy Boyer. Albany, NY: SUNY Press, 1997.

Secondary sources

Patricia Crawford, 'Women's Published Writings 1600–1700', in Mary E. Prior, ed., *Women in English Society, 1500–1800*. London: Methuen, pp. 211–82.

Elaine Hobby, *Virtue of Necessity: English Women's Writing, 1649–88*. Ann Arbor, MI: University of Michigan Press, 1989.

Joan de Jean, *Tender Geographies: Women and the Origins of the Novel in France*. New York: Columbia University Press, 1991.

Women Scientists

Margaret Alic, *Hypatia's Heritage: A History of Women in Science from Antiquity through the Nineteenth Century*. Boston: Beacon, 1986.

Londa Schiebinger, *The Mind has No Sex? Women in the Origins of Modern Science*. Cambridge, MA: Harvard University Press, 1991.

WOMEN AND RELIGION

General

Sherrin Marshall, ed., *Women in Reformation and Counter-Reformation Europe: Public and Private Worlds*. Bloomington, IN: Indiana University Press, 1989.

Protestantism

Martin Luther, *The Marriage Ring: Three Sermons on Marriage*. San Diego, CA: The Book Tree, 2003.

Jane Dempsey Douglas, *Women, Freedom and Calvin*. Philadelphia: The Westminster Press, 1985.

Lyndal Roper, *The Holy Household: Women and Morals in Reformation Augsberg*. Oxford: Clarendon Press, 1989. Takes a more negative view of the impact of the Reformation on women than I do.

Jeffrey R. Watt, 'Women and the Consistory in Calvin's Geneva', *Sixteenth Century Journal* 24 (1993), pp. 429–39.

Joyce L. Irwin, ed., *Womanhood in Radical Protestantism, 1525–1675*. New York: Edwin Mellen Press, 1979. Texts from the radical Protestant sects.

Megan L. Hickerson, *Making Women Martyrs in Tudor England*. Houndmills: Palgrave Macmillan, 2005. Female martyrs.

Phyllis Mack, *Visionary Woman: Ecstatic Prophesy in Seventeenth-Century England*. Berkeley: University of California Press, 1992. English Quakers and sectarians.

Catholicism

The Life of Saint Theresa of Avila by Herself, trans. J. M. Cohen. London: Penguin Books, 1957.

JoAnn McNamara, *Sisters in Arms: Catholic Nuns through Two Millennia*. Cambridge, MA: Harvard University Press, 1996. Nuns and convents.

Elizabeth Rapley, *The Devotes: Women and Church in Seventeenth-Century France*. Montreal: McGill University Press, 1990. The new religious orders of the Counterreformation.

Mary Elizabeth Perry, *Gender and Disorder in Early Modern Seville*. Princeton: Princeton University Press, 1990. The best study of the impact of the Counterreformation on women. There are two works on independent holy women arrested by the Inquisition:

Fulvio Tomizza, *Heavenly Supper: The Story of Maria Janis*, trans. Anne Schutte. Chicago: University of Chicago Press, 1991.

Richard L. Kagan, *Lucrecia's Dreams: Politics and Prophecy in Sixteenth-Century Spain*. Berkeley: University of California Press, 1990.

Other Religions

Natalie Z. Davis, 'Glikl bas Judah heib' in Davis, *Women on the Margins: Three Seventeenth-Century Lives*. Cambridge, MA: Harvard University Press, 1995. Judaism.

Mary Elizabeth Perry, 'Behind the Veil: Moriscas and the Politics of Resistance and Survival', in Magdalena Sanchez and Alain Saint Saëns, eds, *Spanish Women in the Golden Age*. Westport, CT: Greenwood Press, 1996. Islam.

Marie A. Thomas, 'Muscovite Convents in the Seventeenth Century', *Russian History* 10 (1983), pp. 230–42. Russian Orthodoxy.

WITCHES AND WITCHCRAFT

Original sources

Heinrich Kramer and James Sprenger, *The Malleus Maleficarum*, trans. Montague Summers. New York: Dover, 1971.

Secondary sources

Brian P. Levack, *The Witch-Hunt in Early Modern Europe*, 2nd edn. London: Longman, 1995. Still the best general survey.

B. Ankarloo and G. Henningson, eds, *Early Modern European Witchcraft: Centres and Peripheries*. Oxford: Oxford University Press, 1990. Articles showing regional variations.

Robin Briggs, *Witches and Neighbours: The Social and Cultural Context of European Witchcraft*. London and New York: Penguin Books, 1998. Good on the relationships leading to witchcraft accusations.

Lyndal Roper, *Witch Craze: Terror and Fantasy in Baroque Germany*. New Haven: Yale University Press, 2004. A sophisticated treatment especially good on women's history issues.

FEMALE RULERS

Original sources

Elizabeth I: Collected Works, ed. Leah S. Marcus *et al*. Chicago: University of Chicago Press, 2002.

Secondary sources

Lisa Hopkins, *Women who would be Kings: Female Rulers of the Sixteenth Century*. London: St Martin's, 1991.

Carole Levin, *The Heart and the Stomach of a King: Elizabeth I and the Politics of Sex and Power*. Philadelphia: University of Pennsylvania Press, 1994.

Magdalena S. Sanchez, *The Empress, The Queen and the Nun: Women and Power at the Court of Philip III of Spain*. Baltimore: Johns Hopkins University Press, 1998.

Leslie Peirce, *The Imperial Harem: Women and Sovereignty in the Ottoman Empire*. Oxford: Oxford University Press, 1993.

Holly S. Hurlburt, *Dogaresse of Venice 1200–1500: Wives and Icons*. London: Palgrave, 2006.

WOMEN'S LEGAL RIGHTS, CITIZENSHIP AND POLITICAL ACTION

Amy Louise Erickson, *Women and Property in Early Modern England*. London: Routledge, 1995.

Julie Hardwick: *The Practice of Patriarchy*. University Park, PA: Pennsylvania State University Press, 1998.

Thomas Kuehn, *Law, Family and Women: Towards a Legal Anthropology of Renaissance Italy*. Chicago: University of Chicago Press, 1991.

Martha C. Howell, 'Citizenship and Gender: Women's Political Status in Northern Medieval Cities', in Mary Erler and Maryanne Kowalski, eds, *Women and Power in the Middle Ages*. Athens, GA: University of Georgia Press, 1988.

Hilda L. Smith, ed., *Women Writers and the Early Modern British Political Tradition*. Cambridge: Cambridge University Press, 1998. A misleadingly titled collection of essays on women's citizenship and political action in both Britain and continental Europe.

Rudolf M. Dekker, 'Women in Revolt: Collective Protest and its Social Basis in Holland', *Theory and Society* 16 (1987), pp. 337–62.

WOMEN AND WAR

Barton C. Hacker, 'Women and Military Institutions in Early Modern Europe: A Reconnaissance', *Signs* 6 (1981), pp. 643–71.

John R. Hale, *War and Society in Renaissance Europe*. Baltimore: Johns Hopkins University Press, 1985.

M. O'Dowd, 'Women and War in Ireland in the 1640s' in Margaret MacCurtain and Mary O'Dowd, eds, *Women in Early Modern Ireland, 1500–1800*. Edinburgh: Edinburgh University Press, 1991.

Rudolf M. Dekker and Lotte C. van de Pol, *The Tradition of Female Transvestism in Early Modern Europe*. New York: St Martin's Press, 1989.

Dianne Dugaw, *Women Warriors and Popular Balladry, 1650–1850*. Chicago: University of Chicago Press, 1995.

WOMEN IN OVERSEAS EMPIRES

Latin America

C. R. Boxer, *Women in Iberian Expansion Overseas, 1415–1815*. New York: Oxford University Press, 1975.

Asuncion Lavrin, ed., *Latin American Women: Historical Perspectives*. Westport, CT: Greenwood Press, 1978.

Maria Beatriz Nizza da Silva, ed., *Families and the Expansion of Europe*. London: Ashgate, 1998. Excellent article collection.

New France

Allen Greer, *The People of New France*. Toronto: University of Toronto Press, 1997.

Sylvia van Kirk, *Many Tender Ties: Women in Fur-Trade Society, 1670–1870*. Norman, OK: University of Oklahoma Press, 1980.

British North America

Kathleen H. Brown, *Good Wives, Nasty Wenches and Anxious Patriarchs: Gender, Race and Power in Colonial Virginia*. Chapel Hill: University of North Carolina Press, 1996.

Mary Beth Norton, *Founding Mothers and Fathers: Gendered Power and the Forming of American Society*. New York: Knopf, 1996.

INDEX

◆

The Index includes the Introduction, Chapters 1–14, the footnotes and the Conclusion but not the Notes. The filing order is word-by-word and numbers are filed as if spelled out.